Weather, Climate, Culture

Weather, Climate, Culture

**Edited by
Sarah Strauss and Ben Orlove**

Oxford • New York

First published in 2003 by
Berg
Editorial offices:
1st Floor, Angel Court, 81 St Clements Street, Oxford, OX4 1AW, UK
838 Broadway, Third Floor, New York, NY 10003-4812, USA

Berg is an imprint of Oxford International Publishers Ltd.

Library of Congress Cataloging-in-Publication Data
Weather, climate, culture / edited by Sarah Strauss and Ben Orlove.
    p. cm.
Includes bibliographical references and index.
    ISBN 1-85973-692-0 (HB) — ISBN 1-85973-697-1 (PB)
    1. Human beings—Effect of climate on. 2. Human beings—Effect of
environment on. 3. Weather—Social aspects. 4. Weather—Folklore.
5. Climatic changes. I. Strauss, Sarah. II. Orlove, Benjamin S.

    GF71.W43 2003
    304.2'5—dc22

                                                    2003018968

British Library Cataloguing-in-Publication Data
A catalogue record for this book is available from the British Library.

ISBN 1 85973 692 0 (Cloth)
      1 85973 697 1 (Paper)

Typeset by JS Typesetting Ltd, Wellingborough, Northants.
Printed in the United Kingdom by Biddles Ltd, Guildford and King's Lynn.

www.bergpublishers.com

To Rory and Lia, to Jacob, Hannah and Raphael, our children,
who have run with the wind, splashed in puddles, and played in the snow;
and to the glaciers, melting in the sun, that they have seen on long walks in the mountains,
we dedicate this book and our efforts.

Contents

Contents

Acknowledgements

We would like to thank the Cultural Anthropology Program of the National Science Foundation (Strauss) and the Office of Global Programs at the National Oceanic and Atmospheric Administration (Orlove) for support of the projects that have led to this volume.

List of Figures

List of Tables

Notes on Contributors

David M. Ellis has worked with people known as Pawaia in the Pio-Tura region of Papua New Guinea. He was previously a researcher with the Future of Rainforest Peoples programme, sponsored by the European Commission, and was based at the University of Kent at Canterbury. His publications have focused on ethnography of people of the Pio-Tura region and of conservation practitioners and others working on their lands. He is currently engaged in research and advocacy on international environmental, trade and development policy in the UK.

Timothy J. Finan is the director of the Bureau of Applied Research in Anthropology (BARA) at the University of Arizona. His research on climate and society has spanned two decades and three continents. He currently is involved in climate change research in Northeast Brazil and in Bangladesh and has published widely on vulnerability and adaptation to climate variability.

Jan Golinski is professor of History and Humanities at the University of New Hampshire. He is the author of *Science as Public Culture: Chemistry and Enlightenment in Britain, 1760–1820* (Cambridge 1992); and of *Making Natural Knowledge: Constructivism and the History of Science* (Cambridge 1998); and co-editor of *The Sciences in Enlightened Europe* (Chicago 1999).

Trevor A. Harley is senior lecturer in the Psychology Department at the University of Dundee, Scotland. A keen amateur meteorologist, he has kept his own detailed weather records for many years, and maintains a popular website devoted to extreme weather events in Britain. His main area of research is the psychology of language. He is author of the text *The Psychology of Language* (Psychology Press, 2nd ed. 2001).

Anne Henshaw is the director of the Coastal Studies Center and an adjunct assistant professor of Sociology and Anthropology at Bowdoin College. She conducts research in both archaeology and ethnography in several northern communities on Baffin Island, Canada. She has published articles on climate and culture in the Arctic in several journals including *Arctic* and *Journal for Anthropological Archaeology*.

Keith Ingram is an agronomist/crop physiologist with special interests in drought resistance and rainfed farming systems. He has conducted research in South and Southeast Asia and West Africa. He is currently editing a book on controlled environment systems for agriculture.

Christine Jost is an assistant professor of International Veterinary Medicine in the Department of Environmental and Population Health at Tufts University School of Veterinary Medicine. She is also the director of the Tufts University World Health Organization collaborating center for veterinary public health and analysis, and works in Asia and Africa. Her research interests include participatory epidemiology, ecosystem health, and developing community-based methods in research and intervention.

Paul Kirshen is research professor in the Civil and Environmental Engineering Department of Tufts University and Director of the Tufts Water, Sustainability, Health, and Ecological Diversity (WaterSHED) Center. He has conducted research on the use of seasonal rainfall forecasting, long-term climate change impacts and adaptation, integrated water resources management, decision support systems, and hydrology. He has worked in the USA as well as in Africa and Asia. His articles have appeared in both engineering and social science journals.

Gemma Metherell was educated at Sexey's School Bruton, England and then graduated from The University of Birmingham (UK) in 2002 with an Honours degree in Geography. Her work on Monet and his depiction of weather in his London Series reflects her interest in both art and geography. She is now pursuing a career as an officer in the British Army.

Astrid E. J. Ogilvie is a research scientist and fellow of INSTAAR (The Institute of Arctic and Alpine Research) at the University of Colorado, Boulder. She is also Senior Affiliate Scientist at the Stefansson Arctic Institute in Akureyri, Iceland. She is a climate historian and human ecologist with many publications on her main research focus, the Arctic and North Atlantic regions, in particular the climatic and social history of Iceland.

Ben Orlove is a professor of Environmental Science and Policy at the University of California at Davis, and also an adjunct senior research scientist at Columbia University in New York. He has conducted research in Peru and Bolivia, and also has significant field experience in Uganda. His most recent book is *Lines in the Water: Nature and Culture at Lake Titicaca* (California 2002). His articles on climate and society have appeared in *Nature* and *American Scientist*.

Gísli Pálsson is professor of anthropology at the University of Iceland and the University of Oslo. Among his main books are *The Textual Life of Savants* (1995), *Nature and Society: Anthropological Perspectives* (1996, co-editor), *Images of Contemporary Iceland* (1996, co-editor), and *Writing on Ice: The Ethnographic Notebooks of Vilhjalmur Stefansson* 2001, editor). Pálsson's current research focuses on the social implications of biotechnology, medicine and information technology. He is also engaged in research on human-environmental relations, ecological knowledge and the social implications of climatic change. Pálsson has done anthropological fieldwork in Iceland and The Republic of Cape Verde.

Michael Paolisso is an associate professor in the Department of Anthropology at the University of Maryland, College Park. He has conducted fieldwork in several Latin American countries, Kenya, Nepal, and for the past 6 years focused his research on the Chesapeake Bay region. His recent journal publications focus on the cultural construction of environmental problems, cultural models, anthropological research methods, and applied anthropology.

Steve Rayner is director of the ESRC Science in Society Programme, a national research programme based at Oxford University's Saïd Business School, where he also holds the post of professor of Science in Society. He was previously professor of Environment and Public Affairs at Columbia University and has held senior research positions in both the Pacific Northwest and Oak Ridge National Laboratories. He is editor (with Elizabeth Malone) of *Human Choice and Climate Change: An International Assessment* (4 volumes).

Carla Roncoli is the deputy director of the Sustainable Agriculture and Natural Resource Management CRSP and an adjunct assistant professor in the Department of Anthropology at the University of Georgia. She has worked in several countries in West and North Africa. Since 1998 she has conducted research in Burkina Faso for the NOAA-funded Climate Forecasting and Agricultural Resources Project. She has published several articles on livelihood adaptations to climate variability and on farmers' uses of local and scientific climate information.

Todd Sanders is an assistant professor at the University of Toronto. He has taught at the University of Cambridge, the London School of Economics and Political Science, the School of Oriental and African Studies, and the University of California at Santa Barbara. He has published widely on ritual, gender symbolism, witchcraft and neoliberalism in Tanzania and Kenya and has co-edited *Transparency and Conspiracy: Ethnographies of Suspicion in the New World Order* (Duke 2003); *Magical Interpretations, Material Realities: Modernity, Witchcraft and the Occult in Postcolonial Africa* (Routledge 2001); and *Those Who Play with Fire: Gender, Fertility and Transformation in East and Southern Africa* (Athlone 1999).

Sarah Strauss is an assistant professor of Anthropology at the University of Wyoming. Her research themes include globalization, environment, and health in Switzerland, India, and the USA. She has published on the subject of yoga practice in the *Journal of Folklore Research* and *History and Anthropology,* as well as in the forthcoming book, *Positioning Yoga* (Berg 2004). She is now working on a comparative study of water quality and the perceived qualities of waters in the Swiss Alps and the American Rockies, with emphasis on the impact of global climate change on local water resource management.

John E. Thornes is a reader in Applied Meteorology in the School of Geography, Earth and Environmental Sciences at the University of Birmingham. He is currently editor of the journal Meteorological Applications. He runs a final year course in 'Geography and the Visual Arts' and published 'John Constable's Skies' in 1999. He recently helped to define a new branch of climatology: 'cultural climatology'.

Marcela Vásquez-León is a research associate at the Bureau of Applied Research in Anthropology at the University of Arizona. She has conducted research with rural communities in Mexico and the US Southwest. Her articles on climate and society have appeared in *Global Environmental Change* and *Human Organization.*

Colin Thor West is a graduate research associate in the Bureau of Applied Anthropology and a graduate student in the Department of Anthropology, both at the University of Arizona. He has researched climate and society issues in both Burkina Faso and the US Southwest. His co-authored work has appeared in the journal *Climate Research.*

INTRODUCTION

Up in the Air: The Anthropology of Weather and Climate

Sarah Strauss and *Ben Orlove*

All humans experience the variations in atmospheric conditions and in meteor-ological phenomena that we call weather and climate. Indeed, all terrestrial animals, except perhaps cave-dwelling ones, experience these variations as well. It could be argued that, much as the receptor cells in the eyes of humans and other diurnal creatures have evolved to perceive the range of frequencies of radiation from the sun – what we term 'visible light' – so too the receptor cells in the skin have evolved to perceive the range of temperatures in the atmosphere. This atmospheric and meteorological variability is of as great consequence for the activities of humans as it is for other animals.

Unlike other animals, though, humans have unusually varied and elaborate forms of social life and communication that are made possible by language and by culture. Our complex forms of collective life influence the way that we are affected by weather and climate, creating both forms of vulnerability and capacities to reduce impacts. Our highly developed cognitive capacities allow us to recall the past and to anticipate the future. We draw on this strong temporal awareness when we discuss weather and climate. In societies around the world, people talk about the recent weather and the weather that is to come, they remember the conditions months ago and anticipate future seasons, and they discuss the weather far in the past as well. These multiple time frames form a key aspect of human experience of the weather.

Physical experience of the weather provides a common focal point in many societies, through both commiseration and celebration. Many cultures note links between exceptional climate events and historical events. In a related manner, the regular sequence of the seasons often serves as an image for the steadiness of time's passage and the permanence of the fundamental parameters of human existence. Ritual practices integral to the spiritual life of many societies often address these annual cycles. Accounts of cultural or moral change are often associated with narratives of changing climate and vice versa; references to a 'golden age' of prosperity are often accompanied by descriptions of a mild climate. Weather can be called or diverted by human actions, and atmospheric conditions have frequently been explained with reference to a religious context. Here, we think of the Norse god Thor and his thunder hammer, Mjollnir, or, among the African Mbuti people made famous by Colin Turnbull, good weather indicates the favor of the forest god, while a bad storm indicates the reverse. The Great Flood of the Old Testament has parallels among the Tlingit of British Columbia as well as many other cultural contexts. Some present examples of this phenomenon include state governors in Brazil who fear that news of a drought will lead to voters choosing a different candidate in the next election; mishandled snow removal programs in a number of US cities that have deeply angered residents, who believe that adequate management of extreme weather events is the responsibility of public officials; and even debates about global warming that have taken on a novel tinge as adherents of one position paint their opponents as selfish or meddling.

Competing explanations for weather events and conditions have a long and noble history. At the beginning of his *Discourse on Meteorology*, René Descartes suggests that

> Although the clouds are hardly any higher than the summits of some mountains . . . nevertheless, because we must turn our eyes toward the sky to look at them, we fancy them to be so high that poets and painters even fashion them into God's throne, and picture Him there, using His own hands to open and close the doors of the winds, to sprinkle the dew upon the flowers, and to hurl the lightening against the rocks. This leads me to the hope that if I here explain the nature of clouds in such a way that we will no longer have occasion to wonder at anything that descends from them, we will easily believe that it is similarly possible to find causes of everything that is most admirable above the earth. (Descartes 2001 [1637]: 263)

Descartes' desire to render even this most ethereal of subjects explicable in terms of tangible physical processes has, to a great extent, seen fulfillment in the achievements of climatologists and other atmospheric scientists over the past few decades. Yet the explanatory and predictive powers of even the best weather and climate models are still limited, as we see in the case of global climate change. The weather's vagaries and their impact on everyday life remain significant elements of ordinary conversation and of political debate.

The relationship between human communities and the natural environment has been the subject of many academic treatises (e.g.: Rappaport 1968; Netting 1981; Anderson 1996; Ingold 2000; Orlove 2002). In the field of anthropology, particularly over the past thirty years, this research has often been generated from one of two camps, the materially grounded ecologists and the meaning-centered symbolic anthropologists. But of course the notion that either end of this spectrum could fully account for humanity's complex relationships with the natural world is untenable. In this volume, we have made an effort not to exclude one side or the other, but rather to integrate the two in our examination of the wide range of ways that human groups in different places and times think about and respond to meteorological phenomena.

We have often noted a comparison between the study of the human body and the study of the natural world. As recently as the 1970s, relatively few anthropologists thought that the cultural aspects of the human body merited attention; Mary Douglas' elaboration of the notion of the physical and social bodies (1970) was one of the first detailed analyses of this topic. The British Association of Social Anthropologists took on 'The Body' as a central concern in the mid-1970s, producing an edited volume (Blacking 1977) that spurred further interest in the subject. Yet only a few decades later, the body is understood as central to many key issues. Gender studies, taking the lead of Michel Foucault and others, have shown that the separation of physical, social, and political conceptions of the body have significant implications for the distribution of power in a society (Ortner 1974). It was not until 1987, with the publication of both Scheper-Hughes and Lock's 'The Mindful Body' in the first issue of the new series of *Medical Anthropology Quarterly*, and Emily Martin's important work on *The Woman in the Body*, that interest in the body as a primary site for cultural analysis as well as medical analysis really took off. Performance studies have focused attention on the importance of movement and presentation of self (Goffman 1959; Taussig 1987), as well as on the notion of lived experience (Turner 1986). Mauss' work on 'Techniques of the Body' (1973 [1936]) has been used as a platform for expanding studies of bodily practice (e.g. Csordas 1994; Strauss 2004). Many forms of racial distinction and inequality around the world are now understood as centrally linked to concepts of the human body (Stolcke 1993). Part of this shift derives from the internal dynamics of anthropology, and part from broader social concerns, in which bioethics has become a topic of wide concern. It is important to note that anthropologists of many different theoretical orientations have adopted the body as a topic of study.

In a similar way, the natural world has received growing attention from anthropologists (e.g. Descola and Pálsson 1996). Though the concept of environmental adaptation has a long history in anthropology, newer approaches have begun to consider nature in other ways. Where earlier generations of anthropologists looked at animals as resources that could provide food, hides, wool and labor, more recent studies have explored the cognitive, symbolic and ritual dimensions of animals (e.g. Lawrence 1982; Mullin 1999). As anthropologists have turned their attention to nationalism, they have also examined the use of metaphors of soil and of territory as constituents of national or postcolonial identities (e.g. Gupta 1998; Brody 1998; Orlove 1998; Gold and Gujar 2002). Linking local and global concerns, the politics of water resources has also received some attention recently (Donahue and Johnston 1998; Lansing 1991; Gelles 2000). The time, then, is right for a more extended anthropological consideration of weather and climate, key aspects of the natural world. Like the study of the human body, this subject echoes discussion outside academic circles as well, since climate change has become a topic of public debate. And like the study of the human body, a focus on the natural world allows consideration from many different perspectives across the subfields of anthropology (e.g. Butzer 1971; Basso 1996; Fagan 1999; Crumley 2001; Orlove 2002).

The structure of this volume centers on two key issues. First, we examine the different time frames in which weather and climate are experienced. Atmospheric scientists distinguish short-term *weather* events from long-term *climate* patterns, demonstrating one dominant view of this temporal dimension. However, particular social and cultural forms also shape the ways that these phenomena are perceived, recalled, and anticipated. In concrete settings around the world, people experience, discuss, and interpret meteorological phenomena in ways that are dependent not only on the physical characteristics of the events, but also on the cultural frameworks that divide time into current, recent, and distant periods. These frameworks lead us to the second issue, language. To state what may seem obvious, but what nonetheless merits consideration, we note that human responses to weather and climate rest on talking. People communicate through various forms of verbal expression, from proverbs to oral histories and everyday conversations, and on to scientific discourses. Moreover, the social and political responses to specific weather events or climate change reflect these cultural constructions of time. For example, though chitchat about current weather conditions is considered a politically safe subject in many parts of the United States and Europe, ruminations about long-term climate change are highly charged, and often polemic. Our different cultures shape the way that we think and respond to the weather; as we face the impacts that climate change processes bring to our communities, we must recognize that our perceptions as well as our reactions are shaped by our culture.

We suggest that the cognitive and symbolic aspects of weather and climate deserve as much attention as the responses to specific weather events or conditions, since these two are ultimately inseparable; moreover, we argue that it is also important to address historical perspectives (to greater or lesser extents, depending on the orientation of the particular chapter, archaeology, ethnohistory, or simple background for a contemporary study). For these reasons, the authors in this volume present both climatological crises as well as everyday weather-related activities. They also highlight the distinction between what people *think* – for example, data derived from cognitive science, ethnoscience and other kinds of categorical analyses which tend to link up with observed behavior and responses; and what they *feel* about weather and climate conditions – for example, symbolic studies which emphasize cosmology or moral order. Phrased differently, this is the distinction between how people *describe* weather and climate and how people *comprehend* them. For all that weather and climate may seem ordinary and almost trivial, they also evoke strong responses.

The available literature on weather and climate concerns has expanded drama-tically in the last decade. Popular and scholarly books document both specific extreme weather events (Larson and Cline 2000; Drye 2002; Brown 2002), as well as the history of more mundane daily weather phenomena and the techniques and terminologies for describing such natural occurrences (Mergen 1997; Hamblyn 2001; Janković 2001). There are also many excellent social and political histories that document the impact of mid- to long-range climatic conditions on human activities (Ladurie 1971; Worster 1992; Fagan 1999, 2001).

But what are the ways that ordinary people actually talk and write about weather and climate? We use a variety of written and oral forms of communication, and for many of these genres, there exists a particular meteorological variant. For example, the diary is a well-known format for personal history in the western context; since the seventeenth century, as Golinski (this volume) and Pfister et al. (1999) have documented so convincingly, the weather diary has been an important written tool that allows for daily documentation of local conditions. Proverbs, those pithy sayings so easily remembered and reinvented as the circumstances warrant, are common around the world, and provide advice on every subject of importance to human societies. Weather proverbs, usually referring to atmospheric conditions within the range of daily to annual cycles, are a popular category within this genre (Strauss, this volume). A parallel format, the weather forecast, is part of the technical discourse on the weather; weather forecasts are generally local or regional, and predict short-term (less than 10-day) expectations for weather events.

Many typical folk genres express knowledge regarding the full range of weather and climate conditions. Jokes about atmospheric conditions may refer either to singular events or to expected climatic conditions, and help to address emotional responses to unavoidable situations. Myths, and the rituals which frequently accompany them, may refer likewise to a singular but important event (like the Great Flood) or give reasons for climatic conditions perceived to be new or changing from past patterns. They may also explain mid-range phenomena like El Niño or local drought conditions, based on moral or physical trespasses against the gods. So these narrative forms, usually present in oral versions but sometimes also in written varieties, have perhaps the widest range in terms of their temporal relevance for weather and climate. Song and tale traditions, which are often passed orally from one generation to the next, may commemorate a specific extreme event; they are also used to document prior climate conditions and perhaps the reasons for such change.

When we move to the mid- to long-range temporal scale (what we have here labeled 'years' and 'generations'), we find again that both oral and written histories preserve patterns of climate variability, as in the Sagas of Iceland (Ogilvie and Pálsson, this volume) or the stories of Inuit elders (Cruikshank 2001; Henshaw, this volume). In many parts of Europe and Asia, church or community records include narrative documentation of plantings and harvests, with specific reference to the climatic conditions that determined these outcomes (Ladurie 1971). The scientific parallels to these long-range records include ice-core data and, in the future tense, predictive climate models.

Though time passes continuously, it can be broken into units of different lengths. We have selected three major types of time intervals to categorize the varied aspects of human perception and response to weather and climate. The first and shortest time interval that we address in this volume can be termed days. Days are temporal units that people use to discuss events; they are distinctive in their immediacy. This temporal unit corresponds to what meteorologists call weather. We note that this time interval is associated with certain forms of language and communication, such as weather recording, weather proverbs, and ritual responses to unusual weather. Jan Golinski opens the 'Days' section with a study of the weather diaries written by eighteenth century British scholars and gentlemen. He shows how these daily measurements of meteorological phenomena were re-worked into scientific treatises by Enlightenment theorists, and helps us understand the roots of the contemporary weather and climate sciences. Sarah Strauss' exploration of weather forecasting techniques and discourse questions the relationship between 'scientific' meteorology and weather proverbs. Michael Paolisso takes us to the Chesapeake Bay on the east coast of North America, where daily weather conditions and official forecasts receive close scrutiny by local watermen whose lives and livelihoods depend on accurate tracking of these phenomena. Todd Sanders presents a detailed ethnographic example of the performance of a Tanzanian rain-bringing ceremony, giving special attention to the gendered and symbolic meanings of the elements of this ritual practice. Trevor Harley reflects on the concerns and queries of contemporary residents of the United Kingdom regarding the weather, using data collected from his British Weather Internet site. Though these cases are all quite different, they show that even the most routine and apparently banal observation of the weather can serve concrete economic ends and also broader moral concerns about proper conduct.

The second and intermediate temporal unit is termed 'years'. It corresponds to what atmospheric scientists called climate, or, more precisely, climatology: the fact that temperature, rainfall and other meteorological phenomena have a strong annual pattern everywhere in the world. We note that this time interval is also associated with certain forms of language and communication, particularly a great attentiveness to the cycle of the seasons. Ben Orlove analyzes the different ways that various cultures handle the problem of defining seasons in their everyday speech. While the northern European expectation assumes four distinctive annual seasons, not every environment lends itself to such a clear-cut distinction, and not every language has a way of expressing temperature and precipitation variability in the same ways. From John Thornes and Gemma Metherell's discussion of

Monet's paintings of the foggy London scenes, we gain an appreciation for the ways that both artists and policymakers viewed weather conditions, and can see the beauty of the changing atmospheric conditions along with their consequences for health and safety. These studies show that the strong human capacity to form attachments with particular places rests not only on the human affinity for landscapes or vegetation, but for seasonal phenomena as well. Even though weather can be very routine, it still commands human attention.

Much as the section on 'days' includes discussion of how weather shifts from one day to the next, this section on 'years' considers the way that climate patterns can vary, within certain limits, from one year to the next. The impacts of El Niño-induced drought from the perspective of the Pawaia people in Papua New Guinea provides the central problem for David Ellis' chapter. He offers a comprehensive view of how local perceptions of extreme weather events may be viewed within the same framework as national and international perspectives and directives. In a similar vein, Roncoli and her co-authors explore the ways that farmers in the West African nation of Burkina Faso interpret seasonal rainfall forecasts that have been developed for their use by the national weather service in collaboration with Roncoli's research team. They discuss the utility of making probabilistic weather data available to local producers as a method for increasing economic benefits, pointing out that the communication of such information is but one small part of the entire set of changes required for improving the well-being of farmers in this arid portion of the West African Sahel. These cases indicate how people view climate from multiple perspectives, seeing its moral and political significance as well as its economic importance.

The third and longest temporal unit is termed 'generations'. It corresponds to what atmospheric scientists called climate variability and climate change: the fact that temperature, rainfall and other meteorological phenomena in many places shift significantly, whether passing through cycles that are decades or centuries in length, or changing on even longer time scales. We note that this time interval is associated with certain forms of language and communication as well, including formal narrative genres of folk-tales, the use of place-names to record different weather events, and public discussions of changing climate. Indeed, we call this interval 'generations' rather than 'decades' to stress the connection between individual experience and collective conversation. In many parts of the world, people note that the weather was different in the time of their parents, grandparents, and earlier generations; in this way, they refer to the fact that they have heard the oral testimony of people who have lived in those times. Tim Finan looks at the lengthy history of drought mitigation in Brazil, showing that the uses of forecasts by local farmers are limited by the ways that they are perceived and presented by policymakers. Since the nineteenth century, drought has been a commonplace in the Brazilian region of Ceará. Even with the recent effort to add scientific forecasting to the existing local empirical forecasting tradition, the outcomes remain poor, because farmers have few options for changing their growing strategies to accommodate even the most accurate of precipitation predictions. The forecasts become part of the political dynamic of the region and serve as a medium for farmers to voice their views about the state's responsibility to the population.

Anne Henshaw takes us to the far north, with an archaeological and ethnohistorical account of climate change among the Inuit. She presents a case study utilizing a variety of data types to help understand how human groups have adapted to changing climatic conditions. Ogilvie and Pálsson follow a similar route, although their primary reference point is not oral history but the written sagas of Icelanders as compared with ice-core data regarding climate variability in Iceland. West and Vásquez-León look across generations in Arizona to determine whether farmers' perceptions of their local climate match up with scientific assessments of the same period, concluding that there is indeed a significant link between the two. In these cases, the familiarity with a long record of climate variability becomes a key component of local identities.

Having brought forward these two key observations regarding the temporal and linguistic aspects of the relationship between meteorological phenomena and human societies, we must also add a few notes of caution: the boundaries that separate days from years and generations are not hard and fast, nor are the associations between temporal intervals and speech genres fixed. While we have given examples of particular types of speech event that refer to a temporal interval at the immediate, mid-range, or long-term level, this list is by no means exhaustive. Instead of providing a complete typology, our goal is to present an introduction to an emergent area of inquiry, the anthropology of weather and climate, and to demonstrate the significance of using an anthropological eye – and ear – to understand the ways that human societies make sense of this basic aspect of their environment. Even as this volume goes to press, we can see a wide array of topics that invite further research in this area: the attitudes and beliefs of televised weather channel viewing audiences; the shifts in decision-making processes that local farmers and fishermen must make in order to take into consideration new forms of weather and climate information; the economic and political ramifications of the expansion of forecasting divisions within private corporations such as insurance and energy companies; the ways that increasing technical knowledge of climatic processes might influence new generations across the globe to reconsider the many different choices that must be made about future resource use; the recording of memories regarding weather events past; or even the ways that humor is used to convey frustration with or appreciation of meteorological conditions as they are experienced in the present.

We note as well that our discussion can offer a useful perspective on the world-wide concern with climate change. These debates center on the Kyoto Protocol, the key international agreement. Promulgated in 1997, it established the United Nations Framework Convention on Climate Change (UNFCCC) as the forum to discuss this critical issue and to find means to mitigate its effects. The national delegations to this convention have debated the nature of climate change as well as the appropriate means for reducing emissions of greenhouse gasses into the atmosphere and for removing them from the atmosphere into forests, oceans, and other sinks. They have proposed different goals and deadlines for emissions levels, and considered a variety of mechanisms to ensure that these goals and deadlines are met. The UNFCCC meetings have focused primarily on matters of science and politics, so experts in climatology or in international relations might seem more appropriate than anthropologists to discuss this protocol. However, we note that the two key dimensions that we examine, *time* and *talk*, are central for these contemporary debates about climate change. To be sure, the long-term objective of the protocol is to alter human actions in the real world, such as the patterns of energy sources and use that produce emissions of greenhouse gasses. But the major activity of the protocol to date has been the effort to construct a shared narrative, a verbal framework that links specific actors, institutions, and political entities. Within our perspective, we could say that the delegates speak as if they are planning action, but what they are doing first is developing a narrative account, or what we might in general terms call a script. As negotiations continue, the various players debate the shape that the final script will take. What period should it cover? What actions should the different characters perform? Above all, what is the underlying sense of moral responsibility and connectedness that the script should convey? Though this analogy might not be one that the delegates would identify with themselves, its value lies in showing that cultural patterns, centered on language, are important in shaping relations that might otherwise be seen as based entirely on economic and political self-interest.

As we have worked on the development of this project, from first discussions to the production of an Anthropology & Environment Section invited session at the 2001 annual meeting of the American Anthropological Association, and finally to the document now in the reader's hands, we have found that the topic of weather and climate has generated intrigue and approval across many audiences. Based on queries and comments we have received from the popular media, college students, our own relatives, and our academic colleagues, it would seem that the time is right to speak more of what we have to say about the weather!

References

ANDERSON, EUGENE. 1996. *Ecologies of the Heart*. Oxford: Oxford University Press.

BASSO, KEITH. 1996. *Wisdom Sits in Places.* Albuquerque: University of New Mexico Press.

BLACKING, JOHN (Ed.). 1977. *The Anthropology of the Body.* London: Tavistock.

BRODY, HUGH. 1998 [1981]. *Maps and Dreams.* Prospect Heights, IL: Waveland Press.

BROWN, DAVID. 2002. *White Hurricane.* Camden, ME: McGraw-Hill/International Marine Publishing.

BUTZER, KARL W. 1971. *Environment and Archaeology: An Ecological Approach to Prehistory.* Chicago: Aldine Atherton.

CRUIKSHANK, JULIE. 2001. Glaciers and Climate Change: Perspectives from Oral Tradition. *Arctic* 54(4): 377–93.

CRUMLEY, CAROLE. 2001. *New Directions in Anthropology and Environment.* Walnut Creek, CA: Altamira Press.

CSORDAS, THOMAS (Ed.). 1994. *Embodiment and Experience: The Existential Ground of Culture and Self.* Cambridge: Cambridge University Press.

DESCARTES, RENE. 2001 [1637]. *Discourse on Method, Optics, Geometry, and Meteorology.* Trans. Paul Olscamp. Indianapolis: Hackett Publishing Company.

DESCOLA, PHILIPPE and GISLI PÁLSSON. 1996. *Nature and Society: Anthropological Perspectives.* London: Routledge.

DONAHUE, JOHN M. and BARBARA ROSE JOHNSTON (Eds). 1998. *Water, Culture and Power.* Washington, DC and Covelo, CA: Island Press.

DOUGLAS, MARY. 1970. *Natural Symbols.* New York: Vintage Books.

DRYE, WILLIE. 2002. *Storm of the Century: The Labor Day Hurricane of 1935.* Washington, DC: National Geographic Society.

FAGAN, BRIAN. 1999. *Floods, Famines, and Emperors: El Niño and the Fate of Civilizations.* New York: Basic Books.

—— 2001. *The Little Ice Age: How Climate Made History.* New York: Basic Books.

GELLES, PAUL. 2000. *Water and Power in Highland Peru.* Camden: Rutgers University Press.

GOFFMAN, ERVING. 1959. *The Presentation of Self in Everyday Life.* Doubleday: Garden City, New York.

GOLD, ANN and BHOJU RAM GUJAR. 2002. *In the Time of Trees and Sorrows: Nature, Power, and Memory in Rajasthan.* Durham, NC: Duke University Press.

GUPTA, AKHIL. 1998. *Postcolonial Development: Agriculture in the Making of a Modern Nation.* Durham, NC: Duke University Press.

HAMBLYN, RICHARD. 2001. *The Invention of Clouds: How an Amateur Meteorologist Forged the Language of the Skies.* New York: Farrar, Straus & Giroux.

INGOLD, TIM. 2000. *The Perception of the Environment: Essays in Livelihood, Dwelling, and Skill.* London: Routledge.

JANKOVIĆ, VLADIMIR. 2001. *Reading the Skies: A Cultural History of English Weather, 1650–1820*. Chicago: University of Chicago Press.

LADURIE, EMMANUEL. 1971. *Times of Feast, Times of Famine: A History of Climate since the Year 1000*. Garden City, NY: Doubleday.

LANSING, JOHN. 1991. *Priests and Programmers*. Princeton: Princeton University Press.

LARSON, ERIK and ISAAC CLINE. 2000. *Isaac's Storm: A Man, a Time, and the Deadliest Hurricane in History*. New York: Vintage Books.

LAWRENCE, ELIZABETH. 1982. *Rodeo: An Anthropologist looks at the Wild and the Tame*. Knoxville: University of Tennessee Press.

MARTIN, EMILY. 1987. *The Woman in the Body*. Boston: Beacon Press.

MAUSS, MARCEL. 1973 [1936]. Techniques of the Body. *Economy and Society* 2: 70–88.

MERGEN, BERNARD. 1997. *Snow in America*. Washington, DC: Smithsonian Institute Press.

MULLIN, MOLLY. 1999. Mirrors and Windows: Sociocultural Studies of Human–Animal Relationships. *Annual Review of Anthropology* 28: 201–24.

NETTING, ROBERT. 1981. *Balancing on an Alp*. Cambridge: Cambridge University Press.

ORLOVE, BEN. 1998. Down to Earth: Race and Substance in the Andes. *Bulletin of Latin American Research* 17(2): 207–22.

—— 2002. *Lines in the Water: Nature and Culture at Lake Titicaca*. Berkeley and London: University of California Press.

ORTNER, SHERRY. 1974. Is Female to Male as Nature is to Culture? In *Woman, Culture, and Society*. Michelle Zimbalist Rosaldo and Louise Lamphere, eds. Stanford: Stanford University Press.

PFISTER, CHRISTIAN, R. BRÁZDIL, R. GLASER, A. BOKWA, D. LIMANÓWKA, F. HOLAWE, O. KOTYZA, J. MUNZAR, L. RÁCZ, E. STRÖMMER and G. SCHWARZ-ZANETTI. 1999. Daily Weather Observations. In *Climatic Variability in Sixteenth Century Europe and Its Social Dimension*. Edited by Pfister, Chr., Bradzil, R. and R. Glaser. *Climatic Change*, Special Vol. 43(1): 111–150.

RAPPAPORT, ROY. 1984 [1968]. *Pigs for the Ancestors*. Enlarged Edition. New Haven: Yale University Press.

SCHEPER-HUGHES, NANCY and MARGARET LOCK. 1987. The Mindful Body: A Prolegomenon to Future Work in Medical Anthropology. *Med. Anth. Quarterly* n.s. 1(1): 6–41.

STOLCKE, VERENA, (Ed.). 1993. *Mujeres Invadidas. La Sangre de la Conquista de América*. Madrid: Editorial Horas y Horas.

STRAUSS, SARAH. 2004. *Positioning Yoga*. Oxford: Berg Publishers.

TAUSSIG, MICHAEL.1987. *Shamanism, Colonialism, and the Wild Man: A Study of Terror and Healing*. Chicago: University of Chicago Press.

TURNER, VICTOR. 1986. *The Anthropology of Performance.* New York: PAJ Publications.

WORSTER, Donald. 1992. *Rivers of Empire: Water, Aridity, and the Growth of the American West.* Oxford: Oxford University Press.

DAYS

–2–

Time, Talk, and the Weather in Eighteenth-Century Britain[1]

Jan Golinski

The weather is woven into our experiences of modern life in many ways. Remarks about what it is doing or about to do smooth our everyday social interactions. Reports, observations, and predictions punctuate our daily routines. If anything, modern communications have made us more aware of extreme weather conditions and their devastating effects: floods, storms, blizzards, tornadoes, and hurricanes are represented to us in graphic detail, even when they occur on the other side of the world. The circumstances of modern life may have shielded us from some of the threats faced by environmentally more vulnerable communities, but, in other respects, modern conditions have raised new concerns about the weather and how it might disrupt our comfortable lives. In developed countries, people worry that the climate is changing as a result of human activity affecting the natural environment. In this respect, contemporary reflections on the weather express anxieties about modernity itself, especially the fear that nature has been trespassed upon by modern technological civilization and will now wreak its revenge. The French philosopher Michel Serres, who has written extensively on this topic, remarks that, 'Today our expertise and our worries turn toward the weather, because our industrious know-how is acting, perhaps catastrophically, on global nature' (Serres 1995: 27).

The British have a peculiar outlook on the weather, as anyone who has spent time in the country knows. Partly this is because the weather there does have some singular features, and partly it is because certain ways of thinking and talking about it have become deeply embedded in the national culture. It is striking, for example, how many of the things one hears said about the British weather reflect uncertainties about the nation's identity in the modern world. The climate, which is recollected nostalgically as equable and temperate, is said to be changing for the worse. Extreme events, such as violent storms and floods, constitute urgent reminders of this possibility. Wetter springs and autumns seem to be bringing more of these hazards. Winter blizzards also seem to be becoming more common. Warmer summers, which one might imagine would be welcome, are said to bear the threat of invasion by foreign insects and diseases. Poised uncertainly on the edge of the European Union, the British worry that their weather is becoming 'more Continental'. These concerns seem to mirror anxieties about the nation's status and its uncertain future. The good old British weather is apparently passing away. The national climate that has fertilized the crops and toughened the bodily fibers, whose variability strengthened the people's character while its temperateness nurtured commerce and agriculture, may soon be only a memory.

These aspects of the British preoccupation with the weather relate to the country's historical experiences during the last few centuries. Significant shifts in how the weather has been understood have coincided with episodes of social and cultural change. Along with the continuing challenge of defining national identity, the British have experienced conflicts between religious and secular outlooks, and tensions between elite and vernacular cultures. Particularly crucial – I shall argue – was the experience of modernization during the eighteenth-century Enlightenment, when new ideas about the national climate came to the fore. In this period, the country witnessed burgeoning commerce and the beginnings of revolutionary growth in agriculture and industry. Natural resources were exploited on an unprecedented scale, and serious reflection was devoted to how human activities were impinging upon the natural world. There was a new awareness of the environment as a system of relationships in which human beings are implicated, a milieu that affects human life in many ways and can be significantly altered by human action. This was also the period when ideas about the relations between climate and national character were first articulated, when many of the notions recycled in contemporary laments about climate change originated. As part of their experience of enlightenment modernization, the British forged a sense of their national weather, its peculiarities and regularities, and its providential role in the life of the nation.[2]

In this essay, I shall draw upon a larger project in which I am engaged to discuss the relationship between weather and modernization in eighteenth-century Britain. I shall do so under the headings of 'time' and 'talk'. Regarding *time*, I shall point to connections between new notions of the weather and new experiences of temporal order in this period. In the course of the eighteenth century, standard measures of time derived from mechanical clocks gradually displaced the more flexible modes of measurement that had previously governed human activity. A standard civic calendar was also imposed over the customary structure of religious feasts and rural festivals. In 1752, Britain joined continental Europe in using the Gregorian calendar, at the cost of dropping eleven days between September 2 and 14 of that year. These changes in how time was measured formed the backdrop to an enterprise of systematic recording of the weather, which was designed to reduce it to regular order. The aim was to catalogue the weather exhaustively through practices of diary-keeping and journalism, in order to make it *quotidian* – that is to say, an everyday affair sharing the diurnal pattern of daily life. The temporal frameworks of the clock and the calendar were used to subject the weather to rational ordering and normalization. By these means, weather emerged as a public phenomenon, as news events or as history. It came to be seen as the property of the nation, intimately bound up with its character and destiny.

This public weather was the subject of *talk*, in many different social locations. The journalist Joseph Addison, in his daily periodical, *The Spectator* (1711–12), wrote that the discourse in polite companies of men and women frequently turned on 'weather, fashions, news and the like publick topicks'.[3] By becoming a public matter, comparable to fashion and news, the weather had become a fit topic for polite conversation. But talk about the weather was not always so civilized. Certain kinds of talk – that of illiterate or rural people, for example, and also gossip and proverbial speech among the educated – tended to subvert the program of reducing the weather to systematic order. Even polite conversation would frequently resort to oral lore and vernacular traditions dating from before the spread of enlightenment culture. Although 'vulgar superstitions' were regularly denounced in polite discourse, traditional oral wisdom was often resorted to. When it came to forecasting the weather, proverbial lore gave the best advice available. In addition, the weather continued to throw up monstrous and inexplicable phenomena, which were widely reported and commented upon. The weather remained stubbornly irregular and unpredictable, notwithstanding the efforts of enlightened investigators; and of course, it remains to a significant degree beyond the reach of human understanding and control to this day. The point has been made in our own time in the idiom of postmodernism (Andrew Ross's 'strange weather') or chaos theory (the unpredictable effects of the butterfly flapping its wings) (Ross 1991). But the observation was already a familiar one to reflective intellectuals in the eighteenth century. By considering the part played by the weather in eighteenth-century Britain's experience of modernization, we can gauge the extent to which it has always escaped comprehension within the systems of enlightenment rationality.

I shall begin with a dramatic event, the 'Great Storm' of 1703, which has remained present in the national memory ever since. On the night of 26–27 November 1703, an especially violent tempest tore across southern England and the Low Countries, uprooting trees, tearing down houses, and sinking ships. Hundreds of thousands of trees were uprooted, and hundreds of houses destroyed; estimates of human fatalities ran into the thousands, most of them lost at sea. The storm forcefully impinged on the lives of the entire population and demanded some kind of explanation from intellectuals. In the whirlwind of printed pamphlets that followed, the central question was whether the event was to be seen as a divine admonition or punishment, or as the result of regular natural causes. Sermonizing clergy and the authors of moralistic tracts insisted that the storm was God's punishment for the sins of modern life. One anonymous author particularly fingered the depravities of the London theatre, and condemned those who advanced alternative naturalistic explanations for the devastation, along the lines 'That the storm was nothing but an Eruption of *Epicurus's* Atoms; a Spring-Tide of Matter and Motion.' According to this author, the tempestuous wind had acted abnormally, and, 'when Natural Agents act in a strange, unusual manner . . . this is from the Lord.'[4] The storm was thus to be regarded as a departure from the normal course of nature, one of the abnormal atmospheric events that were agents and messengers of God. As another anonymous writer explained, phenomena of this kind were appropriately located in the heavens to communicate the divine omen to all who saw them: 'strange and amazing Tempests, Storms, and Thunders, . . . Excessive Inundations of Water, . . . Alterations in the Heavens, strange Appearances of the Sun and Moon . . . [are] set in the fair and spacious Theatre of Heaven as the fittest place to represent those Divine shews to the view of all' (Anon. 1692: 15).

This interpretation of the storm was opposed by a number of natural philosophers. Reviewing the event several years later, another anonymous author insisted that 'there is nothing in all this which supposes or implies any immediate Interposition of God' (Anon. 1711: 16). At the time of the event itself, natural causes were emphasized by the correspondents who reported on its effects in the pages of the Royal Society's *Philosophical Transactions*, including the Essex clergyman William Derham, and the Dutch merchant Anton van Leeuwenhoek (Derham 1704–5; Leeuwenhoek 1704–5). The natural philosophers did not deny God's role altogether, but they emphasized that the event unfolded according to regular natural laws, which were the results of God's ordinary providence rather than of His occasional miraculous interventions. A programmatic statement of this way of thinking was written two decades later by John Pointer, chaplain of Merton College, Oxford. In his *Rational Account of the Weather* (1723), Pointer called for the meteorological realm to be reduced to natural law as Newton had tamed the motions of the planets and comets by making them accountable to the law of gravity: 'For Natural Causes do Naturally (i.e. according to the settled Order and Nature of things) produce Natural Effects' (Pointer 1723: vii). For Pointer, God's ordinary providence, by which He sustained the laws of nature, was not to be disparaged by postulating miracles to explain unusual phenomena. Those who emphasized strange or unique meteors (such as auroras or visions of armies fighting in the air), and who interpreted them as miraculous, were guilty of 'a kind of enthusiasm' – an error both theologically culpable and politically dangerous, in Pointer's view (Pointer 1723: 196). The more secure path was to uncover the workings of natural causation, revealed by the underlying regularity of meteorological events.

Pointer spoke for those who saw the weather as governed by regular laws of nature. For him, and for those intellectuals who thought like him, a rational view of the natural world regarded it as uniform and harmonious. A good and wise God was thought to uphold universal laws producing regular – perhaps ultimately predictable – phenomena. The weather would therefore be expected to follow some recurring pattern, like the movements of the planets. Unusual events were simply the exceptions that proved the rule; they should not be accorded any special significance. To do so would be to succumb to popular superstition and fear of the unknown. Pointer's argument took its place in a widespread movement, analyzed by the historians Lorraine Daston and Katharine Park, in which enlightened intellectuals denigrated the popular fascination with – and fear of – various kinds of marvels and wonders.[5] In place of this 'kind of enthusiasm', those who advocated a naturalistic understanding of the weather sought to domesticate its spectacular phenomena by showing how divine providence underwrote a uniform order of nature.

The way this was to be done had already been mapped out by 1703: if every day's weather was recorded, not just extreme or unusual events, it could be reduced to the formulaic and routine. This was the rationale for the compilation of systematic weather diaries, begun among the members of the Royal Society of London in the 1660s. Robert Hooke published a 'Method for Making a History of the Weather' in Thomas Sprat's *History of the Royal Society* in 1667, laying out the format for a daily journal (Hooke 1667). At the urging of Robert Boyle, the young physician and philosopher John Locke began to keep a weather diary in June 1666 and continued (with some gaps) until May 1703. To begin with, Locke took two or more readings of thermometer, barometer, and wind gauge on almost every day for the first six months.[6] His dedication was later matched by William Derham, vicar of Upminster, whose annual journals, including instrumental readings for every day from 1697 to 1702, were published in the *Philosophical Transactions* (Atkinson 1952). In rural Worcestershire, an obscure gentleman, Thomas Appletree, compiled a diary of the weather during the year of the Great Storm itself, attempting to discern amidst the apparently chaotic torrents of the atmosphere the guiding hand of divine providence.[7] Later in the eighteenth century, weather diaries for a month at a time became standard features of periodicals ranging from the *Philosophical Transactions* to the *Gentleman's Magazine*. Dozens of journals, sometimes extending for a decade or longer, were published during the century, and many more survive in manuscript repositories.

The diarists frequently claimed that the moderation of the British weather was an example of God's providential benevolence to their country. A commentator on the 1703 storm, who criticized the notion that it was a direct act of God, nonetheless thought it appropriate to give thanks that the normal temperateness of the English climate prevented this kind of event occurring very often (Anon. 1711: 21). Thomas Appletree, recording the weather in the same tempestuous year, wrote: 'I doubt not God whom winds and seas obey disposes of clouds & Rain to use & benefit of that corner it is directed to.'[8] The Irish Quaker physician John Rutty, who recorded the weather in Dublin from 1725 to 1766, denounced 'Lazy men' who complained that the weather was capricious and lacking in periodical patterns. According to Rutty, the diligent observer could readily discern 'the footsteps of divine Wisdom and Goodness, presiding over these seemingly irregular operations' (Rutty 1772, II: 275, 280–281). Those who complained about extreme or unpredictable weather were turning their backs on the blessings of providence, which had in fact bestowed a benevolent climate on Ireland, as disciplined observation had shown. In England, also, the providential benefits of the national climate, including its goodness for human health, were said to emerge clearly from systematic records of the weather. Extreme and violent events were found to be rather infrequent. For the most part, the English weather displayed a gentle variability in temperature and pressure, visible to the investigator who followed events day by day. The physician John Arbuthnot, author of an *Essay Concerning the Effects of Air on Human Bodies* (1733), thought this variation was particularly healthy for the inhabitants of the British Isles. John Fothergill agreed that the English people had 'abundant cause to be satisfied' with their climate. William Falconer, an Edinburgh-trained physician who wrote about the influence of climate on national character, observed that the very fact that the English were interested in this field of research was itself testimony to the influence of the English weather on the intellectual character of the inhabitants. The diurnal mutability of the climate stimulated mental alertness, Falconer claimed, while its general temperateness fostered good judgment.[9]

The enterprise of systematic weather observation emphasized the normal regularities of the atmosphere rather than violent peculiarities like the 1703 storm. To quote Michel Serres again, this kind of normalization integrated even the rarest of events into a secular continuum, 'where the irregular becomes all but normal' (Serres 1995: 4). Weather was to be seen as a continuous process rather than as occasional dramatic events, as the domain of constant providential supervision rather than as an arena of spectacular divine interventions. Instead of providing graphic descriptions of unique meteoric incidents, recorders of the weather mapped its daily routines. Studied in this manner, the British climate was found to be generally temperate overall but punctuated by bracing diurnal variations. In both features observers discerned the special dispensations of a providence favorably disposed to the British people.

In casting their records in the form of daily journals, the weather observers had adopted the temporal framework of the public calendar. Diarists placed events within a chronological structure, established prior to the incidents recorded, which could be extended indefinitely to encompass any occurrence. The availability of this framework made the composition of a diary, more or less, a matter of routine – a practice that demanded a degree of discipline and perseverance, but where the formal outlines of the writing were laid down in advance. The weather diarists often established the calendrical outline graphically by drawing lines on a blank page to mark spaces for each day in the month to come. Later in the century, printed forms became available in which observers could fill in the blanks to compile a daily record of the weather. These methods provided the formal structure within which a record of the British climate was compiled.

They also reflected the trend in eighteenth-century Britain toward the wider adoption of uniform measures of time, defined by the clock and the civic calendar. As Stuart Sherman has shown, middle-class literary genres, including diaries and novels, had manifested a growing consciousness of public time since the mid-seventeenth century (Sherman 1996). The increased availability of watches and public clocks, and the greater awareness of the calendar communicated by almanacs, periodicals, and newspapers, consolidated the ascendancy of public standards of time. For the urban middle-classes, at least, work and social activity were increasingly regulated by clock-time and the calendar rather than by the rhythms of agricultural life. The authority of a single civic calendar was asserted against surviving rural and local practices. Elite agitation for calendar reform culminated in the official adoption of the Gregorian system in 1752, following a legal statute that was justified by reference to enlightened ideals of science and social progress. There was a significant degree of reluctance in some quarters to abandon the traditional Julian calendar, which had tied such customary events as rural festivals and fairs to the cycle of the seasons and the harvesting of crops. In many rural locations, the 'old style' dates continued to be used, or the dates of festivals were shifted back in the calendar so they would continue to occur at the same season. Although it seems that stories of widespread riots – with protesters complaining they had been deprived of eleven days of their lives – were mythical, there is no doubt that the calendar reform was at least tacitly resisted.[10]

The civic calendar might have been resented by some, but it was critical to the self-consciousness of enlightened intellectuals. It implied a single chronological scale that extended indefinitely into the past and the future. In relation to the past, it allowed for the application of what Donald J. Wilcox identified as Newtonian 'absolute time' to the understanding of history (Wilcox 1987). The *General Chronological History of the Air* (1749), by Thomas Short, a Sheffield physician and statistician, went all the way back to the biblical flood, which the author dated to the year 1657 after the creation of the world. Beginning at that point, he embarked on a lengthy catalogue of plagues, floods, pestilences, earthquakes, famines, and other extreme meteorological and epidemic events. Events perceived by Christians and Jews as providential interventions were included in a single series with the marvels recorded by pagan historians. All were reduced to routine episodes in a single chronological sequence. Volume one of the two-volume work took 494 pages to reach AD 1717; volume two picked up at 1711 and included in a seamless continuum the records of observers such as Clifton Wintringham (based in York) and John Huxham (in Plymouth). Short stitched the records of these contemporary weather observers into a single continuous temporal fabric, extending back to the time of the biblical patriarchs. His work extrapolated the public calendar to construct a chronological framework for meteorological phenomena even of the distant past. The approach could normalize even the most extraordinary weather events by placing them in a regular table of dates (Short 1749).

As regards the future, the uniform framework of the public calendar replaced the apocalyptic expectations that previously surrounded strange meteorological events with a confident anticipation of uniform unending progress. Eschatology gave way to the prospect of time stretching indefinitely into the future. The practice of compiling chronological weather records was consistent with very long-term views of the incremental accumulation of knowledge and with a vision of natural inquiry as a collective public enterprise. The weather diarists expected that the project of compiling data would go on for a long time and involve many observers. Weather journals were necessarily limited in location and temporal range, so it could always be argued that more were needed before general laws could be extracted from them. As early as December 1700, when Locke sent his weather journal to Sir Hans Sloane for possible publication in the *Philosophical Trans-actions*, he wrote: 'This I know that I did not keep this register for my own sake alone.' Other observers called for the compilation and comparison of as many 'histories' of weather as possible. The physician and weather observer William Hillary wrote, in 1740: '[T]here must be many Collections, and of much longer Continuation, obtained with the greatest Exactness, before we can draw such Aphorisms as are certain and conclusive from them.'[11]

In the view of many investigators, systematic records compiled over extended periods would contribute to a public enterprise that would confirm the rule of a benevolent providence over an orderly world. It was suggested that the keeping of such records showed the discipline, industry, and refinement of the society in which they were kept. Short proposed that the compilation of weather diaries was a sign that at least a certain level of enlightenment had been achieved. In non-European regions, he complained, 'the barbarous Natives' had no inclination to produce such records and, even in countries where learning existed, 'the Generality of People have been too idle to collect such Histories' (Short 1749: viii). Journals of the weather were thus a sign of politeness, improvement, and refinement – a cluster of values seen as opposed to rusticity, superstition, and religious fanaticism. Polite knowledge of the weather was contrasted with what was identified as 'low,' 'barbarous,' or 'vulgar' knowledge: the kind that exaggerated how good or bad things had been in the past, or interpreted peculiar meteorological phenomena as divine portents. Thus, Pointer denounced stories of visions of armies fighting in the air as 'too credulously believ'd by the Vulgar' (Pointer 1723: 199). Rutty remarked that 'In the last Century it was . . . a prevailing Opinion among the Vulgar, that the Winds were in some measure, under the direction of infernal spirits.' Such barbarous notions were to be replaced by recognition of 'the super-intendency of a Providence in these seemingly irregular commotions of our Atmosphere' (Rutty 1772, II: 417). Rutty also castigated the idea that the moon had an influence on winds and rain; such superstitions, he claimed, 'have no better a Foundation than heathenish Idolatry . . . [and] cannot stand the test of the growing light of Christianity and sound Philosophy' (Rutty 1772, II: 486). Diaries of the weather would rescue it from enthusiasm and exaggeration, unreliable memory and vulgar gossip. Samuel Say, vicar of Lowestoft in Essex at the beginning of the eighteenth century, noted that he had begun to compile a weather diary, 'to be able to contradict some common & groundless Observations and Superstitions.' In the 1770s, Gilbert White introduced his journal of weather and natural history as a weapon in the fight against 'superstitious prejudices . . . too gross for this enlight-ened age,' such as those held by the 'lower people' of his district.[12]

Such manifestos expressed a desire to demarcate polite understanding of the weather from popular or vernacular beliefs – to set it in opposition to traditional notions of the weather. A general separation of elite from popular cultures has been taken by many historians as characteristic of this period of British history and of the Enlightenment in general. As social divisions widened and bourgeois affluence increased, the middle classes seem to have distanced themselves from many aspects of popular behavior and customs. Those who identified themselves as 'polite' pursued new hobbies, patronized new forms of the creative arts, and adopted 'refined' manners. They withdrew from the rural festivals and rough sports still popular among the mass of the population, while contrasting their enlight-ened ways of thinking with what they castigated as 'ignorance' or 'vulgar super-stition.'[13] The widening gulf between elite and vernacular beliefs was reflected in intellectuals' denunciation of popular fear of weather phenomena. Great winds, atmospheric visions, and other extraordinary meteors had provoked apprehension among the ignorant, but such anxieties would be soothed as more people under-stood the overall regularity and moderation of the British climate. Fear of God's wrath would be replaced by calm appreciation of His general providential benev-olence.

It was not possible, however, to exclude anomalous weather events from public consciousness. Conversation about the weather, as Samuel Johnson noted, was frequently provoked by its unexpected turns. People talked of it, as they talked of fashion and news, because it offered surprising novelties. Violent storms, torn-adoes, lightning strikes, strange cloud formations, auroras, and other bizarre lights in the sky, all continued to draw widespread interest. They seemed to exist outside the prepared framework of the weather diaries, calling for a different kind of recording and analysis. They found their place, alongside routine weather records, in periodical journalism and in pamphlet publications. In fact, the growth of journalism in the eighteenth century provided the media outlets for expanding the public interest in these events. Again, the 'Great Storm' of 1703 established the pattern; this was the first weather event to become a news story on a national scale. Special-issue broadsheets, such as *The Amazing Tempest* (1703), gave details of the extensive damage to property and stories of the people who had been killed. A compilation entitled *The Storm* (1704), traditionally attributed to Daniel Defoe, collected accounts of the deaths and destruction from all parts of the country, drawing upon newspapers and correspondents to supply a series of graphic narratives.[14] Readers were assured that any story included in the collection, 'tho' it may be related for the sake of its Strangeness or Novelty, . . . shall nevertheless come in the Company of all its Uncertainties, and the Reader [be] left to judge of its Truth' (Defoe 1704: 33). With appropriate assurances of authenticity, 'strange but true' stories found their place in journalistic practice (McKeon 1987). Subsequent extraordinary weather events received similar journalistic treatment, whether they were waterspouts or lightning strikes, hailstorms or heat waves. Even among the natural philosophers of the Royal Society, such phenomena remained respectable topics of reportage. Tornadoes, haloes around heavenly bodies, balls of fire, and thunderstrokes were often described in papers in the *Philosophical Transactions*, at least through the 1780s. As Vladimir Janković has shown, such events were prized especially by provincial investigators as features of the peculiar atmospherics of their localities. Though no longer seen as divine portents or preternatural wonders, they retained much of their singular fascination in a supposedly enlightened age (Janković 2000).

Public interest in extraordinary meteorological events was not diminished by the appearance of regular journals of the weather. The project of meticulous cataloguing of weather patterns could not suppress these anomalies, though it did perhaps lessen the degree to which they were seen as divine interventions. While diarists and record-keepers struggled to reduce the weather to providential law and order, journalism and conversation continually brought extraordinary and spectacular meteors into the public domain. The summer of 1783 was especially noted for a gloomy haze that hung in the atmosphere, obscuring the sun and setting off spectacular thunderstorms. Strange weather was widely reported across northern Europe, though the cause – a volcanic eruption in Iceland – was not generally recognized at the time (Grattan and Brayshay 1995). In Hampshire, Gilbert White reflected that such events reawakened old fears; he mentioned 'a superstitious kind of dread, with which the minds of men are always impressed by such strange and unusual phenomena' (White 1813: 298). One might say that weather of this kind showed the limitations of what enlightenment was able to accomplish. Turbulent clouds continued to surround the sun of reason and could not be entirely dispelled.

In another connection, also, the project to forge a new science of the weather ran into difficulties. Those who were keeping systematic records made no progress in learning how to make predictions; in fact, they rarely attempted any kinds of forecasts. Even the most promising new meteorological instrument – the barometer – proved a disappointment in this respect. After some rashly optimistic claims were made around the turn of the eighteenth century, the consensus came to be formed that the barometer could only yield probable forecasts of the weather to come, and only for a few days at most. It was generally interpreted by combining its indications with traditional prognostic signs, such as the appearance of the sky and the behavior of animals. John Smith, an early writer on the instrument, recommended that the movements of the mercury in the tube should be watched together with the sun, cloud formations, the phase of the moon, the wind's strength and direction, and the actions of owls, bats, crows, and pigs.[15] The new device was only as useful as the traditional proverbs and maxims that had long been resorted to. Weather forecasting could do no better than to use the rules preserved by a popular – pre-Enlightenment – tradition, the vernacular lore of what was called 'weather-wising.' Such oral lore could not be entirely dismissed, even by those who were most keen to develop a scientific approach to studying the weather. Evidence about the content of this tradition was preserved by the work of folklorists, who collected proverbs and popular sayings about the weather beginning in the early nineteenth century. M. A. Denham's pioneering compilation of 1846 was followed by those of Richard Inwards, Charles Swainson, and others.[16] Many of the maxims they recorded were already centuries old; some go back to the period of the New Testament.[17] They comprise both rules for short-term prognosis, making reference to visible signs in the atmosphere or on earth, and methods for forecasting the weather of a particular season up to several months ahead. For example, it was said that the yield of the coming harvest could be known by the weather in the preceding summer, spring, or even winter. Conversely, the early ripening of apples was thought to foretell an early and snowy winter to come.

The seasonal maxims reflected a popular understanding of time, which was rooted in the practices of rural life and tradition. Many sayings deduced the character of a forthcoming season from the weather on a particular day: Christmas Eve, for example, or All Saints' Day, or the day of the new moon. St. Swithin's day (July 15) was probably the best known of many supposedly prognostic days, mostly chosen from the ecclesiastical calendar. The weather on Candlemas Day (February 2) was thought in many European countries to be a predictor of how soon spring would arrive. Bears or badgers were supposed to show by their behavior on that day whether or not winter was over, a tradition preserved even now in 'Groundhog Day' in the United States. A similar significance was ascribed to St. Bartholomew's Day (August 24), the weather on which was thought to foretell that of the autumn as a whole. Other prognostic days moved about in the civic calendar with the changing dates of Easter, Lent, and Whitsuntide. Popular belief even countenanced 'borrowed days', when days in one month seemed to manifest the kind of weather typical of another. On the days that March borrowed from April, it was reported, Scottish people would not lend or borrow household articles, lest they be used for witchcraft against their owners.[18] The uniform public calendar being imposed by civic authority could not accommodate such beliefs; and when the shift was made from the Julian to the Gregorian system, they were rendered literally 'out of date'. Nonetheless, 'old style' dates were still sometimes invoked by country people, and seasonal prognostic maxims continued to be quoted. In 1824, Thomas Forster recorded that 'the popular Belief in the Rules outlived the Change of Style, and the Husbandman and the Astrologer still consult the critical Days as heretofore.'[19] Astrological almanacs were one outlet in which the practices of seasonal forecasting continued throughout the eighteenth century. The almanacs traditionally gave weather predictions for the seasons of the year to come, based on the phases of the moon and the angular separation of the planets.[20]

Popular methods of short-term weather prediction also continued in widespread use. In fact, they were hailed by some writers as the fruits of a genuine rural wisdom that city-folk would do well to take seriously. The anonymous *Knowledge of Things Unknown* (1743) included numerous weather maxims ascribed to husbandmen and shepherds (Anon. 1743a). The most widely read compilation of weather signs was the so-called *Shepherd of Banbury's Rules*, composed by John Claridge in 1670, and republished in a second edition by John Campbell in 1740. Campbell's introduction to the later edition lauded the abilities of the shepherd who spent his whole life outdoors: 'Every thing in Time becomes to him a Sort of Weather-Gage. The Sun, the Moon, the Stars, the Clouds, the Winds, the Mists, the Trees, the Flowers, the Herbs, and almost every animal with which he is acquainted. All these I say become to such a Person Instruments of real Knowledge' (Claridge 1744: ii). As natural 'instruments,' the shepherd's weather signs were more reliable than artificial instruments, such as the barometer, and they had the advantage of forecasting conditions for days, weeks, even months ahead. Campbell's aim in expanding Claridge's book was to recuperate and rehabilitate a body of popular knowledge. He did this, not by disputing the credentials of natural philosophy, but by trying to explain the shepherd's maxims in scientific terms. John Mills, an agricultural writer who published his own remarks on the shepherd of Banbury's rules thirty years after Campbell's edition, took a similar line, arguing that natural philosophy would never make progress in understanding the weather unless it paid attention to the accumulated wisdom of uneducated country people (Mills 1770). Campbell and Mills insisted that vernacular knowledge was not 'superstition,' but rather a kind of 'natural' natural philosophy, revealed to individuals through their unmediated experience of the normal pattern of climatic events.

Publications of this kind made vernacular lore available for conversational use even among the social elite. The weather provided a rich topic for polite discourse, to initiate encounters with strangers or to fill embarrassing silences, as novelists from Daniel Defoe to Jane Austen confirm. Authors of advice manuals on the art of conversation generally cautioned against resort to the subject, suggesting its banality would reflect poorly on the speaker. *The Lady's Preceptor* (1743) warned: 'If the Occasion of the Visit does not afford you a Subject for Conversation, take care not to be so unprovided with one, as to be obliged to the Weather or the Hour of the Day for your Discourse' (Anon. 1743b: 49). For the insufficiently prepared conversationalist, however, the weather was one of the most obvious topics. It was common knowledge, about which opinions were not likely to differ too drastically; it was neither political nor sectarian. It therefore fulfilled the requirement that polite conversation should not be pedantic or divisive. As Addison noted, it was a 'publick topick,' especially suitable for social intercourse in large and heterogeneous gatherings. Samuel Johnson thought it peculiar that, 'when two Englishmen meet, their first talk is of the weather; they are in haste to tell each other, what each must already know'; but the social value of such platitudinous talk was clear. A century later, Inwards noted: 'The state of the weather is . . . the usual text and starting-point for the conversation of daily life.' Weather-talk is an example of what linguists call 'phatic' communication, in which the primary meaning lies not in what is referred to but in the social bonds strengthened by the exchange. As Mark Twain quipped, 'Everyone talks about the weather, but nobody does anything about it.'[21]

Satirists observed that conversation, even in the most refined circles, was frequently filled with proverbs and clichés. Jonathan Swift wrote a satirical *Treatise on Polite Conversation* (1738) entirely filled with the overused phrases found in elite discourse, including a number of weather sayings that have their origins in popular culture (Swift 1963). Notwithstanding the attempts by some writers to purge polite speech of traditional proverbs, they evidently persisted in use.[22] Indeed, they persist to this day. Folklorists and anthropologists have mapped the incidence of proverbial weather wisdom in contemporary conversation.[23] Television weather-forecasters are still heard to interject maxims such as: 'March comes in like a lion, and goes out like a lamb,' and 'An English summer – two fine days and a thunderstorm,' which have been in documented usage for centuries.[24] It seems likely that adages of weather-wising like the shepherd of Banbury's often made their way into polite discourse. Addison and Arbuthnot both noted how frequently people would tell one another that rain was coming because they felt it in their joints or in the corns on their feet.[25] In the early nineteenth century, the Quaker meteorologist Luke Howard remarked on the prevalence of popular lore even in learned discourse on the weather: 'There is no subject on which the learned and the unlearned are more ready to converse, and to hazard an opinion, than on the weather – and none on which they are more frequently mistaken' (Howard 1818–20, I: xxxvi). The indications are that conversation about the weather was pervasive and frequently permeated by traditional lore.

Even those who attempted to study the weather scientifically often understood the value of oral traditions and drew upon them. In 1785, Benjamin Franklin discussed the proverb 'As the day lengthens, the cold strengthens.' He explained – as had John Ray, who mentioned the same saying more than a century earlier – that the phrase referred to the sun's rays being too weak to warm the air significantly during January.[26] Howard's engagement with popular weather lore was more substantial than this. He insisted that the weather followed God's providential guidance; notwithstanding 'perpetual fluctuations, and occasional tremendous perturbations, the balance of the great Machine is preserved' (Howard 1818–20, II: vi). In his two-volume study, *The Climate of London* (1818–20), he proposed to rescue meteorology from 'empirical mysteriousness, and the reproach of perpetual uncertainty', by diligent measurement and meticulous record-keeping (Howard 1818–20, II: vi). Memory alone was an unreliable source of information, Howard explained; people always tended to think that the character of the seasons was changing because their recollections of the weather a few years back were quite imperfect. Nonetheless, he noted repeatedly that meteorologists had much to learn from those with practical experience. Farmers and mariners, for example, 'become weather-wise by tradition and experience; and are often able to communicate the results of a certain local knowledge' (Howard 1837: 1). Concerning the course of the winds, indeed, 'the experience of our navigators . . . outruns science' (Howard 1818–20, II: 161). Even proverbial sayings that might appear to be pure superstition, like the well-known adage about rain on St. Swithin's Day forecasting forty days' rain to follow, were worthy of serious discussion. Howard was keen to 'do justice to popular observation' on this matter, and concluded that a showery period frequently would begin about that time, though it was unlikely that the preceding weeks would have been much drier in a typically wet English summer (Howard 1818–20, II: 198). Overall, Howard's attitude to vernacular weather lore was far from dismissive; though he clearly saw scientific meteorology as something different, he believed it could only benefit from an openness to popular knowledge.

Howard's willingness to incorporate oral tradition indicates the complex relationship between meteorological science and vernacular lore. His stance was shared by rural and urban observers of the period, from Thomas Appletree to Gilbert White. When it came to the weather, elite and popular cultures did not inhabit separate worlds; the history is at least as much one of contact and engagement between them as of differentiation and confrontation. The weather remained a common experience for society as a whole, and middle-class intellectuals understood that popular wisdom had much to offer regarding it. Proverbial weather-wisdom did not necessarily contradict basic providential assumptions about nature; in fact it could be seen as entirely consistent with them. Some weather maxims could be traced back to classical writers like Theophrastus, Aratus, and Seneca, providing a learned pedigree for what might otherwise be taken for vulgar lore.

And, as we saw with Campbell and Mills, bourgeois interest in popular wisdom could also benefit from a kind of primitivism that became increasingly fashionable from the middle of the century. For these reasons, even at the heart of the Enlightenment, polite knowledge of the weather continued to draw heavily upon popular culture.

The program of systematic weather recording had been initiated by leading members of the community of experimental natural philosophers in the late seventeenth century. Among the factors that drew intellectuals to it in the context of events like the 1703 storm was a desire to overcome popular fears of unusual weather phenomena. Elite individuals sought to replace the politically destabilizing consequences of popular superstition and enthusiasm with an awareness of the uniformity of divine providence. Systematic recording promised to show that the weather was generally temperate and providentially benevolent to the British population; it would perhaps even exhibit regularities that would allow for reliable prediction. In these respects, the project participated in the movement of the Enlightenment, sometimes explicitly proclaiming its opposition to the preceding culture of 'vulgar ignorance' and error. As the project developed over several decades, it generated a set of weather records that is still found useful by those studying how the climate has changed during the last three centuries.[27] But it could not entirely normalize anomalous and extreme phenomena, which remained topics of widespread fascination and press coverage. Howard, for example, recognized the value of popular reports of spectacular weather events. He complained about the lack of specificity in such reports: 'The *language* of these accounts is . . . commonly vague and unphilosophical: a hard gale of wind is too often "a tremendous hurricane," and frost and floods, hail and thunder, are too frequently stated to have been the most severe and destructive "in the memory of the oldest persons living!"' (Howard 1818–20, I: xxxiv–xxxv). But he found himself unable to resist the temptation to introduce such dramatic narratives into his work. In April 1807, he quoted a newspaper report from Lancashire of 'the most tremendous thunder and lightning ever remembered by the oldest persons.'[28] On later occasions, freezing rain and hailstorms, tornadoes, and lightning bolts found their way into his monthly summaries, accompanied by incidental details of witnesses and victims. The narrative appeal of such unusual and extreme events evidently outweighed the difficulty of reconciling them with the demands of scientific exactitude and normalization.

In addition, as we have seen, hopes for weather prediction from systematic recording remained unfulfilled. Popular oral traditions provided the best available resources for practical forecasting. Even intellectuals involved in weather research turned on occasion to vernacular lore. Traditional maxims and proverbs – known to everyone – gave rules for predicting the weather for the immediate future or for the whole season ahead. Oral wisdom retained its pre-Enlightenment authority when it came to predicting the weather, either for a few hours hence or for the months to come. Thus, the enlightened project of regular weather recording had only limited success, remaining strongly challenged by other kinds of discourse that derived from older structures of belief. The new science of the weather remained unstable and insecure. But this situation did not only apply in the eighteenth century. In fact, that age holds up a mirror to our own. In today's conversation, we still resort to oral maxims and proverbs about the weather. People will still tell you they feel a change of weather in their bones. Seasonal forecasts are still offered by the compilers of almanacs and by pundits who lack formal credentials but nowadays appear on television. Few of us have complete confidence in official forecasts or even entirely trust the official record-keepers. Spectacular and catastrophic meteorological events receive more media coverage than ever. In relation to the weather, we have never been completely enlightened.

Looking at the eighteenth century, we thus recognize a reflection of our own ambivalence about enlightenment and modernity. Thinking about the weather obliges us to acknowledge the incompleteness of modernity, even its questionable value as an ideal. We read climatic change as a sign of the damage wrought by humans on the environment and of the inherent problems of the modern drive toward continual scientific progress. Our society's vulnerability to environmental catastrophes and unpredictable crises is viewed as an unintended consequence of social development. From the Romantic period on, environmental degradation has been read as an indictment of enlightenment – of its obsession with reducing nature to order. But I have suggested that the eighteenth century had already perceived some of the limitations of the project to order the weather and was by no means as uniformly enlightened as we have sometimes assumed. Jean Baudrillard has written: 'Meteorology is chaotic; it is not a figure of destiny.'[29] Certainly, the weather evaded enlightened attempts to encompass it within the destiny of modernity. Recognizing that this was so might help us to deal with the issues we face in our own time.

Notes

1. For their comments, I thank the audiences at University College London, at the University of California Davis, and at the University of Cambridge, where earlier versions of this chapter were presented as seminar papers. I am also grateful to the editors of this volume, Sarah Strauss and Ben Orlove, for their suggestions.

2. For a comprehensive survey of the Enlightenment in Britain, see Porter 2000.
3. *The Spectator*, no. 68 (18 May 1711).
4. Anon. 1705: 8–10. Other sources on the storm include: Anon. 1703; Anon. 1704; Defoe 1704; Gifford 1733.
5. Daston and Park 1998, chap. 9. For weather wonders in this period, see also: Janković 2000, chaps. 2, 3; Fara 1996.
6. Dewhurst 1963: 18–19, 300–301. Locke's weather register from 1666–67, 1669–75, and 1681–83 was printed in Boyle 1692: 104–132.
7. For a discussion of the Worcestershire diary and identification of its probable author, see Golinski 2001.
8. Appletree quoted in Golinski 2001: 161.
9. Arbuthnot 1733: 151–152; Fothergill 1784: 96; Falconer 1781: 50, 73.
10. On the calendar reform, see: Poole 1995; Poole 1998. A classic study of time-measurement and social experience is Thompson 1967.
11. Locke quoted in Dewhurst 1963: 301; Hillary 1740: x.
12. 'A Journal of the Weather at Lostaff [Lowestoft] in Suffolk, from 1695 to 1724, by the Rev. Mr. Say,' Bodleian Library, Oxford, MS 35448, p. [1]; White 1813: 203.
13. On the distancing of elite from popular culture during the Enlightenment, see: Burke 1978, chaps. 8, 9; Malcolmson 1973, chaps. 6, 7, 8; Barker-Benfield 1992.
14. Anon. 1703; Anon. 1704; Anon. 1705; Defoe 1704.
15. Smith 1694; and, on the barometer in general, see Golinski 1999.
16. Denham 1846; Inwards 1898; Swainson 1873. Other works on weather lore and proverbs include: Sloane 1963; Benstead 1940; Dufour 1978; Galtier 1984; McWilliams 1997; Shields 1987; Wilson 2000: 51–87.
17. See Matthew 16: 2–3 and Luke 12: 54–55, in the Authorized Version. The former verses have been dropped from the Revised English Bible.
18. On Candlemas day, see: Denham 1846: 28; Swainson 1873: 42–50; Inwards 1898: 20. Borrowed days are discussed in Swainson 1873: 65–66. On rural calendar customs in general, see: Malcolmson 1973, chap. 2; Bushaway 1982.
19. Forster 1824: xix. On continuing observance of the old-style dates, see also: Poole 1995: 120; Poole 1998: 152–157.
20. Sources on almanacs in the eighteenth century include: Capp 1979; Curry 1989; Perkins 1996.
21. Johnson in *The Idler* (24 June 1758), reprinted in Bate, et al. 1963, II: 36–37; Inwards 1898: v; Twain quoted in Sloane 1963: 11.
22. On the attempts to purge proverbs from polite speech, and their limited success, see Obelkevich 1987; Davis 1975; and Matthews 1936–37.
23. Studies of modern weather proverbs include: Widdowson 1980; Arora 1991; Ward 1968.

24. These are both in Denham 1846: 31, 48.

25. *The Spectator*, no. 440 (25 July 1712); Arbuthnot 1733: 63.

26. Ray 1678: 48; Franklin 1785.

27. See, for example, Kington 1988.

28. Howard 1818–20, I: unnumbered pages following Table 6.

29. Baudrillard quoted in Fara 1996: 240.

References

[ANON.] 1692. *A Practical Discourse on the Late Earthquakes*. London: J. Dunton.

—— 1703. *The Amazing Tempest*. London: P. Mead.

—— 1704. *A Wonderful History of all the Storms, Hurricanes, Earthquakes, &c.* London: A. Baldwin.

—— 1705. *The Terrible Stormy Wind and Tempest*. London: W. Freeman.

—— 1711. *A True and Particular Account of a Storm of Thunder & Lightning*. London: John Morphew.

—— 1743a. *The Knowledge of Things Unknown*. London: for J. Clarke and A. Wilde.

—— 1743b. *The Lady's Preceptor: Or, a Letter to a Young Lady of Distinction upon Politeness*. London: J. Watts.

ARBUTHNOT, JOHN. 1733. *An Essay concerning the Effects of Air on Human Bodies*. London: J. Tonson.

ARORA, SHIRLEY L. 1991. Weather Proverbs: Some 'Folk' Views. *Proverbium* 8: 1–17.

ATKINSON, A. D. 1952. William Derham, F.R.S. (1657–1735). *Annals of Science* 8: 368–392.

BARKER-BENFIELD, G. J. 1992. *The Culture of Sensibility: Sex and Society in Eighteenth-Century Britain*. Chicago: University of Chicago Press.

BATE, W. J., et al. (Eds.). 1963. *The Yale Edition of the Works of Samuel Johnson*. New Haven: Yale University Press.

BENSTEAD, C. R. [1940]. *The Weather Eye: An Irreverent Discourse upon Meteorological Lore, Ancient and Modern*. London: Robert Hale.

BOYLE, ROBERT. 1692. *The General History of the Air*. London: Awnsham and John Churchill.

BURKE, PETER. 1978. *Popular Culture in Early Modern Europe*. London: Temple Smith.

BUSHAWAY, BOB. 1982. *By Rite: Custom, Ceremony and Community in England 1700–1880*. London: Junction Books.

CAPP, BERNARD. 1979. *Astrology and the Popular Press: English Almanacs 1500–1800*. London: Faber and Faber.

CLARIDGE, JOHN. 1670. *Shepheards Legacy: Or, John Clearidge, his Forty Years Experience of the Weather*. London: John Hancock.

CLARIDGE, JOHN. 1744. *The Shepherd of Banbury's Rules to Judge of the Changes of the Weather*. London: W. Bickerton.

CURRY, PATRICK. 1989. *Prophecy and Power: Astrology in Early Modern England*. Princeton: Princeton University Press.

DASTON, LORRAINE and KATHARINE PARK. 1998. *Wonders and the Order of Nature, 1150–1750*. New York: Zone Books.

DAVIS, NATALIE ZEMON. 1975. 'Proverbial Wisdom and Popular Errors,' in Davis, *Society and culture in early modern France*, pp. 227–267. Stanford: Stanford University Press.

[DEFOE, DANIEL.] 1704. *The Storm: Or, a Collection of the Most Remarkable Casualties and Disasters which Happen'd in the Late Dreadful Tempest*. London: G. Sawbridge.

DENHAM, M. A. 1846. *A Collection of Proverbs and Popular Sayings Relating to the Seasons, the Weather, and Agricultural Pursuits*. London: Percy Society.

DERHAM, WILLIAM. 1704–5. A letter . . . containing his Observations concerning the Late Storm. *Philosophical Transactions* 24 (no. 289): 1530–1534.

DEWHURST, KENNETH. 1963. *John Locke (1632–1704), Physician and Philosopher: A medical biography*. London: Wellcome Historical Medical Library.

DUFOUR, LOUIS. 1978. *Météorologie, calendriers et croyances populaires*. Paris: Librarie d'Amérique et d'Orient.

FALCONER, WILLIAM. 1781. *Remarks on the Influence of Climate . . . [on] Mankind*. London: C. Dilly.

FARA, PATRICIA. 1996. Lord Derwentwater's lights: Prediction and the Aurora Polaris. *Journal of the History of Astronomy* 27: 239–258.

FORSTER, THOMAS. 1824. *The Perennial Calendar and Companion to the Almanack*. London: Harding, Mavor, and Lepard.

FOTHERGILL, JOHN. 1784. *The Works of John Fothergill, M.D.*, ed. John Coakley Lettsom. London: Charles Dilly.

FRANKLIN, BENJAMIN. 1785. Meteorological Imaginations and Conjectures. *Memoirs of the Literary and Philosophical Society of Manchester* 2: 357–361.

GALTIER, CHARLES. 1984. *Météorologie populaire dans la France ancienne*. Le Coteau: Horvath.

GIFFORD, A. 1733. *A Sermon in Commemoration of the Great Storm*. London: Aaron Ward.

GOLINSKI, JAN. 1999. 'Barometers of Change: Meteorological Instruments as Machines of Enlightenment,' in *The Sciences in Enlightened Europe*, ed.

William Clark, Jan Golinski, and Simon Schaffer, pp. 69–93. Chicago: University of Chicago Press.

—— 2001. 'Exquisite Atmography': Theories of the World and Experiences of the Weather in a Diary of 1703. *British Journal for the History of Science* 34: 149–171.

GRATTAN, JOHN and MARK BRAYSHAY. 1995. An Amazing and Portentous Summer: Environmental and Social Responses in Britain to the 1783 Eruption of an Iceland Volcano. *The Geographical Journal* 161: 125–134.

HILLARY, WILLIAM. 1740. *A Practical Essay on the Small-Pox*, 2nd edition. London: C. Hitch.

HOOKE, ROBERT. 1667. 'Method for Making a History of the Weather,' in *The history of the Royal Society of London*, ed. Thomas Sprat, pp. 173–179. London: T. R. for J. Martyn.

HOWARD, LUKE. 1818–20. *The Climate of London, deduced from Meteorological Observations*, 2 vols. London: W. Phillips.

HOWARD, LUKE. 1837. *Seven Lectures on Meteorology*. Pontefract: James Lucas.

INWARDS, RICHARD. 1898. *Weather Lore: A Collection of Proverbs, Sayings, and Rules concerning the Weather*, 3rd edition. London: Elliot Stock.

JANKOVIĆ, VLADIMIR. 2000. *Reading the Skies: A Cultural History of English Weather, 1650–1820*. Chicago: University of Chicago Press.

KINGTON, JOHN. 1988. *The Weather of the 1780s over Europe*. Cambridge: Cambridge University Press.

LEEUWENHOEK, ANTON VAN. 1704–5. Part of a Letter . . . giving his Observations on the Late Storm. *Philosophical Transactions* 24 (no. 289): 1535–1537.

MALCOLMSON, ROBERT W. 1973. *Popular Recreations in English Society, 1700–1850*. Cambridge: Cambridge University Press.

MATTHEWS, WILLIAM. 1936–37. Polite Speech in the Eighteenth Century. *English: The Magazine of the English Association* 1: 493–511.

McKEON, MICHAEL. 1987. *The Origins of the English Novel, 1600–1740*. Baltimore: Johns Hopkins University Press.

McWILLIAMS, BRENDAN. 1997. 'The Kingdom of the Air: The Progress of Meteorology,' in *Nature in Ireland: A Scientific and Cultural History*, ed. John Wilson Foster, pp. 115–132. Montreal: McGill-Queen's University Press.

MILLS, JOHN. 1770. *An Essay on the Weather; With Remarks on the Shepherd of Banbury's Rules for Judging of its Changes*. London: S. Hooper.

OBELKEVICH, JAMES. 1987. 'Proverbs and Social History,' in *The social history of language*, ed. Peter Burke and Roy Porter, pp. 43–72. Cambridge: Cambridge University Press.

PERKINS, MAUREEN. 1996. *Visions of the Future: Almanacs, Time, and Cultural Change 1775–1870*. Oxford: Clarendon Press.

POINTER, JOHN. 1723. *A Rational Account of the Weather, shewing the Signs of its Several Changes and Alterations*. Oxford: L.L. for S. Wilmot.

POOLE, ROBERT. 1995. 'Give us our Eleven Days!': Calendar Reform in Eighteenth-Century England. *Past and Present*, 149: 95–139.

—— 1998. *Time's Alteration: Calendar Reform in Early Modern England*. London: UCL Press.

PORTER, ROY. 2000. *The Creation of the Modern World: The Untold Story of the British Enlightenment*. New York: W. W. Norton.

RAY, JOHN. 1678. *A Collection of English Proverbs*, 2nd edition. Cambridge: John Hayes.

ROSS, ANDREW. 1991. *Strange Weather: Culture, Science and Technology in the Age of Limits*. London: Verso.

RUTTY, JOHN. 1772. *An Essay towards a Natural History of the County of Dublin*, 2 vols. Dublin: W. Sleater.

SERRES, MICHEL. 1995. *The Natural Contract*, trans. Elizabeth MacArthur and William Paulson. Ann Arbor: University of Michigan Press.

SHERMAN, STUART. 1996. *Telling Time: Clocks, Diaries, and English Diurnal Form, 1660–1785*. Chicago: University of Chicago Press.

SHIELDS, LISA. 1987. 'Popular Weather Lore in Ireland,' in *The Irish Meteorological Service: The First Fifty Years, 1936–1986*, ed. Shields, pp. 56–58. Dublin: Stationery Office.

[SHORT, THOMAS.] 1749. *A General Chronological History of the Air, Weather, Seasons, Meteors, &c.*, 2 vols. London: T. Longman and A. Millar.

SLOANE, ERIC. 1963. *Folklore of American Weather*. New York: Duell, Sloan, and Pearce.

SMITH, JOHN. 1694. *Horological Disquisitions concerning the Nature of Time*. London: Richard Cumberland.

SWAINSON, CHARLES. 1873. *A Handbook of Weather Folk-lore*. Edinburgh: William Blackwood.

SWIFT, JONATHAN. 1963. *Swift's Polite Conversation*, ed. Eric Partridge. London: Andre Deutsch.

THOMPSON, E. P. 1967. Time, Work-discipline and Industrial Capitalism. *Past and Present* 38: 56–97.

WARD, DONALD J. 1968. Weather Signs and Weather Magic: Some Ideas on Causality in Popular Belief. *Pacific Coast Philology* 3: 67–72.

WHITE, GILBERT. 1813. *The Natural History and Antiquities of Selbourne*, new edition. London: White, Cochrane, and Co.

WIDDOWSON, J. D. A. 1980. 'Form and Function in Traditional Explanations of Weather Phenomena', in *Folklore Studies in Honour of Herbert Halpert*, ed. Kenneth S. Goldstein and Neil V. Rosenberg, pp. 353–376. St. John's, Newfoundland: Memorial University of Newfoundland.

WILCOX, DONALD J. 1987. *The Measure of Times Past: Pre-Newtonian Chronologies and the Rhetoric of Relative Time*. Chicago: University of Chicago Press.

WILSON, STEPHEN. 2000. *The Magical Universe: Everyday Ritual and Magic in Pre-modern Europe*. London: Hambledon and London.

–3–

Weather Wise: Speaking Folklore to Science in Leukerbad

Sarah Strauss

[T]here are many who say that once the climate across the land was much milder, there was scarcely a trace of the glaciers, and in the high mountains fruit trees, vineyards, paved streets, villages, and even cities could be found. Then others have come along and thought that the whole of Wallis was once a great lake and only the mountains could be seen at the edges. And finally there are the learned geologists, who have written about the famous gray glaciers which once filled all of the valleys and extended far beyond the boundaries of Wallis. Who is right? I believe that all of them are.[1]

This tale, recorded in 1872, discusses the changing climate in Wallis/Valais,[2] the great Rhone river valley of Switzerland. Located between the Berner Oberland to the north and the massive 4,000-meter peaks of the southern European Alps, Wallis is a geographically dramatic setting. Nowadays, vineyards dominate the dry south-facing slopes, but large glacier systems can be found only 20 kilometers from the Mediterranean climate of the valley floor. As one moves in and up through the various ecological zones, vegetation drops off, leaving only grass and evergreens surrounding the small villages nestled in the higher reaches. These changes in elevation bring with them changes in weather and climate that are often both extreme and rapid, and so it is unsurprising to find that the inhabitants of this mountain region are constantly noting and commenting upon meteorological conditions.

The story related above can safely be linked with the 'Little Ice Age' of European history, roughly from 1570 to 1870. Indeed, in the Medieval Warm Period (~1000–1300 AD) preceding that time of extreme cold and advancing glaciers, it may well have been possible to find fruit trees and human occupation at much higher altitudes, and both the excessive flooding of the Rhone and the many Ice Ages prior to the most recent one ending about 12,000 years ago are well known (cf. Ladurie 1971). This passage also speaks to the relationship between folk knowledge passed through generations as part of an oral tradition, and the technical expertise used by the 'learned' scientists in describing natural phenomena, as well as for predicting change. Evaluating such story traditions and other forms of weather talk can help us to reflect upon the different understandings that human groups, both within and across cultures, hold regarding the control of natural phenomena. In this chapter, I use two kinds of historical data, the first concerning the development of weather science in the Euro-American context, and the second concerning the development of farmer's rules, or *Bauernregeln*, in the Germanic context. These historical data are then discussed in light of information gleaned from ethnographic interviews with Leukerbad's own direct link to the Swiss Meteorological Society, a gentleman I have called Matti. My goal is to compare one aspect of the historical development of scientific knowledge about the weather – the use of synoptic charts for weather forecasting – with typical forms of local knowledge exhibited by individual predictions, including 'farmer's rules' as well as personal observations and recording of local weather conditions in Leukerbad. The object is therefore neither straight historical narrative nor extensive ethnographic representation, but rather a comparative project in which the production of different but interrelated ways of knowing and communicating knowledge about the weather is examined.

The manner in which people from different societies talk about the weather varies across cultures and through time. Speculations about weather and climate, and the ways that such phenomena have been inscribed on the landscape, are common topics for talk in the Swiss Alps, as in other locations around the world. In this chapter, I will explore two types of organizational frameworks that we can use to describe the ways that people talk about the weather. My primary examples come from Switzerland and the United States, but these frameworks could easily be applied to any other context as well. The first of these frameworks is what I will call the 'popular-expert speech continuum,' using insights from the ethnography of communication. Members of a speech community, whether one based on technical expertise or geographic proximity, share commonalities of lexicon as well as of genre and key (Hymes 1988: 59). That is, people who work or live together use similar vocabularies and styles of speaking which, while perfectly recognizable, may not be particularly *meaningful* to those outside the group. I am here talking about the verbal expression of two coexisting (and often competing) types of knowledge: what has been called 'folk' or 'indigenous' knowledge, and its presumed opposite, 'scientific' knowledge. The ways that people in a community talk about things that are important to them – and the weather is surely one of the most relevant of all topics in all but the most seasonless of places (cf. Orlove, this volume) – refract personal experience, local history, and shared culture in identifiable ways. More importantly, speech communities are never isolates. Rather, they comprise intersecting circles of individuals who may communicate with each other in a variety of ways that change over time and in response to other external factors. I begin with the example of the development of scientific meteorology for popular consumption, to represent the technical end of this continuum, and the weather proverbs used by generations of ordinary people to explore the popular side of weather communication, though even this seemingly clear division is subject to question.

The second of these frameworks is a shapeshifting axis that has gone under the name of the tradition–modernity spectrum. Sometimes this axis is meant to address changes over time in the same region, sometimes changes over space, usually from rural to urban regions within a broader geographical area; often the two are conflated, especially when the speaker chooses to follow a nineteenth-century notion of unilinear progress towards a singular modernity, generally the one defined by urban Euro-American technological innovation (e.g. Smelser 1958; Rostow 1960). This axis, or – more accurately – plane of experience (to continue with the mathematical metaphor), does not intersect the first in only one location, but rather weaves in and out of the field defined by the linguistic framework as described above. As I think about the ways in which the concept of modernity has been understood, I focus on the relationship between Foucault's (1979) usage of Bentham's Panopticon and the late- to post-modern notion of the Synopticon. The Panopticon is a construct that allows a single individual (or collective serving as an institutional representative) to observe many others simultaneously, as in a modern prison setting; Foucault's use of Bentham's original idea of the Panopticon extends this notion further as a metaphor of modernity, in which powerful govern-mental institutions have the ability to observe, monitor, and control populations of citizens. The Synopticon has two variants: one in which many individuals simult-aneously observe one or a few others, as occurs with a television viewing audience (Mathiesen 1997), and one in which many perspectives are melded into a single vision or representation, which is the approach I explore below. The creation of a synoptic chart for weather forecasting requires the compilation of multiple data points, most of which are collected by individual human volunteers, even in this age of highly automated information gathering.

Within the European context, this framework is especially interesting. I want to emphasize here that there is no simple progression from 'traditional' personal obeservation of climatic conditions and subsequent generation of folk knowledge about the weather to 'modern' instrument-based scientific weather forecasting to be demonstrated. Rather, Switzerland, and especially its Alpine core, is what I have elsewhere called a 'central periphery' (Strauss 1999). Located physically in the heart of western Europe, Switzerland has nonetheless worked hard at maintaining an identity that can only be seen as rigidly outside the bounds of Europe; it is both ultra-modern in its urban financial centers, and ultra-traditional in its continued insistence on community property and other local political institutions. By dint of dialect as well as politics, Switzerland has been able to maintain this inside–outside stance up until the twenty-first century. Where it will take this identity in the coming decades remains to be seen, although the 2002 vote for the Swiss to join the United Nations may be a harbinger. Moving from urban to rural locations in Switzerland engages the two axes noted above in an explicitly self-conscious way – the German Swiss value both their traditional roots in the rural areas, and their stereotypically modern urban institutions. They encourage the paradoxical maintenance of both of these identities simultaneously, as can be seen in such efforts as the cow art campaign in Zurich during the 1990s, in which businesses sponsored noted contemporary artists in projects involving decoration of a standardized, life-size cow statue. These art-cows, festooned with everything from leopard skins to traditional bells, were placed throughout the center of the city for the course of a year. While this traditional/modern identity is accentuated in Germanic Switzerland, it is certainly also present in other German-speaking European contexts; attention to both 'progress' in the modern sense, as well as the romantic roots of folk identity and rural values are of course well documented from the early decades of the twentieth century in Germany and elsewhere (Bramwell 1992).

Although the cities of Zurich and Geneva are often considered to be among the most modern and cosmopolitan centers on the planet, outsider views of the Swiss Alps hearken back to Heidi and the simple life of the traditional peasant. Weather conditions are perhaps incidental to the former, demonstrating the ideal that modernity can erase all dependence on environmental factors. Weather conditions absolutely determine the latter: no matter how much high-tech effort may go into producing weather forecasts and other products used by the tourism industry, the bottom line is still the same: too much or too little snow, too early or late in the season, the availability of panoramic views from trains that travel across alpine passes – all of these have demonstrable impacts on the economic potential of Swiss tourism. Indeed, Switzerland's economy depends heavily on both of these images – the first for its finance and precision instrument industries, the second for tourism.

'Time and talk', as Golinski has outlined for eighteenth century Britain (this volume), are thus also the guiding themes for my discussion of weather and climate in Leukerbad. Attention to details of weather conditions and even to longer-term climate variability cannot be anything but an important component of human discourse. These discourses and narratives can also shed light on the differential valuation of various forms of knowledge about the natural world. In this chapter, I want to explore the spectrum of weather and climate knowledge as it moves from the local to the global, in this case spanning the bridge between experiential and practical weatherlore of rural individuals in Switzerland, to the development and practice of the science of weather forecasting in western Europe and North America more generally. I recognize that these two arenas of knowledge might seem to share little more than a general theme in common, but I want to demonstrate that their relationship is partially grounded in an unexpected irony, which I have used to demonstrate the notion of the Synopticon: in many, if not most cases, the production of scientific knowledge regarding the weather relies on subjective documentation of local conditions by individuals who, though engaged in stand-ardized practices, still offer views of atmospheric conditions that are decidedly personal. I begin with a discussion of the scientific approach to understanding atmospheric conditions, and then move on to review popular forms of local weather knowledge.

The Science of Weather: Moore's Meteorological Almanac

An examination of the history of medicine and public health practice since the nineteenth century in North America and Europe offers a useful model for thinking about the development of weather forecasting and lore. As American biomedical practitioners professionalized, their collective voice became the dominant force in what had previously been a multivocal conversation across a variety of 'folk' medical practitioners. Many effective and locally meaningful health beliefs and practices were squelched, succumbing to the hegemony of capitalist-oriented 'dominative' medicine (Baer 2001). Similar histories hold true for the western European nations, although in Europe there was greater continuity between the folk/alternative traditions, and less complete dominance by biomedicine.

The post-Enlightenment project of weather prediction likewise emerged from a milieu rich with local folk traditions. The Swiss national weather service began operations in 1881, after approximately sixty years of weather data collection under the auspices of the Swiss Nature Research Society (SNG). From 1860 on, the SNG had utilized a network of weather observers to produce daily weather reports, and by 1879 was producing daily forecasts.[3] Taking a comparable path within the same decade, the United States Weather Service began operation in 1869, building on more than twenty years of support for such an institution by the national scientific community (Moore 1900). Moore's Weather Almanac for the year 1901 serves as a demonstration of the transformative progression from weather lore to meteorology over the nineteenth and twentieth centuries, highlighting a shared sentiment found across the Euro-American academic community, namely that scientific measurement and analysis of atmospheric conditions was superior to local use of folk oral traditions concerning the weather.

Professor Willis Moore, Chief of the U.S. National Weather Bureau, went to considerable effort in the publication of his weather almanac for the turn of the new century. Moore's explicit goal was to correct the misguided perceptions held by the public, and to inform them about the techniques of the modern science of meteorology:

> It will be the object of *Moore's Meteorological Almanac* to present in concise form such weather data and facts relative to meteorological phenomena as will be at once

interesting and profitable . . . Effort will be made to correct many popular but erroneous assumptions relative to climate and weather. Where but a few years ago we thought that chaos reigned supreme, we are now able, by the aid of daily simultaneous observations of the weather and the wonderful telegraph joining our cities by an electric touch, to trace out the harmonious operations of many physical laws that previously were unknown. (Moore 1900: 1)

He continues his treatise, not with the expected predictions of an almanac (to which the reading public had, following Poor Richard and his successors, long since become accustomed), but with a listing of historical weather data, history of the meteorological profession, and instructions for learning to command the technical tools of the weatherman. Moore admonishes his readers that:

You can forecast the weather. Any intelligent person, by studying the few simple principles on which the daily weather map is founded, can make an intelligent estimate of the general character of the weather for his region . . . You may ask: Why has this not been done by the laymen whose crops, whose perishable produce in transit, whose vessels exposed to the fury of wave and tempest, and whose health and pleasure are so dependent upon the weather . . . In answer it may be said that many members of com-mercial associations . . . make a fairly accurate forecast of the weather from the large daily weather maps displayed on blackboards before all the important commercial exchanges of the country, and in a pecuniary way largely profit therefrom. (Moore 32–3)

Moore concludes his volume with the following panoptical statement: 'The grand meteorological panorama of which hurriedly I have endeavored to give you a bird's eye view, should inspire all with greater wonder and admiration for the Grand Architect of Nature who creates and controls all things'. (Moore 1900: 128).

Moore believed that even if the abilities of science were at that time still limited, they would eventually develop more reliable outcomes. As Chief of the National Weather Bureau, it was his job to shape the public's understanding of the science of meteorology so that the people would be primed to consume that expert know-ledge. Moore introduces the scientific staff members in his office, and asks pointedly, 'Does not the reader suppose, if there were any information to be derived from the position of the planets or the phases of the moon that would enable them to make weather forecasts months in advance, that these scientific men would make use of it?' (1900: 54).

Surely the most popular of these other publications to which Moore referred was the *Old Farmer's Almanac*, published now by *Yankee Magazine*. The *Old Farmer's Almanac* commenced publication in 1792 under the direction of Robert B. Thomas, who wanted to continue the tradition of Ben Franklin's *Poor Richard's Almanac*. In recent years, it has claimed an 80 percent accuracy rate for its secret weather prediction algorithm, as determined by comparison with official US meteorological data; Stevens (1999) suggests that the actual accuracy is in the 50 percent range. While that is of course no better than would be expected by random chance, it is also the case that the long-range forecasts of the US National Weather Service have averaged about the same. An exception to this average was the winter of 1997–98; because of the strong El Niño effects, models were more accurate, and forecasters achieved an all-time high of 75 percent accuracy.

Moore's goal, as noted, was to correct the public's erroneous ideas about the weather. Elsewhere he makes specific reference to the 'long term weather prophets' who publish long term forecasts in almanacs (1900: 54), warning the public to avoid these charlatans who 'prey on the credulity of the people' (1900: 53). The notion that individual members of the public could have access to – indeed, have developed for themselves – empirically accurate knowledge about their local weather conditions, is not even remotely addressed. This was, after all, the turn of a new century – the twentieth – and the division of labor in this *Gesellschaft* required the accession of specialized knowledge to the designated experts in the field. In terms of the framework outlined above, Moore's effort clearly falls into the category of expert speech that has as its primary purpose the promotion of a modern scientific outlook for all, and the concomitant eradication of traditional knowledge.

Moore promotes the idea that the laity could use these new technical tools as well as the experts, saying that anyone can forecast the weather, given the right tools (1900: 32). He asks why the farmers don't do this, while suggesting that the businessmen who know what's good for them do in fact pay attention to the weather maps at the stock markets, and learn to interpret this technical information for fun and profit. Again there is no irony in his presentation – he never acknowledges the fact that individual farmers and sailors had been making a living based on their own observations for centuries, and that accurate knowledge of weather conditions must have been developed. Although the folk system was not perfect, neither (as Moore freely admits) was the National Weather Service.

Nearly a century later, we can see that current edicts about scientific meteorology are still quite consistent with Moore's view. The Swiss National Weather Service, MeteoSchweiz, has the following statement on its website:

Some examples of systematic documentation of the weather in Switzerland in the past can be found, but still those that are interesting from a scientific perspective in today's sense are rare. With the invention of measurement tools such as the thermometer and the barometer in the seventeenth century, it became possible to compare measurements from different locations with each other. Meteorology as an exact science was born.[4]

Although the 'Statement on Weather and Forecasting' adopted by the American Meteorological Society Council on August 17, 1998 tells us that there has been 'a revolution in the accuracy and utility of weather forecasts in the past several decades,' not one sentence in the following three pages of the statement gives any sense, precise or relative, of the actual improvements made. It is on the whole a defensive but optimistic piece, identifying the difficulties of the endeavor, and the value of numerical models and rapid communications systems for the ultimate goal of improving profits and the overall quality of life for the nation's citizens. In contrast with the universalist scientific approach emphasizing comparability of data, local knowledge of weather events and patterns tends to highlight familiarity with a specific place. With that difference in mind, I now turn to the community of Leukerbad, Switzerland.

Weather and Climate in Leukerbad

Over the past three years, I have spent eight months conducting fieldwork on water and weather in Leukerbad, in the canton of Wallis. Tourists both Swiss and foreign travel to this canton for skiing and taking the waters at the thermal baths in Leukerbad and a few other spots, not to mention visits to that signature landmark, the Matterhorn. Leukerbad, a village of about 1500 residents lies pressed against the back of a 16-kilometer-long valley – a box canyon, as it would be called in the American West. A journey to Leukerbad takes a traveler as far into the main spine of the Alps as she can go without coming out again on the other side.

The Dalatal, the valley of the river Dala that flows down from the glaciers above Leukerbad, opens southward to the main valley of the Rhone River. This valley marks the dividing line between the French- and German-speaking regions of the canton. Unlike the wine villages of the south-facing slopes of the Rhone, Leukerbad lacks the typical Valaisan climate: dry, sunny, and in need of constant irrigation to support the viticulture that has brought the region great fame. Leukerbad does have its share of sun, but its climate seems more often to be controlled by its proximity to the Berner Oberland, an area known for cool and foggy weather. On the positive side, this means that Leukerbad has not suffered the effects of the water scarcity that characterizes most other south-facing Walliser communities. Water is life, as we all know, but in Leukerbad abundant water is truly the town's lifeblood.

The economy of Leukerbad depends entirely on its varied water resources, which include thermal springs, used commercially since the sixteenth century; a ski area; and a small hydroelectric system fed by the Dala that provides power for all of the community's summer electrical needs, and one-third to one-half of these needs in winter. Until the late 1950s, every family in Leukerbad had a cow or two, a few goats, and a large garden plot. Subsistence was supplemented by wage labor, often available only by seasonal (winter) outmigration, and perhaps by some summer tourist income. As with other Swiss alpine communities (cf. Netting

1981), grazing land, as well as forest and water use rights, were held in common, and access distributed across the *einheimische*[5] families, who in turn constituted a powerful elite citizenry with rights that exceeded those of ordinary 'civil' citizens.

Weather-dependent threats to home and livelihood have always been central concerns for the inhabitants of this valley. Surrounded by steep, shale cliffs, Leukerbadners live in the shadow of a thousand avalanche chutes, and indeed the history of the village is one of repeated destruction by thundering rock and snow-slides (see Figure 3.1). The first protective walls were erected in the eighteenth century, and the following 250 years have seen the implementation of increasingly sophisticated systems of fences and other avalanche management techniques.

In 1958, a large medical clinic capitalizing on the thermal springs was built with funding from the northern cities of Zurich, Winterthur, and Lucerne. Since that time, an influx in foreigners (not just from other countries, but also *Ausserschweiz*, or non-Valaisan Swiss) has been accompanied by a rapid decline in subsistence-level smallholdings. Now, there are very few stock animals left in the valley; seven

Figure 3.1 The steep chute coming down the mountain on the far right side of this picture marks the avalanche path of 1719, in which more than fifty people died. This etching, from 1769, makes it clear that the central portion of Leukerbad village, as well as other grazing and economically significant lands, were all at high risk from destruction by avalanches.

or eight families make their living at least partly by farming, and almost no one else maintains animals year round. In most parts of western Europe and the United States during the year 2000, less than 5 percent of the population was engaged in full time agriculture. A century ago, that figure was around 40 percent in the United States. Statistics for Switzerland are similar, but there the shift was much more recent, extending to the mid-twentieth century.

Because of its water-based economy, Leukerbad is an excellent location to study weather, climate, and water resources. Despite the shift from a subsistence-oriented economy, weather and climate have continued to be important determinants for the economic health of the valley. The short- to mid-range consequences of altered precipitation patterns for the ski area, as well as the long-term impact of global environmental change on the glaciers that permit a stable flow of water through the Dalatal, make attention to water and weather crucial concerns for Leukerbad. As a self-designated 'Berg-Stadt', or mountain city (Andereggen n.d.), Leukerbad embodies the tensions between nature and culture, as well as tradition and modernity, that are central to German Swiss identity.

Weather Lore

When people in the village of Leukerbad were asked to tell any weather proverbs (*Bauernregeln*, or farmer's rules) or stories they could recall, most laughed, but nearly everyone had a contribution to make. Some shrugged and offered the popular parody of a *Bauernregel*, 'Wenn der Hahn kräht auf dem Mist, so ändert sich's Wetter oder bleibt wie es ist!' (If the rooster crows on the dungpile, the weather will change – or it won't);[6] more often than not, this was accompanied by a comment regarding the unpredictability of the weather. Weather lore in the form of easily remembered proverbs, though often associated with simpler times in centuries past, is still an important part of Euro-American cultures today. In Germanic lands, these *Bauernregeln* are the subject of countless popular books (see, for example, Eisbrenner 2000; Lussi 1994; Malberg 1999; Weingaertner 2000). I recently encountered a website with the following saying recorded on a virtual 'guest book': '"Donner am Morgen, der Taliban Sorgen' – Relativ neue afghanische Sprichwoerter' (roughly, Thunder in the morning, Taliban take warning – Relatively new Afghani proverb).[7] As this comment demonstrates, these pithy sayings, remembered over generations, are 'good to think' (cf. Levi-Strauss 1983) and so are constantly being developed anew. There are *Bauernregeln* covering a wide range of folk knowledge topics, but weather, particularly in conjunction with calendrical details, is one of the most common themes (see also Golinski, this volume). They are frequently quoted in everyday conversations, not to mention actually used as a forecasting method for the remaining farmers and shepherds, as well as hobby gardeners and sports enthusiasts. When I entered a local grocer's shop one day in May, the checker greeted me with the phrase 'Alles neu macht der Mai'; she had noticed that I had just gotten a haircut, and her comment on that observation – roughly, 'May brings a new start' – was couched in typical *Bauernregel* format. In terms of the 'tradition–modernity' axis mentioned above, *Bauernregeln* definitely fall toward the 'tradition' side of the scale; with regard to the 'popular–expert' speech axis, they likewise tend to fit into the popular category.

The wide array of popular books on this subject in both English and German tend to feature rules which vacillate between being so general as to be irrefutable: 'First love and the month of May seldom pass without a frost',[8] and so specific to a particular calendar day that they are rarely accurate: 'The weather on St. Urban's Day (May 25) foretells the Fall weather';[9] or, 'If it rains on Bibian's Day, it will rain for forty days plus a week thereafter.'[10] There are, however, also locally specific rules, based on observable environmental indicators, that are part of regional oral traditions, and these frequently yield trustworthy forecasts.

Bauernregeln were one of the earliest forms of knowledge to be put to press following the Bible. The date given for first publication of *Bauern-Praktik*, an almanac which forecast the year's weather, based on the twelve Days of Christmas and other specific days from the church calendar traditionally thought to be important determinants for planting and harvesting, is said to be 1508 (Hellman 1896). *Bauern-Praktik* was a bestseller in its day – though authorship is uncertain, it was probably first published in Augsburg, Germany, with twenty-nine different German impressions produced between 1530 and 1590 alone (Weingaertner 2000).

Weather proverbs, stemming from Germanic as well as other origins, have been the subject of much discussion by linguists and folklorists (Mieder 1993; Taylor 1931). In one running debate, Alan Dundes (1991) claims that these rhyming predictions that many people call weather proverbs are not in fact 'proverbs' at all, but rather 'superstitions' because they are often meant literally, while in his opinion proverbs are always meant to be understood metaphorically. The utility of his take on the matter has since been contested, at least for many non-English speaking contexts (Arora 1995). Leaving aside the scholarly classification of this speech genre, the fact remains that these often-rhyming predictive statements about topics of general interest – weather, health, love, food, life – have been the subject of much discussion by both technical specialists and the lay public.

Research concerning the reliability of these weather rules relative to meteorological knowledge is plentiful (e.g. Moore 1900; Rebetez-Beniston 1992; Linacre and Geerts 1997; Freier 1989; Malberg 1999). While many weather rules refer to observed phenomena – wind direction, animal behavior, etc. – others are based on calendar details. Saints' days and other specific holidays from the church calendar are frequently cited as presages of later seasonal or specific weather events; some examples include 'Green Christmas, White Easter' or 'Rain on St. Gorgon's Day

[September 9] means bad weather for the rest of the Fall.' During the winter of 2000, there was indeed a Green (or at least Brown) Christmas, and over a foot of snow fell on Easter weekend; I cannot count the number of times that the appropriate proverb was recited to me over the course of that week! Those *Bauernregeln* with a general basis in observable phenomena, like rainbows or red skies – whether at morning or night – often do reflect accurate knowledge of frequently experienced weather patterns. Other examples of such reliability include assessments of humidity ('Thunderstorms follow humid weather'[11]); cloud types (mare's tails or mackerel skies); or wind patterns ('When the north wind blows in June, storms tend to be late'[12]). Animal behavior also appears quite frequently as an indicator of near or mid-range weather conditions, as in: 'When the mosquitoes are playing in January, the farmers are in big trouble!'[13]

Malberg (1999), a geophysicist and meteorologist, has explicated many of the more common weather rules in terms of current scientific knowledge, reflecting atmospheric conditions that might be found in a wide variety of locales. Martine Rebetez-Beniston (1994) has made a thorough analysis of perceptions of weather and climate in the French-speaking part of Switzerland, using weather proverbs as her primary data. She also compares recorded weather patterns with perceptions of the same. Rebetez-Beniston classifies these weather proverbs, or *dictons*, into three main categories (1994: 7): agro-meteorological, astronomical, and meteorological. The last is further divided into those proverbs that require fulfillment of a condition, whether based on the actual weather or on other events ('When the moon is new, the weather changes'; 'Friday's weather is Sunday's weather'), and those that are unconditional statements ('Saturdays are always sunny').

In America, as in Europe (indeed, following the examples brought by many German and English immigrants), popular weather lore has continued to be a dominant form of folk knowledge. At the same time, local as well as global (e.g. CNN and The Weather Channel) professional meteorologists have expanded their role from mere forecasting to education of the public regarding the technical expertise required for weather prediction. They show us maps, and we learn to distinguish warm from cold fronts, swirling storms and tightly clustered isobar lines. Such an effort to demonstrate the utility of the expert knowledge that the clan of the weatherpeople brings to the public arena is certainly not new, but has been a constant effort since the earliest days of the profession, as we have seen with the example of Moore's *Weather Almanac*. Well before the organized science of meteorology existed, lay audiences counted public lectures on atmospheric phenomena as the highest form of what today might be called 'edutainment' (Hamblyn 2002). This educational mission is not merely an attempt to help the lay public understand the complexities of weather forecasting, but also a way of developing a market for a wide assortment of weather products. The commodification of weather and climate includes marketing of past weather datasets as well as a range of local to global short- to long-term forecasts, synoptic charts, and market-based speculation on future weather. Such products extend interest in weather from personal activities at a daily or seasonal level to a much broader range of applications, including short- to mid-term personal and corporate investments in 'weather futures.'

From Synoptic Charts to the Synopticon

While large segments of the population consider minimal attention to the weather forecast to be useful for planning activities in their daily lives, there exists a smaller group for whom weather watching is an avocation that is practiced daily. Though the history of amateur weather observation is extensive (see Golinski and Harley, both in this volume), less has been said about the relationship between the daily work of individual amateurs and that of regional or national institutions, who use a variety of sources to generate official forecasts. Such an inquiry offers insight into the shift from meteorological knowledge produced by and for local communities to the national and global production of scientific forecasts.

How do the weather forecasters obtain their data? The 'daily simultaneous observations' mentioned by Moore are still made and transmitted by a corps of amateur weather observers, in both the United States and Switzerland. One of these is Matti Bergmann. Matti is the local weatherman in Leukerbad. He is an outsider, an Austrian from the south Tirol, a region that came under Italian control following World War II. Matti arrived in Leukerbad in the 1970s after living in Canada for fifteen years, where he had met and married a Leukerbad woman. Together Matti and I have spent many hours reviewing his carefully kept daily records of rainfall and wind direction, barometric pressure and cloud cover, talking about life as well as the weather. A small, spry man more than eighty years old, Matti has never failed to greet me with a lively smile. On nice spring and summer days, he can often be found working in his extraordinarily rich garden, weeding the strawberry patch or staking out tomatoes. The rain gauge and anemometer are prominent features of his backyard, from which vantage point he can survey most of the village, viewing the length of the Dalatal as it reaches out toward the Matterhorn. Before his retirement, Matti was employed as a warden for the village, performing a range of tasks from giving parking tickets to caretaking public buildings. Until the local paper went out of business, Matti used to write a daily weather column; he even read the column on the regional radio station for a few years.

For the past dozen or so years, Matti has kept records for MeteoSchweiz. He records observations from his backyard twice a day, and faxes them to the national weather headquarters. He keeps monthly and annual summaries of the weather conditions in Leukerbad, and makes up his own *Bauernregeln* – as he told me, anyone can make these up, all you have to do is look around, and wait to see if you were right. What is important to note about the records Matti relays to Zurich is that his data, which are recorded using a standardized procedure and format, represent but one point of hundreds on the weather map of Switzerland. MeteoSchweiz takes this kind of locally produced information and incorporates it simultaneously into a synoptic chart or map, comprised of all of the other weather observation station data in the country. The product of this simultaneous viewing of local conditions is a tool that claims a higher level of accuracy and predictive value than any one of the readings could possibly give. By making several of these synoptic maps in a timed sequence, one can track the movement of storms and determine the probability for weather changes in various regions of the country.

These 'daily simultaneous observations' are the key to what I here term the 'Synopticon,' in direct contrast to Foucault's (1979) use of Bentham's Panopticon. Mathiesen (1997) and Bauman (2000) have spoken of the shift from the modern Panopticon-based society, in which the few observe – and by observing, control – the many, to what Mathiesen first called the Synopticon. Rather than concentrating the power of observation in the hands of a small number of powerful individuals, the Synopticon describes a situation in which the many observe the few. The type case for this transformation, according to Mathiesen, would be the large audiences who use public media to watch celebrities of various sorts, from athletes to movie idols and even television weather personalities.

The Weather Channel is certainly one example of this version of the Synopticon in action, but I would like to propose a somewhat different, though equally late modern, reading. By the mid-nineteenth century, the technology of the telegraph allowed the simultaneous transfer of local weather data to centralized points, and thus a picture of the atmospheric conditions across a region, or indeed an entire continent, could emerge: the synoptic map ('seeing together' all of the data points observed only by the eyes of individual weather collectors). The synoptic weather map highlights the production of local knowledge about the weather, exemplified by Matti's daily efforts, as it is joined simultaneously with other bits and bytes of local knowledge and panoptical satellite data, to produce a translocal or even global image. This image, in turn, circulates via the Internet with minimal boundaries of time or space. The key here is that the global informational product cannot be produced without local input; satellites are often limited in what kinds and degrees of local ground conditions they can identify. So, expert meteorologists are dependent on amateurs for their controlled and specialized knowledge. There is an inherent irony in the notion of having individuals as 'weather collectors' who supply the data points for the creation of a weather map. The presentation of this finished product – the synoptic map – creates a fiction that masks its reliance on the observations made by the laity, without which the expert's data products could not exist. Folk knowledge, as well as individual practice, is embedded into the scientific process, rendering these elements invisible to the consumer of weather forecasts.[14] Rather than the many viewing the few, as also occurs, this Synopticon is a metaphor for the joint production of image/knowledge/ideology – the cyborg that, though resolutely late modern, still breathes through the face-to-face *Gemeinschaft*, or community, of individual actors engaged in their immediate environments.[15]

Highlighting the importance of maintaining intimate knowledge of particular places, as opposed to using selected points across a region to identify general trends, gives us some insight into the differences between institutionally and locally produced forecasts. In considering categories of weather knowledge, I find a stark contrast between synoptic charts and the *Bauernregeln* with specific local geographical referents. The accuracy of certain weather proverbs can be linked to the specificity of the environment and conditions within which they arose: in Leukerbad, 'Wenn der Balmhorn hat ein Hut, wird das Wetter gut' (When the Balmhorn wears a hat [ring of clouds near the summit], the weather will be good'). With a specific geographical referent, the local nature of this proverb is clear, but even without such a physical anchor, it may also be the case that prediction only for a local region is meant. In Leukerbad, a north wind is known to bring clear, cold weather; that might not be the case in other locales, such as those that border on open water to the north. Storms usually come in from the west in this location, and the clouds hanging by the mountains on that side indicate the right conditions for rain or snow. These local rules tend to be based on observed phenomena, and they are most likely to be good predictors of actual weather. With this, we are leaving aside the need to predict, for example, exactly how much rain falls, or the duration of the storm. Knowing that there will be rain is different from knowing exactly when, how much, and for how long. But considering our axis of popular to expert speech, one could argue that such explicit local knowledge (which might be identified as Indigenous Knowledge, or IK, in a non-European context) is as technical as an official weather forecast by the Swiss or American meteorological bureau, in that it has special meaning for a select audience, and can be tested effectively only within that context.

Producing knowledge of and for local contexts is a markedly different thing from the local consumption of globally prepackaged probabilities of specific outcomes or events. Risk perception for natural hazards, including the weather, has been strongly shaped by the development of expert knowledge over the past century,[16] but the predictive use-value of non-locally produced weather forecasts, in contrast to many other forms of scientific discourse, often seems to be literally laughable – for example, the chance that the urban forecaster will get it right for a specific rural community may well be less likely than the chance that a native endowed with a substantial body of local lore will. And even the local bungler may have a decent chance. As weathermen will tell you, regardless of the models, the single best predictor of the next day's weather (averaging 70 percent accuracy) is simply the reiteration of today's experience – something for which no skill, and only a limited amount of experiential knowledge, is required.

As with other oral traditions, the transmission of weather proverbs over generations and through migrations from place to place may result in the codification of ever more generic forms of the expression, with a resultant decrease in meaningful information within the new context. Reversals of this trend, including customization of generic forms to fit new locales, are also possible. When residents of a particular locale migrate to a very different geographic setting, as was the case with many German-speaking settlers in the American Midwest, the rules that were learned for local predictions in the country of origin ceased to be valuable for the new conditions.

Rather than looking only to nostalgia, 'tradition,' and a longing for simpler lifeways as an explanation for the continued use of *Bauernregeln* in Switzerland and elsewhere, I suggest that we think about the relative value of relinquishing control over different types of knowledge. The distribution of specialized knowledge is certainly one of the hallmarks of modernity, and in cases where expertise can be demonstrated to make a difference (brain surgery comes to mind), then the non-specialists are usually happy to abdicate responsibility. On the other hand, if no apparent or immediate benefits seem forthcoming, and if the experience of one's own senses, or one's neighbor, or the almanac on the newsstand, appear to provide equally useful informational products, then the consumer has no reason to give up his own control over the production of that specialized knowledge. This, I would argue, is the case with the weather, and is one reason why local weather lore remains a strong feature of everyday experience, both in Switzerland and elsewhere.

Another good reason for maintaining local control over knowledge of the weather is that of the immediacy of shared experience. As one experiences the weather on any given day, it is only to be expected that others who have shared in the same experience would use that commonality to build and support social bonds. The experience of past weather, as against the prediction of future weather events, provides a basis for discussion with little dispute, and again an opportunity for the type of phatic communication described elsewhere (e.g. Golinski, this volume). Leaving the everyday experience of expectable weather aside, there is one caveat regarding the relinquishment of local control of this type of knowledge. Advance notice of extreme weather events is a key concern for meteorologists, and one which the lay public greatly appreciates – even revels in, to judge by the videos of disastrous weather one can purchase on the weather channel. Such concern is warranted when one considers the lives and livelihoods at stake, but the voyeuristic sensibility that accompanies this attention speaks perhaps more to the late modern society of the spectacle (Debord 1997) than to actual risk management strategies.

While meteorological science has made great advances over the past several decades, chaos still (or again) reigns supreme. At the turn of the twentieth century, Moore and his colleagues sought to banish the uncertainties of nature so abhorrent to post-Enlightenment thinkers. To this end, their aim was to demonstrate regularities in the weather, and to a degree, they did find some. But now, at the beginning of the twenty-first century, the core of weather science is grounded in chaos theory. There is general recognition that the best models in the world, made by the fastest supercomputers with the most comprehensive satellite data, will lose accuracy after two weeks (and probably well before) because the production of weather is inherently chaotic (Lorenz 1963), meaning that it is extremely sensitive to initial conditions, and so the slightest change at any point may have dramatic effects on later outcomes.

Conclusion

If the goal of indigenous-knowledge research is, as Sillitoe (1998: 224) suggests, 'to make connections between local people's understandings and practices and those of outside researchers and development workers . . . seeking to achieve a sympathetic and in-depth appreciation of their experience and objectives and to link them to scientific technology', then the study of *Bauernregeln* certainly meets these criteria. When comparing the present-day use of such folk sayings in contrast to the sophisticated forecasting by meteorologists using synoptic charts, computer models, and multi-sited datasets, it strikes me that the modern scientific approach, explained so nicely by Dr. Moore, takes on the shape of both a Panopticon as well as a Synopticon, in contrast with the singularly local perspective of the observation-based weather proverbs. Modern weather forecasting requires data input from many different on-the-ground geographic locations at once, as well as data collected from outer space via weather satellites; these various weather observation stations provide the bases for the synoptic maps used by weathermen to show regional and global weather fronts. Weather forecasting technology is both panoptic in its satellite-based external vantage point, and synoptic in the simultaneity of its multiple-locale reporting. Though modern forecasts offer statistical probabilities of certain outcomes for selected regions, they may not be as good as direct, personal observation of local phenomena for an accurate short-term account of impending weather. Yet farmers, sailors, mountain guides, and others who make their living by their skills at navigating nature's complex rhythms and random disturbances, know that to trust the weatherman's forecast *alone* is to cast one's lot to the wind – there is no substitute, no matter how sophisticated, for being there.

Sarah Strauss

Acknowledgements

This research has been supported since 1997 by a variety of sources: a University of Wyoming International Travel Grant (1997), a University of Wyoming College of Arts and Sciences Basic Research Grant (1998), a University of Wyoming Faculty Research Grant-in-Aid (1998), and a grant from the Cultural Anthropology Program of the National Science Foundation (#BCS-0078891; 2000); the author gratefully acknowledges all of these funding agencies. In addition, thanks are due to Bonnie Zare, Lin Poyer, and Ben Orlove, as well as the participants in the 2001 Invited Session on Weather, Climate and Culture at the annual meeting of the American Anthropological Association.

Notes

1. M. Tscheinen and P.J. Ruppen, *Walliser Sagen*, 1983[1872]; this and all other translations by author unless otherwise noted.
2. The canton is known as Wallis in German, and Valais in French.
3. For a more detailed history of the Swiss weather service, see http: //www. meteoschweiz.ch/de/Portrait/Aufgabe/IndexAufgabe.shtml, accessed on 16 October 2002.
4. http: //www.meteoschweiz.ch/de/Portrait/Aufgabe/IndexAufgabe.shtml, accessed 21 October 2002. The German original reads: 'Systematische Auf-zeichnungen über das Wetter in der Schweiz lassen sich in der Vergangenheit einige finden, von wissenschaftlichem Interesse im heutigen Sinne sind jedoch nur die wenigsten. Mit der Erfindung von Messgeräten wie Thermometer und Barometer im 17. Jahrhundert war es möglich, Messwerte verschiedener Orte miteinander zu vergleichen. Die Meteorologie als exakte Wissenschaft war geboren.'
5. *Einheimische* is usually translated as 'native' – which in this context means having been settled in Leukerbad for significantly longer than 100 years!
6. For an extended discussion of 'anti-proverbs' or parodies of this sort, see Mieder and Litovkina 1999.
7. http: //www.schlue.de/gaestebuch/ Bruss, Will ES, Donnerstag, 11 Oktober, 2001 um 16: 18: 51; accessed 22 October 2002.
8. Original: 'Die erste Liebe und der Mai, gehen selten ohne Frost vorbei'.
9. Original: 'Die Witterung auf St. Urban zeigt des Herbstes Wetter an'.

10. Original: 'Wenn's regnet am Bibianstag (December 2), regnet's vierzig Tag' und eine Woche danach'.

11. Original: 'Auf schwüle Luft folgt Donnerwetter'.

12. Original: 'Wenn im Juni Nordwind geht, kommt Gewitter oft recht spät'.

13. Original: 'Wenn die Mücken spielen in Januar, so kommt der Bauer in grosse Gefahr'.

14. This is also linked to another issue – how new strategies in weather forecasting depend on consensus forecasts created by pooling individual forecasts (see, for example, http: //www.e-acumen.com/knowledge/weather_risk/consensus. html; see also Hendry and Clements 2002). In this case, idiosyncratic forecasts produced by lone weatherpeople are shown to be far less accurate than those generated by combining several individually made forecasts.

15. One question suggested by this model is whether it would still be useful if all of the Swiss weather collectors were to be replaced by mechanical or computerized instrumentation. Movement to total automation in weather data collection could be seen in one of two ways. On the one hand, because this would seem to remove the element of unique human observation to the production of the whole weather picture, the notion of the late modern Synopticon might be brought into question. On the other hand, since the decentralized collection of information at dispersed sites would continue, even if by automated rather than manual means, we might simply regard this kind of transformation as an indicator of the shift from the late-modern to the post-modern situation imagined by such authors as Baudrillard. In this instance, human observations are replaced by those that are simulacra, hyper-real technological products that re-create a person's senses of sight, sound, and touch. This feature of hyper-reality is important:

> 'The real is produced from miniaturized cells, matrices, and memory banks, models of control – and it can be reproduced an indefinite number of times from these. It no longer needs to be rational, because it no longer measures itself against either an ideal or a negative instance. It is no longer anything but operational. In fact, it is no longer really the real, because no imaginary envelops it any more. It is a hyperreal, produced from a radiating synthesis of combinatory models in a hyper-space without atmosphere.' (Baudrillard 1994[1981]: 2).

Cartwright's discussion of fetal and maternal monitor use in hospitals provides a cogent example of how automated data production is often taken to be 'more true' than that produced by individual humans; she provides ethnographic documentation of the extent to which hospital staff rely on monitor data rather than on women's own verbal reports of their labor experiences (1998).

16. For extended discussions of the relationship between expert knowledge and risk assessment, and of both for modernity in general, see Lupton 1999; Douglas 1992; Beck 1992; Giddens 1991.

References

AMERICAN *Meteorological Society. 1998. Statement on Weather and Fore-casting. Bull. Amer. Met. Soc., 79,* 2161–2163; also at http://www.ametsoc.org/AMS/. Accessed 21 October 2002.

ARORA, SHIRLEY. 1995. Weather Proverbs: Another Look. *de Proverbio* 1: 2; http://info.utas.edu.au/docs/flonta/. Accessed 21 October 2002.

ANDEREGGEN, STEPHAN. n.d. *Leukerbad: Thermen, Themen und Tourismus.* Visp: Verkehrsverein Leukerbad und Rotten Verlag.

BAER, HANS. 2001. *Biomedicine and Alternative Healing Systems in America.* Madison: University of Wisconsin Press.

BAUDRILLARD, J. 1994[1981]. *Simulacra and Simulation.* Trans. Sheila F. Glaser. Ann Arbor: University of Michigan Press.

BAUMAN, ZYGMUNT. 2000. *Liquid Modernity.* Cambridge: Polity Press.

BECK, ULRICH. 1992. *Risk Society: Towards a New Modernity.* London: Sage Publications.

BRAMWELL, ANNA. 1992. *Ecology in the 20th Century.* New Haven: Yale University Press.

CARTWRIGHT, ELIZABETH. 1998. 'The Logic of Heartbeats: Electronic Fetal Monitoring and Biomedically Constructed Birth', in *Cyborg Babies: From Techno-Sex to Techno-Tots.* Edited by Robbie Davis-Floyd and Joseph Dumit, pp. 240–254. New York: Routledge.

DEBORD, GUY. 1997. *Society of the Spectacle.* New York: Zone Books.

DOUGLAS, MARY. 1992. *Risk and Blame: Essays in Cultural Theory.* London: Routledge.

DUNDES, ALAN. 1991. Weather Proverbs: Some 'Folk' Views. *Proverbium* 8: 1–17.

EISBRENNER, RUDOLPH (Ed.). 2000. *Das grosse Buch der Bauernweisheiten.* Würzburg: Stürtz Verlag GmbH/Flechsi-Buchvertrieb.

FOUCAULT, MICHEL. 1979. *Discipline and Punish.* New York: Vintage Books.

FREIER, GEORGE. 1989. *Weather Proverbs.* Tucson, AZ: Fisher Press.

GIDDENS, ANTHONY. 1991. *Modernity and Self Identity.* Cambridge: Polity Press.

HAMBLYN, RICHARD. 2002. *The Invention of Clouds: How an Amateur Metor-ologist Forged the Language of the Skies.* New York: Picador.

HENDRY, D.F. and M.P. CLEMENTS. 2002. Pooling of Forecasts. *Econometrics Journal* 5: 1–26.

HELLMANN, G. 1896. *Die Bauern-Praktik* von L. Reynman 1508. Neudrucke von Schriften und Karten ueber Meteorologie und Erdmagnetismus. Berlin: Asher.

HYMES, DELL. 1988. 'Models of the Interaction of Language and Social Life', in *Directions in Sociolinguistics*. Edited by J. Gumperz and D. Hymes, pp. 35–71. Oxford: Basil Blackwell.

LADURIE, EMMANUEL. 1971. *Times of Feast, Times of Famine*. Garden City, NY: Doubleday & Company.

LEVI-STRAUSS, CLAUDE. 1983. *The Raw and the Cooked*. Chicago: University of Chicago Press.

LINACRE, EDWARD and BART GEERTS. 1997. *Climate and Weather Explained*. London: Routledge.

LORENZ, E. N. 1963. Deterministic Nonperiodic Flow. *Journal of Atmospheric Science* 20: 130–141.

LUPTON, DEBORAH. 1999. (Ed.) *Risk and Sociocultural Theory*. Cambridge: Cambridge University Press.

LUSSI, KURT. 1994. *Wind und Wetter: die bäuerliche Wettervorhersage und Unwetterabwehr.* Wollerau: Schellen-Verlag.

MALBERG, HORST. 1999. *Bauernregeln aus meteorologischer Sicht*. 3rd Edition. Berlin: Springer Verlag.

MATHIESEN, THOMAS. 1997. The Viewer Society: Michel Foucault's 'Panopticon' revisited. *Theoretical Criminology* 12: 215–234.

MERGEN, BERNARD. 1997. *Snow in America*. Washington, DC: Smithsonian Institution Press.

MIEDER, WOLFGANG. 1993. *Proverbs Are Never Out of Season: Popular Wisdom in the Modern Age*. New York: Oxford University Press.

MIEDER, WOLFGANG and ANNA T. LITOVKINA. 1999. *Twisted Wisdom: Modern Anti-Proverbs*. Supplement to *Proverbium*, no. 4. Burlington: University of Vermont Press.

MOORE, WILLIS. 1900. *Moore's Meteorological Almanac for 1901*. Chicago and New York: Rand McNally & Co.

NETTING, ROBERT. 1981. *Balancing on an Alp*. Cambridge: Cambridge University Press.

REBETEZ-BENISTON, MARTINE. 1994. Perception du temps et du climat: une analyse du climat de suisse romande sur la base des dicton populaires. Ph.D. Dissertation, University of Lausanne.

ROSTOW, W. 1960. *The Stages of Economic Growth: A Non-Communist Manifesto*. Cambridge: Cambridge University Press.

SILLITOE, ALAN. 1998. The Development of Indigenous Knowledge. *Current Anthropology* 39: 223–252.

SMELSER, NEIL. 1958. *Social Change in the Industrial Revolution*. London: Routledge & Kegan Paul.

STEHR, NICO and H. VON STORCH. 1999. *Klima, Wetter, Mensch*. Munich: C.H. Beck Verlag.

STEVENS, WILLIAM. 1999. *The Change in the Weather*. New York: Delacorte Press.

STRAUSS, SARAH. 1999. Urbane Nature: Shapeshifting in a Central Periphery. Paper presented at the Annual Meeting of the American Ethnological Society, Portland, OR, March 25–28, 1999.

TAYLOR, ARCHER. 1931. *The Proverb*. Cambridge, MA: Harvard University Press.

WEINGAERTNER, HARALD. 2000. *Wenn die Schwalben niedrig fliegen*. Munich: Piper Verlag.

4

Chesapeake Bay Watermen, Weather and Blue Crabs: Cultural Models and Fishery Policies[1]

Michael Paolisso

Introduction

You listen to a lot of talk about weather if you study commercial fishermen. During my fieldwork with Chesapeake Bay commercial fishermen, known throughout the region as watermen, the topic of weather kept surfacing in interviews and participant observation. At first, what watermen said and knew about the weather did not seem related, at least in any serious manner, to my research focus on watermen's knowledge and views about the blue crab (*Callinectes sapidus*) fishery. However, it is not possible to spend time with watermen and not become engaged in conversations about the weather. Slowly and almost imperceptibly, I found myself becoming increasingly interested in everyday discussions about the weather

And I was not at a loss for opportunities to listen and ask questions of watermen about the weather. Talking about the weather is an early-morning ritual for watermen. Before casting off, most watermen I know stop at the local general store for coffee, maybe a smoke, and talk with other captains. Invariably, this talk includes discussion of different radio and television forecasts of the day's weather, along with their own commentary on current conditions outside. Included in this talk are comments and observations about how the weather will affect the day's work. Will it be hot and humid? If working near the shoreline, will there be breezes strong enough to keep biting greenhead flies away? Will strong winds make it difficult to keep boats on course while pulling up a line of crab pots? Will the winds kick up swells high enough that the day's already exhausting work will be made more difficult as the boat pitches and rolls?

There were mornings when talk of the weather dominated the discussion. These were days of beautiful or stormy weather: the warm, slightly breezy and sunny days that reminded watermen why they loved 'working on the water' or, conversely, mornings when high winds, waves, and rain made a captain anguish over the decision whether to stay in and lose a day's catch or 'head out' and risk gear, boat or, in the extreme case, life.

As fieldwork progressed and my understanding of watermen culture improved, I realized that there was much more significance and meaning to those early morning weather conversations than I had originally detected. I now suspect that, even as each waterman discussed weather and work conditions, he was also thinking about how the day's weather would affect the movement and molting of crabs. In fact, probably since the moment they awoke early that morning, the captains were applying a wealth of experience-based knowledge of the effects of weather on crabs to the specifics of their current fishing situation: where their crab pots are located, water depth, sand or shoal bottom, when they last 'fished up' their pots, the stage of the current crab run, molting stage of crabs already in the onshore floats, etc. Of interest is the fact that most of this weather and crab knowledge is implicit, taken-for-granted knowledge slowly acquired by watermen through years of close observation and study of crab behavior as part of their work on the water. Although widely shared, it is knowledge that watermen assume each other have, and thus is not often discussed and talked about, unless there is a pestering anthropologist about. And for the anthropologist, in order to ask questions regarding weather and crabs, you first need some understanding of crab ecology, fishing economics, and a holistic understanding of the cultural importance of 'working the water' for Chesapeake Bay watermen and their families.

In this chapter my aim is to present a cultural analysis of watermen's knowledge of the role of weather in the blue crab fishery. Drawing on interview and observation data from my ongoing fieldwork with Maryland watermen on the lower Eastern Shore of the Chesapeake Bay, I will provide examples of the type of associations watermen see between different weather patterns and crab behavior. Understanding the weather's effect on crab behavior has obvious economic implications for watermen in terms of the fishing and the marketing of blue crabs. However, for watermen this understanding also has ecological and political significance: unpredictable weather changes affect crab behavior in ways that protect the crab from overharvesting. According to watermen, the randomness of weather creates unpredictable changes in crab behavior, which in turn function to prevent watermen from overharvesting crabs. Watermen's strong beliefs in the biological effectiveness of weather's beneficial contribution to sustaining the fishery is part of the reason for watermen's resistance to recent scientific and state regulatory actions implemented to protect the blue crab reproductive stock.

I begin by providing a description of the blue crab fishery, followed by a brief overview of the focus of my research and fieldwork. Next, I present examples provided by watermen of how weather affects blue crab behavior, which in turn directly influences crab fishing and marketing practices and ultimately, to no small degree, watermen's livelihood. I follow this with discussion of the current controversy over the biological status of the bay's blue crab population, contrasting the views and knowledge of scientists and state resource managers with the knowledge and views of watermen. As part of the discussion of watermen's position, I present a cultural model of watermen's reasoning about the blue crab fishery. In this model, weather plays a major role as an agent of God's management of nature, including the blue crab. I conclude with a few general observations and comments about the multiple meanings of weather to watermen and to broader discussions about knowledge, science, and environment on the Chesapeake Bay.

Chesapeake Bay, Blue Crabs, and Watermen

The largest estuary in the contiguous United States, the Chesapeake Bay is an unparalleled and multi-faceted natural resource. Encompassing portions of six states, its watershed drains approximately 64,000 square miles of land through five major rivers. Both rural and urban populations from the surrounding states of Maryland, Delaware and Virginia, and the District of Columbia have come to rely upon the Chesapeake Bay's abundant resources and natural beauty. Home to nearly 27,000 species of plants and animals, its fertile watershed and waterways provide livelihoods for both watermen and farmers.

Today, the livelihood of the bay's watermen depends on the annual harvest of blue crabs, which in Maryland was 46 million pounds annually for the period 1982–99 (Chesapeake Bay Commission 2001). The annual harvest in Maryland of hard crabs from the Chesapeake Bay accounts for over 50 percent of total U.S. landings. For the Chesapeake Bay alone, harvests during the 1990s averaged more than $50 million a year – and that is just the dockside value. In 1999, blue crab harvests accounted for over 60 percent (or $38.9 million) of Maryland watermen's fishing income (Maryland Sea Grant 2001).

Blue crabs are harvested as hard shell crabs, peeler crabs (i.e. those about to molt), and soft shell crabs. Watermen fish for soft and peeler crabs using scrapes, pots (wire cages), and bank traps. Hard crabs are caught using baited trotlines and pots. Recreational gear includes baited hand lines, collapsible traps, trotlines, dip nets, and bank traps. Table 4.1 describes in more detail the type of fishing gear used by watermen and recreational crabbers.

Study Background

The geographical focus of my work with watermen is the Maryland portion of the Lower Eastern Shore of the Chesapeake Bay. I began this work in the summer of 1998, as part of an initial study of cultural beliefs about *Pfiesteria piscicida*, a dinoflagellate that bloomed toxic in three bay tributaries in this area (Paolisso and Chambers 2001). In July 2000, I expanded my research among watermen to include a wider range of environmental issues. After exploring a number of areas

Table 4.1 Crab harvesting gear.

Fisher Type	Gear Type	Description
Commercial	Hard Crab Pot	A wire mesh pot, usually a cube measuring 2 feet per side, with four openings for crabs to enter into. The pot is baited (using things such as eel, chicken necks, or fish), and when the crab enters it floats up into a second compartment of the pot and cannot escape.
Commercial	Peeler Pot	Very similar to a hard crab pot, except that instead of using bait to lure the crabs in, which is illegal in peeler pots, a large male crab, or Jimmy, is used to attract peelers into the pot.
Commercial	Crab Scrape	A metal frame shaped somewhat similarly to a hockey goal, but measuring about 3 feet wide by a foot tall. A long net is attached to the frame, and the entire thing is dragged along the bottom of the bay, collecting crabs as it goes.
Commercial	Bank Traps	Consist of a leader made of wire netting strung out between poles in a line along the shore. Crabs hit the leader, follow it, and then enter a large heart. In an attempt to exit the heart, the crab is funneled into a large trap, measuring about five feet tall and four feet square. The trap is then lifted out of the water and emptied into another container where the crabs are sorted out from other animals caught in the trap.
Commercial and some Recreational	Trot Line	A long nylon (usually) rope weighted with chains at either end, and each end is attached to an anchored buoy. Bait is tied to rope at intervals. The rope is lifted out of the water by a roller or hook mounted at the back of a boat, and the crabs are collected using dip nets.
Recreational	Collapsible Traps	A cubical wire box whose sides will open up to allow crabs to enter the trap. Bait is placed in the center of the trap, and by pulling up on a line attached to the top of the trap, the sides will close and trap the crab. It can be used in shallow water (off piers) or by boat.
Recreational	Dipping, Chicken Lining or Hand Lining	The use of a long string with a lead weight and some form of bait attached to the end to catch crabs. The crab nibbles at the bait and is slowly pulled out of the water or until it is close enough to be caught by a dip net.
Recreational	Dip Nets	Long handled net, preferably of wire mesh, used to catch crabs under piers or bulkheads, or to scoop up crabs in shallow water from a boat.

on the Lower Eastern Shore, I selected the communities of Chance, Deal Island, and Wenona. The communities are located at the end of a peninsula surrounded by the Tangier Sound, approximately 15 miles west of Princess Anne, which is the government seat for Somerset County (see Figure 4.1). These are relatively small, contiguous communities with a combined population of 955 (U.S. Census Bureau 2000).

While the three communities maintain somewhat unique social and cultural identities, they are similar in that they are communities where being a waterman is the most important local profession. Although some men and women work 'down the road' in Princess Anne and beyond, the majority of families in the area are economically dependent on the harvest of soft and hard crabs.

The Tangier Sound is a fertile area for the harvesting of crabs. From April until early September, most men in the communities fish for soft crabs using pots and many of the women work full or part-time shedding soft crabs in the family crab shanties, located near the boat docks. Some hard crabbing is done throughout the season, but it becomes the dominant form of crabbing from September through November. A few men trotline and scrape for crabs, but potting is by far the most common form of crab fishing. In winters, many of the local watermen dredge for oysters.

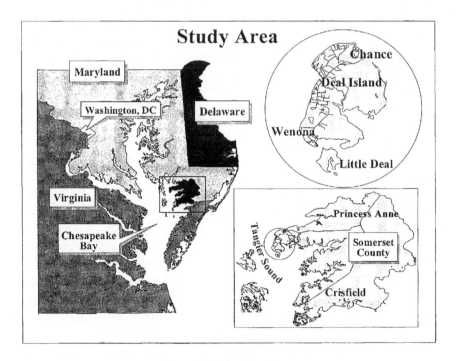

Figure 4.1 Map of Study Area.

Cultural Model Approach

One important applied challenge for anthropologists studying contemporary environmental issues, including topics related to weather, is to make explicit the roles of beliefs, values, and experiences in the formation of cultural models that enable individuals to make sense of or understand today's complex environmental problems. Since beginning fieldwork on the Chesapeake Bay, I have been using theories and methods from cognitive anthropology to identify the cultural models used by Chesapeake Bay watermen, farmers, and environmental professionals to understand and respond to environmental problems such as toxic algal blooms, farm nutrient runoff, declines in water quality, and reduced fishery production.

In an oft-quoted definition, Quinn and Holland (1987: 4) describe cultural models as 'presupposed, taken-for-granted models of the world that are widely shared (although not necessarily to the exclusion of other, alternative models) by members of a society and that play an enormous role in their understanding of that world and their behavior in it.' A fundamental assumption of cultural modeling is that when individuals engage the world they cannot possibly attend to it in all of its complexity. Consequently, individuals use models to reason with or calculate by mentally manipulating the parts of the model in order to solve problems or interpret situations or events (D'Andrade 1995). Cultural models frame experience, supply interpretations of that experience and inferences about it, and provide goals for action (Quinn and Holland 1987). For the individual, the cultural models deployed are largely tacit and unexamined and often highly resistant to change (Quinn and Holland 1987).[2]

An effective approach to identifying underlying cultural models of knowledge is to focus on explanations offered as part of natural discourse on the topic or domain at hand (Blount 2001, D'Andrade 1995, Quinn and Holland 1987). In offering explanations for why something is the way it is, respondents often present their understanding of a situation in terms of propositions and theories. A proposition is a statement asserting or proposing a state of affairs (Shore 1996). Following D'Andrade (1995: 180), 'a proposition is the sense of something said about something (typically a sentence) and involves the integration of a relatively small number of separate schemas into a more complex schema; a proposition asserts the relationship between this integrated schema and the complex world.' Propositions are culturally codified as slogans, clichés, wise words, maxims, and other formulaic statements (D'Andrade 1995). A theory is an interrelated set of propositions that describe the nature of some phenomena. Cultural theories are explicit formulations in language. Cognitive anthropologists analyze propositions and theories in order to identify underlying cultural models and schemas.

The results of recent research I have conducted with colleagues suggest that bay stakeholders, mainly environmental professionals, farmers and watermen, understand pollution and natural resource problems within broader encompassing cultural models. These models integrate values and beliefs about religion, spirituality, nature, morality, work, independence, and responsibility with experienced-based ecological and economic knowledge (Paolisso 2002; Paolisso and Chambers 2001; Paolisso and Maloney 1999, 2000a, 2000b, 2001).

In terms of field methodology, analysis of interviews and natural discourse is very useful for identifying explicit and implicit cultural model information (Blount 2001, D'Andrade 1995, Quinn and Holland 1987, Shore 1996). Also, participant-observation data fills in cognitive gaps in verbal and linguistic information (cf. Gatewood 1985). In my work among watermen, I have used a combination of methods, including semi-structured interviews, in-depth and extensive conversations, and participant-observation during all phases of commercial crabbing operations. Since July 2000, I have completed close to fifty semi-structured interviews and more than thirty days of participant observation with watermen on their boats. Equally important, I have spent countless days in the communities, visiting families, attending church and social events, and drinking coffee in the local general store (see Paolisso 2002 for a more detailed discussion of field methods and sample).

Weather and Blue Crab Behavior

Well, I'm a commercial waterman. I start off April with crabbing and we'll crab right through, a lot of years, to November. It's just according to the weather.

(Deal Island waterman)

In Maryland, the crabbing season currently runs from April 1 through December 15. During the first month of the season, watermen catch hard crabs, which are awakening from a long winter slumber in the deeper parts of the bay and working their way toward shallow waters in search of food and, for many, mates. The harvest begins slowly and the catch is not substantial, but market prices are at some of their highest levels for the season. Once you have your pots overboard, the 'fishing up' is relatively straightforward. Legal-size hard crabs are easily sorted (culled) into baskets according to sex, and sold immediately to local buyers, who may even meet returning watermen dockside to transfer the crabs to refrigerated trucks.

Hard crabbing in April marks a transition for watermen in their work. For months watermen have been working to prepare their pots and boats for months of daily use. This work is unpaid, tedious, and can be costly if new pots need to be purchased or significant boat repairs are required. The income earned from April's hard crabbing is a welcome financial relief, and the change in work from preparation to fishing is much appreciated by watermen.

The first molt of season or 'peeler run' occurs during an approximately two-week period in May. Watermen anxiously await this first peeler run, which typically produces the most soft crabs of the three to four runs during the season. The first crabs to molt are immature male crabs, or what watermen call 'he-crabs'. Typically the catch of male peelers is small – a good catch is a few crabs per pot – but steady throughout the run. However, what makes the first peeler run particularly productive is the presence of doubler crabs: female crabs undergoing their final molt and seeking to mate with a jimmy crab, a mature, male hard crab. During mating, male and female crabs double up, as the jimmy crab cradles the female underneath him in what anthropomorphically could be called a prolonged and protective embrace. To catch doublers – the term refers only to the female partner – watermen either dredge using crab scrapes or use pots baited with jimmies.

It is not uncommon to catch hundreds of doublers a day during the first peeler run. Once shed, each crab can be worth between one and two dollars, depending mainly on size. No other time in the year can you catch doublers in such quantities. Also, market prices for soft crabs are typically near the highest in the early spring.

The general rule of thumb is that the peeler run begins in mid-May, but the actual date varies from year to year depending on when the air and water temperatures increase. As one waterman stated:

> [crabs] got internal clocks . . ., but the weather is key. If the weather is really pretty, I've seen that first run of crabs come on as early as the 6th of May, or between the 6th and the 10th. But most of the time, it's right around the 17th. And, then again, I've seen it a little bit later than that. I've seen it come on about the 21st or 24th of May. But like I say, it just [depends], the weather is a key factor.

Thus, as May approaches watermen become very attentive to changes in the weather that might signal a warming trend. They also begin to check undersized crabs in their hard crab pots for signs that they will molt soon. It is a very busy time for watermen, since they are both fishing for hard crabs while also trying to ready any remaining peeler pots and the crab shanty. It is a stressful and anxious time for watermen. Given the economic importance of the first peeler run, coupled with the fact that the run lasts only for about two weeks, watermen worry about not being ready and missing some of the run.

As May's weather warms, at some point each waterman decides to switch from hard to peeler crabbing. The timing of decision carries with it significant economic implications. If the peeler pots are set out too early, hard crabs that would have been sold are instead used as bait for doublers. If the pots are set out even a few days late, then a significant portion of the run's total harvest will have been lost. Moreover, going after doublers is a risky strategy, since male peeler crabs will not enter a pot baited with a large jimmy crab. If you bait up your peeler pots too early, your catch of male peelers drops off.

While the first peeler run is the most dramatic example of weather affecting crab behavior and watermen's harvest strategies, throughout the season weather plays a major role in determining the crab harvest. Winds from the west and south increase crab movement on the bottom, and generally lead to periods of higher catches in pots. Harvests drop off dramatically when easterly winds blow, causing crabs to move less, and northeast winds cause crabs to bury in the bottom. Cooling water temperature generally causes crabs to move less, except if this occurs in the autumn when cool weather signals that winter is approaching, and it is time for crabs to migrate to deeper waters in the bay and Atlantic Ocean for overwintering. And finally, warmer temperatures cause peeler crabs to molt faster, both in the bay itself and in the onshore crab shanties where shallow tanks of circulating water, known as floats, are used to hold peeler crabs until they shed. In shedding, women and children assist in fishing up the floats and packaging the now soft crabs for sale. Warm weather makes it necessary to fish up the floats every few hours in order to remove the crabs while soft, or else they will begin to harden again.

Increased Regulation of Blue Crab Fishery

It is tough enough battling the weather, and then you have to fight against regulations too.

(Deal Island waterman)

Findings from recent research and monitoring efforts indicate that blue crab spawning stock in the Chesapeake Bay is near its recorded lowest level, which occurred in 1968, from which the crab population recovered (Chesapeake Bay Commission 2001). Of concern to scientists and resource managers is the absence of historical experience to demonstrate the crab population's ability to recover. Concerned that the stock was reaching dangerously low levels, in 2000 the Bi-State Blue Crab Advisory Committee (BBCAC) advised state policymakers and natural resource managers to establish minimum blue crab fishing thresholds, based on information from fisheries-independent monitoring (particularly the bay-wide winter dredge survey) and levels of fishing effort.[3] The specific thresholds recommended by BBCAC are a minimum catch threshold that preserves 10% of the blue crab's spawning potential and a more restrictive fishing target level that would preserve 20% of spawning potential, which adds a margin of safety to fishery management decisions. It was estimated that a decrease in blue crab fishing pressure of 15% would be needed to preserve 20% of the spawning potential (Chesapeake Bay Commission 2001).

Commercial fishing is a major source of blue crab mortality, and Maryland natural resource managers argue that regulation of the fishery is the most effective policy response to protect the spawning stock. Even if the low crab stock could be explained by environmental factors, such as increased fish predation, current state policy is directed toward reducing fishing pressure to avoid shrinking the stock even further. Furthermore, improvements in crab habitat and water quality, also recognized as important actions needed to reduce crab mortality, will take years to implement before any noticeable improvement in crab reproduction would be achieved. The current situation is seen as risky because of low biomass and high fishing mortality. Thus, under present environmental conditions, scientists and resource managers argue that the prudent policy response is to reduce commercial fishing mortality (Greer 2000).

Accepting the BBCAC minimum stock threshold and target fishing recommendations, and after a number of public hearings to discuss with watermen and crab processors how best to achieve the 15% reduction in fishing pressure, the Maryland Department of Natural Resources (DNR) enacted new commercial harvest regulations for the 2001 and 2002 crabbing seasons. These regulations require watermen to take one day off per week from commercial crab fishing and to limit their daily time on the water to a maximum of eight hours. For the 2001 season, the new regulations required watermen to take one day off per week from commercial crab fishing and to limit their daily time on the water to a maximum of eight hours. Additional regulations for the 2002 season include increased minimum size limits for peeler crabs from 3 to 3.5 inches, for soft crabs from 3.5 to 4 inches, and for male hard crabs, beginning in August, from 5 to 5.25 inches. Moreover, the number of allowable undersized crabs per harvest basket was reduced from twenty to five crabs.

Most watermen did not object to the mandatory one day off, since many of Maryland's watermen, for religious and family reasons, do not work on Sundays. Reactions were much stronger to the proposed eight-hour day. Many watermen argued, for example, that weather and tide conditions, plus the occasional mechanical breakdown, make it difficult to fish up pots or trotlines consistently in the same eight-hour period. Watermen opposed an increase in the minimum legal size for peelers, fearing the loss of their market for smaller soft crabs, which many people say taste better than the larger soft crabs. Watermen also expressed concern that the difference between a 5- and a 5.25-inch hard crab would be difficult and time consuming to discern, resulting in a disruption of the flow and pace of work on their boats.

Nature and Weather Manage Crabs

They want to regulate everything and you can't regulate nature. I mean, nobody knows what the weather is going to be from one year to the next.

(Deal Island waterman)

While willing to do their part to protect the fishery, watermen felt unfairly targeted by the new harvest regulations. Watermen agreed with scientists that recent harvests have been down, but argued at public hearings and in the media that this decline was due more to a combination of factors, principally increased fish predation on juvenile crabs, a decrease in submerged aquatic vegetation where crabs can hide and reproduce, and declining water quality.

Watermen also expressed their strong belief that fluctuations in the size, composition, and distribution of the blue crab population are ultimately unpredictable and cyclical. From their perspective, changes in the blue crab population are a part of nature that is not knowable to a significant degree by either watermen or scientists. Rather, consistent with strong religious convictions, most watermen believe that only God can determine whether there will or will not be crabs in any given year. While admitting that humans, including watermen, can do great harm to the fishery and need to use nature's resources in a sustainable way, in interviews, conversations, and at public hearings, watermen repeatedly argued that natural cycles in the blue crab population are an unpredictable part of God's plan for nature and humans.

The unpredictability of nature's management of the blue crab fishery is operationalized in part through changes in weather and the resulting effects on crab mortality and behavior. On many occasions, watermen have explicitly challenged the ability of science and natural resource managers to predict or model changes in the blue crab population and to develop effective regulations based on such information. Instead, watermen have used examples of weather's sudden effect on crab behavior and mortality to illustrate the unpredictability of nature and blue crabs. For example, a waterman from Deal opined:

> I don't see any great difference [before the current period of low harvests and before]. Crabs up and die; fish up and die. You take it in cycles and everybody knows that and the state knows it . . . You don't know if you're going to get a hurricane, you just don't know. Weathermen can't predict the week ahead of time, much less years. And nature depends on it all. I mean, what the weather is determines when you're going start [daily and for the season overall], and when you're going to finish, it just determines it all.

Watermen cannot predict God's stewardship of nature, which ostensibly is expressed as changes in tides, winds, spawnings, etc. They do not expect to predict it, and to be a successful waterman you need to plan on not being able to predict God's stewardship. According to watermen, you might have an idea that it will be a good year based on the spring doubler run, but there is no guarantee that the crabs will remain plentiful throughout the season. Fluctuations in crab populations are simply not predictable, and weather plays a major role in varying crab population characteristics. A waterman from Wenona expressed the following:

I mean, who knows when a hurricane is going to blow through here, going to stir the bottom up? . . . if you would get a storm in March, if it warms up like it's warmed up now, and you get an awful storm by the middle of March, there would be more damage to the crabs than anything in the world because they [crabs] are coming out, when it gets warm they start coming out.

The unpredictable nature of weather helps protect the crab from overharvesting by watermen and helps ensure that there will always be crabs. This is all part of God's plan for the watermen and blue crabs. Weather is one of nature's most important tools for randomizing the size and distribution of crabs. The best watermen can do is work with basic generalities about what should happen in terms of crab behavior given certain weather conditions, and, according to watermen, scientists need to recognize the role of weather and the limits to a scientific study of blue crab population. As one Deal Island waterman expressed:

Scientists are smart . . . but you have to know . . . the weather conditions . . . the wind and rain. I mean, you just cannot predict [weather]. You might have a rainy season. The water is not salty. Then you're liable to have a dry summer and the water's so salty that your [boat] windows are covered with dry salt after you come in on a rough day . . . But I mean, it's just nature, if you could predict how much rain we're going to have in a month or something like that, scientists could do good, but it can't be done. And I mean, the more rain there is, the crabs will do things differently. The more wind, the cool weather, the hot weather, crabs move place to place and you just can't predict it!

A Cultural Model of the Blue Crab Fishery

Scientists, state resource managers, and the general public are not unfamiliar with watermen's arguments that nature manages the blue crab, including watermen's explicit views on the effects of weather on blue crab mortality and behavior. However, these statements have been ineffective in influencing public discourse and fishery policymaking. While not denying the existence of natural cycles in the blue crab population, the scientific and regulatory approach to managing the blue crab fishery has been widely perceived as the safer and more 'sound' approach. The reasons for this dismissal of watermen's argument are complex and beyond this chapter's focus on weather. What is important to the discussion at hand is to situate watermen's statements about weather, unpredictable nature, and blue crabs within a broader fishery management approach that integrates watermen's beliefs, values, and knowledge.

As described earlier, my research among watermen focuses on identifying cognitive models of implicit and shared cultural knowledge about environment and pollution. On the basis of extensive analysis of interview transcripts and participant observation, I believe that watermen do share an implicit cultural model for managing the blue crab fishery. In its entirety, this model represents an underlying cognitive structure, which assists watermen to frame, interpret, and give meaning to human and nature dynamics in the blue crab fishery. The model is tacit and assumed; it is what watermen see *with* rather than see (Quinn and Holland 1987).

A diagrammatic representation of a cultural model of watermen's reasoning about the management of the blue crab fishery is presented in Figure 4.2. The model frames a number of underlying cultural propositions and theories about blue crabs, regulations, science, and human interventions that surfaced in my interviews and informal conversations with watermen. The cultural model integrates and links these beliefs and statements in a manner that is consistent with watermen's explicit statements about what determines crab population dynamics.

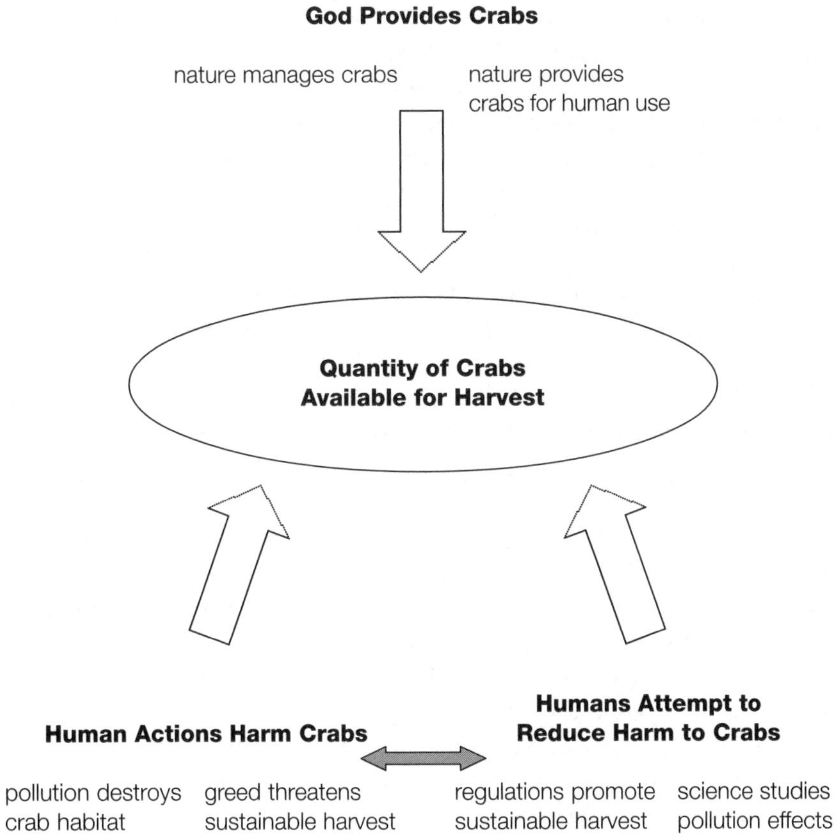

God Provides Crabs

nature manages crabs   nature provides
                                              crabs for human use

**Quantity of Crabs
Available for Harvest**

                    Humans Attempt to
Human Actions Harm Crabs   **Reduce Harm to Crabs**

pollution destroys   greed threatens   regulations promote   science studies
crab habitat   sustainable harvest   sustainable harvest   pollution effects

Figure 4.2 Cultural model of watermen's reasoning about blue crab management.

In watermen's reasoning, the quantity of crabs that are available for harvest is determined by three general propositions: 'God Provides Crabs,' 'Human Actions Harm Crabs,' and 'Humans Attempt to Reduce Harm to Crabs.' The model also consists of six more specific propositions, which are more detailed articulations of the meanings and emphasis of the general propositions and are closer to watermen's explicit knowledge and statements about the blue crab fishery. Of particular relevance to this chapter is the specific proposition 'nature manages crabs,' examples of which include statements and observations by watermen about the effect of weather on crab behavior, the intelligence of crabs and how they learn and adapt, and the natural cycles of abundance and scarcity of all species. The specific proposition 'nature provides crabs for human use' includes watermen's firm belief that they can trust and depend on God to provide crabs (and other species) for their use. This dependence creates a personal and close relationship with God, one where God is in control, a fact watermen are reminded of in times of storms and other dangers inherent in working on the water.

The two specific propositions of 'science studies pollution effects' and 'pollution destroys crab habitat' are easily recognizable by watermen, and their instantiation in terms of studying and controlling the effects of sewage on crab habitat has been at the center of watermen's recommendations about what role science and regulations should play in managing the blue crab fishery. The specific propositions 'regulations promote sustainable harvests' and 'greed threatens sustainable harvest' are more complex and contentious among watermen, although almost all the watermen I interviewed admitted in the end that some regulations are necessary for the fishery to survive. The types of regulations that promote sustainable harvests include laws to set size and gear limits, for watermen and recreational crabbers alike, which help to ensure that the crabs provided by God are used in the best possible ways to guarantee enough crabs for all commercial and recreational fishers. Among watermen, the implicit sense of what is enough is perhaps best defined by what they perceive as necessary to continue a livelihood of working on the water.

Even more sensitive is the specific proposition 'greed threatens sustainable harvest.' While watermen recognize the right of an individual to work hard and make a living by being a waterman, there is also recognition that watermen can be greedy and that such greed hurts watermen in general. The instances of greed are excessive harvesting of undersized crabs and the use of significantly more crab pots than allowed by licence. The same instances would be true for recreational crabbers. What is key here, and illustrated by the model, is that this greed is not directly linked to God's provisioning of crabs, but rather reduces the availability of crabs that God has provided for watermen. The greed is linked to the sustainability of watermen's livelihood, not to the sustainability of the blue crab population. Thus, the greed hurts watermen themselves, making it difficult for all to catch enough crabs to sustain their livelihood. It results in an escalation of gear to remain competitive and economically viable, and it can create ill feeling even among watermen toward those watermen who routinely and by a wide margin ignore gear and minimum size regulations.

The model in Figure 4.2 helps us account for watermen's strong belief that you can never predict crab harvests (or the size of the crab population), since a significant component of what determines crab availability is under God's control, and ultimately not understandable by watermen or scientists. However, improved human management can result in better utilization of the crabs provided by God. Thus, the size of the circle 'Quantity of Crabs Available for Harvest' can expand and contract for any period, and, most importantly, good secular management can keep the crab harvest high even in years when God provides fewer crabs.

Broader Bay-Wide Relevance

Although a detailed discussion of the relationships between watermen's cultural and environmental knowledge and broader bay-wide ecological, economic, political, and socio-cultural changes is beyond the principal focus of this chapter, I would like to briefly mention a few issues and concerns. First, it is widely reported that the Chesapeake Bay is one of the most studied estuaries in the world. Along with continued population growth and urban sprawl in the watershed has come an even greater emphasis and reliance on science to monitor anthropogenic effects on the bay's ecology and natural resources. Blue crabs are certainly no exception to this trend, and in fact may be one of the most visible examples of science-based efforts to monitor human impacts, for example due to increased fishing pressure, pollution, and shoreline development, and provide guidance to policymakers and resource managers charged with ensuring a sustainable Chesapeake blue crab population and fishery. An issue that warrants more explicit consideration is how watermen's cultural and environmental knowledge is perceived and used (or misused) compared to science-based research on blue crabs.

In interviews and in responses to a recent survey we conducted among watermen, scientists, and resource managers, one of the most consistent and strongest responses by all groups was the felt need to integrate the scientific and watermen knowledge on blue crabs. It was also clear that the information groups were seeking from each other was behavioral: what do crabs do, where do they go, and watermen's fishing responses to crab movements and abundance and to different regulatory actions. Not surprisingly, watermen, scientists and resource managers were less interested in acquiring more information on the underlying explanatory models that each group uses to understand, to the best of its ability, blue crab reproduction and behavior. Watermen did not ask questions about the biological assumptions of scientific models to estimate blue crab spawning stock biomass or about the economic principles implicit in analyses of the potential impacts of latent effort (commercial fishing licences held but currently not being used) on future harvests if conditions improve in the fishery. Scientists and resource managers did not express much interest in understanding, in any detail, watermen's religious beliefs and values or their epistemological assumptions about nature and natural cycles that, for example, situate weather's effects on crab behavior in a broader explanatory paradigm or model that is a theoretical alternative to science-based models. That watermen, scientists and resource managers did not seek in-depth information on each other's theories and models of blue crabs should not be seen so much as a criticism or failure to communicate, but as evidence of the difficulties and challenges inherent in eliciting and communicating implicit and complex cultural environmental knowledge, both science- and religious-based.

Second, the cultural model analysis of weather and blue crabs could be used for the purposes of integrating a focus on cultural factors into bay environmental education programs. Talking about weather can serve as an entry point for establishing rapport as part of an expanded dialogue on bay environmental issues. For example, recreational boaters (fishermen and sailboat owners) share much of watermen's interest in weather. It is hard to imagine a discussion of weather as not being of strong interest to recreational boaters, who in general respect and admire watermen for their decision to fish commercially. Moreover, the discussions of weather may also involve personal experiences and viewpoints based on past boating experiences in inclement weather. These experiences can reinforce the relevance and personal meaning of practical weather information, and also help establish rapport among groups who at times disagree with each other on Bay environmental issues.

For recreational boaters and watermen alike, this interest in weather is clearly less for weather's own sake but more for the effects of weather on fishing and boating. With appropriate facilitation, dialogue could be moved from weather and boating to, for example, discussions of how weather affects crab behavior, watermen livelihoods, and the role of God and nature in managing natural resources. Recreational boaters may not share or even agree with watermen's viewpoints on weather, crabs, God and nature. Nonetheless, the linking of watermen cultural beliefs about nature and God, for example, to weather and crabs may make such beliefs more palatable to others. At the very least, it may be possible to achieve improved cross cultural understanding, for both recreational boaters and watermen. In subtle and implicit ways, the understanding and views of participants in such dialogues could evolve, thus creating improved cultural awareness and understandings as well as correcting some of the existing cross-cultural misconceptions. Thus, the topic of weather may be an ideal medium for conversation and a bridge for communication on a wider range of cultural and environmental topics for the bay.

Third, dialogues on such topics of shared interest as weather and blue crabs can also be used in expanded environmental education programs to sensitize and educate bay stakeholder groups on how environmental issues are also cultural constructions. These cultural constructions in turn can become politicized. An environmental issue of particular importance is the political and public valuing of different types of environmental knowledge. For example, watermen's experiential knowledge about crab behavior is unquestioned by all as peerless. On the other hand, science-based, experimental knowledge about blue crab reproduction and population dynamics is widely valued. Both types of knowledge – experiential and experimental – are incorporated into political decision making for managing the bay's natural resources.

Topics such as cultural knowledge of weather and blue crabs can serve as case studies of the conditions and situations in which both types of knowledge are integrated or not into environmental decision making. Such case studies could highlight a host of important environmental questions: How is experiential and experimental information complementary or in conflict? What is the political process whereby one type of knowledge achieves intellectual dominance over the other? What broader cultural and social changes are occurring in the bay area that privilege one type of knowledge over another? These questions and others can be used in turn to generate more general discussions on underlying and implicit cultural-environmental assumptions for all participating stakeholder groups. In part through a focus on broader cultural-environmental beliefs and values, it may be possible to begin a process of collective critical assessment of the underlying, implicit cultural and political elements of the bay's environmental decision making. The goal would be to assist bay stakeholders in reflexive pursuit that would make more explicit the fact that natural resource management issues for the bay are much more than biological or ecological issues, but in fact have strong cultural roots that implicitly can define and shape bay environmentalism. The role that cultural factors play in constructing bay environmental issues, along with the ecological and biological conditions, is embedded and used in the politics of defining and managing the bay as a natural resource for the region's stakeholders. An important overall goal of such discussions would be to raise public and political awareness about the power of different types of cultural-environmental knowledge, and what is gained and lost in situations where one type of cultural knowledge becomes hegemonic.

Finally, we recently organized three workshops with watermen, scientists and resource managers where we aimed to promote nonjudgmental dialogue on the status and challenges in the bay's blue crab fishery. Using a collaborative learning approach that has been applied to environmental conflict situations (Daniels and Walker 2001), we made progress in facilitating open discussions of underlying cultural beliefs and values associated with participants' views and work (i.e., fishing, studying or managing) with the blue crab. Throughout the workshops, we metaphorically and repeatedly expressed our goal as attempting to 'dredge up' cultural environmental knowledge of the blue crab in terms of participants' cultural beliefs and values. We also emphasized the importance of understanding implicit and underlying knowledge, which we framed in the language of cultural models.

We feel the workshops and our ongoing work to promote the open exchange of cultural and environmental knowledge among blue crab stakeholder groups are important social science complements to scientific and regulatory efforts and to watermen's interests in understanding, in a more comprehensive manner, these efforts. Perhaps most importantly, these workshops and our anthropology on the Chesapeake Bay have begun to illustrate that many of the differences among stakeholder groups on how to manage key natural resources are less a difference on what individuals see, in terms of actual population dynamics and behavior, but more a difference of what they see with (i.e., cultural models). Focused on implicit cultural models of nature, environment and pollution, our work seeks to promote dialogue, improve cultural understanding and foster collaborations among watermen and environmental professionals, while monitoring how and why these cultural models evolve and change.

Conclusions

Watermen depend on their knowledge of weather to make key fishing decisions. Weather is one of the most important topics they discuss in terms of weather patterns and the effects of weather on crab behavior. Even if a waterman is not talking about the weather, you can be sure that he is aware of it, monitoring it with multiple senses, and processing the possible changes he will make in his fishing in accordance with changes in weather. This relationship between weather patterns and fishing is strongly exemplified in the blue crab fishery, where weather has many effects on crab behavior based on crab life cycle changes and time of year.

That weather is an important factor in the livelihood of watermen should come as no surprise. What is perhaps novel and unanticipated is the extent to which watermen see weather as part of God's plan for nature and the blue crabs in particular. Humans cannot predict the weather or much else about nature. That is not to say that science and management policies do not have a role. In fact, the cultural model in Figure 4.2 situates science and regulations in the domain of secular management: science and regulations should focus on studying and controlling how humans through pollution and greed can hurt the blue crab fishery. From the watermen's perspective, weather is part of God's way to ensure that crab behavior is not understandable to the point that humans would be tempted to overharvest. Trusting in the management effects of the weather on the blue crab population is one of the watermen's policy responses to help manage the blue crab. Conversely, for scientists and resource managers, weather, particularly a hurricane, is seen as a natural event that might drive down the crab population to levels where recovery may not occur. This difference in perspectives is just one indication of the conceptual and knowledge differences currently separating watermen and scientists and natural resource managers in terms of the status and management of the blue crab fishery.

From an ethnographic perspective, my unexpected interest in weather has greatly enriched my understanding of watermen culture and the blue crab fishery. In fact, it is now difficult not to see the linkages, both direct and indirect, to so much of what it means to be a waterman. As my fieldwork continues, both in conversations and while out working with watermen on their boats, I find myself engaging in weather conversations, more to explore my own, implicit cultural knowledge rather than to verify explicit information already collected. And my early morning coffee in the local general store is the richer for it.

Notes

1. The fieldwork on which this chapter is based would not have been possible without the cooperation and support of many Maryland watermen. In particular, I would like to thank Eldon Willing Jr., Grant Corbin, Roy and Ryan Ford, David and Linda Horseman, Sonny Benton, and Paul Holland. Thanks also to my colleagues Erve Chambers, Ben Blount, Jack Greer, Amanda Ritchie, Stacey Hockett-Sherlock, Charles Petrocci and Mary Winterbottom for their participation in broader research efforts within which the study of watermen is being undertaken, and for their helpful comments and suggestions on earlier drafts of this chapter. Finally, the material presented in this article is based upon work supported by the National Science Foundation and the U.S. Environmental Protection Agency under Grant No. 9904928 and Grant No. 9975825. The Maryland Sea Grant College provided additional program development support.
2. In the cultural model literature in anthropology, the term 'cultural model' is often used synonymously with the term 'schema'. An important exception to this practice includes D'Andrade (1995) who defines schemas as the organization of cognitive elements into an abstract mental object with default values or open slots that can be variously filled in with appropriate specifics. Furthermore, according to D'Andrade schemas are not models when the collection of

elements is too large and complex to be held in short-term memory (D'Andrade 1995).

3. The Bi-State Blue Crab Advisory Committee (BBCAC) was created by the Chesapeake Bay Commission (CBC), which is a tri-state legislative group created to advise the General Assemblies of Maryland, Virginia, and Pennsylvania on matters of bay-wide concern. In 1996, the CBC created the BBCAC to coordinate management of the blue crab fishery by Maryland, Virginia, and the Potomac River Fisheries Commission. BBCAC is comprised of legislators, resource managers, watermen, seafood processors, researchers, and conservationists. BBCAC is charged with providing advice to the governors, legislatures, and resource management agencies of Maryland, Virginia, and the Potomac River, and in turn is advised by a Technical Work Group of twenty-nine scientists.

References

BLOUNT, BEN G. 2001. Key Words and Cultural Models in Representation of Environmental Knowledge. Department of Anthropology. University of Georgia. Unpublished MS.

CHESAPEAKE BAY COMMISSION. 2001. Taking Action for the Blue Crab. Managing and Protecting the Stock and its Fisheries. Report of the Bi-State Blue Crab Advisory Committee. Annapolis, Maryland.

D'ANDRADE, ROY. 1995. *The Development of Cognitive Anthropology*. Cambridge: Cambridge University Press.

DANIELS, STEVEN and GREGG WALKER. 2001. *Working Through Environmental Conflict: The Collaborative Learning Approach*. Westport, CT: Praeger.

GATEWOOD, JOHN. 1985. 'Actions Speak Louder than Words', in *Directions in Cognitive Anthropology*. Edited by Janet W. D. Dougherty, pp. 199–219. Chicago: University of Illinois Press.

GREER, JACK. 2000. The Bottomline on Blue Crabs: Setting Thresholds for the Last Great Fishery. *Marine Notes* 18: 5–6.

HORTON, TOM. 1996. *An Island out of Time: A Memoir of Smith Island in the Chesapeake*. New York: W.W. Norton and Co.

MARYLAND SEA GRANT. 2001. 'Research Needs for Sustainable Blue Crab Production in Maryland.' Workshop Report. College Park, Maryland.

PAOLISSO, MICHAEL. 2002. Blue Crabs and Controversy on the Chesapeake Bay: A Cultural Model for Understanding Watermen's Reasoning about Blue Crab Management. *Human Organization* 61(3): 226–239.

PAOLISSO, MICHAELand ERVE CHAMBERS. 2001. Culture, Politics, and Toxic Dinoflagellate Blooms: The Anthropology of Pfiesteria. *Human Organization* 60: 1–12.

PAOLISSO, MICHAEL and R. SHAWN MALONEY. 1999. Toxic Algal Blooms, Nutrient Runoff, and Farming on Maryland's Eastern Shore. *Culture and Agriculture* 21: 53–58.

—— 2000a. Farmer Morality and Maryland's Nutrient Management Regulations. *Culture and Agriculture* 22: 32–39.

—— 2000b. Recognizing Farmer Environmentalism: Nutrient Runoff and Toxic Dinoflagellate Blooms in the Chesapeake Bay Region. *Human Organization* 59: 209–221.

—— 2001. Building a Constituency for Applied Environmental Anthropology through Research. *Practicing Anthropology* 23: 42–46.

QUINN, NAOMI and DOROTHY HOLLAND. 1987. 'Culture and Cognition,' in *Cultural Models in Language and Thought*. Edited by Dorothy Holland and Naomi Quinn, pp. 3–40. New York: Cambridge University Press.

SHORE, BRADD. 1996. *Culture in Mind*. New York: Oxford University Press.

UNITED STATES CENSUS BUREAU. 2000. Census 2000: Profile of General Demographic Characteristics. <http://www2.census.gov/ census_2000/datasets/ demographic_profile/Maryland/2kh24.pdf>.

5

(En)Gendering the Weather: Rainmaking and Reproduction in Tanzania

Todd Sanders

It was yet another sweltering day in Ihanzu, north-central Tanzania. Although it was mid-February, the sun shone down on us with a vengeance, the rains long overdue. Having wound our way through the bush and up the hill on a narrow, serpentine path earlier in the morning, we now sat in a small, dusty clearing. We had come to this secluded sacred site – most with great hopes, many in sheer desperation – to carry out an ancestral offering for rain.

The sheep had already been sacrificed, and the grandchildren were now moving into the centre of the clearing to start the fire. The grandson grasped a long, slender stick between his outstretched palms. Placing its tip into a small hole in a second flat stick that the granddaughter held on the ground, he twirled the firedrill determinedly. At the same time he theatrically intoned an address to the spirits.

Just then, as I scribbled hurriedly in my notebook, an elderly man who had been sitting silently next to me all morning leaned over. 'Do you see those two sticks?' he asked. Ever the anthropologist, I continued to write, thinking this was an inopportune moment to deliberate over a couple of sticks. Smoke began to rise from the point where the sticks met, a certain sign that the fire would soon ignite and that the addresses would be over.

When the addresses finally finished, I turned to the man. 'What was that about the sticks?' I asked. Smiling wryly, he spoke: 'The long, slender stick, that's the male. And the short, fat stick with the hole in it, that's the female.' Apparently my expression betrayed puzzlement. He elaborated: 'Look: the male is active, the female passive. Still, can either do anything alone? No, of course not. But if they cooperate, if they have sex, fire is born.' Grinning as if he had just given away the game, he leaned back and said no more. Although this elder no doubt felt otherwise, for me this was the beginning, not the end, of my musings over the relationship between rainmaking, gender, and ritual power.

As the months passed, I participated in many such ancestral rain offerings. And at each, men and women spontaneously explained to me in nearly identical ways the centrality of the firedrill to those rites and, of course, the gendered and sexual symbolism that came with it.

The aim of this chapter is to come to terms with those two sticks or, more broadly stated, to delve into the relationship between the cultural construction of gender, sexuality, and rainmaking rites and beliefs in Ihanzu. Although my interest in rainmaking, gender, and fertility derives from one particular ethnographic encounter,[1] the theoretical implications move well beyond it. Most anthropologists concerned with rainmaking in Africa, as good empiricists, have noted the centrality of gender and sexual symbolism in these rites and beliefs. More often than not, however, they have been puzzled by this, and have therefore either de-emphasized the topic or ignored it altogether, focusing instead on more instrumental social, political, and economic aspects surrounding rainmaking (e.g. Beemer 1935; Evans-Pritchard 1938; Colson 1948, 1977; Wollacott 1963; Larson 1966; James 1972; O'Brien 1983). Important though these topics undoubtedly are, our understanding of African rainmaking will remain impoverished until we pay more careful attention to locally informed understandings.

Rainmaking in Africa

Rainmaking in Africa has long interested Western observers, academic and otherwise.[2] And for as long as such observers have reported on African rainmaking rites and beliefs, they have reported on their blatant sexuality and the presence of things gendered.

All across the continent, for example, we find gendered rainstones (Rogers 1927; Hartnoll 1932: 738; 1942: 59; Cooke and Beaton 1939: 182; Middleton 1971: 196; James 1972: 38; Packard 1981: 69), some of which are themselves allegedly 'capable of reproducing' (Avua 1968: 29). Also common are gendered rain pots (Cory 1951: 51n.; Hauenstein 1967b: 13); male and female rain drums (Weatherby 1979); male and female rain statuettes (Ntudu 1939: 85; also Johnson 1948: 41, 96 [plate]); and even male and female rains (Bleek 1933: 308; Ginindza 1997: 152; Holas 1949; Marshall 1957; Sanders 1998).

Moreover, rain rituals themselves, much like the implements used in them, frequently hint at the cultural salience of gender and sexuality (e.g. Hauenstein 1967a, 1967b; Hoernlé 1922; Jellicoe *et al.* 1968; Lindström 1987: 77; Murray 1980; Schoeman 1935; Ten Raa 1969; Vijfhuizen 1997; Håkansson 1998: 276). Songs sung during such rites are often sexually explicit or, if not, highly suggestive (Evans-Pritchard 1929; Jacobson-Widding 1990: 71, n. 7; Krige 1968).

Similarly, the opposite of rainmaking – that is, 'rain-breaking' – is frequently associated with sexuality or the breach of taboos using genitalia. In some places a man may destroy the rain by urinating on a fire (Marshall 1957: 237) or 'by raising his posterior to the clouds' (MacDonald 1890: 130).

It is not difficult to imagine why gender and sexuality might feature centrally in most, if not all, African rain rites. For in most places and most cases, rain equals fertility on the grandest scale: without rain, people, plants, and animals whither and die. Rain equals life. It might therefore seem banal – if not palpably tautological – to point out that rain rites, which are after all rites of fertility, are full of fertility symbolism. What is altogether more puzzling is why so few scholars have dwelt on this.[3]

Take, for instance, Elizabeth Colson's landmark paper on rainmaking among the Tonga of Northern Rhodesia (today Zambia). In it she describes at some length Tonga rain rites, but only to tell us that she is 'frankly puzzled as to why some are considered appropriate to the occasion. In one the dancer limped sadly about the shrine . . . Other dances were obscene' (Colson 1948: 279–280).

In one of the few, full-length monographs devoted to the topic, Isaac Schapera repeatedly records, but then either ignores or fails to appreciate the significance of sexuality in rainmaking. He was told that:

'In the old days' widows and widowers were 'doctored in groups outside the village', in the presence of the whole tribe. Their clothing was removed, and when they were absolutely naked the doctors smeared their bodies with the juice of 'stinging bulbs' (*digwere tsedibabang*). They were then made to cohabit together sexually in public; if they refused . . . they might be killed on the spot. They were thought to be holding off the rain, and unless they were so treated the country would become 'spoiled' by the heat of the sun.

(Schapera 1971: 123)

Regrettably, Schapera seems to have made no further inquiries into the local logic that lay behind this and other statements like it.[4] Nowhere in his excellent monograph, in fact, does he provide any coherent account of how the themes of sexuality, gender and fertility might be linked to rainmaking rites and beliefs more generally.

Still others writing about rainmaking seem to shy away from sexuality altogether, even though the topic is, by their own accounts, not absent. In their monumental study, *The Realm of a Rain-Queen*, Krige and Krige (1943) have almost nothing to say about sexuality in rainmaking rituals, except this:

In ritual, sex is symbolized to some extent, but only as an aspect of fertility, not as a sensual pleasure, while obscenity is inconspicuous and must sometimes be rationalized, as if it were questionable even under the auspices of the ritual. The fertility theme is itself pushed far back, so that it is unrecognizable in the symbolic background.

(Krige and Krige 1943: 290).

We might be justified in wondering just how sex is symbolized as an aspect of fertility if at the same time it is 'unrecognizable in the symbolic background'. Or why obscenities, if they are really so inconspicuous, must be rationalized at all.

And to whom, exactly, must they be rationalized (except to their ethnographers)? But whatever the case, the important point is that it has been common for scholars writing about rainmaking to note the presence of gender and sexuality, only to dismiss these themes as insignificant for its comprehension. We can only guess at how many others might have failed completely to report similar themes in rain rites for their apparent irrelevance. It is only recently, after all, given impetus from feminist scholarship, that sexuality has been 'rediscovered' in anthropology as a topic worthy of theoretical consideration (Lindenbaum 1991; Tuzin 1991; Vance 1991).

This chapter aims to show how, amongst the Ihanzu of north-central Tanzania, people's ideas about gender, sexuality, and transformative processes inform and give meaning to certain rain rituals and everyday practices and vice versa. On the one hand, in the Ihanzu everyday world, gender representations and practices are multiple, contradictory, and contested. There are three Ihanzu notions of gender: male superiority, female superiority, and gender equality. Of these, the first is most commonly foregrounded in men's and women's day-to-day lives. Even so, men and women frequently find themselves engaged in a tacit struggle over the relative position of the genders. Resolution is always situationally defined and is thus fleeting. This is the state of affairs in the mundane world.

In the ritual realm of rainmaking matters are different. Disputes over the relative statuses and powers of the genders are temporarily resolved; the gendered state of affairs is agreed to by all. It is here that the ideology of gender symmetry or gender complementarity eclipses all others and becomes hegemonic (Ortner 1996). To be sure, this eclipse is not total. In rain rites there are still traces of gender asymmetries to be found. Competing gender representations are comprehensible only when defined one against the other (Moore 1994: ch. 3). Yet on balance, when it comes to Ihanzu rain rites, men and women stress gender complementarity, by which I mean interdependence and equality.[5]

The reason people foreground notions of gender complementarity during rain rites, both conceptually and in practice, has to do with their ideas about reproductive processes broadly defined (also Sanders 1997, 1998, 2000). In Ihanzu eyes, cosmological transformations result only from the complementary combination of the cultural categories 'male' and 'female'. In other words, power comes in differently gendered pairs; and these pairs must combine as equals to ensure efficacy (cf. Heald 1995). This is as true for making rain as it is for making babies. Underlying all Ihanzu transformative processes we find the same cosmological model, what might be termed a 'procreative paradigm' (Herbert 1993).[6]

Such broad notions of reproductive processes are sometimes formulated discursively, as the elder's statement about 'male' and 'female' firesticks above reminds us. Yet it would be unwise to speak of culturally specific ideas of fertility and transformative processes as 'folk models', if this requires that we reduce such understandings to verbal exegesis alone (Holy and Stuchlik 1981; Jacobson-Widding and Beek 1990). To limit our understandings in this way is to ignore the fact that many rituals are meaningful precisely because they *do*, rather than *say* things (Moore 1999). In this context, it is their illocutionary force that is at issue. Rituals, for those who perform them, are culturally appropriate ways of acting upon the world. They are meant to make things happen. And this is particularly so in the context of rainmaking, where the issue is not simply one of symbolic representation, but of animating the cosmic and divine powers of the universe and effecting change (Buxton 1973: 358–359). In fact, it is precisely this practical engagement with the world that enables such rites convincingly to range across, and draw their cosmic powers from, a number of separate yet interrelated cultural domains. Making babies requires the genders to combine equally. So, too, does rainmaking. Before showing how and why this is so, we need to elaborate on Ihanzu notions of gender, and how they are operationalized in different everyday and ritual settings.

The Ihanzu of Tanzania

The Ihanzu are a Bantu-speaking, matrilineal people numbering around 30,000. Most live in northern Iramba District, north-central Tanzania. In the same district, to the south and west, live the Iramba, a larger Bantu-speaking matrilineal agricultural group with whom the Ihanzu share close affinities socially, culturally, and linguistically. To the east in Mbulu District, atop the Rift Valley escarpment, live the Southern Cushitic-speaking, agro-pastoral Iraqw. The hunting and gathering Hadza live to the north, as do the agro-pastoral Sukuma, one of Tanzania's largest ethnic groups.

While some Ihanzu keep cattle, goats and sheep, they are primarily agriculturalists and largely imagine themselves as such. Sorghum, millet, and maize are the staple crops and, together with an assortment of wild greens, milk, and dried fish, provide the bulk of their diet. But farming and herding in this arid Ihanzu region have never been easy. Annual rainfall averages a meagre 20–30 inches. Even in the best of years rainfall is unpredictable and patchy. Moreover, there are no year-round rivers that might alleviate or lessen these difficulties. Consequently, droughts and famines are common. That the rains arrive on time and fall regularly is – quite literally – a matter of life or death.

The precarious environment is something that Ihanzu villagers and successive colonial and postcolonial administrations have had to deal with for over a century. German, British and postcolonial administrators have all seen Ihanzu as a labor reserve for more fertile and promising parts of the country. Thus, from the early 1900s, the Ihanzu have routinely done migrant labor to urban centers like Singida, Arusha and elsewhere to provide for their families at home in the villages. Another way villagers have managed drought for well over a century is through rainmaking rites and beliefs.

There are two Ihanzu ritual leaders (*akola ihĩ*) whose job it is to organize and orchestrate all rain rites. One of these leaders is male, the other female. While neither of these leaders is today officially recognized by the state, both are and long have been crucial to nearly all Ihanzu villagers. To understand the significance of this royal gendered duo, and the pivotal role they play in the Ihanzu cultural imagination and rain rites, it is helpful to explore briefly Ihanzu gender notions and practices.

There are three discernible Ihanzu notions of gender, each of which is salient in different contexts.[7] The first notion, that male is superior to female, permeates much of the Ihanzu lived-in world and informs people's ideas and ideals about an array of daily practices. This is most commonly the picture Ihanzu men and women provide when asked to sum up gender relations among them.

This discourse asserts the frivolity of the feminine, suggesting that women are sometimes simple, often irresponsible, and largely lacking in foresight. Many daily activities are justified on these grounds alone. The when's, where's and what's of planting, for instance, are almost always decisions men make, often on the grounds that women cannot understand the complexity of these matters. Similarly, owner-ship of and control over livestock fall roundly into men's domain; women are often said to be incapable of caring for them. Men inherit livestock, use it for bride-wealth, and make all-important decisions concerning its sale and slaughter. To a large extent, livestock – especially cattle – is 'men's business' and is thus male-coded.[8] In the political domain, too, it is generally men and not women who play an active role.

Whatever salience this first disparaging discourse about male–female relations might possess, it is, in other situations, thoroughly undermined by another suggest-ion: that females are superior to males.

Together a man and his wife farm their fields. Yet once the grain has been harvested and safely stowed in the grainstore, a wife gains close to total control over its allocation within and outside the household. With her grain, a woman must budget from one harvest to the next. She must decide how much she can afford to give away to needy neighbours, kin, and others, and still have enough to provide for herself, her husband, and children.[9] She must also make decisions about when and how many times to brew beer, the single largest contributor to household income, the foundation of day-to-day social life in the villages, and the bedrock of the local cash economy. Beer brewing is associated with women since it is always they, not men, who brew. It is also women who control the proceeds of any given brew.

For these reasons, in domestic contexts, women are often symbolically assoc-iated with grain and especially with stiff porridge and beer, the indispensable grain products of everyday life. Moreover, control over grain is a source of women's power and status. Women regulate the ebb and flow of the local economy and village sociality by controlling grain and its by-products.

In still other contexts, Ihanzu emphasize a third notion of gender: compl-ementarity or symmetry. Here, male and female each has his or her own unique abilities and tasks, and no relative evaluation of gender categories is implied. Male is said to be active, female passive; male leads, female follows; male is above, female below. In these cases male and female complement and give meaning to one other. There are several cultural and social arenas in which people strongly emphasize this particular representation of the genders, one of the most evident being procreation beliefs.

The Ihanzu believe that both men and women possess fertilizing fluids (*manala*) which are required in equal amounts to create a child. These fluids, frequently referred to euphemistically as 'waters' (*mazĩ*) or 'seeds' (*mbeũ*), are virtually identical, but are nevertheless gendered. Men have male fluids; women have female fluids. In concert, though not separately, the two are potent. When it comes to human reproduction in the abstract, all I spoke with agree that male and female are equal (Sanders 1998).

At life's end, as at its beginning, notions of gender complementarity are man-ifest. When people in Ihanzu die their souls (*nkolo*) are said to enter the under-world (*ũlũngũ*), immediately becoming ancestral spirits (*alũngũ*; sing. *mũlũngũ*).[10] These spirits do not dissolve into any androgynous collectivity (Bloch 1987: 326–328) but instead maintain their distinctive gender identities. Both male and female spirits are equally thought capable of afflicting the living (see also Kohl-Larsen 1943: 293). In Ihanzu, there is no apparent preponderance of afflictions by either maternal or paternal spirits, nor are there any discernible differences between types or severity of afflictions caused by male and female spirits. More often than not, in fact, it is male and female spirits together that are ultimately responsible for any given affliction, be it personal or communal, like drought.

To sum up so far, both at life's beginning and at its end male and female are often viewed as equal and complementary. It is only in-between that things are much less decided, the actual statuses and relative powers of the genders being questioned and contested. Resolution is context-dependent and hence, at best, temporary. Household grain – and more especially, grain transformed into stiff porridge or beer – embodies ideas of female power and status, in the same way that livestock, as part of the male domain, symbolically asserts male power and status. Procreation beliefs and death, on the other hand, tend to emphasize symmetry between the genders. So, too, as we shall see in the remainder of this chapter, do rainmaking rituals and beliefs.

Ancestral Rain Offerings

The Ihanzu have many different rain rites. Some are performed annually, at the onset of each new farming season. Others are performed only in those years when the annual rites fail to bring the rain. Whatever type they may be, all such rain rites are informed by the same underlying logic of reproduction, what I have called gender complementarity (Sanders 1997, 1998, 1999, 2000).

This chapter focuses on one particular remedial rain rite: ancestral offerings for rain (*mapolyo a mbula*).[11] Ancestral offerings for rain take place only when the rains have utterly failed and it has been divined that the royal *Anyampanda* clan spirits have demanded such an offering. Offerings take place over two days, though the entire ritual sequence often lasts a month or more. It is only the two *Anyampanda* royal leaders, and no one else, who can bring such rain offerings to fruition.

To initiate the offering (*kŭkŭmbĭka*), which is done the evening of the day of the divination session, a few 'grandchildren' are summoned to the male ritual leader's homestead. These grandchildren (always classificatory grandchildren) play a central role in all such rain offerings. They must initiate all ritual activities. It is imperative, too, informants stress, that at least one grandson and one grand-daughter participate. Both genders must be present.

The grandchildren place some white sorghum flour and water, together with some ritually significant tree branches, into a special long-necked calabash (*mŭmbŭ*). While addressing the royal clan spirits, they set the calabash in the door-way of the male ritual leader's homestead. Both grandchildren address the spirits; the grandson's addresses always precede the granddaughter's. Such addresses are brief, usually stating the obvious – 'We are now putting your beer here in the door-way', etc. – and are made throughout the offering whenever the grandchildren initiate a new task. There are three addresses, above all others, that are of particular importance in these offerings. I will discuss these presently.

Several days later the grandchildren begin brewing beer. Unlike in everyday contexts, however, where it is only women who brew beer, for these offerings granddaughter and grandson must brew beer together. Over the course of a few weeks, at each stage in the brewing process – addressing the spirits, digging the beer brewing trench, collecting firewood and so forth – these two must cooperate (*kiunga*) and 'reside together harmoniously' (*wikiĩ ŭza palŭng'wĩ*). For reasons that will become apparent below, it is worth noting that the beer brewing trench (*ilŭngŭ*) must be dug on an east–west axis, which again differs from everyday beer brewing.

On the final day of brewing, the grandson and granddaughter set aside a small amount of ritually significant beer (*kĩnyaŭlŭngŭ*). Just before sundown, they visit a few significant places where, as before, they address the spirits. The places normally visited are, first, the royal clan offering sight itself and, second, the graves of a few former ritual leaders, both male and female.

The following morning, the male ritual leader leads the way from his homestead to the royal offering site, a small mountain called *Ng'waũngu* in the village of Kirumi. Everyone follows him in single file, walking slowly, deliberately, speaking either in quiet tones, or not at all.

Most of the party ascends the mountain with the male ritual leader to a small clearing. The female ritual leader, for her part, remains at another clearing at the bottom of the mountain with a number of elderly women. It is their job to prepare castor-seed oil (*mono*) to be used later in the offering. Throughout the offering these women sing songs they conventionally sing at the birth of twins (*ipaha*), the women's rain dance (*isĩmpũlya*) and girl's initiation ceremonies (*mũlĩmũ*). Most of these songs are blatantly sexual. Many are considered obscene.

In the principle offering clearing, people sit in distinct groups. Diviners, together with the male ritual leader and some male elders, sit at the highest point in the clearing. Most elderly men sit slightly below them. Women sit further down the clearing and in the path, while those who have never before attended such an offering, young men and women, sit in the lowest position.

When everyone is seated, the grandson continues up the path with some beer (sometimes with a rainmaking assistant) to one of two sacred clan caves. After removing his shirt, he sprays some of the ancestral beer over the cave entrance and briefly addresses the spirits.

The grandson then collects a number of tree branches and places them in the centre of the clearing, cut ends to the east, leaves to the west. The two grand-children lay down the sacrificial animal – most commonly, a black sheep born at night – with its head to the west, atop the leafy branches. Together the grand-children smother the animal until it passes out, at which time a Muslim slits its throat.

After skinning the animal, the grandchildren start a fire 'in the traditional way' (*kijadi*) by twirling a long, slender firedrill (*kĩlĩndĩ*) into a hole in a smaller, stationary hearth (*kiziga*). While so doing, each addresses the spirits aloud. One such address, the one that began this Chapter, went as follows:

> You, Mũnyankalĩ, who come from your senior house and are going to your junior one, you have passed through Ihanzu and have seen we are carrying out an ancestral offering, an offering in the cave. We have an offering for rain. We are offering [you] water [i.e. beer], and a sheep that was born at night. Take good news to the place you are going; and the bad, toss it into the waters of Lake Victoria.

These addresses are always made to *Mũnyankalĩ*, the name used for the sun in ritual contexts. Being neither God nor spirit, *Mũnyankalĩ* may be understood as 'a visible and tangible symbol of a supernatural world about which nothing can be known' (Adam 1963: 22). In these addresses, reference is customarily made to the fact that *Mũnyankalĩ* – who is unequivocally said to be male – is moving from one wife's house in the east to another wife's house in the west (Adam 1963: 11–12, 22; Kohl-Larsen 1943: 303–305). As he does so, grandchildren urge him to make it known to the spirits that an offering is in progress in Ihanzu. Typically, too, they tell *Mũnyankalĩ* to remove whatever evil there might be, like witchcraft, and to cool it in the waters of Lake Victoria, the (perhaps mythical) homeland of the Ihanzu people.

Following this comes one of the most significant addresses of offering: giving meat to the spirits (*kũtagangĩla*). Collecting several roasted pieces of the sacrificial meat, the grandchildren make an address to each of the four cardinal points, tossing, before each address, a piece of meat in that direction. As always, the grandson's address precedes the granddaughter's.

This sequence of addresses completed, the diviner reads various entrails in an oblong, divining bowl (*ntua*). The bowl must be oriented east–west, like the beer trench and sacrificial animal. The entrails invariably tell of the spirits' gratitude for the offering, of plentiful rains and of other things auspicious (Adam 1963; Obst 1923: 221–222).

Following the divination session, the women from the base of the mountain dance and sing their way up the path, through the main clearing, to the cave. Both grandchildren take a handful of chyme from the sacrificial sheep and join them. At the cave, one at a time, the grandchildren address the spirits and toss the chyme around the entrance, 'to cool' (*kũpola*) the spirits. The grandson then descends to the clearing. The female ritual leader, the granddaughter and a few other elderly women of the royal clan remove their clothes and, carrying the half-gourd of castor-seed oil, enter the cave. After the granddaughter addresses the spirits, the women anoint some ancient cave drums with oil.[12] They enter a second, nearby sacred cave too, naked, where they anoint an enormous ancestor-snake (usually described as a python) that allegedly lives there. The women then don their clothes and join the other women in the clearing below.

At this point, the grandchildren roast and dole out meat from the sacrificial animal. Most eat in their respective groups, while a few ad hoc groups visit and feast on the royal graves visited the previous day by the grandchildren. The loin, which people explicitly associate with giving birth, is always eaten on a female ritual leader's grave, while the a front leg is eaten on a male ritual leader's grave. When all have eaten, they return to the male ritual leader's homestead.

Once there, people sing rain songs, many of which are sexually explicit or suggestive. In preparation for the second major address of the offering – giving beer to the spirits (*kũlonga shalo*) – the male ritual leader sits in the doorway to his house. The grandson initiates the offering. He stands in the centre of the courtyard holding a ritual whisk; at his feet sits a divining bowl (again, placed east–west) filled with ancestral beer and water. Dipping the whisk into the bowl and splashing it to the east, he begins his theatrically intoned address to the spirits, repeating this procedure to the west, south, and then north. When he finishes, the granddaughter does the same. The day's events are brought to a close by addresses from the royal leaders' classificatory father and, finally, a jester. People continue to drink beer, often late into the night, and are expected to sleep on the ritual leader's homestead.

The next morning, the final day of the offering, the grandchildren arise early. The granddaughter starts cooking stiff sorghum porridge, while the grandson roasts the meat remaining from the previous day's sacrifice. The grandson and grand-daughter divide the stiff porridge in half and put the two portions into two separate calabash bowls. They also divide the roasted meat in this way. Each takes a bowl of stiff porridge and meat.

At sunrise, in the centre of the courtyard, the grandson begins the third and final significant address of the offering. He tosses a piece of roasted meat to the east, immediately followed by a piece of stiff porridge. As the previous day, he addresses *Mũnyankalĩ* in the east. He repeats the sequence to the west, then to the north and south. The granddaughter follows the grandson, doing the same.

Addresses completed, the grandchildren feed small pieces of roasted meat and stiff porridge to the male and female ritual leaders who sit idle throughout. They then feed a few others from the royal clan, as well as a group of senior men and the diviner. From inside the house the grandchildren bring out bowls of roasted meat and stiff porridge – two each – which are then served to the group of younger men, and finally, the women.

Following the meal the grandchildren distribute ancestral beer likewise: clan elders, younger men, and then women. A few elderly men and women, including the male and female ritual leaders, then enter and drink beer inside the house. The beer is served from two ritually significant long-neck calabashes or *mũmbũ*, also the word for 'womb'. These calabashes wear white beads around their necks, beads that are today associated both with the ancestors who wore them in abundance (Obst 1923: 222), and with the powers of fertility the ancestors control.

The grandchildren briefly address the spirits, one last time, and cover over the beer trench they used to brew the beer. This rite officially marks the end of the offering.

Discussion

Ihanzu ancestral offerings for rain are lengthy, complicated affairs. If one takes into account ancestral beer brewing, these rites can easily last a month, sometimes longer. It is equally evident that Ihanzu ancestral offerings are replete with fertility and sexual symbolism. Throughout, ritual participants play, sometimes in rather striking ways, on themes of gender difference and complementarity.

One of the more obvious ways this is done is by using two differently gendered grandchildren to initiate and conduct each step in the ritual process. They must 'cooperate', so people say, and 'reside together harmoniously' in everything they do. It is also they, and they alone, who must use the gendered firedrill: to cause the sticks to have 'sex' so fire is 'born'. Grandchildren's addresses similarly allude to locally inflected understandings of gender and sexuality by focusing much attention on *Mũnyankalĩ*, the this-worldly male symbol who moves each day between his two wives' houses. Finally, the songs sung also hint at the salience of fertility and sexuality in these rites.

Yet to note simply that these rain rites, or any others, are full of fertility and sexual symbolism, as many Africanist scholars have done, provides few clues as to *why* this might be so. Nor does it explain why ritual participants feel such rites are both appropriate and efficacious. In other words, the question of interest is 'Why do Ihanzu rain rites, or similar rites elsewhere in Africa, often play on themes of gender, sexuality and fertility?' The answer, I suggest, is because such rites are linked to, and broadly informed by, local conceptions of reproductive processes. As noted above, in Ihanzu eyes, this implies the notion of gender complementarity. It now remains to trace explicitly the linkages between Ihanzu notions of reproductive processes on the one hand, and ancestral offerings for rain on the other. The task, more specifically, is to demonstrate that Ihanzu rain rites foreground themes of gender symmetry or gender complementarity, while simultaneously de-emphasizing themes of gender hierarchy and difference. Since *Mũnyankalĩ* features centrally in all ancestral offerings for rain, we can begin with him.

Ihanzu men and women have surprisingly little to say about *Mũnyankalĩ*. All seem to agree that he is male,[13] and that the sun is his visible, this-worldly representation. But no one I spoke with could say more. This paucity of information, however, is itself instructive. For what people do say goes a long way towards explaining why they need say no more.

Mũnyankalĩ is male and, as the sun, moves from east to west each day between his two wives' houses. All spatial references during the offering, including the orientation of the beer trench and divining bowl, as well as the tossing of meat and porridge, people relate explicitly to *Mũnyankalĩ*'s daily movements across the sky.

Each day, *Mũnyankalĩ* moves from east to west, a movement associated with cycles of life and death. For the Ihanzu, the east and morning are associated with birth, upwards, growth and renewal. *Mũnyankalĩ* is reborn each morning. For this reason the east is auspicious. Life-giving rains come from the east. Each year the royal rainshrine is opened in the morning, when the sun is rising. And divination sessions, which usually occur in the morning, face east. All ancestral offerings, too, take place in the morning.

The west, in contrast, is inauspicious. It is commonly associated with death, downwards, and decay. *Mũnyankalĩ* dies here each evening. Ihanzu graves have east–west orientations, and the head is invariably placed to the west. When, on occasion, the wind causes rain to fall from the west, as infrequently happens, people say this is bad rain (*mbula mbĩ*) that brings aphids, lightning and other things unpropitious. When the rainshrine is closed each year, it is done in the evening, when the sun is setting in the west.

Ancestral addresses to *Mũnyankalĩ*, like all east–west spatial references in these rites, therefore serve as a spatial commentary on an idealized gender order. This is an order, as the Ihanzu see it, of gender complementarity. Male and female work and live together harmoniously. Here, male (the sun) is 'active'. Female (his wives) is 'passive'.

Likewise, during these offerings, grandchildren address both male and female spirits. Male and female spirits are generally said to cooperate. All this-worldly spiritual afflictions, drought included, are thought to be caused by male and female spirits working together. It is for this reason that, in Ihanzu, male and female spirits must be addressed and placated together to heal the ill or to bring rain.

If the contents of ancestral addresses and the spatial layout evoke an idealized order of gender complementarity, then so, too, does the temporal sequence of these addresses. Grandson and granddaughter make all addresses jointly, but never simultaneously. The grandson must go first, the granddaughter second. This alludes once again to an idealized gender order of complementarity where male precedes female. Both work together; each fulfils his or her role. The overall sequence of addresses operates likewise.

The grandchildren make numerous addresses throughout the offering. These are brief addresses, stating the obvious (i.e. we are brewing beer; we are digging a trench; etc.). There are three addresses, however, that people identify as more significant than others. In the order they occur these are, first, giving meat to the spirits (*kũtagangĩla*); second, giving beer to the spirits (*kũlonga shalo*); and third, on the final day, giving the spirits meat and stiff porridge simultaneously. Given the symbolic associations between female and grain on the one hand, and male and livestock on the other, the emphasis on gender complementarity is once again manifest.

Grandchildren make the first of these addresses by tossing meat which, given its association with men's control over livestock, is symbolically male-coded. This address condenses within it the male elements of the Ihanzu cosmological universe. The second significant address is made with sorghum beer. Given the everyday symbolic associations between grain, beer, and women, this second address might be seen as embodying feminine elements of the cosmos. Taken together, the two addresses realize the idealized gender order in which male precedes female. Lest there be any ambiguity as to the relative status of gender categories in these two addresses, the final address to the spirits, made on the final day of the offering, is a blatant assertion of gender equality. Here, the grandchildren combine as equal masculine and feminine elements by tossing meat and stiff porridge in the same address.

Concluding Remarks

This chapter has shown some of the ways Ihanzu ancestral offerings for rain, in varied ways, play on themes of gender and sexuality. The reason for this, I submit, is that such rain rites are informed by a particular cultural logic of transformative processes, a logic of gender complementarity. It is this culturally specific notion of transformation that makes such sexual symbolism both meaningful and necessary in these rites. If rain rites are to be effective, if they are to bring rain, then the Ihanzu cultural categories 'male' and 'female' must combine as equals. Ritual participants thus pay close attention to acting out, through ritual practice, this particular proposition.

Identical cultural notions of reproductive processes underpin Ihanzu men's and women's ideas about procreation. To create children, male and female must unite as equals. Men and women each have semen, and these differently gendered semens must combine in equal amounts. Once again, male and female must cooperate to bring about change.

This cosmic congruence between rainmaking beliefs and ideas about procreation is not the result of one leading directly to the other. Ihanzu speak of the gendered 'waters' required for procreation, and the sexuality of rainmaking, but no one would confuse sex with rainmaking. The point worth stressing, rather, is that underlying both reproductive and transformative processes is the same notion: that cosmic power comes in differently gendered pairs. And to accomplish their respective goals, these pairs must combine as equals. What is more, such principles need not be explicitly stated in order to do what they purportedly do. To discuss sex, after all, will not bring a child any more than discussing sexually laden rain rites will bring the rain. In both cases action speaks louder than words.

It is simply not enough to note that African rainmaking rites play on themes of gender and sexuality, patently true though such observations may be. To stop here is to ignore most of what is interesting about rain rites in Africa. Instead, as this chapter has tried to do, we must interrogate and problematize these issues – which means coming to terms with locally inflected notions of reproduction and transformative processes, always, of course, situating them soundly within specific cultural and social contexts. For at the end of the day, male and female firesticks may be just two more sticks, like any others. But they promise to be so much more.

Notes

1. The chapter is based on fieldwork carried out in Ihanzu, Tanzania, between August 1993 to May 1995 and June to September 1999. A longer version of it appeared in *Cahiers d'études africaines* 166 (2002). I thank the UK Economic and Social Research Council, the US National Institute of Health, the University of London, the Royal Anthropological Institute and the London School of Economics for funding different portions of this research; the Tanzania Commission for Science and Technology for granting me research clearances; and, above all, the men and women of Ihanzu for their unflagging hospitality. Comments by Albert Schrauwers and the anonymous reviewers helped to sharpen the argument though of course I alone am responsible for any short-comings that remain.

2. Writings on African rainmaking are copious. See bibliographies in Sanders (1997), Petermann (1985) and Zimon (1974). For some early accounts of various African rain rites, most of which offer interesting but decontextualized accounts of various rain rites, see Driberg (1919), Dornan (1928), Hartnoll (1932), Ntudu (1939), Cooke and Beaton (1939), Wright (1946), Ludger (1954), and Feddema (1966).

3. For some noteworthy exceptions see Feierman (1990), Packard (1981), Jacobson-Widding (1985, 1990) Kaspin (1996), Middleton (1971, 1978), and Kaare (1999).

4. Elsewhere, when examining a Tswana rain song, Schapera (1971: 100) says: 'I cannot explain the allusions in the second song to 'whores' . . .'.

5. The term 'complementarity', I am well aware, does not logically demand equality. Different social classes or people in a caste system, for example, might well be considered 'complementary' in that they are mutually defined and interdependent, but as unequal partners. How complementary elements fit together is ultimately an empirical not theoretical question. I use the term as it relates to Ihanzu understandings of transformative processes.

6. This is not to argue, however, that 'transformative processes invoke the human model as the measure of all things' (Herbert 1993: 5); that the human body – with its universal physiological attributes and processes – necessarily provides a shared 'primordial psychobiological experience' (Turner 1967: 90) that subsequently allows for higher order modes of social classification. Nor is it to suggest that society invariably provides a template for making the body (Mauss 1973). More likely, it would seem, is that both positions are correct: that 'the opposition between masculinity and femininity . . . constitutes the fundamental principle of division of the social and the symbolic world' (Bourdieu 1990: 78) and that neither bodies nor society can be given logical priority.

7. It would be inaccurate to see any one of these gender models as exclusively held by either men or women, for both genders subscribe to all three perspectives at different times and in different contexts.

8. Practices sometimes belie these ideals. For example, young girls and women often herd sheep and goats. And a woman has disposal rights over the milk of her husband's livestock. Further, a very few women have inherited and own livestock.

9. Nor is this just an ideal. On several occasions I spoke with men who ruefully related to me instances of their being denied access to their grainstores by their wives. Without exception, somewhat surprisingly, these men accepted their wives' decisions.

10. As elsewhere in Africa, it is only certain categories of persons whose souls may become spirits. On death, in theory, everyone's soul (*nkolo*) becomes a spirit (*mŭlũngŭ*). In practice it is generally the spirits of the elderly – both male and female – that afflict people and are thus remembered.

11. For a description of a very similar ancestral offering to heal cattle (*ipolyo la ndwala*), see Sanders (1999).

12. There are many caves in Ihanzu and surrounding areas where giant drums are found (Hunter 1953). The Ihanzu do not know who made the drums, but claim that they were already there when they migrated into the area long ago (Kohl-Larsen 1943: 168). It is the sacred caves, not the drums in them, that people find most significant in these offerings.

13. Associations between the sun and masculinity are common among the Ihanzu's neighbours. This is so amongst the Turu (Jellicoe et al. 1967: 28), Sandawe (Ten Raa 1969: 28), Sukuma (Tanner 1956: 51–52), and Iramba (Pender-Cudlip c.1974: 14). The Iraqw, on the other hand, who live to the east of the Ihanzu, associate the sun (*Looaa*) with femininity and the earth spirits (*neetlaamee*) with masculinity (Snyder 1999: 227–228).

References

ADAM, V. 1963. Rain Making Rites in Ihanzu. Conference Proceedings from the East African Institute of Social Research, Makerere College.

AVUA, L. 1968. Droughtmaking among the Lugbara. *The Uganda Journal* 32 (1): 29–38.

BEEMER, H. 1935. The Swazi Rain Ceremony (Critical Comments on P. J. Schoeman's Article). *Bantu Studies* 9: 273–280.

BLEEK, D. F. 1933. Beliefs and Customs of the /Xam Bushman. Part 5: the Rain. *Bantu Studies* 7: 297–312.

BLOCH, M. 1987. 'Descent and Sources of Contradiction in Representations of Women and Kinship', in *Gender and Kinship: Essays Toward a Unified Analysis*.

Edited by J. F. Collier and S. J. Yanagisako, pp. 324–337. Stanford, CA: Stanford University Press.

BOURDIEU, P. 1990. *The Logic of Practice*. Stanford, CA: Stanford University Press.

BUXTON, J. 1973. *Religion and Healing in Mandari*. Oxford: Clarendon Press.

COLSON, E. 1948. Rain-shrines of the Plateau Tonga of Northern Rhodesia. *Africa* 18: 272–283.

—— 1977. 'A Continuing Dialogue: Prophets and Local Shrines among the Tonga of Zambia', in *Regional Cults*. Edited by R. P. Werbner, pp. 119–139. London: Academic Press.

COOKE, R. C. and BEATON, A. C. 1939. Bari Rain Cults. Fur Rain Cults and Ceremonies. *Sudan Notes and Records* 22: 181–203.

CORY, H. 1951. *The Ntemi: the Traditional Rites in Connection with the Burial, Election, Enthronement and Magic Powers of a Sukuma Chief*. London: Macmillan.

DORNAN, S. S. 1928. Rainmaking in South Africa. *Bantu Studies* 3: 185–195.

DRIBERG, J. H. 1919. Rain-making among the Lango. *Journal of the Royal Anthropological Institute* 49: 52–73.

EVANS-PRITCHARD, E. E. 1929. Some Collective Expressions of Obscenity in Africa. *Journal of the Royal Anthropological Institute* 59: 311–331.

—— 1938. A Note on the Rain-makers among the Moro. *Man* 38: 53–56.

FEDDEMA, J. P. 1966. Tswana Ritual Concerning Rain. *African Studies* 25: 181–195.

FEIERMAN, S. 1990. *Peasant Intellectuals: Anthropology and History in Tanzania*. Madison: University of Wisconsin Press.

GININDZA, T. 1997. 'Labotsibeni/Gwamile Mduli: the Power behind the Swazi Throne 1875–1925', in *Queens, Queen Mothers, Priestesses, and Power: Case Studies in African Gender*. Edited by F. E. S. Kaplan, pp. 135–158. New York: The New York Academy of Sciences.

HÅKANSSON, N. T. 1998. Rulers and Rainmakers in Precolonial South Pare, Tanzania: Exchange and Ritual Experts in Political Centralization. *Ethnology* 37(3): 263–283.

HARTNOLL, A. V. 1932. The Gogo Mtemi. *South African Journal of Science* 29: 737–741.

—— 1942. Praying for Rain in Ugogo. *Tanganyika Notes and Records* 13: 59–60.

HAUENSTEIN, A. 1967a. Rites et coutumes liés au culte de la pluie parmi différentes tribus du Sud-Ouest de l'Angola. *Boletim do Instituto de Angola* 27: 5–23.

—— 1967b. Rites et coutumes liés au culte de la pluie parmi différentes tribus du Sud-Ouest de l'Angola. *Boletim do Instituto de Angola* 29: 5–27.

HEALD, S. 1995. The Power of Sex: Some Reflections on the Caldwells' 'African Sexuality' Thesis. *Africa* 65(4): 489–505.

HERBERT, E. W. 1993. *Iron, Gender, and Power: Rituals of Transformation in African Societies.* Bloomington–Indianapolis: Indiana University Press.

HOERNLÉ, A. W. 1922. A Hottentot Rain Ceremony. *Bantu Studies* 1: 20–21.

HOLAS, B. 1949. Pour faire tomber la pluie (Nord du Togo). *Notes africaines* 41: 13–14.

HOLY, L. and STUCHLIK, M. (Eds). 1981. *The Structure of Folk Models.* London: Academic Press.

HUNTER, G. 1953. Hidden Drums in Singida District. *Tanganyika Notes and Records* 34: 28–32.

JACOBSON-WIDDING, A. 1985. *Private Spirits and the Ego: A Psychological Ethnography of Ancestor Cult and Spirit Possession among the Manyika of Zimbabwe.* Working Papers in African Studies 24. Uppsala: African Studies Programme, University of Uppsala.

—— 1990. 'The Fertility of Incest', in Jacobson-Widding and van Beek 1990: 47–73.

JACOBSON-WIDDING, A. and Beek, W. van (Eds.). 1990. *The Creative Communion: African Folk Models of Fertility and the Regeneration of Life.* Uppsala: Acta Universitatis Upsaliensis.

JAMES, W. 1972. 'The Politics of Rain Control among the Uduk', in *Essays in Sudan Ethnography: Presented to Sir Edward Evans-Pritchard.* Edited by I. Cunnison and W. James, pp. 31–57. London: Hurst and Company.

JELLICOE, M., PUJA, P. and SOMBI, J. 1967. Praising the Sun. *Transition* 31(6): 27–31.

—— 1968. The Shrine in the Desert. *Transition* 34(7): 43–49.

JOHNSON, V. E. 1948. *Pioneering for Christ in East Africa.* Rock Island: Augustana Book Concern.

KAARE, B. T. 1999. 'Saisee Tororeita: an Analysis of Complementarity in Akie Gender Ideology', in *Those who Play with Fire: Gender, Fertility and Transformation in East and Southern Africa.* Edited by H. L. Moore, T. Sanders and B. Kaare, pp. 133–152. London: The Athlone Press.

KASPIN, D. 1996. A Chewa Cosmology of the Body. *American Ethnologist* 23(3): 561–578.

KOHL-LARSEN, L. 1943. *Auf den Spuren des Vormenschen (Deutsche Afrika-Expedition 1934–1936 und 1937–1939).* Stuttgart: Strecher & Schröder.

KRIGE, E. J. 1968. Girls' Puberty Songs and their Relation to Fertility, Health, Morality and Religion among the Zulu. *Africa* 38(2): 173–198.

KRIGE, E. J. and KRIGE, J. D. 1943. *The Realm of a Rain-Queen: a Study of the Pattern of Lovedu Society.* London: Oxford University Press.

LARSON, T. J. 1966. 'The Significance of Rainmaking for the Mbukushu. *African Studies* 25(1): 23–36.

LINDENBAUM, S. 1991. Anthropology Rediscovers Sex. *Social Science and Medicine* 33(8): 865–866.

LINDSTRÖM, J. 1987. *Iramba Pleases Us: Agro-pastoralism among the Plateau Iramba of Central Tanzania*. Ph.D. Dissertation, University of Göteborg.

LUDGER, K. 1954. Rainmakers in Teso. *The Uganda Journal* 18(2): 185–186.

MACDONALD, J. 1890. Manners, Customs, Superstitions, and Religions of South African Tribes. *Journal of the Anthropological Institute* 20(2): 113–140.

MARSHALL, L. 1957. N!ow. *Africa* 27 (3): 232–240.

MAUSS, M. 1973. Techniques of the Body. *Economy and Society* 2(1): 70–88.

MIDDLETON, J. 1971. 'Prophets and Rainmakers: the Agents of Social Change among the Lugbara', in *The Translation of Culture. Essays to E. E. Evans-Pritchard.* Edited by T. O. Beidelman, pp. 179–201. London: Tavistock Publications.

—— 1978. 'The Rainmaker among the Lugbara of Uganda', in *Systèmes de signes: textes réunis en hommage à Germaine Dieterlen*, pp. 179–201. Paris: Hermann.

MOORE, H. L. 1994. *A Passion for Difference: Essays in Anthropology and Gender.* Cambridge: Polity Press.

—— 1999. 'Gender Symbolism and Praxis: Theoretical Approaches', in Moore, Sanders, and Kaare 1999: 3–37.

MOORE, H. L., T. SANDERS, and KAARE, B. (Eds.). 1999. *Those who Play with Fire: Gender, Fertility and Transformation in East and Southern Africa.* London: The Athlone Press.

MURRAY, C. 1980. Sotho Fertility Symbolism. *African Studies* 39: 65–76.

NTUDU, Y. 1939. The Position of Rainmaker among the Wanyiramba. *Tanganyika Notes and Records* 7: 84–87.

O'BRIEN, D. 1983. Chiefs of Rain – Chiefs of Ruling: a Reinterpretation of Pre-colonial Tonga (Zambia) Social and Political Structure. *Africa* 53(4): 23–42.

OBST, E. 1923. Das abflußlose Rumpfschollenland im nordöstlichen Deutsch-Ostafrika (Teil II). *Mitteilungen der Geographischen Gesellschaft in Hamburg* 35: 1–330.

ORTNER, S. B. 1996. 'Gender Hegemonies', in *Making Gender: the Politics and Erotics of Culture.* Edited by S. B. Ortner, pp. 35–80. Boston: Beacon Press.

PACKARD, R. M. 1981. *Chiefship and Cosmology: an Historical Study of Political Competition.* Bloomington-Indianapolis: Indiana University Press.

PENDER-CUDLIP, P. c.1974. God and the Sun: Some Notes on Iramba Religious History. Unpublished Manuscript at British Institute in Eastern Africa, Nairobi.

PETERMANN, W. 1985. *Regenkulte und Regenmacher bei Bantu-sprachigen Ethnien Ost- und Südafrikas.* Berlin: Express Edition GmbH.

ROGERS, F. H. 1927. Notes on some Madi Rain-Stones. *Man* 27: 81–87.

SANDERS, T. 1997. *Rainmaking, Gender and Power in Ihanzu, Tanzania, 1885–1995.* Ph.D. Thesis, London, London School of Economics and Political Science.

—— 1998. Making Children, Making Chiefs: Gender, Power and Ritual Legitimacy. *Africa* 68 (2): 238–262.

—— 1999. '"Doing Gender" in Africa: Embodying Categories and the Categorically Disembodied', in Moore, Sanders, and Kaare 1999: 41–82.

—— 2000. Rains Gone Bad, Women Gone Mad: Rethinking Gender Rituals of Rebellion and Patriarchy. *Journal of the Royal Anthropological Institute* (n.s.) 6(3): 469–486.

SCHAPERA, I. 1971. *Rainmaking Rites of Tswana Tribes*. Cambridge: African Studies Centre.

SCHOEMAN, P. J. 1935. The Swazi Rain Ceremony. *Bantu Studies* 9: 169–175.

SNYDER, K. 1999. 'Gender Ideology, and the Domestic and Public Domains among the Iraqw', in Moore, Sanders, and Kaare 1999: 225–253.

TANNER, R. E. S. 1956. An Introduction to the Northern Basukuma's Idea of the Supreme Being. *Anthropological Quarterly* 29(4): 45–56.

TEN RAA, E. 1969. The Moon as a Symbol of Life and Fertility in Sandawe Thought. *Africa* 39 (1): 24–53.

TURNER, V. 1967. 'Color Classification in Ndembu Ritual: a Problem in Primitive Classification', in *The Forest of Symbols: Aspects of Ndembu Ritual*, pp. 59–92. Ithaca: Cornell University Press.

TUZIN, D. 1991. Sex, Culture and the Anthropologist. *Social Science and Medicine* 33(8): 867–874.

VANCE, C. S. 1991. Anthropology Rediscovers Sexuality: a Theoretical Comment. *Social Science and Medicine* 33(8): 875–884.

VIJFHUIZEN, C. 1997. Rain-making, Political Conflicts and Gender Images: a Case from Mutema Chieftaincy in Zimbabwe. *Zambezia* 24(1): 31–49.

WEATHERBY, J. 1979. 'Raindrums of the Sor', in *Chronology, Migration and Drought in Interlacustrine Africa*. Edited by J. B. Webster, pp.317–331. London: Longman and Dalhousie University Press.

WOLLACOTT, R. C. 1963. Dziwaguru – God of Rain. *NADA* 40: 116–121.

WRIGHT, A. C. A. 1946. A Rainmaking Ceremony in Teso. *The Uganda Journal* 10(1): 25–28.

ZIMON, H. 1974. *Regenriten auf der Insel Bukerewe (Tanzania)*. Freiburg: Universitätsverlag Freiburg.

–6–

Nice Weather for the Time of Year: The British Obsession with the Weather[1]

Trevor A. Harley

When, on a summer evening, the melodious sky growls like a tawny lion, and everyone is complaining of the storm, it is the Méséglise way that makes me stand alone in ecstasy, inhaling, through the noise of the falling rain, the lingering scent of invisible lilacs.

(Proust 1983)

Introduction

The British are notorious for their casual interest in the weather. Indeed, a parody of a national stereotype of the British is a portrayal of a person who is very reserved, yet who can happily chat about the weather with strangers.

The weather is a safe topic of conversation because we can discuss it while avoiding sensitive or personal matters. There is more to the weather as a conversational topic than safety, however: the British person's interest in the weather is not without good reason. Britain's weather is particularly fascinating because it is so variable and unpredictable throughout the year. These features are a consequence of its position: it is an island, on the edge of a continent, and its weather is profoundly influenced by the Gulf Stream. The most important consequence of the Gulf Stream is that Britain's climate is much more mild than that of most locations at the same latitude (e.g. it is meteorologically remarkable that Britain is on the same line of latitude as Hudson Bay). Furthermore, because of its position at the edge of a continent, it is often a battleground between maritime and continental air masses. The mild westerlies usually win, but when the continental mass dominates we often see spells of exceptional weather. Severe weather events are still discussed decades later (e.g. the winter, spring, and summer[2] of 1947, the Lynemouth flood of August 1952, the Great London Smog of December 1952, the North Sea floods of winter 1953, the Great Freeze of 1962–63, the Hampstead Storm of August 1975, and the exceptional summer heat and drought of 1976 are among those often talked about more than a quarter of a century later; see Eden 1995, for descriptions of these events).

In this chapter, I examine in detail what British people talk about when they talk about the weather. Although people have surprisingly strong memories of the weather, these memories are not always correct, and I will consider some reasons why these faulty memories occur. I will also argue that the weather occasionally plays a role in organizing autobiographical memory.

What do People Talk about when they talk about the Weather?

Several characteristics of the weather make it an interesting, frequent, and safe conversational topic. These characteristics include its unpredictability, variability, environmental prominence and importance, and impersonal nature. Yet for many British people, the weather is more than a casual topic to discuss with strangers: it borders on an obsession.

Examination of the British weather newsgroup, *uk.sci.weather*, which is among the most active in the world (indeed, it is probably the most active), provides evidence for this claim. Each day may see hundreds of messages about the weather. But what do people talk about when they talk about the weather? What are British 'weatherphiles' most interested in?

I collected data to answer these questions in two ways. First, *uk.sci.weather* is an active and unmoderated newsgroup devoted to the British weather. The news-group is open to anyone who can access the *uk.sci* newsgroups. Although some of the contributors are professional meteorologists, most are not. There is some technical discussion, but many postings reflect items of current popular interest in the weather. I saved a random sample (the content determined by throwing a die) of all messages from fifteen days' worth of postings to the newsgroup. The sample contained nearly 2000 messages.

Second, I run a website devoted to the British weather which emphasizes severe weather events (http: //www.personal.dundee.ac.uk/~taharley/britweather.htm). I often receive emails about the weather from people who have accessed my site. I stored all weather-related emails for five months (October 2001 to February 2002), and analyzed their content. The sample contained almost 200 messages.

Collecting data from the Internet involves special methodological problems. There are three problems of particular importance. First, in the case of both emails and newsgroups, it is difficult to uncover much meaningful personal information about the newsgroup posters and email correspondents because so many people use a handle rather than a name, and because people do not supply personal information in these settings. Nevertheless, it is possible to draw a few provisional conclusions. First, in the public newsgroup, the great majority of contributors are male (probably in excess of 95 percent), but in my private emails, the distribution is more evenly balanced (with about 60–70 percent being male). Furthermore, and unsurprisingly given that the topic of the newsgroup is the British weather, the vast majority of contributors are British, although again the bias is less pronounced in my private emails (with most of the difference being made up from people from North America asking about the Scottish weather in the light of a possible vacation). There is a clear geographical bias to both contributors and correspondents, with more coming from the southeast of Britain, where the population density is highest. It is also difficult to say much about the ethnic origins of the contributors, although examination of the non-handle names suggest that most are Caucasian. It is my impression that contributors are on average older than the population of computer users as a whole. It is similarly difficult to say much about the educational level and social class of the samples, except to say that clearly both presume at least a rudimentary level of computer literacy. One might speculate that given that the name of the newsgroup includes 'science', contributors will probably have a higher level of education in general, and in science in particular, than people in the population at large, or even than people in the sample of private correspondents. This speculation is consistent with the tone of the messages.

The second methodological problem is that the Internet is a dynamic system. In particular, it is an interactive system with feedback. People's beliefs and interests are shaped by what they read on it; this shaping process in turn influences what they write, which goes on to influence what others believe and write, and so on. The newsgroup generates its own issues (which are occasionally picked up on by the press and form the basis of newspaper articles – an illustration that it is possible to jump outside the system). At least some of the readers of the weather newsgroup may come to believe that the newsgroup is in some sense definitive and authoritative (which, if the reader applies caution and reads many posts on a topic, it can be).

On a related matter, the third problem is that in some cases the contributor may be posting a contribution that violates one or more of Grice's (1975) maxims: it may be more or less informative than necessary, it may not be true, it may not be relevant, and it may be obscure, ambiguous, or in some other way difficult to follow. There are few opportunities to assess the formal credentials of contributors, so some casual readers may come away with incorrect beliefs.

Consideration of these problems suggests that some caution is necessary when drawing conclusions about people's understanding of the weather based on observational data collected from the Internet. The sample of contributors is unlikely to be representative of the population as a whole, the Internet is a dynamic system, and some contributions may be in some way faulty. On the other hand, there are reasons for supposing that we should not place too much store on these problems. The newsgroup is to some extent a self-correcting system: errors are rapidly – and often strongly – pointed out by other contributors; pseudo-scientific beliefs are criticized (or even ridiculed); and in general all but the most casual reader is likely to get a more up-to-date and accurate picture of the current status of theorization about the weather, and a more accurate rendition of the facts, than from many outlets of the media.

Naturally discussion on the weather newsgroup is more wide-ranging than the content of my private emails, although similar main themes emerge from both data sources. The first common theme is speculation about what the weather is going to be like in the near future. The second common theme is related to the first: there is an obsession with extreme weather events. This obsession takes the form of discussion about whether severe weather is likely, how severe it is going to be, and who will be affected by it and for how long. I discuss this particular obsession in more detail below. The third common theme is the presence of reminiscences of past weather events.

Hardly surprisingly, given the supposedly science-based nature of the newsgroup, questions about the physical mechanisms involved in producing the weather are prominent on it. Geographical comparisons are also frequent: how much colder or wetter (or warmer or drier) is one place than another (with occasional discussion of comparisons of pressure and humidity). Reports of comparisons of weather records across time are also frequent. It is strikingly obvious that we are particularly obsessed with weather extremes, and the setting of new records (highest and lowest daily and monthly temperatures, rainfall, and pressure). Fortunately, my sample spanned the setting of one particularly striking record: October 2001 was the warmest ever recorded in Britain. ('Ever recorded' means in the Central England Temperature (CET) series.)[3] Other unusual atmospheric phenomena excite much discussion (and envy from those who missed them): in the recent past, these have included noctilucent clouds, haloes and arcs, persistent and bright rainbows, meteors, and particularly aurora. In all of these cases, rapid access to information generates excitement and indeed awareness in readers: they may be more likely to go out and look for and measure these phenomena. There are instances of people becoming weather observers, and purchasing observing equipment, on the basis of Internet exchanges – thus providing new sources of data for the newsgroup to discuss (which is an example of positive feedback in the Internet, as discussed above).

Naturally there has also been much discussion of the causes of extreme weather events (or lack of them): do they arise from chance variation, natural climatic change, or man-induced global warming? Although the bulk of the correspondents find the data cited as supporting the global warming hypothesis overwhelmingly convincing, there is some scepticism, and a few antagonistic contributors, and this topic provokes perhaps the most acerbic debates and exchanges.

My personal emails largely reflect these general topics, although two additional types of communication dominate the emails that are not mirrored in the newsgroup. The first type is a request for information about what the weather was like on a particular day in the past, and the second type a request for speculation on what it will be like on a particular day in the future. People do not always give reasons for their interest, but the reasons for requests for past weather information are more heterogeneous than those for the future, which are dominated by weddings and holidays (in addition to optimistic desires for extreme weather). Reasons for asking about past weather include: insurance claims, completing school projects, finding out for an elderly relative, identifying the time and place of weather events (I return to this below), and a surprisingly large number of domestic disputes about the weather. For example, LS wrote: 'I was trying to find out what the weather was like between 16 and 21 August 2000. This is to settle an argument I had with my husband on when it actually rained and when his things got wet in the yard.'

Another common question concerned the date of England's last White Christmas. Many correspondents clearly do not realize how local weather phenomena such as snow can be, or that the notion of a White Christmas is quite a vague one, with a number of possible definitions. In the newsgroup, there is often discussion about what really constitutes a 'White Christmas': for bookmakers, it is usually a single flake of snow falling at the meteorological recording site of the appropriate town – in London, it is the roof of the London Weather Centre. Unsurprisingly, this definition is not adequate for most people. Instead, for many a White Christmas means a significant snowfall on Christmas Day – something that has in fact not happened in lowland Britain since 1970! Others are just satisfied with the presence of extensive snow cover. Such matters are obviously a source of discussion – and yet again argument – at home: AP wrote to me saying, 'you will settle a battle between myself and my partner if you can answer this question!'

Another frequent inquiry concerns the best place to live in Britain to get or avoid certain types of weather. People are perhaps surprisingly prepared to move to get certain types of weather. Not surprisingly, elderly people generally want to retire to somewhere sunny, warm, and dry. It is surprising, however, how frequently younger people want to live somewhere where there is a particular type of weather. The most striking example is living somewhere to either avoid or maximize the likelihood of experiencing thunderstorms. Discussion of thunderstorms is very popular in summer on newsgroup, mirroring winter interest in snow, although outside on the newsgroup thunderstorms are widely disliked.

I received numerous requests about measuring and observing the weather. I run my own amateur weather station, and the details of my station are published on my website. These details clearly prompt questions from people keen to begin their own observations. Questions about amateur automatic weather stations are particularly frequent.[4]

In stark contrast to the level of casual interest, most people who have not studied the subject know relatively little about the weather, forecasting, observing, or how the weather works. This is very apparent in that the less knowledgeable people tend to have greater faith in long-range forecasting.

Finally, I received a surprisingly large number of requests asking me to supply data about particular weather events because they were of personal significance. I will discuss this in more detail later.

The Obsession with Severe Weather

In autumn and winter months, the obsession with severe weather takes the form of speculating about and expressing a wish for a severe winter. As a result of the dominant westerlies, severe winters are unusual in Britain; the last truly exceptional winter was 1962–63, and the last exceptionally cold winter months were February 1986 (with a Central England Temperature average of $-1.1C^5$) and January 1987 (CET +0.8C). Snow in lowland Britain has recently been a rare event; although there have been occasional and locally severe wintry outbreaks, the last time snow covered more than 50 percent of the country was for a short spell in February 1991. Nevertheless, it is rare for a day to pass in winter without someone commenting upon the prospects of severe winter weather based on analysis of the latest long-range or medium-range forecast. Daily updates of forecasts for the two weeks ahead are now freely available on the Internet, and each day these are scrutinized for signs of severe winter weather. Model forecasts are compared and the slightest hints of a change to extreme cold and snowy weather are discussed at length.

My survey period covered the winter of 2001–2. Earlier in the autumn of 2001, there were a number of long-range forecasts that predicted an exceptionally severe forthcoming winter, perhaps akin to that of 1947,[6] with extreme cold setting in from mid-January. It should be said that the more scientific members of the newsgroup, or those with more meteorological experience, do not always hold these long-range forecasts (often made by amateurs) in high esteem. The more scientific members criticize many of these long-range forecasters for failing to provide and discuss their methods, and for not providing verification data. Global warming and long-range forecasts generated the only really vituperative and personal debates. Nevertheless, the forecasts generated a state verging on what can best be described as near hysteria in much of the readership. Sadly, however, the sceptics were right, and winter 2001–2 turned out to be an unremarkable one in Britain – being mild and wet, particularly in the second half.

The interest in severe winter weather peaked before Christmas: in addition to the interest in severe weather, there was a secondary obsession with having a 'traditional' White Christmas. I return to the topic of a White Christmas below.

Nostalgia: 'The weather isn't what it used to be'

Nostalgia, meaning 'the pain that people feel when they are no longer in their native land', was first described by the Swiss physician Johannes Hofer in the later seventeenth century. Hofer observed the condition of nostalgia in young soldiers who had little hope in returning to their homelands. He noted that affected people became 'sad and taciturn, listless, solitary, full of sighs and moans, and neither medicaments or argument nor promises no threats' helped to make afflicted people any better. Napoleon's military surgeon, Dominique Larry, observed that soldiers affected by nostalgia during the retreat from Moscow would recall their homes and villages as 'being delightful and enchanting, no matter how rude and poverty-stricken they may be'.[7] The past is seen through rose-colored spectacles, and this saw is also true of people's memory of the weather. It is clear from my data that nostalgia plays an important role in people's interest in the weather. But it is a curious sort of nostalgia, because the events that give rise to it are relatively rare.

Perhaps the best example of nostalgia, in both sources of data, is that correspondents generally expressed a strong desire for a White Christmas. There is much nostalgic talk of snow in childhood and White Christmases of the past. However, snow around Christmas is rare in lowland Britain (occurring in fewer than one in ten years), so where does this obsession come from? It should be noted that a desire for snow at Christmas is widespread, and not restricted to weather-philes; people who would curse heavy snow and the disruption it brings at any other time of year express a desire for it at Christmas. (This desire is even reflected in a change in tone of the BBC weather forecasts around this time.) Doubtless there are many reasons for this obsession, including nostalgia, mass hysteria, and specific prompts such as Hollywood films, memories of a *Christmas Carol*, and the description of Christmas in Charles Dickens' *The Pickwick Papers* (which was probably based on the winter of 1830). Statistically, this expectation of a snowy Christmas Day is totally wrong: the most likely weather for Christmas Day in lowland Britain is cold, dry, and sunny. Indeed, many of the younger contributors will never have experienced a severe winter or an instance of the White Christmas for which they yearn! Instead of individual memories, the drive seems to be a collective nostalgia for how people think things used to or should be. Extrapolating from my own case, and discussions with others, there is also a yearning for an idealized experience: the perfect Christmas is white.

In addition to nostalgia for a White Christmas, there is also marked nostalgia for 'real winters'. Table 6.1 shows the top ten coldest winters of the twentieth century in Britain.

Table 6.1 shows a marked absence of recent cold winters: the most recent was 1985. Furthermore, let us consider the distribution of severe winters, defined by two criteria. The first criterion is that of severe months with an average temperature

Table 6.1 The top ten coldest winters of the twentieth century in Britain.

Years	Mean temperature C
1962–63	–0.3
1946–47	1.1
1939–40	1.5
1916–17	1.5
1978–79	1.6
1928–29	1.7
1941–42	2.2
1940–41	2.6
1981–82	2.6
1984–85	2.7

less than 2°C. In the first half of the century, there were 14 severe months, and two occasions (January and February in 1917 and 1929) when there were consecutive severe months. In the second half, there were actually a few more, seeing 17 severe months, with two occasions (1963 and 1979) when there were two consecutive severe months, and only one occasion with three consecutive severe months (1916–17).[8] This difference, however, is statistically insignificant. Second, I define exceptionally severe months as those with average temperature beneath freezing. In the first half of the century, there were only two very severe months (January 1940 and February 1947). In the second half, there were five (February 1956, January 1963, February 1963, January 1979, and February 1986; and December 1981 came very close).

In spite of the data, there is a perception that 'winters are not what they used to be', and this perception is one drive behind the nostalgia. In spite of the absence of very recent severe winters, in general this belief does not have a very strong foundation (although the basis is stronger than the belief that summers are not what they used to be). For example, there were more exceptionally severe winter months in the second half of the twentieth century than in the first. Where, therefore, does the belief come from? First, older people's memories are distorted by the exceptionally severe winters of 1947 and 1962–63, in particular. Second, and perhaps most importantly, I think the recency effect where there have not been many severe winter episodes in the last few years has had a profound influence. Consider Table 6.2, which shows the distribution of the number of severe winter months across the decades of the twentieth century:

Table 6.2 The distribution of severe winter months across decades of the twentieth century.

1900s	1910s	1920s	1930s	1940s	1950s	1960s	1970s	1980s	1990s
1	4	2	1	6	4	5	2	5	1

Older people's perceptions might be affected by the bump in the middle of the century (particularly the war years, which were exceptional) and compare those winters with those of the 1990s. There is no overall trend, however: note the scarcity of severe months in the zeroes and thirties. It is also possible that central heating means that we are less sensitive to cold weather when it happens.

Hence the nostalgia for severe winters seems to arise from a nexus of reasons; because severe winter weather is rare, but does occur intermittently, and yet has not done so very recently.

As some recompense for the lack of real winter weather, there is frequent discussion of past severe winter weather. For example, there have been daily postings about the events of each day in the Great Freeze of 1962–63. Such postings doubtless help drive the nostalgia, and particularly help influence the perceptions of what 'winter should be like' in the young.

There has also been considerable discussion of the reverse of severe winters: the consequences of an early spring. Manifestations of this include early bird migration and the early blooming of flowers, particularly daffodils. More humorous discussion has centred on when lawns have first to be mowed in different regions.

In spring and summer the obsession with severe weather is manifested by speculation about a prolonged, hot summer with record-breaking temperatures; the pattern is similar, but interest in severe winters is more pronounced. I think there are several reasons for this emphasis on winter weather, including the fact that statistically we have had several very hot summers in recent years, but have not had cold winters, and presumably, given global warming, this pattern is likely to continue. The lack of real winter weather contrasts with the pattern of recent summers. In recent years Britain has seen several hot summer months (e.g. the reading of 37.1C at Cheltenham on August 3, 1990 was the highest temperature ever recorded under standard conditions in Britain, and the exceptionally hot months of July and August 1995 and August 1997, with August 1995 being the hottest August ever recorded, and the second hottest month of any sort – after July 1983 – were most notable). From late winter and spring onwards, there is discussion about the likelihood of exceptional summer weather, with some desire for prolonged warm, sunny weather, exceptional hot days, and severe thunderstorms. There is also not as prominent a nostalgic core to summer in the way that there is in the form of a White Christmas for winter. There is also more division about what constitutes interesting summer weather, with different people preferring settled long, warm spells, others violent thunderstorms, and others exceptional heat. Many people of course find hot, humid weather very uncomfortable. (People would also presumably find exceptional cold unpleasant, but perhaps because of its rarity do not remember what it is like!)

There is one particularly interesting nostalgic aspect to summer: the idea commonly held and vocalized by older people in Britain that 'summers aren't what they used to be'. However, the hottest summer of the twentieth century was relatively recent: 1976 (which was hottest overall by a considerable margin), and the summers of 1990, 1995, and 1997 were all exceptional. Table 6.3 shows the means for the top ten hottest summers (June, July, and August) of the twentieth century.

Table 6.3 Mean temperatures for the hottest ten summers of the twentieth century.

Year	Mean temperature C
1976	17.8
1995	17.4
1983	17.1
1947	17.0
1933	17.0
1911	17.0
1975	16.9
1997	16.6
1959	16.6
1955	16.5

This list of hot summers is dominated by recent years. Furthermore, consider Table 6.4, which shows the distribution of the number of hot summer months across the decades of the twentieth century.[9] I count as a 'hot month' one whose CET is 17.5°C or greater.

Table 6.4 The distribution of hot summer months across decades of the twentieth century.

1900s	1910s	1920s	1930s	1940s	1950s	1960s	1970s	1980s	1990s
2	2	2	3	1	2	0	3	3	6

Furthermore, the dates of exceptionally hot months (which I define as 18.5°C or hotter) are also dominated by recent years: July 1921, August 1947, August 1975, July 1976, July 1983, July 1995, August 1995, August 1997. (Before the twentieth century, summers were generally worse. The only very hot month before 1921 was July 1852, with a mean of 18.7°C, since records began in 1659.) Therefore it is reasonable to conclude that the belief that summers 'aren't what they used to be' is just wrong.

Hence once again people's nostalgia for a particular weather event is based upon statistically incorrect data. It is likely that the source of this incorrect belief is a combination of unquestioning subscription to a popularly held myth, and generalization from one or two prominent but unrepresentative examples. Of course, there have been some recent poor summers: 1985–88 was a pretty lean spell, and July and August of 1993 were disappointing. We may also remember counter examples to the average pattern and because of their prominence consider them to be average. I have noticed this tendency in my own weather memories: the 1960s were marked by general cooling and a sequence of poor summers, yet I remember many fine summer days. It is likely that many of them came from one or two relatively fine months (e.g. July 1967 and 1969), or even just occasional fine days. It is also likely that people misidentify the time of weather events (e.g. remembering a sunny spring or autumn day as a hot, sunny summer's day). It is also well known that people's memories for personal events can be highly unreliable (e.g. see Baddeley 1999; Loftus 1979). It is of particular note that people's memory for weather forecasts is usually very poor (Ayton 1988). It is worth noting here that in general, people's memory for everyday objects is surprisingly bad. For example, people are very poor at recalling features and their locations of coins (Nickerson and Adams 1979). Indeed, the data show that rather than remembering specific instances of everyday objects, people remember an average aggregate; Rosch 1973; Rubin and Kontis 1983; see Harley 2001, for a review). Such averages of exemplars are called *prototypes*, and they have played an important role in theorization throughout cognitive psychology and psycholinguistics. Although I am unaware of any specific research on their application to the weather, it is reasonable to suppose that prototypes should operate in the same way when talking about weather categories (e.g. memory for average months) as they do when considering other natural kind categories. People remember the average tendency, even though the average of many instances may not itself have actually occurred (in the same way that the prototypical bird may not correspond to any particular species of bird). People also remember exceptions, and if all they remember are exceptions, they might come to think of those exceptions as typical.

Remembrance of weather events

One of the most frequent queries in my sample is that a person has a particularly strong memory of some non-weather event, and is trying to discover the weather that went with it; or has a vivid memory of some weather event, and is trying to date and amplify it. This observation suggests that weather can be a source of important childhood memories, and can even be a component of 'flashbulb memories'. Indeed, the weather can be the focus of the memory. A flashbulb memory is a particularly vivid memory of what a person was doing at a particular time, often when the person discovers important news, such as hearing about the Kennedy assassination (Brown and Kulik 1977) or the Challenger space shuttle disaster (Bohannon 1988). Some researchers have speculated that strong emotions can lead to the storage of particularly vivid memories, although this idea has proved controversial (e.g. McCloskey et al. 1988). Certainly in my sample, and in my experience, not all vivid memories are associated with moments of heightened emotion.

The observation that people try to discover the weather associated with particular events suggests that the weather provides a *metacognitive role* in organizing memories, in that weather events can provide a framework for searching and dating memories (see Karmiloff-Smith 1986 for a discussion of metacognition). For example, I remember some striking thunderstorms in London that were probably in September 1961 or August 1962 (when I was 3 or 4; these were notably thundery months in the south, and I would be unlikely to remember events any earlier). Even at this age, I clearly remember the light cast by the lightning as being brilliant yellow-white. My father tried to comfort me (I think) by saying that it was the sound of angels banging together; this upset me even more. I can date this memory because of my knowledge of the distribution of severe thunderstorms in the London area in the early 1960s. I also have a clear image of making a snowman in my grandmother's garden: the snow was thick and white. Again, my knowledge of the weather enables me to date this event to the winter of 1962–1963. These examples show that we can organize memories on the basis of their weather content. Such mnemonic techniques are not restricted to people obsessed with the weather. A correspondent emailed me with memories of violent thunderstorms happening while she was sailing off the Isle of Wight in Hampshire when she was a child. (I was able to provide the date for this event as August 1956.) Much more recently, I remember August 1995 in the Midlands just being hot and sunny all the time. I remember getting off a bus and thinking 'wow'. This instance shows how fallible memory is, because I do not see how I could have been on a bus then. Once again, this finding echoes that of other memory research: memories might be very clear, but might also have never happened. We may have particularly vivid memories, but the memories might be false (Schachter 1999). Indeed, on the basis of such errors, Neisser (1986) argued that accuracy in vivid memories can be quite poor, and in any case accuracy is not of paramount importance: instead, vivid memories serve a symbolic function. This argument is consistent with my weather data and the literature on the unreliability of eye-witness testimony. We may have vivid memories of the weather, but they are not always accurately to other events we might remember. Although it may be stretching the point, we might for example remember the weather as being hot and sunny at a time when we were particularly happy, or pouring with rain when we were unhappy. Even if we do not always misremember the weather, we might only remember it if it is consistent with our emotions at the time of encoding.

I note on my website that in memories of my own childhood, all winters were cold and snowy, and all summers hot and sunny. Again, these memories are just wrong – or at least I am remembering a few instances. In particular, as discussed above, British summers in the 1960s (which cover my early childhood years) were cool and wet. The only truly severe winter in my childhood was 1962–63, with a few other cold, snowy months (most notably January 1966 and February 1968 and 1969). People – including me, who should know better – are clearly remembering occasional prototypical events (e.g. one cold winter) and then attributing whole categories to this prototype (e.g. they remember one cold, snowy January and think that all Januarys are like that). This observation suggests that there might be a top-down influence on prototype formation: we do not just aggregate memories, as our beliefs also have an effect on how the prototype is formed. These beliefs, as we saw in the discussion of White Christmases, may have a cultural rather than memorial origin.

The idealization seen in our memories of the weather mirrors that shown in other types of nostalgia. Larry's remark about soldiers longing for their home villages, no matter how grim those villages were, might equally be applied to the weather: we long for the weather of our past, no matter how grim or atypical it might have been.

Conclusions

From an analysis of postings to the British weather newsgroup, my personal emails, and my own introspections, it is clear that the weather is much more than just a topic of casual conversation. When people talk about the weather, one of the topics that is discussed most frequently is memory of past extreme weather events. In addition to being a source of memories, at least some of the time weather can provide a framework for accessing and structuring memory. That is, the weather plays a metacognitive role in organizing cognition. People are also nostalgic about past weather events when they have few statistical grounds for doing so. There might be a number of reasons for this nostalgia, about which one can only speculate. The weather is a 'safe' topic for childhood memories, in the same way that it is a safe topic of conversation: it is impersonal. There is an element of idealization and romanticism about the past in which the weather can play a surprisingly central role. Finally, although people can have vivid memories of past weather events, these memories can often be wrong.

Notes

1. Please send correspondence to Dr Trevor Harley, Psychology Department, University of Dundee, Dundee DD1 4HN, UK, or by email to t.a.harley@dundee.ac.uk.
2. The seasons are defined meteorologically as follows: spring: March, April, May; summer: June, July, August; autumn (fall): September, October, November; winter: December, and January and February of the following year. I follow this usage in this chapter.
3. The Central England Temperature series, abbreviated to CET, provides an estimate of the average temperature of southern and central lowland Britain. The series dates from 1659; the earlier temperature estimates were constructed by Professor Gordon Manley in a paper of exceptional importance – see Manley (1974).
4. See my web pages on my experience of building my own weather station, http://www.personal.dundee.ac.uk/~taharley/my_weather_station_adven.htm.
5. C is an abbreviation for the Celsius temperature scale, used throughout this chapter. To convert degrees Celsius to Fahrenheit, multiply by 1.8 and add 32.
6. In Britain 1947 was probably the most remarkable year, meteorologically speaking, of at least the twentieth century. The winter was generally the snowiest of the century, although, unusually for a severe winter, the prolonged severe weather did not set in until relatively late (20 January); February was the coldest on record; the severe winter persisted well into March, when rapid thawing led to widespread flooding; yet by May 3 the temperature reached 34.4C in the south. The summer was exceptionally hot, sunny, and dry. There was a drought in autumn, and to end the year, there was a thunderstorm on Christmas Day with marble-sized hail (which would be exceptional in Britain in summer).
7. This description of the medical condition of nostalgia comes from a medical column in the *Sunday Telegraph* newspaper by Dr James Le Fanu (2002).
8. Here are the severe months (mean < 2.0°C): February 1902, December 1916, January 1917, February 1917, February 1919, January 1929, February 1929, December 1933, January 1940, January 1941, January 1942, February 1942, January 1945, February 1947, December 1950, February 1955, February 1956, December 1962, January 1963, February 1963, February 1968, February 1969,

January 1979, February 1979, December 1981, February 1983, January 1985, February 1986, January 1987, February 1991. Here again are the very severe months (mean < 0C): January 1940, February 1947, February 1956, January 1963, February 1963, January 1979, February 1986.

9. Here are the hot months (mean ≥ 17.5C): July 1900, July 1901, July 1911, August 1911, July 1921, July 1923, July 1933, August 1933, July 1934, August 1947, July 1955, August 1955, August 1975, July 1976, August 1976, July 1983, August 1984, July 1989, August 1990, July 1994, July 1995, August 1995, August 1997, July 1999.

References

AYTON, P. 1988. Perceptions of Broadcast Weather Forecasts. *Weather* 43: 93–197.

BADDELEY, A. 1999. *Essentials of Human Memory*. Hove: Psychology Press.

BOHANNON, J. N. 1988. Flashbulb Memories for the Space Shuttle Disaster: A Tale of Two Theories. *Cognition* 29: 179–186.

BROWN, R. and J. KULIK. 1977. Flashbulb Memories. *Cognition* 5: 73–99.

EDEN, P. 1995. *Weatherwise*. London: Macmillan.

GRICE, H. P. (1975). Logic and conversation. In P. Cole and J. Morgan (Eds.), *Syntax and Semantics: Vol. 3. Speech Acts*, pp. 41–58. New York: Academic Press.

HARLEY, T. A. 2001. *The Psychology of Language* (2nd ed.). Hove, Sussex: Psychology Press.

KARMILOFF-SMITH, A. 1986. From Meta-processes to Conscious Access: Evidence from Children's Metalinguistic and Repair Data. *Cognition* 23: 95–147.

LE FANU, J. 2002. Nostalgia is More than a Longing – It's a Condition. *The Sunday Telegraph* (14 April): 4.

LOFTUS, E. 1979. *Eyewitness Testimony*. Cambridge, MA: Harvard University Press.

MANLEY, G. 1974. Central England Temperatures: Monthly Means from 1973. *Quarterly Journal of the Royal Meteorological Society* 100: 389–405.

McCLOSKEY, M., C. G. WIBLE and H. J. COHEN. 1988. Is there a Special Flashbulb-Memory Mechanism? *Journal of Experimental Psychology* 117: 171–181.

NEISSER, U. 1986. Remembering Pearl Harbor: A reply to Thompson and Cowan. *Cognition* 23: 285–286.

NICKERSON, R. S. and M. J. ADAMS. 1979. Long-term Memory for a Common Object. *Cognitive Psychology* 11: 87–307.

PROUST, M. 1983. *Remembrance of things past*. Trans. C. K. Scott Moncrieff and Terence Kilmartin. Harmondsworth, Middlesex: Penguin Books.

ROSCH, E. 1973. Natural Categories. *Cognitive Psychology* 4: 28–349.

RUBIN, D. C. and T. C. KONTIS. 1983. A Schema for Common Cents. *Memory and Cognition* 11: 35–341.

SCHACHTER, D. L. 1999. The Cognitive Neuropsychology of False Memories: Introduction. *Cognitive Neuropsychology* 16: 193–195.

YEARS

–7–

How People Name Seasons
Ben Orlove

Do people everywhere in the world divide the year into seasons? This question seems straightforward enough. Certainly many languages have terms for seasons. It might seem that such terms are a simple way to note and to name specific portions of the annual cycle of the year. In areas far from the equator, the shifts in the weather and the changes in day length are striking phenomena. At the equator, the length of the day does not shift, but in many tropical areas precipitation varies; temperatures can also rise and fall, though to a lesser extent. Even at the equator, the wettest months receive more than 150 percent of the rainfall of the driest months; the only exceptions are northern Sulawesi and the island of Halmahera in Indonesia, and a portion of western South America on the eastern slopes of the Andes in Ecuador and southern Colombia, where precipitation is not concentrated at any time of year.[1] Nor are these apparently seasonless places lacking in shifts that occur regularly throughout the year. Since these regions are strongly influenced by El Niño events, there are certain months of the year when droughts or heavy flooding occur, usually once or twice a decade, and other months when these extreme events are much less common. Even in normal years, unaffected by El Niño events, these relatively seasonless zones experience shifts in wind speed and direction. Moreover, the sun's path across the sky varies during the year. At the equator, where the length of the day is fixed, the sun's highest point in the sky is to the north during the northern hemisphere spring and summer and to the south in the northern hemisphere autumn and winter. People in different cultures around the world have noted this apparent movement. Taking all these phenomena into account, it can be stated that no portion of the earth is truly without an annual cycle of seasons.

This chapter represents an initial effort to examine the question of the ways that speakers of different languages name seasons. It presents information on twenty-six languages from six continents. It explores commonalities and differences in the ways that speakers of these languages name seasons. To summarize these preliminary findings as concisely as possible, the results from these twenty-six languages suggest that the question posed above can be answered in the affirmative: in all these cases, people divide the year into seasons, though they do so in a number of different ways.

The research for this chapter has unfolded in an inductive fashion. The initial impulse for the work grew out of a study of traditional forecasting methods in highland Peru and Bolivia. In that region, indigenous farmers look at the Pleiades, a star cluster in the constellation Taurus, at a specific date in June, in the middle of the dry season. On the basis of the appearance of this cluster, they predict whether the coming rainy season will begin around the usual time in October, or whether it will be delayed, and whether the amount of rain will be sufficient or scanty. Research showed that there is a solid empirical basis to these forecasts – El Niño events influence the atmospheric conditions that affect both stellar visibility in June and rainfall later in the year (Orlove, Chiang and Cane 2000, 2002). In looking for other cases of such traditional forecasts elsewhere in the world, the question arose whether cultures looked to predict the conditions in coming seasons. This question, then, led to the question of whether cultures speak of seasons at all, or whether they divide time up in some different fashion. They might simply count days or months. Alternatively, they might measure time in relation to a series of temporal points, which in turn could be diverse in nature – salmon runs or rice planting times or a certain festival or the appearance of a certain star in the eastern sky before dawn. (Some indigenous calendars indicate twelve or thirteen months, each with a name that corresponds to a natural feature, such as 'Snow Moon' and 'Grass Moon'; these may reflect a tendency to mark such temporal points, rather than to tally cycles of the moon.)

This question of the universality of seasons, in turn, led to a review of anthropological sources on local systems of classification of weather and climate. A set of categories was developed to record cases of terminology about seasons. Researchers at CIESIN, the Center for International Earth Science Information Network, at Columbia University, provided helpful advice on establishing the categories. Twenty-eight cases were compiled, most from the anthropological literature and a few from queries to researchers who were fluent in local languages around the world.

Before presenting the cases themselves, it bears mentioning that many anthropologists at present are skeptical of efforts to look for cultural universals. The efforts to generalize about human cultures have largely been replaced by a concern to explore the differences among cultures. However, there has been a longstanding interest within anthropology on the subject of classification. For a number of decades, anthropologists looked at systems of classification as a kind of cultural order that might shape, or reflect, social action. Durkheim's work on totemism, published early in the twentieth century, showed a correspondence between certain kinds of social groups, such as clans, and certain natural objects, which were their totemic signs (1995[1912]). The adherents of structuralism in the 1960s and 1970s conducted a number of studies that showed the parallelism or congruence of classification in many domains. The growth of post-structuralist approaches led to different accounts of classification. Rather than being part of a shared culture, it was an element in an ideology that served as an instrument of control. Social power was exercised through the imposition of systems of categories.

To take one example, structuralist studies looked at the categorization of space and types of vegetation. They showed that oppositions between different types of spaces corresponded to other culturally significant contrasts. Zimmermann (1987) discusses the importance in South Asian thought of the difference between moister forest zones and drier grassland zones. He shows that this opposition corresponds to other contrasts in political, ritual, culinary, and medical realms; order – whether political stability, moral balance, appropriate foods or good health – depends on a balance of these two poles. By contrast, post-structuralist approaches have challenged the view that concepts can be ordered into neat systems, preferring to study looser associations of metaphors; these approaches also reject the view that such systems of meaning are widely shared and politically neutral, showing how metaphors can support social inequality. The post-structuralists often argue that political hierarchies can be established and maintained, and at times challenged, through the use of key metaphors. Continuing with the example of forests, Grinker (1994) argues that the dominance of settled agricultural peoples in central Africa over nomadic hunting groups rests in part on their claims that forests are inherently uncivilized places and that the inhabitants of forests are backward. Similar claims for the relative savagery and inferiority of the forest have been found on other continents as well, such as Asia (Peluso 1992) and South America (Orlove 1993). Much as structuralist theory suggested that rituals could enact and reinforce oppositions, post-structuralist theory emphasizes performance as a way that symbols can be enacted. Sahlins (1994) offers a particularly detailed example of the use of the metaphoric association of forests and wildness by rural social movements in nineteenth-century France.

The shift from structuralism to post-structuralism has eroded some of the support for the anthropological study of systems of categorization. Nonetheless, research on cultural systems of classification has remained relatively strong, particularly in the area of research on classification of the natural world. One important study examines the terminology for color, surely a basic attribute of objects. In their key work, Berlin and Kay (1969) define a color space that includes all possible colors within the visible spectrum. They work with a set of 320 color chips, a bit like the color inserts that appear in some dictionaries. These chips are arrayed in a rectangle that contains forty columns of hues, comprising the full range of the rainbow, and eight rows of brightness from light to dark. Berlin and Kay found that speakers of all languages could distinguish between basic colors (in English, red, orange, yellow, green, blue, purple, black, gray, white, brown, and pink) and non-basic or secondary colors such as beige, rust, magenta, mustard, blue-green and salmon-colored. The basic terms are more general, more widely applicable, and more psychologically significant to informants; in addition, they have certain linguistic properties. When presented with the array of chips, individuals could quickly identify the ones that lay at the core, or focus, of a color; they could show which chips were the very greenest ones. They had more difficulty locating the boundaries of the colors; they deliberated a long time before distinguishing between the green chips that, though yellowish, were still green, and the yellow chips that, though greenish, were still yellow. The authors' principal finding was that they could arrange all languages into a set of seven stages corresponding to the basic color terms that they used. They presume that all people share the same biological capacity to perceive color, in the sense of hue and brightness; they just use different words for these colors. The first stage, corresponding to only a few languages in Papua New Guinea, has terms only for black and white, in essence distinguishing between all objects only by their relative darkness and lightness; the second includes red as well. In such systems, objects that English-speakers would call blue would be categorized as black (if dark blue), white (if light blue), and perhaps red (if a kind of rich blue that veers towards reddish-purple). The third stage adds either yellow or green, which are both present in the fourth stage. By the fifth stage, blue is included, or, more precisely, separated from green. The sixth stage adds brown to give a total of seven color terms. The seventh stage adds one or more of the last colors: pink, gray, purple, or orange.

Berlin also conducted extensive research on classification of plants and animals. He summarizes much of this work, as well as studies conducted by other anthropologists, in a book, *Ethnobiological Classification: Principles of Categorization of Plants and Animals in Traditional Societies*. He shows that this knowledge is often detailed, and that the classification systems concentrate on certain plants and animals, and pay less attention to others – a phenomenon that bears some resemblance to the ways in which informants can quickly state with assurance that a particular chip is a certain color, but take longer to puzzle out which color might best describe another chip. Berlin notes that the systems of ethnobiological classification in virtually all cases follow a tight hierarchical structure: the most general categories can be divided into subcategories which can in turn be broken down into sub-subcategories. These hierarchical divisions apply to all sorts of living things, so that the hierarchical system of classification for plants would be similar to the system for birds or reptiles. In particular, these structures consist of ranks, usually six in number. Berlin assigns names for these ranks. Ranging from most to least inclusive, they are kingdom, life form, intermediate, generic, specific and varietal. Though many particular criteria could be used to distinguish, for example, crows from robins or oaks from maples, these generally can be reduced to features of morphology and behavior. Berlin notes as well some specific linguistic properties of names of different levels. He discusses as well two accounts of such classificatory systems: an intellectualist view, in which humans, endowed with an inherent curiosity, observe and categorize plants and animals, and an utilitarian view, in which humans observe and categorize plants and animals because so many of them have distinct uses or consequences (they can be used for food, clothing, medicines, building materials and the like, or they can be harmful, dangerous, or annoying).

These studies of color terminology and classification of plants and animals provide suggestive models for the study of terms for seasons. In particular, they suggest that systems of classification can be compared for speakers of many different languages, and they also indicate that some regularities in the structure of such systems can be found. Seasons might seem a similar case, since all languages could classify different types of weather, just as they classify color and living things. Color is an observable attribute of material objects, and, moreover, virtually all humans have at least some exposure to a wide range of colors: they see blood, urine, leaves and skies, even if they do not use four separate words for red, yellow, green and blue, and they would see other colored objects – different ones in different settings – which they could also classify. Similarly, virtually all humans see a large variety of plants and animals. The particular kinds of plants and animals differ from place to place, but everywhere there would be many individual fish or birds or flowering bushes, each of a particular species, that could be grouped into various hierarchical categories. However, seasons differ in at least three ways. The first two stem from the temporal nature of seasons. First, they are not physically continuous and present the way objects and living things are. To be in one season is not to be in the other seasons. In contrast, to have a red object in view does not exclude having other objects in view, and to see an oak tree does not mean that one cannot also see a daisy. Second, seasons are not objects or things; they are parts or segments of an entity – the year. Third, seasons can be categorized along many dimensions. For Berlin and Kay, the various permutations of only two variables, hue and intensity, gave all possible colors; color chips could be arrayed in a simple rectangle. The numerous criteria by which particular kinds of plants and animals can be divided also correspond to two broad dimensions, morphology and behavior. As discussion of the twenty-eight cases shows, seasonal classification seems far more variable.

These features that distinguish seasons raise certain methodological issues. Berlin and Kay were able to study color terminology by showing their informants a set of standardized color chips. Similar tasks can be constructed for ethno-biological classification by presenting informants with pictures of organisms, or, in some cases, with actual animals or plants, whether living or preserved. There is no similar means of presenting people with sample atmospheric conditions and asking them to name the seasons to which they correspond. Even if a generous individual were to provide a researcher with the funds to construct a climate-controlled chamber which could replicate a variety of conditions of temperature, humidity, wind, light and precipitation, this device would not fully recreate the variety of conditions that people use to name seasons, as the cases discussed here show. Instead, it is necessary to construct verbal tasks (for example, asking people to name the parts of a year, or to start at one point and to list the parts) – or to infer, from ordinary conversation and interaction, which names are the most salient.

This chapter represents an allocation of research effort in a way that might be described as broad and shallow. It is broad because it considers a relatively large number of cultures, and shallow because it considers relatively little information about each. Such an effort can direct attention to some variation among systems of terminology for seasons. However, such effort will also inevitably miss some detail in each case, and might miss variation that exists at the level of detail. A different allocation of research effort, one that is narrow and deep, would complement this chapter.

This task required guidelines to define what is meant by a season. The word itself can have several referents, as can be illustrated with examples drawn from English. On the one hand, English-speakers understand that the words 'spring' 'summer' 'fall', and 'winter' refer to periods of the years that occur in a fixed sequence. They understand as well that each season is characterized by particular attributes – weather, length of day and night, stages of plant growth. English-speakers would not seriously dispute that these are the four seasons in English. On the other hand, English speakers also understand that 'Christmas season' is the period around December 25 and that 'strawberry season' refers to the time when fresh berries are available. This contrast between what might be called basic and minor seasons is not unique to English, since other languages also have minor seasons.

It bears mentioning that the year may be defined and discussed in different ways in different languages. Though the year is a natural unit, cultures vary greatly in the extent to which they emphasize or even recognize the year. Western cultures lie close to one end of a continuum of emphasis on the year. Calendars are ubiquitous, historical events are known by the year in which they occurred, an individual's age influences activities and obligations. Indeed, when physicians in the United States wish to assess the mental acuity of someone who has suffered a stroke or an accident, they often ask the victim to state his or her age and the year. Along with the victim's own name, and the name of the president, these are taken as the most basic questions possible, whose answers are the facts most firmly retained in the mind. For other cultures, however, the year is a far less salient unit. These cases lie closer to the opposite end of the continuum, in which years are not emphasized. Schieffelin (2002) describes the Bosavi of Papua New Guinea. Until the influence of missionaries in the 1970s led to a radical reconceptualization of time, they had no word for 'year'. The staples on which their subsistence system rested did not grow in an annual cycle. Root crops could be planted and harvested throughout the year, and trees bore fruits and nuts at different months. Pigs, too, could be slaughtered at any time. The absolute age of an individual was not an important fact, since it was sufficient to keep track of the relative seniority of individuals. Nor were historical events recorded or recollected in relation to a chronological sequence of years. When the missionaries, with their emphasis on linear and eschatological time, pressed for the inclusion of a word that meant 'year', the Bosavi adopted the word *dona*, the name of the longest of their seasons. In a similar fashion, the Baganda of what is now Uganda did not have a word for 'year' in pre-colonial times. The agriculture led them to speak of varying time frames rather than of the year. Like the Bosavi, they raised root crops and tree crops. They also cultivated grains and legumes. Both of the rainy seasons, from March to June and from August to November, were long enough to support agriculture, so they had two harvests a year. Though it might be supposed that cultures that do not emphasize the year as a unit of time also do not reckon seasons, these cases, at least, do have well-established terms for seasons. They did not tally years, but they divided them into their component sections. As with the Bosavi, the Baganda adopted a term, agricultural season, *mwaka*, to mean year.

Moreover, a single culture may contain multiple frameworks for marking and counting years. A single cycle of the seasons may not coincide with a single cycle of the progression of the constellations in the night sky – a celestial year, or, more precisely, a sidereal year, since the weather that characterizes a particular season might start earlier or later than usual in a given year. Agricultural calendars, ritual calendars and political calendars can vary from these climatological and sidereal years, and from each other.

This question of the definition of the year was one issue that arose in setting up the parameters of the study of seasonal terminology. To remain open to the potential variability in the ways that languages divided the year into seasons, the particular kind of year was not chosen. This matter was left open, in order not to assume that seasons refer to segments of a climatological year.

Nonetheless, to set up a database of cases, a definition of season was required, specifically a definition that would include basic seasons but not minor seasons. After trial efforts with other wordings, the following rather lengthy definition was included in the codebook: 'Seasons are defined as the periods that the year is divided into, each of which is characterized by specific natural conditions or phenomena; these conditions and phenomena are usually, but not always, atmospheric. Taken together, the seasons "fill up" the year with at most brief inter-seasonal periods. Seasons can vary in length.'

This definition has served as the basis for assembling twenty-eight cases in a kind of ethnoclimatology database. These cases are listed in Appendix 7.1. Some cases were taken from articles and monographs in the anthropological literature. Others were derived from a major anthropological database, the Human Relations

Area Files, available at http: //www.yale.edu/hraf/. Still others came from queries of field researchers. In all these sources, researchers report directly on seasons. It seems to strike researchers as a natural and unproblematic category. Researchers might wonder which local activities could be construed as 'law' or 'economics' but they assumed that the local people had a set of seasons. This assumption itself merits attention – the topic, perhaps, of a future paper. At present, it is sufficient to say that it may simply reflect the universality of the pattern of dividing the year into seasons, though it may also reflect the profound extent to which North Americans and Europeans have internalized their own systems of seasons. It might also demonstrate the nature of conventions of ethnographic writing, in which it is common to report on annual cycles of activities.

For each record in the database, certain information was obtained, centered on a list of the names of all the seasons. For each season, the beginning and ending were recorded; it was left open whether these were taken as fixed or as occurring over a certain range. The most important characteristics of each particular season were recorded, as were any specific features that were taken to herald its onset. The specific meanings, if any, of names of seasons were included. If a language included terms for sub-seasons – periods within particular seasons with charact-eristics of their own – these were also recorded. Information about forecasts was also recorded, including the particular feature that served as a basis of the forecast, the timing of the forecast, and the predicted outcomes. In addition, the presence or absence of local weather experts was recorded as well. Appendix 7.2 contains a full list of variables that are included for each case in the database. If a source was complete enough to document the name, timing, and characteristics of seasons, it was included. Some sources were brief, and did not describe any forecasting practices, or mention any weather experts. Since the absence of evidence is not necessarily evidence of absence, it cannot be assumed that these cases lack seasonal forecasting and weather experts. Nonetheless, these sources were included. Other complementary sources may be located later that would either describe these practices and experts, or document their absence more firmly.

The records are assembled on the basis of language. Language seemed a more effective basis than ethnic group, culture, or society; there was less disagreement over the names of languages than over the names of ethnic groups. To preserve information on variability of seasonal terminology, a record can contain inform-ation on more than one site within a particular country. Since some languages are spoken over a large area, though, each combination of language and country forms a specific record. For example, the database includes two sets of seasonal terms in Arabic, one from Libya and one from Saudi Arabia.

Some effort was made to draw the initial set of twenty-eight cases from a wide range of areas, including low-latitude tropical areas, mid-latitude temperate areas, and high-latitude areas closer to the poles. However, it cannot be claimed that these cases are fully representative of the languages of the world, since some areas are underrepresented. The greater presence of other areas reflects the interests of the people who collected the cases.[2]

In entering the cases in the databases, a question arose about how to distinguish between seasons and sub-seasons. Once again, some examples from English may be helpful at this point. In much of the United States and Canada, 'Indian summer' is a stretch of dry mild weather that occurs in the fall. It is not a season at all, but rather a segment of fall. Indian summer cannot occur during any season other than fall, and it does not cease to be fall during Indian summer. In much of Vermont, 'mud season' is a period in spring when snow is melting, the ground is often bare, and thick mud makes roads difficult to pass. Mud season cannot occur during winter (since the weather is too cold; there is often snow on the ground, and bare ground would be hard), nor in the summer (since the weather is too warm; the ground is softer, but no longer so muddy); 'mud season' is a part of spring. An analogy might be drawn with the discussion of color terminology. Seasons are like basic colors such as red or blue, and sub-seasons are like secondary colors, such as scarlet or sky-blue.

As these cases suggest, sub-seasons can be distinguished from seasons by several characteristics. A sub-season is a part of a season. It does not replace the season in which it is inserted, but rather is a phase of that season. Sub-seasons are shorter than seasons. A compound name may also suggest that a time interval is secondary in nature, a sub-season rather than a season. As research in ethnoclimatology progresses, and more cases are included in the database, this distinction between seasons and sub-seasons may be refined, but at present these rules seems to be effective.

It may seem arbitrary to decide which of the great number of minor seasons will be counted as sub-seasons. If 'Indian summer' is part of fall, and 'mud season' part of spring, should 'peach season' be part of summer – or 'silly season', the period in August when newspapers often carry stories of quirky or amusing events, because national and global politics often slow down at this time? For the time being, it seems possible to include the variety of sub-seasons for each case; if a number of cases prove to have a large number of sub-seasons, some principle of selection will need to be established.

I will provide two examples. The Nuer of southern Sudan, one of the best-known cases in the ethnographic literature, reckon two seasons of the year. The name of the first, *mai*, means 'drought'. It refers to the dry period from mid-September to mid-March, when little or no rain falls, the rivers shrink, and wet areas dry up. The other season, from mid-March to mid-September, is called *tot* or rains, for the precipitation that occurs regularly in these months. In this period, the rivers rise and many low-lying areas become inundated. At least in the relatively halcyon days that Evans-Pritchard described, before the brutal wars in that region, many activities of Nuer life were shaped by these seasons. In *tot*, the Nuer, along with their herds, moved to villages on ridges; they spread out more widely to scattered camps during *mai*. Indeed, this annual movement is marked by the sub-seasons; *jiom*, a word that means 'wind', is the time of the first movements from the ridge-top villages to camps. (It is also the time of fishing, in the retreating streams, and of harvest.) Correspondingly, *rwil* is the time of the reverse movement, from camp to village, and of planting.

J	F	M	A	M	J	J	A	S	O	N	D
1				2					1		
			2a						1a		

1. *mai* 2. *tot*

1a. *jiom* 2a. *rwil*

Nuer/Sudan

The speakers of Gundjeihmi, an Indigenous Australian language in coastal western Arnhemland in the Northern Territory, reckon six seasons. The first season, *gunnmeleng*, runs from October through December. This is a period of high humidity. It marks the arrival of the first storms of the year; they are often intermittent but violent, with extensive lightning. It is followed by *gudjeuk*, which begins in January and continues into March; it can end early or late in this month. This is the time of the greatest amount of rains, when moist winds blow from the northwest. The next season, in March and April, is *banggerreng*. In this season, the winds sometimes shift, blowing from the southeast and bringing in drier air. May and June are the months of the fourth season, *yegge*, a time of no rain, cool nights, humid days, and steady winds from the southeast. The season of *wurrgeng* starts in June – its onset can occur at different times in this month – and continues into August. The lowest temperatures of the year occur during nights in this season, and there is little wind. Two important species of eucalyptus, *Eucalyptus tetrodonta* and *E. miniata*, begin to flower. The sixth and final season, *gurrung*, from August to October, brings hot, dry weather.

Several observations emerge from the twenty-eight cases that are included in the preliminary database. It is quite possible that they will be revised as more cases are included.

J	F	M	A	M	J	J	A	S	O	N	D
2		3		4		5		6		1	

1. *gunnmeleng* 2. *gudjeuk* 3. *banggerreng* 4. *yegge* 5. *wurrgeng*
6. *gurrung*

Gundjeihmi/Australia

The first point is that all the languages have names for seasons. The speakers of these languages list a set of intervals that recur in a fixed sequence. Moreover, some names of seasons are arbitrary, in the sense that they have no other meaning. As far as the sources indicate, for example, the Gudjeihmi names for seasons are arbitrary, in that they have no other meaning. In other cases, the season names refer to natural phenomena. The Etolo of highland Papua New Guinea reckon two seasons: *genegi* or 'clouds exist' from mid-April till September, and *gaheoi* or 'fruit pandanus exists' from September till mid-April.

J	F	M	A	M	J	J	A	S	O	N	D
2			1						2		

1. *genegi* 2. *gaheoi*

Etolo/Papua New Guinea

Another characteristic of the seasons is the relative fixity of their positions within the year. In some cases, the timing of the onset or close of a particular season varies little from the normal or ideal date. In others, it can vary as much as three or four weeks in either direction, but not more. It is possible that the sources underestimate this fixity of the seasons and underreport both the variability from one person to another and from one year to another; they may report beliefs about what seasons should be, rather than the actual use of seasonal terminology.

An aspect of the variability of the cases is the extent to which seasons are sharply bounded, so that the shift from one season to the next is brief. The contemporary Western system, in which the shift can be assigned to a particular minute of a particular day, is extreme in its boundedness, but it is surely not unique. When the first rain showers fall at the end of the dry season in southwestern Uganda, speakers of Rukiga and related languages discuss whether they mark the beginning of the rainy season, or whether they are false rains that happen to fall in the dry season. They have a number of terms for these false rains, such as 'quick visitors'. Even in Western cases, though, people can speak of having certain times when seasons grade into one another. In many parts of the United States, for example, it would make sense to say: 'With that cool weather last week, I was sure that summer was over and that fall had already begun. But that last hot spell made me think that we weren't finished with summer yet.' In other words, a spell of cool weather in the United States could correspond to false rains in Uganda. This issue raises the question of the temporal boundary of seasons. This subject is a difficult one to study. It is possible to gather some information about color terminology by showing a set of color chips to speakers of a language, and asking them to classify these chips; it would be less productive to show them a calendar and ask them to mark off seasons, or to bring them to a series of climate-controlled chambers and ask them which ones felt like a particular season.

In addition, there may be a significant level of uncertainty about the boundaries of the seasons. Seasons can be separated by some time that is unclassified. To offer another example from the United States, it would be possible, but somewhat odd, to say: 'The weather this last week has been strange. It feels like winter is over, since the days are getting longer and it's been warmer. But it doesn't quite seem like spring has started yet.' As Berlin and Kay noted, people could quickly indicate color chips that were very blue or very green, but had a hard time deciding which blue-green chips would count as blue and which as green. It is possible that some languages classify only parts of the year as seasons, and would consider some time between seasons as altogether unclassified. There are no cases in the database that contain intermediate, unnamed time between seasons, but it is possible that such examples exist; it is also possible that some researchers simply assumed that a year can be wholly divided into seasons, and so they have imposed this view on cases where it does not fit. Such cases would change, but not wholly invalidate, the study of seasonal terminology. In a related vein, the fact that some individuals might be unable to decide what color term they would use for a certain object does not invalidate the study of color classification. Color terminologies do not disappear just because a hazy sky, though surely not blue, is also not white or yellow or gray, or because a dry leaf, no longer green, has not become something that could be called orange or yellow or brown.

These cases show that seasons are usually, but not always, described by atmospheric phenomena. The exceptions are clustered in tropics, where day length does not vary much throughout the year, particularly in the humid regions where no month is likely to lack rain entirely. Some languages name seasons by botanical, or, more properly, phenological characteristics. The Kaluli of highland Papua New Guinea reckon three seasons. The first, *dona*, named for the *dona* tree that fruits in this season; the name of the second season, *imou*, also means 'tree base,' since some trees shed their leaves at this time, and the leaves accumulate near the bases of trees. The third season, *tan*, bears the name of the pandanus tree, whose fruit ripens at this time.

There are also examples of what could be called hydrological seasons. Portuguese-speaking villagers, sometimes called caboclos, in some portions of the Amazon basin trace four seasons that are based on stages of the river. January and February are the months of *subida*, rising waters, as the flow in the rivers increases. March through June mark the *enchente* or flood, also known as *agua cheia* or full water. The months of June, July and August are the *baixa da agua*, the falling or lowering of the water; this season can continue into September. The fourth season marks the lowest level of the river, known as *vazante*, empty water or *seca*, drought. The economic and social activities of the villagers are conditioned by the level of the rivers: they plant their fields in the lands that are exposed during the falling water, and they fish at low river levels.

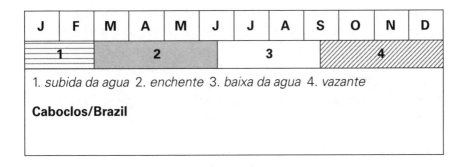

1. *subida da agua* 2. *enchente* 3. *baixa da agua* 4. *vazante*

Caboclos/Brazil

Most languages give each season a unique name, but this feature is not universal. The Rukiga language, spoken by the Bakiga people in several districts in south-western Uganda, has only two words for seasons, *orugazi* or rainy season and *ekyanda* or dry season. However, a year may have more than one of each of these seasons. The Bakiga in Kitumba sub-county of Ndorwa county, Kabale district, recognize two rainy seasons of each year, roughly of equal length: the first runs from late September through December and the second from March through May. Both of these rainy seasons are long enough to permit a full agricultural cycle from field preparation and planting through weeding to harvesting. They have two dry seasons as well; the first includes the months of June, July, and August, as well as the first part of September. The second occurs in January and February. When they wish to distinguish between the first and second rains, they can call them first rainy season, *orugazi orwokubanza¸* and second rainy season, *orugazi orwakabiri*.

However, they more frequently refer to the seasons in sequence, speaking of the current rainy season, the previous rainy season, and the rainy season that will come next, rather than by the terms for first and second rainy season. Similarly, they sometimes use ordinal numbers to distinguish between the first dry season and the second dry season, *ekyanda eky'okubanza* and *ekyanda ekyakabairi*. However, if they wish to speak specifically of the second dry season, they are more likely to use the term *echanda*, which is the diminutive for *ekyanda*.

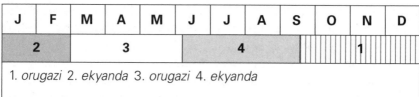

1. *orugazi* 2. *ekyanda* 3. *orugazi* 4. *ekyanda*

Bakiga/Uganda (Kitumba sub-county)

The Bakiga in Rubaya sub-county of the same county and district, about 25 kilometers to the southwest, use these words *orugazi* and *ekyanda* differently. Their lands lie at a higher elevation, about 2,100 meters rather than 1,800 meters, and are somewhat closer to the moist Congo basin. The first rains start about one month earlier, in August rather than in September, and the second rains end one month later, in June rather than May. More importantly, these Bakiga do not speak of an *ekyanda*, a dry season, that occurs between these two rainy seasons; the second follows immediately after the first. The one *ekyanda* that they name is the one in July and August. In other words, the Bakiga in Kitumba, when asked to list the seasons of the year in order, would state the equivalent of 'rainy season, dry season, rainy season, dry season,' and those in Rubaya would say 'rainy season, rainy season, dry season'. They note that the two rainy seasons correspond to the two crops that they raise during the ten months or so of rain.

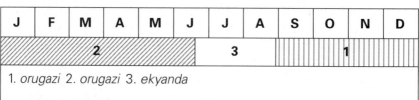

1. *orugazi* 2. *orugazi* 3. *ekyanda*

Bakiga/Uganda (Rubaya sub-county)

It may also be noted that there is some range in the number of seasons, as illustrated in the table below. Since these cases form only a small sub-sample of all seasonal systems, it would be premature to describe trends. Some tendencies may reflect the sampling; for example, four of the six cases that register six seasons are of Australian languages. Still, it is striking how few cases there are of an odd number of seasons.

number of seasons	*number of cases*
2	9
3	3
4	8
5	2
6	6

Within any particular case, the seasons may be about the same length, or of varying lengths. To construct a rough measure of the variability of length of seasons, one may divide the length of longest season by the length of the shortest season. If the seasons are all equal, this ratio equals 1. The case of the seasons of least equal length is that of a Bedouin group in Libya, illustrated below. Their system starts with *ishta* in September or October, when the first rains fall and temperatures drop; it runs until February. The second season, *luwaiya*, begins in March and continues into May. It is the time of drying pastures and ripening grain. The third season, *saif*, extends from May into August or September. It is the time of great heat and dryness. The ratio in this case is 3:1. Though this figure should not be taken as a precise measure, since the length of seasons cannot be pinned down precisely, it does suggest the great range of the length of seasons. The short *luwaiya* is a time of specific activities – the harvest of grain and the movement away from the pastures of the long cold wet season.

J	F	M	A	M	J	J	A	S	O	N	D
1		2			3				1		

1. *ishta* 2. *luwaiya* 3. *saif*

Bedouin/Libya

The final characteristic of seasonal terminology that may be noted is that there are cases of local or regional variation within particular languages. This pattern has already been noted for the Bakiga in Uganda, but is not unique to them. The system of seasons that was recorded for a Bedouin group in Saudi Arabia differs from the Libyan case. They also start counting, with a season of falling temperatures and rain, *al-asferi*, which runs from mid-September to December or early January. It is also followed by a drier time, a season with less rain, *ash-shita*, from late December or mid-January to March. The third season, bearing a similar name, *as-seif*, is a time of rising temperatures, when plants wither. Hot sandstorms come in this season. These Bedouin count a fourth season, *al-gaidh*, which means 'halting' in Arabic. This is the hottest season, a time in which the temperatures, in this portion of Saudi Arabia, exceed those of Libya.

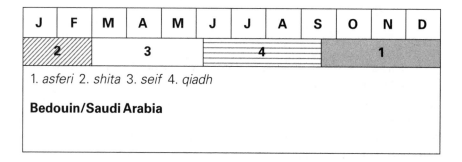

1. *asferi* 2. *shita* 3. *seif* 4. *qiadh*

Bedouin/Saudi Arabia

In sum, the tendency to name seasons seems a widespread characteristic. Seasonal names vary considerably. It is hoped that a widening of the database, and a closer inspection of particular languages, will provide further understanding of this matter. It might be possible to explore the relative weight of the intellectualist and utilitarian accounts of systems of classification that Berlin discussed for the case of ethnobiology. As the first approach suggests, humans display an attentiveness to the natural world, and note its features and rhythms. And, as the second approach indicates, humans name the things that they need to speak about to conduct their daily lives. To this second approach, the case of seasons might add what could be termed a conversational or discursive aspect: to speak of seasons is to stress a temporal dimension of human activity and experience. To recall the weather conditions of the past and to anticipate them in the future, humans must be able to call upon the names of seasons.

Notes

1. Source: International Research Institute for Climate Prediction data library, Columbia University: http: //iridl.ldeo.columbia.edu/
2. I would like to thank Cralan Deutsch, Jules Keane, Aaron Petty and Renn Schnute, the research assistants who compiled the cases. Petty's interests in Melanesia and Australia are reflected in the cases from these areas.

References

BERLIN, BRENT. 1992. *Ethnobiological Classification: Principles of Categorization of Plants and Animals in Traditional Societies*. Princeton: Princeton University Press.

BERLIN, BRENT and PAUL KAY. 1969. *Basic Color Terms: Their Universality and Evolution*. Berkeley and London: The University of California Press.

DURKHEIM, EMILE. 1995. *The Elementary Forms of Religious Life*. Translated by Karen E. Fields. New York: Free Press.

GRINKER, ROY RICHARD. 1994. *Houses in the Rainforest: Ethnicity and Inequality Among Farmers and Foragers in Central Africa*. Berkeley: The University of California Press.

ORLOVE, BENJAMIN S. 1993. Putting race in its place: order in colonial and post-colonial Peruvian geography. *Social Research* 60: 301–336.

ORLOVE, BENJAMIN S., JOHN C. H. CHIANG, and MARK A. CANE. 2000. Forecasting Andean Rainfall and Crop Yield From the Influence of El Niño on Pleiades Visibility. *Nature* 403: 68–71.

—— 2002. Ethnoclimatology in the Andes. *American Scientist* 90: 428–435.

PELUSO, NANCY LEE. 1992. *Rich Forests, Poor People: Resource Control and Resistance in Java*. Berkeley: The University of California Press.

SAHLINS, PETER. 1994. *Forest Rites: The War of the Demoiselles in Nineteenth Century France*. Cambridge: Harvard University Press.

SCHIEFFELIN, BAMBI B. 2002. Marking Time: The Dichotomizing Discourse of Multiple Temporalities. *Current Anthropology* 43(S): 5–17.

ZIMMERMANN, FRANCIS. 1987. *The Jungle and the Aroma of Meats: An Ecological Theme in Hindu Medicine*. Berkeley: The University of California Press.

Appendix 7.1: Case Studies

Cases	Language	Ethnic group	Country	Latitude	Longitude
Case 1	Arabic	Bedouin	Libya	32° 30' N	22° E
Case 2	Gunwinggu	Gunei	Australia	12° 20' S	133° 35' E
Case 3	Etolo	Etolo	Papua New Guinea	6° S	142° E
Case 4	Awa	Ilaka Awa	Papua New Guinea	6° 10' S	145° 20' E
Case 5	Kodi	Kodi	Indonesia	9° 48' S	119° 5' E
Case 6	Gunwinggu	Gunwinggu	Australia	12° 28' S	134° 10' E
Case 7	Gundjeihmi	Gundjeihmi	Australia	15° 30' S	129° 30' E
Case 8	Lau	Lau	Fiji	18° 40' S	178° 50' W
Case 9	Aymara	Aymara	Peru/Bolivia	17° S	69° W
Case 10	Aymara	Aymara	Bolivia	17° S	68° W
Case 11	Dogon	Dogon	Mali	14° 20' N	3° 30' W
Case 12	Lifu	Lifuan	New Caledonia	20° 75' S	167° 20' E
Case 13	Saami	Saami	Norway	69° N	23° 10' E
Case 14	Portuguese	Caboclos	Brazil	1° 75' S	55° 37' W
Case 15	Rukiga	Bakiga	Uganda	1° 20' S	30° 10' E
Case 16	Yup'ik	Yup'ik Inuit	United States	61° N	162° 30' W
Case 17	Arabic	Bedouin	Saudi Arabia	20° N	50° E
Case 18	Kaluli	Bosavi kalu	Papua New Guinea	6° 22' S	142° 40' E
Case 19	Nuer	Nuer	Sudan	9° N	31° E
Case 20	Bororo	Bororo	Brazil	20° S	54° W
Case 21	Somali	Somali	Somalia	10° N	45° E
Case 22	Wik-Mungkan	Wik-Mungkan	Australia	18° S	14° 20' E
Case 23	Walabunnba	Walabunnba	Australia	20° S	133° E
Case 24	Yanyuwa	Yanyuwa	Australia	16° S	136° E
Case 25	Songola	Songola	Dem. Repub. Congo	2°S	26° E
Case 26	Jawoyn	Jawoyn	Australia	15°S	133° E
Case 27	Bwari	Bwari	Dem. Repub. Congo	3°S	30° E
Case 28	Swahili	Shirazi	Tanzania	6°S	39°30' E

Appendix 7.2: Ethnoclimatology database

Each record contains data for the following variables or fields.

1. language
   e.g. Rukiga
2. dialect
3. ethnic group
   e.g. Bakiga
4. country
   e.g. Uganda

5. place name
   e.g. Kitumba county, Kabale district
6. latitude
   e.g. 1° 20' S
7. longitude
   e.g. 30° 10' E
8. elevation
   e.g. 1800'
9. author of article
   e.g. Ben Orlove and Ronald Kabugo
10. first year of study
    e.g. 2001
11. last year of study
    e.g. 2001
12. number of seasons
    e.g. 4
13. existence of weather lore experts
    e.g. no

(numbers 14 through 29 are repeated in each record for every season, with a maximum of seven seasons)

14. season name
    e.g. *ekyanda*
15. beginning month *(the earliest month the season normally begins in)*
    e.g. June
16. time in beginning month *(the time in the month when the season normally begins, i.e. early, mid or late)*
17. second beginning month *(the latest month the season normally begins in)*
18. time in the second month *(i.e. early, mid or late)*
19. ending month *(the earliest month the season normally ends in)*
    e.g. September
20. time in ending month *(i.e. early, mid or late)*
    e.g. mid
21. second ending month *(the latest month the season normally ends in)*
22. time in second ending month *(i.e. early, mid or late)*
23. attributes *(characteristics of the season)*
    e.g. dry season
24. indicator type *(classification of the characteristics that indicate that the season has started, i.e. astronomical, atmospheric, botanical, hydrologic or zoological)*
    e.g. botanical

25. indicator description
    e.g. flowering of yellow flower
26. predictor type *(classification of the characteristics that are used to predict the characteristics of the upcoming season i.e. astronomical, atmospheric, botanical or other)*
    e.g. botanical
27. predictor description
    e.g. coffee trees flower
28. predicted outcome *(what the predictor effects)*
    e.g. precipitation in season 2
29. outcome effect *(the type of change predicted)*
    e.g. greater

(numbers 30 through 41 are repeated in each record for every sub-season, with a maximum of three sub-seasons)

30. subseason
31. subseason beginning month *(the month during which the subseason generally begins)*
32. time in beginning month *(i.e. early, mid or late)*
33. subseason ending month *(the month during which the subseason generally ends)*
34. time in subseason ending month *(i.e. early, mid or late)*
35. subseason attributes
36. subseason indicator type
37. subseason indicator description
38. predictor type
39. predictor description
40. predicted outcome
41. outcome effect
42. notes

–8–

Monet's 'London Series' and the Cultural Climate of London at the Turn of the Twentieth Century

John E. Thornes and *Gemma Metherell*

Over the last few years there has been a growing interest in the environmental and social history of air pollution sparked by the topical concerns of climate change and the sustainability of the air that we breathe. Smoke pollution and the permanent smoke haze that enveloped the Victorian cities of Britain not only ruined people's health through rickets, bronchitis, pneumonia and asthma, it also altered the climate, reducing sunshine and increasing the number and severity of fog episodes. Climate change in the nineteenth century was far more dramatic and visual than it is today as smoke blotted out the sky and gave the air a filthy smell and taste. The horrors of smoke pollution, and the growth of legislation to try and deal with it, have been well documented not just in Britain (Brimblecombe 1988; Mosley 2001; Luckin 2002) but also in Germany (Brüggemeier 1994) and the United States (Stradling 1999).

The critical examination of the dialectic between air pollution and society is well under way therefore and the broader links between weather and climate and society are also beginning to take shape (Janković 2000; Hamblyn 2001). Indeed the term cultural climatology has been suggested very recently (Thornes and McGregor 2003) to encourage this new approach.[1] One aspect of cultural climatology that has been around somewhat longer concerns the representation and deconstruction of weather, climate and air pollution in art (Thornes 1979, 1999; Brimblecombe 2000; Brimblecombe and Ogden 1977; Gedzelman 1991) and the recognition of the symbolism of atmospheric effects. Bonacina (1939: 485) defined 'landscape meteorology' to be 'those scenic influences of sky, atmosphere, weather and climate which form part of our natural human environment . . . whether the natural scenery is merely received and carefully stored in the memory, or is photographed, painted or described'. This chapter is concerned with the relationship between the climate of London and the French artist Monet at the turn of the twentieth century. Monet's 'London Series' will be deconstructed in the light of contemporary weather, climate, and culture. Do Monet's images of London at this time represent reality or are they figments of the artist's imagination or a combination of the two? The distinction between art and nature is never clear. The term 'Realism' was coined in France with respect to the French artist Gustave Courbet (1819–77), who produced 'The Realist Manifesto' in 1855 (Nochlin 1966). Baudelaire stated that the Realists 'Want to represent things as they are, or as they would be, supposing that I (the perceiving subject) did not exist' (quoted in Rubin 1996: 53). However Realism in art developed beyond just a representation of real and existing things, it became a movement to overturn the established view of art and paved the way for the Impressionist movement by hastening the departure of the hitherto dominant 'classical' school. Realism attempted 'to create objective representations of the external world based on the impartial observation of contemporary life' (Rubin 1996: 53). Realists could therefore paint their own vision of nature, although their observations were rarely impartial and the movement became closely associated with wider socio-political views. As a result the term 'Naturalism' arose to describe art without a particular socio-political significance. In its broadest sense, Naturalism refers to any work of art that depicts actual rather than imaginary or exaggerated subject matter. The subject that is represented by the artist is done as naturalistically as possible, without deliberate idealization or stylization. In England we would describe Turner as a realist and Constable as a naturalist despite the fact that both artists had died well before the terms were defined. Turner strove to incorporate his own emotions and ideas into his art whereas Constable found his art under every hedge and within every cloud. Can Monet best be described as an exponent of realism or of naturalism, or of both?

English weather has always attracted the attention of artists due to its transitory nature which constantly challenges their ability to catch the 'atmosphere' on canvas.[2] As the weather and climate of England have changed over the centuries, so this is reflected in the art of the times, which offer unique visual 'weather diaries' of transition. Lamb (1967) and Neuberger (1970) have shown,[3] by examining landscape paintings from around the world, that artists have faithfully reproduced the changes of climate, for example the 'Little Ice Age', in their works. Obviously, one has to be aware that artists may freely use their 'artistic license' to exaggerate and invent, and this makes their study even more fascinating as we attempt to unravel the embedded culture as well as the realities of the weather and climate in their paintings. Pevsner (1955: 20) in his classic book *The Englishness of English Art* suggests that although the English loved to complain about the weather at that time, they did nothing about it: 'Perhaps this staunch conservatism in the teeth of the greatest discomforts is English?'[4] The 'stiff upper lip' and indifference to the domestic and industrial pollution in England suggested that the London fog did not exist. The London Particular was ignored by all except the patrons of the arts: 'At present, people see fogs, not because there are fogs, but because poets and painters have taught them the mysterious loveliness of such effects. There may have been fogs for centuries in London. But . . . They did not exist till Art had invented them' (Wilde 1889: 925).[5]

It is to the foreign visitors that we owe the description of the changes of the English climate as the smoke and the fog combined in increasing quantities as the nineteenth century progressed. For example, Monet's fascination with the London fog is represented in his 'London Series'. His ninety-five paintings of 'The Big Smoke' are deconstructed using a version of content analysis and by examining Rose's (2000) sites of production, sites of the images themselves, and sites of audiencing.[6] It is ironic that we must turn to a Frenchman for the visual representation of the London Particular and that none of Monet's 'London Series' are on permanent display in London galleries today. Perhaps the English do not want to be reminded that 'Hell is a city much like London – a populous and a smoky place'.[7]

The climate and culture of London at the end of the nineteenth century represent a fascinating enigma. London was the imperial metropolis of the world and the capital of a British Empire serving 400 million people, the biggest empire the planet had yet seen (Schneer 1999). London invented culture and then exported it to the rest of the world. However there was a hefty price to pay for all this power, industrial production and trade. London invented the 'urban climate' (Howard 1818) and was the most polluted city in the world. It had become affectionately known around the globe as 'The Big Smoke' and the word smog (a combination of smoke and fog) was first coined in 1905 with reference to London fog. Unfortunately, London could not export its smog to some distant colony and Londoners and the many visitors had to live with it. Ruskin (1884) in 'Storm Cloud of the Nineteenth Century' notes his diary entry for Tuesday February 20, 1872:

> There has been so much black east wind lately, and so much fog and artificial gloom, besides, that I find it is actually some two years since I last saw a noble cumulus cloud under full light. I chanced to be standing under the Victoria Tower at Westminster, when the largest mass of them floated past . . . and I was more impressed than ever yet by the awfulness of the cloud-form, and its unaccountableness, in the present state of our knowledge. The Victoria Tower, seen against it, had no magnitude: it was like looking at Mount Blanc over a lamp-post.
>
> (40)

Ruskin was convinced that he had discovered a new meteorological phenomenon to go with the fog: 'This wind is the plague-wind of the eighth decade of years in the nineteenth century; a period that will assuredly be recognized in future meteorological history as one of phenomena hitherto unrecorded in the courses of nature' (43). This plague-wind looks partly as if it were made of poisonous smoke; very possibly it may be: there are at least two hundred furnace chimneys in a square of two miles on every side of me. But mere smoke would not blow to and fro in that wild way. It looks more to me as if it were made of dead men's souls- . . .

(47)

Ruskin's claim that he had discovered a new type of 'plague' wind and 'storm' cloud was of course a myth – Athena raped by political economy (Cosgrove and Thornes 1981). Ruskin was harking back to the pre-modernist days when meteorology was concerned with classical 'meteoric reportage' – when the atmosphere was totally 'unaccountable' and unique. Also the skies had been richly coloured in 1883 by the eruption of the volcano Krakatoa.

Janković (2000) suggests that the end of classical meteorology was marked, between 1794 and 1803, by the acceptance of 'the cosmic origins of meteoric stones'. Fireballs were finally recognized to be of extraterrestrial origin and not ignited terrestrial vapours. Aristotle's *Meteorologica* as the source of wisdom was finally put to rest and meteorology could also cease to exist – as the study of meteors was left to astronomers. The study of the atmosphere was passed to chemistry – and meteorology – a classical discipline – was moved under the heading of 'chemical philosophy', along with chemistry and geology, in the journal *Philosophical Transactions*. The atmosphere was then considered to be a vast chemical laboratory, which suited the growth of laboratory science at the beginning of the nineteenth century.

Janković states that in the seventeenth and eighteenth centuries, 'English air was the cause of the mutability of English thought and thus the source of national characteristics such as newfangledness, rashness and love of rebellion' (2000: 3).

The dominant form of engagement with the weather was the reporting of *unusual* weather events at specific places – meteoric reportage. 'Meteoric' in the classical sense could include any unusual weather events such as storms, earthquakes, fireballs, waterspouts, flying dragons, or northern lights. 'Meteoric' captures the unusual discrete meteorological events that are separated by 'anonymous' interludes of atmospheric tranquility.

This pre-1800 meteorology was a far cry from the content of modern and postmodern meteorology. The history of meteorology at this time was intimately linked to bodily pain, death, financial loss and dream-mongering and the early modern clergy explained such events in terms of divine intervention, sin, and the devil. Meteoric events were publicized in pamphlets, almanacs, broadsheets, ballads, poetry, newspapers, drama, oral culture and even in the scientific journals of the time. Meteorology was about the unique, the unexplainable, the astonishing and was completely unfathomable.

How could a science of the weather be constructed amongst such unique events? Janković (2000: 4) points out that such grand meteorological phenomena were considered privileged philosophical 'facts' because according to Bacon 'nature spoke more clearly when it sported itself in the "out of the ordinary"'. The inductive collection of unusual events in an area was considered to lead to a better understanding through encouraging networks and exchanges of information.

Those individuals who networked and exchanged information were mostly Anglican clergymen and members of the gentry – working out in the country well away from the laboratories and observatories of London. The London antiquarian Roger Gale, having received some letters from provincial correspondents, wrote: 'who could have expected such a learned correspondence and so many curious observations . . . made by a set of virtuosi almost out of the world!' (quoted in Janković 2000: 6).

Ruskin could not accept that science would ever explain how the atmosphere worked, especially as the success of astronomers in predicting future events such as eclipses was not mirrored by the meteorologists. Certainly there was no evidence of success in forecasting the onset of London Particulars. The modernist view that the behaviour of the atmosphere was predictable did not make significant strides until the beginning of the twentieth century when Bjerknes in Norway led the way for Richardson (1922) in England to publish *Weather Prediction by Numerical Process.*

Victorian London fog (the London Particular or London Peasouper) was probably the most famous global meteorological phenomenon of the nineteenth and twentieth centuries. This cultural enigma was a symbol of power, mystery and prosperity that defied the truth of the smoke-poisoned lungs and badly bowed limbs due to rickets, caused by the lack of light, that afflicted tens of thousands of Londoners at any one time.

In the Victorian winter a million coal fires mixed smoke and sulphur dioxide with the industrial outpourings of a myriad of chimneys, furnaces, processing plants, railway engines, steam-driven barges and boats on the Thames, to produce a London Particular more than 200 feet (60 meters) thick. In 1873 it was noted that over 3 days in December there were up to 700 extra deaths, 19 of them as a result of people walking into the Thames, docks, or the canals and drowning (Brimble-combe 1988: 123).

Coal was first brought to London in appreciable quantities from Newcastle in the early thirteenth century, being used as ballast for boats returning from Tyneside to London. By 1620 it was estimated that 100,000 tonnes per year were being imported and as supplies of wood dwindled so the sales of 'sea-coal' continued to rise. The first serious indictment against the deleterious effects of smoke from the running of sea-coal came in 1661 from John Evelyn in *Fumifugium*:

> That this Glorious and Ancient City . . . should wrap her stately head in clouds of smoke and sulphur, so full of stink and darkness, I deplore with just Indignation.

> . . . the City of London resembles the face rather of Mount Etna, the Court of Vulcan, Stromboli or the suburbs of Hell, than an Assembly of Rational Creatures.

The adverse effect of smoke mixed with accompanying sulphur dioxide was also noted by Evelyn:

> For is there under Heaven such coughing and sniffing to be heard, as in the London churches and Assemblies of the People, where the barking and the spitting is most importunate.

> . . . but the chance for life in infants, who are confined in the present Foul Air of London, is so small, that it is highly prudent and commendable to remove them from it as early as possible.

John Evelyn was a cultural climatologist centuries ahead of his time. He suggested moving industries downwind of the city and planting gardens along the Thames. His ideas were ignored and coal fired the industrial revolution in London and became the domestic fuel for all classes of society. By the middle of the eighteenth century a perpetual mist or fog enveloped London in winter and those sepia faded-looking photographs of London in the second half of the nineteenth century, show the perpetual mist not a fading photograph. In the summer months the sun did break through and the mist was temporarily lifted. On September 3, 1802 Wordsworth wrote his poem *Composed Upon Westminster Bridge* in which he notes:

> Ships, towers, domes, theatres and temples lie
> Open unto the fields, and to the sky;
> All bright and glittering in the smokeless air.

London was not oblivious to the smoke and fog. In 1819 a committee was appointed by Parliament to inquire 'how far persons using steam engines and furnaces could erect them in a manner less prejudicial to public health'. In 1853–56 the Smoke Abatement Acts came into force relating to Metropolitan areas, but the impact on smoke levels was probably more imagined than real. In 1858 and 1866 the Sanitation Acts authorized sanitary authorities to take action against smoke nuisance, but legislation did not seem to work. Smoke levels and the frequency of fogs continued to rise.

The relationship between smoke and fog was still not completely understood. There had always been fogs along the Thames in London and as the number increased, so people thought that they were obviously caused by the increasing smoke. There were no observations of smoke levels and meteorological observations recorded fogs but not their cause. The first serious study of the increase in fogs, based on proper observations rather than on conjecture, was published by Brodie (1892). He showed that there had been a steady increase in the prevalence of fog in London between 1870 and 1890.

However in 1905 he published a further article (Brodie 1905: 15) stating: 'In the 13 years which have since elapsed the tendency has been so strongly in the opposite direction that little apology is needed for bringing the subject once more before the notice of the society.'

The fog frequency was recorded at the Meteorological Office's official London site in Brixton, and data were presented for the years between 1871 and 1903. The highest total of 86 was recorded in 1886 and the lowest was just 13 in 1900, with a mean of 55. Brodie suggests a number of reasons as to why the fog levels had fallen, including the success of the Coal Smoke Abatement Society; modern grates and stoves that were more efficient at burning the smoke; the introduction of incandescent gas and electric lights; and the increasing use of gas stoves for heating and cooking.

Brodie's paper caused quite a stir at the meeting of the Royal Meteorological Society at which it was presented. The discussion was held over to the next meeting, allowing the Fellows to prepare some statistics of their own. Mr Marriot said that Mr Brodie needed to define what he meant by a fog. He assumed that Mr Brodie's data related to what was popularly called 'London Fog' and not to ordinary meteorological fogs. Mr Marriot presented his own findings in comparison for days of fog at West Norwood some 3 miles from Brixton as shown in Figure 8.1. The fog frequency for the 26 years of comparison averages 57 days at

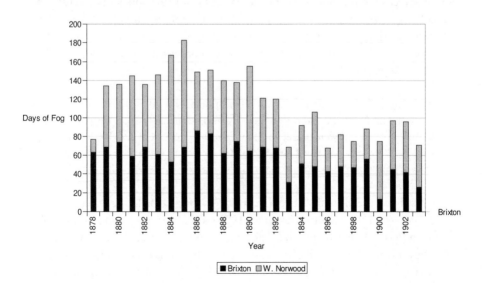

Figure 8.1 Days with fog in London at Brixton and West Norwood, 1878–1903.

Brixton and 116 days at West Norwood. Although it is clear that visibility varied enormously across London these discrepancies are more likely to be due to differing definitions of what constitutes a fog. The two series are correlated (r = 0.72) and both show a steep decline starting in 1893.

The modern definition of fog used by today's meteorological observers is based on visibility in meters and distinguishes between Dense Fog < 40 m; Thick fog 40m–200m; Fog 200m–1000m and Mist 1000m–2000m. It is not clear what definition of fog was used by the Meteorological Council in Brixton or by Mr Marriot in West Norwood.

During the winter of 1901/2 'The London Fog Inquiry' was carried out by the Meteorological Council funded by a grant of £250 from the County Council of London (Shaw 1901). Gaslights were gradually yielding to electric lights and the new owners of the electricity generators were frustrated by unexpected fluctuations in demand due to the changing daylight as the fogs displayed remarkable spatial variation. One house would be in darkness whilst the sun shone upon another across the street. It was estimated that during fogs more than £10,000 a day was being spent on additional lighting in daylight hours. The Fog Inquiry was not set up to research methods of getting rid of the fog but to see if its formation and movements could be forecast up to an hour in advance (Bernstein 1975).

Captain Carpenter was hired to carry out the inquiry and quickly established an observing network of 30 fire stations throughout the County of London. Daily sheets were to be completed and a definition of surface fog was agreed: Light Fog – not sufficient to require artificial light in the daytime; Moderate Fog – when ordinary gas lamps, though visible at 60 yards, are invisible at 440 yards; and Thick Fog – in which street gas lamps are invisible at 60 yards or less. This definition led to problems, however, as several of the fire stations were in narrow streets where there was no clear view. A new, more practical definition was then derived (Bernstein 1975: 199):

> Thin Fog or Mist was defined as visibility of objects at 200 yards or more, slightly hindering traffic by rail and river but not by road. Moderately Thick Fog was taken to mean that observers were unable to discern a man by day more than 100 yards away, a house at 200 yards, or a street light by night at 440 yards. Dense Fog meant inability to discern objects across the road by day or lights of street lamps 60 yards distant by night.

This shows the difficulty of getting observers to agree on the occurrence of fog. The findings of the Inquiry (Carpenter 1903) were broadly as follows. First, the London fogs were locally generated and not imported from the Essex marshes, nor did they travel up or down the Thames. Second, there was some evidence that fogs formed in some areas before others and that the fogs moved, but no regular pattern of movement was found. Third, in winter light fogs, largely caused by smoke, were permanent in parts of London and the best visibility in London was no more than 1½ miles.

> The contamination of the air by smoke has been very forcibly brought to my notice by the ascents of Victoria Tower and of St. Paul's. In the 10 ascents made as yet, none of which were made during fogs, and several of which were made on days of great visibility in the country, the visibility has ranged from ½ mile to 1¼ miles only. St. Paul's has not yet been seen from Westminster nor Westminster from St. Paul's, although their distance apart is but 1½ miles.
>
> (MPMC 1902: 114)

Fourth, if the minimum temperature was above about 42 degrees Fahrenheit then fogs were unlikely to form. Fifth, if the wind speed was above 13 miles per hour then the fog dispersed. These results were interesting but did not suggest a way of forecasting the fog accurately. The Meteorological Council decided to extend the survey for another winter, at their own expense, but the results did not lead to any prospect of prediction. It is ironic that the first scientific study of the London fog should take place at a time when the fog frequency was declining for the first time in several hundred years.

The London fog was making its mark in other areas, particularly in literature, and its description included other features apart from the poor visibility. For example the fog could take on a variety of colours according to the time of day and the thickness of the fog. Ackroyd (2000: 432) gives a useful list from a variety of sources:

> There was a black species, 'simply darkness complete and intense at mid day'; bottle green; a variety as yellow as pea-soup, which stopped all the traffic and 'seems to choke you'; 'a rich lurid brown, like the light of some strange conflagration'; simply grey; 'orange-coloured vapour'; a 'dark chocolate-coloured pall'.

The Particular became a source of vivid literary description such as Benson (1905):

> A sudden draught apparently had swept across the sky, and where before the thick black curtain had been opaquely stretched, there came sudden rents and illuminations. Swirls of orange-coloured vapour were momentarily mixed with the black, as if the celestial artist was trying the effects of some mixing of colours on his sky palate, and through these gigantic rents there suddenly appeared, like the spars of wrecked vessels, the chimneys of the houses opposite. Then the rents would be patched up again, and the dark chocolate-coloured pall swallowed up the momentary glimpse. But the commotion among the battling vapours grew ever more intense: blackness returned to one quarter, but in another all shades from deepest orange to the pale grey of dawn succeeded one another.
>
> (quoted in Brimblecombe 1988: 125)

Brimblecombe (1988: 125) suggests that the fine smoke particles in the atmosphere filtered out the blue wavelengths of the sunlight above the fog in such a way that the ground was illuminated by yellow and orange light and occasionally green. At night the fog appeared yellow due to the yellow light of the gas lamps and glare from shop windows.

The fogs were sometimes accompanied by oily, tarry, yellow deposits as noted by Conan Doyle in the Sherlock Holmes story 'The Adventure of the Bruce-Partington Plans' set in November 1895: 'We saw the greasy heavy brown swirl still drifting past us and condensing into oily drops upon the window panes' (Doyle 2002: 390).

The London fog had became an integral character of Victorian fiction. It became a metaphor that embodied confusion, foreboding, and uncertainty about the future. Several stories such as Robert Barr's 'The Doom of London', published in *The Idler* in 1892, predicted that the Metropolis would be wiped out by asphyxiation in an everlasting fog. Ruskin's non-fiction confirmed such gloom and openly declared that the fog was God's punishment. Wheeler (1995: 166) points out that Ruskin's apocalyptic view refers to the last book in the Bible 'in which the world is brought to judgement and the glory of God is uncovered in the last days'. Perhaps the greatest novel that hinges on the London Particular is *The Strange Case of Dr Jekyll and Mr Hyde* by Robert Louis Stevenson published in 1886.

Not all writers agreed, however, that the fog was evil. For example, Dziewicki (1902) wrote a chapter in a book on London by 'Famous Writers' entitled 'In Praise of London Fog'. To some foreign visitors the fog was a definite winter tourist attraction and made London seem more immense and unique than ever.

Of course the fog appealed to artists. Turner was the first great artist to paint London fogs and the term 'phantasmagoria' was totally appropriate in relation to his skies (Thornes 1999). The famous image of Maidenhead Bridge over the Thames, *Rain, Steam and Speed* (1844), shows how the smoke from the railway engine is blended into the opaque atmosphere.

Whistler, an American artist living in London, also loved the London atmosphere. His *Nocturnes* utilized the night-time fog to give an eerie light and color to the scenes. Chaleyssin (1995: 41) suggests that 'The *Nocturnes* force the viewer to try and enter into the picture, to penetrate the fog'. *Nocturne in Black and Gold: The Falling Rocket* (1875) was criticized by Ruskin in his magazine *Fors Clavigera* (Letter 79: 11): 'I have seen and heard much of cockney impudence before now, but never expected to hear a coxcomb ask two hundred guineas for flinging a pot of paint in the public's face.'

Whistler was outraged and sued Ruskin for libel. The libel action opened on November 25, 1878 and lasted for two days. Ruskin was too ill to attend, but witnesses included Rossetti and Edward Burne-Jones. The jury awarded in Whistler's favor the symbolic damages of one farthing but no costs, which soon bankrupted him.

Whistler was a great friend of Monet's and introduced him to the Savoy Hotel with its superb accommodation and wonderful views of the Thames (Shanes 1994). Monet was obsessed with the weather and its changing moods. He has immortalized the London fogs, not only in his 'London Series' but also in his letters (Kendall 1989):

> I so love London! But I love it only in the winter. It's nice in the summer with the parks, but nothing like it is in the winter with the fog, for without the fog London wouldn't be a beautiful city . . .
>
> (quoted in Shanes 1994: 130)

> I love London . . . I adore London. But what I love more than anything . . . is the fog.
>
> (quoted in Shanes 1994: 114)

> The Thames was all gold. God it was so beautiful . . . I began to work in a frenzy, following the sun and it's reflections on the water.
>
> (quoted in Kendall 1989: 191)

Monet first visited London during 1870–71 as an exile from the Franco-Prussian war. During that time he painted three views of the Thames cloaked in winter fog, including *The Thames and the Houses of Parliament*.[8] These foggy views of the Thames were a precursor of the smoke-laden *Impression, Sunrise* (1873), a view of the Seine at Le Havre, from which the word Impressionism was derived. Monet was determined to return to London in the 1890s to embark upon a 'London Series'. He had already completed a number of other 'series' such as the Grainstacks, the Poplars near Giverny, Rouen Cathedral and Mornings on the Seine. Why he chose to go to London and paint bridges, factory chimneys, and railway engine smoke after such blissful rural series is open to debate. Monet was resolute that he would make his mark in England and produce a series that would rank him alongside Turner as one of the greatest landscape painters.[9] Monet also respected the English and London and the political stability that the Houses of Parliament represented at a time of political turmoil in France. In the middle of September 1899, Monet arrived in London on holiday with his wife and her daughter Germaine to visit his son Michel who was in London to improve his English. He took a suite on the sixth floor of the Savoy Hotel, on the north bank, with a balcony overlooking the river. Below him to the east was Waterloo Bridge and to the south Charing Cross Bridge. The Houses of Parliament were just a kilometer to the south. From his room he could see the sun rise over Waterloo Bridge and by midday the sun would be fully illuminating the Thames from the south, silhouetting Charing Cross Bridge.

During this visit Monet painted exclusively Charing Cross Bridge with the Houses of Parliament in the background. The winter fog set in during October 1899 and the weather observations recorded at 8 a.m. at Brixton show that there were fourteen mornings when fog or mist was recorded (7th–11th and 17th–25th) and on the October 17 Monet wrote that he was 'trying to do a few views of the Thames.' He was entranced with the images before him and although he left London in early November he was determined to return as soon as possible. He went back to France with at least eleven canvases, all of which he was still working on.

He returned to London alone, in the middle of February 1900 and embarked upon his major London campaign, this time from the fifth floor of the Savoy. He began work on the 11th February and his working habits are well documented in the many letters he sent home to his wife.[10] He tried to stick to a strict daily routine working on Waterloo Bridge in the early morning as the sun moved around from the southeast. Then he moved on to Charing Cross Bridge for the midday and early afternoon sun. Then he would pack up his things and move to a small balcony at St Thomas's Hospital opposite the Houses of Parliament to catch the sunset. He would work on a number of canvases each corresponding to a position of the sun in the sky and rapidly progress through them, adding a bit more each day. However, as the weather conditions were different each day it was a struggle to maintain such a demanding schedule.

Wednesday February 14, 1900:
'I had a better day than I expected, I was able to work before and after lunch from my window and at 5, with the sun setting gloriously in the mist, I started work at the hospital.'

(188)

Monday February 26, 1900:
'In the early hours of this morning there was an extraordinary yellow fog; I did an impression of it which I don't think is bad.'

(188)

Friday March 9, 1900:
'as I had predicted, the sun already sets a long way from the place I'd wanted to paint it in an enormous fireball behind the Houses of Parliament; so there must be no further thought of that.'

(189)

Sunday March 18, 1900:
'The only shortage I have is of canvases, since it's the only way to achieve something, get a picture going for every kind of weather, every colour harmony . . . I have something like 65 canvases covered with paint.'

(189)

Monday March 19, 1900:

'it became terribly foggy, so much so that we were in total darkness, and I had to have the lights on until half-past ten; then I thought I'd be able to work but I've never seen such changeable conditions and I had over 15 canvases under way, going from one to the other and back again, and it was never quite right; a few unfortunate brushstrokes and in the end I lost my nerve and in a temper I packed everything away in crates.'

(189)

Wednesday March 28, 1900:

'Just imagine, I'm bringing back . . . eighty canvases'

(190)

Monet returned to France in the first week of April 1900 and didn't return until the end of January 1901 again staying alone on the fifth floor of the Savoy.

Sunday February 3, 1901:

'I can't begin to describe a day as wonderful as this. One marvel after another, each lasting less than five minutes, it was enough to drive one mad. No country could be more extraordinary for a painter.'

(191)

Saturday March 2, 1901:

'The weather's terrible . . . Torrential rain and it's beating so hard on the windowpanes that I can barely see anything at all. Yesterday I was happy and full of energy and was looking forward to a good day; yesterday evening the weather was perfect, but as I've said before, it is not possible to work on the same paintings two days in succession . . .'

(192)

When Monet returned to Giverny at the beginning of April 1901 he had in total more than 100 canvases of the Thames, of which 95 survive today spread around the art galleries of the world. He was far from satisfied with them, however, and he continued to work on them, from memory, over the next few years. This could have created a dilemma for Monet, as the impressionists were only supposed to paint from nature, but the many months immersed in the London atmosphere had given him sufficient experience to finish the pictures in the studio. Just twelve of the 95 surviving pictures are dated at between 1899 and 1901, 57 between 1902 and 1904 and 26 are undated, suggesting that most of those that were dated, were dated when Monet sold them rather than when he painted them. However, it is impossible to say how many of the canvases brought back from London were actually finished and how many Monet painted entirely in Giverny.

On May 9, 1904 an exhibition of thirty-seven London pictures opened in Paris entitled *Séries de vues de la Tamis à Londres (1900–1904)*. There were eight views of Charing Cross Bridge, eighteen of Waterloo Bridge and eleven of the Houses of Parliament. The exhibition was an immediate success and the critics duly declared that Monet's atmospheric renditions of London were equal to those of his hero Turner. It was also a commercial success and Monet sold twenty-three pictures to the gallery owner Durand-Ruel, who sold many of them on to the United States. Monet had planned an exhibition in London in 1903 but it had failed to materialize – otherwise perhaps some of the pictures, rather than none, would be hanging in London galleries today.

We must now ask ourselves how accurate a rendition of London's winter skies 1899–1901 do Monet's paintings provide? Are they accurate impressions or just commercial representations of a popular theme? Monet was asked many times to defend his London and other pictures, especially the range of colors. In January 1905 an article appeared in a French magazine *La Revue Blue* entitled 'La Fin de l'impressionnisme' (The End of Impressionism) and subsequent discussions included a criticism of Monet's Rouen Cathedral paintings which suggested that they had been copied from a photograph. One could hardly suggest that the 'London Series' were copies of photographs, but Monet was not worried and wrote to Paul Durand-Ruel on February 12:

> You are quite wrong to worry about what you tell me, indications of nothing but bad feeling and jealousy which leave me quite cold. I know . . . only Mr Harrison, whom Sargent commissioned to do a small photo of Parliament for my benefit which I was never able to use. But it is hardly of any significance, and whether my Cathedrals and my London paintings and other canvases are done from life or not, is none of anyone's business and is quite unimportant. I know of so many artists who paint from life and produce nothing but terrible work.[11]

There are two aspects of Monet's paintings of London that we can examine for truth: first, the visibility in the pictures; and second, the colors. It has already been stated that the London Fog Inquiry in the winter of 1901/2 showed that the winter visibility in London at that time was never more than about 2 km. The visibility depicted in Monet's Charing Cross Bridge pictures can be gauged by estimating the furthest point clearly visible in the pictures. Figure 8.2 shows the result of this analysis which gives a mean visibility of 1127 m (maximum 2000 m, minimum 600 m).[12] These estimates are taken from photographs of the pictures, but they nevertheless show that Monet's pictures are entirely consistent with contemporary meteorological accounts. He did not paint in dense fogs, as he would not even have been able to see the bridges. The ideal weather was when the sun was breaking through the mist and smoke and the visibility was about 1 km and he could just see the Houses of Parliament in the background. The best visibility of 2000 m is shown in the undated *Charing Cross Bridge, Reflections on the Thames*, now owned by the Baltimore Museum of Art, which clearly shows a visibility beyond the old Lambeth suspension bridge, which was about 1700 m south.

The colours in the pictures are much more difficult to estimate without access to the originals. The range of colours describing the London fogs has already been given and although Monet may have exaggerated what he saw his basic colours are true. When he was asked to list the composition of his 'London Series' palette he replied: 'I use flake white, cadmium yellow, vermillion, deep madder, cobalt blue, emerald green and that's all.'[13]

The colors can be divided between the water, the sky and the bridges and buildings. In many of them the sky is directly reflected in the water and the colour of the whole picture is controlled by the color of the atmosphere. In others the sun is visible, or sunlight bursts through the mist to give islands of color. Like Turner, Monet has portrayed unique moments of color and time. Like Constable, whose skies are so typically English, Monet has also portrayed the general typical winter climate of London at that time, which any Londoner would have instantly recognized.

Monet's 'London Series' was painted at a time when the fog frequency in London was declining, having peaked in the mid-1880s. They serve as a constant reminder of how polluted the city of London was in its glory days as the capital of the world. It was a price that Londoners were prepared to pay and we would have

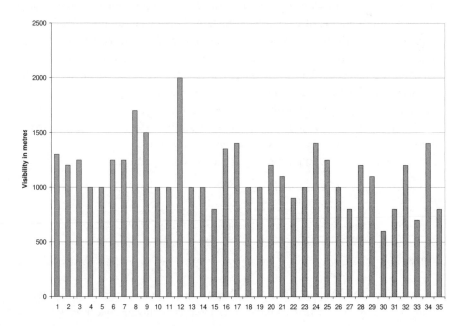

Figure 8.2 Visibility in the 35 Charing Cross Bridge pictures (mean = 1127m).

forgotten about the full glory of the London Particular had it not been for a Frenchman who was obsessed with the weather.

Having discussed in detail the sites of production and sites of the images themselves it remains to briefly consider the sites of audiencing. Of the ninety-five paintings in the 'London Series' forty-one are in private collections, which are occasionally lent to galleries and exhibitions. Of the remaining fifty-four there are twenty-nine in American galleries and the rest are spread around the galleries of the world (France 7, Japan 4, Canada 3, Switzerland 3, Germany 2, Russia 2, Denmark 1, Egypt 1, Ireland 1, and Wales 1). Not one is housed in an English gallery although currently (in 2003) *Houses of Parliament, Sunset*, owned by a Japanese private collector, is on temporary loan at the National Gallery in London. It is as if Londoners do not want to be reminded of their foul polluted past. Of the American galleries The Art Institute of Chicago owns three pictures, one of Charing Cross Bridge, one of Westminster Bridge and one of the Houses of Parliament. It is the only gallery in the world to have a complete sample of the series. The National Gallery of Art in Washington D.C. has four pictures – three of Westminster Bridge and one of the Houses of Parliament. The only other gallery to have three pictures is the Musée Marmottan in Paris – two of Charing Cross Bridge and one of the Houses of Parliament. It is ironic that this remarkable 'London Series', unlike the London Particular, has been exported to the rest of the world.

The deconstruction of Monet's 'London Series' has shown that its paintings are an accurate souvenir of the perils of air pollution in London and as such they are a unique representation of the winter climate of London at that time, combining realism and naturalism. Smoke is a visible reminder of air quality, whereas today many pollutants are invisible but nevertheless just as dangerous if air quality standards are exceeded. The air we breathe is the most valuable resource on earth and we must insure that its quality is sustained. And yet the glorious colors and mystique of Monet's paintings of the London fog awaken a nostalgic yearning that is saddened by its loss. We must content ourselves with the visual images and strive to insure that the air of our cities and countryside is not only protected but also restored to its original composition before the London Particular.

Notes

1. Thornes and McGregor (2003: 178) discuss the concept of cultural climatology as follows: we advocate that climatology should not only be concerned with the study of physical processes at various space and time scales but with evaluating

and understanding climate society interactions and feedbacks as manifest by societal response and how society may interpret climate information. Therefore, we view climate as an integral part of culture and as such we contend that there is a need to develop a sub-discipline within climatology that we will refer to as cultural climatology.

2. The landscape artist Turner (1775–1851) spoke of the advantages of the British climate for landscape artists:

> In our variable climate where [all] the seasons are recognizable in one day, where all the vapoury turbulence involves the face of things, where nature seems to sport in all her dignity and dispensing incidents for the artist's study . . . how happily is the landscape painter situated, how roused by every change in nature in every moment, that allows no languor even in her effects which she places before him, and demands most peremptorily every moment his admiration and investigation, to store his mind with every change of time and place.
>
> (Wilton 1979: 107)

3. Lamb examined 200 Dutch and British paintings from 1550 to 1939. Neuberger examined 12,284 paintings in 41 art museums in 17 cities of 9 countries. He examined directly the weather in the paintings (clouds, visibility, etc.) and indirectly the clothing of the people depicted to give an indication of the season, etc.

4. The first chapter of Pevsner's book is called 'The Geography of Art' in which he gives a 'whole string of facts from art and literature tentatively derived from climate' (Pevsner 1955: 19).

5. Oscar Wilde (1889: 925) suggested that nature imitates art: 'Where, if not from the impressionists, do we get those wonderful brown fogs that come creeping down our streets, blurring the gas lamps and changing the houses into monstrous shadows? . . . The extraordinary change that has taken place in the climate of London during the last ten years is entirely due to a particular school of art.'

6. Rose's book is an excellent introduction to the critical interpretation of visual images. She suggests a methodological framework that involves the examination of the site of production, the site of the image itself, and the site of audiencing. In order to try to understand the different, sometimes controversial, approaches to these aspects, she defines three modalities: (1) technological ('any form of apparatus designed either to be looked at or to enhance natural vision, from oil painting to television and the internet'); (2) compositional ('when an image is made, it draws on a number of formal strategies: content, colour and spatial organization'); (3) social ('the range of economic, social and political relations, institutions and practices that surround an image and through which it is seen and used').

7. Quoted from Shelley (1819).
8. This painting is in the National Gallery, London. To see images of all of Monet's works see Wildenstein (1996).
9. A thorough discussion of the various reasons why Monet undertook the London Series is given by Tucker (1989).
10. The following quotes are taken from Kendall (1989).
11. Kendall (1989: 196).
12. These visibilities have been estimated from the illustrations in Wildenstein (1996). This exercise would have been conducted with the real paintings but they are not accessible in sufficient numbers. The illustrations are good enough to decipher buildings, bridges and the Houses of Parliament, etc., so the results are unlikely to be significantly affected.
13. Kendall (1989: 196). Note that Monet's eyesight did not deteriorate due to cataracts until after 1905.

References

ACKROYD, P. 2000. *London – The Biography*. London: Vintage Press.

BARR, R. 1892. The Doom of London, *The Idler*: 397–409.

BENSON, E. F. 1905. *Images in the Sand*. London: Heinemann

BERNSTEIN, H. T. 1975. The Mysterious Disappearance of Edwardian London Fog, *The London Journal* (1): 189–206.

BONACINA, L. C. W. 1939. Landscape Meteorology and its Reflection in Art and Literature. *Quarterly Journal of the Royal Meteorological Society*. 65: 485–497.

BRIMBLECOMBE, P. 1988. *The Big Smoke, A History of Air Pollution in London since Medieval Times*. London and New York: Methuen.

—— 2000. Aerosols and Air Pollution in Art. *Proceedings of the Symposium on the History of Aerosol Science*. Vienna.

BRIMBLECOMBE, P. and C. OGDEN. 1977. Air Pollution in Art and Literature. *Weather* 32: 285.

BRODIE, F. J. 1892. The Prevalence of Fog in London during the Twenty Years 1871–1890. *Quart. J. Roy. Met. Soc.* 18: 40–45.

—— 1905. Decrease of Fog in London in Recent Years. *Quart. J. Roy. Met. Soc.* 31: 15–28.

BRÜGGEMEIER, F.-J. 1994. A Nature Fit for Industry: The Environmental History of the Ruhr Basin 1840–1990. *Environmental History Review* 18: 35–54.

CARPENTER, A. 1903. *London Fog Inquiry*. Report to Meteorological Council. HMSO.

CHALEYSSIN, P. 1995 *James McNeill Whistler – The Strident Cry of the Butterfly*. Bournemouth: Parkstone Press.

COSGROVE, D and J. E. THORNES. 1981. 'Of Truth of Clouds: John Ruskin and the Moral Order in Landscape'. In *Humanistic Geography and Literature*, pp. 20–46. Edited by D.C.D. Pocock. London: Croom Helm and Totowa.

DOYLE, A. C. 2002. *The Complete Works of Sherlock Holmes* New York: Gramercy Books.

DZIEWICKI, M. H. 1902. *In Praise of London Fog*. In *London – as Seen and Described by Famous Writers,* Edited by Singleton. New York,: Dodd Mead.

EVELYN, J. 1661. *Fumifugium, or The Inconvenience of the Aer and Smoak of London Dissipated*. London: printed by W. Godbid for Gabriel Bedel and Thomas Collins.

GEDZELMAN, S. D. 1991. Atmospheric Optics in Art. *Applied Optics*. 30: 3514–3522.

HAMBYLN, R. 2001. *The Invention of Clouds*. London: Picador Press.

HOWARD, L. 1818. *The Climate of London*. Vol 1. London: W. Phillips.

JANKOVIĆ, V. 2000. *Reading the Skies –A Cultural History of English Weather 1650–1820.* .Manchester: Manchester University Press.

KENDALL, R. 1989. *Monet by Himself*. Boston: Little, Brown and Company.

LAMB, H. H. 1967. Britain's Changing Climate. *Geographical Journal* 33: 445–466.

LUCKIN, B. 2002. 'Demographic, Social and Cultural Parameters of Environmental Crisis: The Great London Smoke Fogs in the Late 19th and Early 20th Centuries', in *The Modern Demon: Pollution in Urban and Industrial European Societies*. Edited by C. Bernhardt and G. Massard-Guilbaud. Clermont-Ferrand: Blaise-Pascal University Press.

MOSLEY, S. 2001. *The Chimney of the World: A History of Smoke Pollution in Victorian and Edwardian Manchester*. Cambridge: White Horse Press.

MPMC. 1902. *Minutes and Proceedings of the Meteorological Council 1901–02*, 17 January 1902, Met Office Library, Exeter.

NEUBERGER, H. 1970. Climate in Art. *Weather* 25: 46–56.

NOCHLIN, L. 1966. *Realism and Tradition in Art 1848–1900*. London: Prentice-Hall.

PEVSNER, N. 1955. *The Englishness of English Art*. London: Penguin Books.

RICHARDSON, L. F. 1922. *Weather Prediction by Numerical Process*. Cambridge: Cambridge University Press.

ROSE, G. 2000. *Visual Methodologies*. London: Sage Publications.

RUBIN, J. H. 1996. 'Realism', in *The Dictionary of Art*. Vol. 26. Edited by J. Turner. London: Grove Publishers.

RUSKIN, J. 1884. *The Storm Cloud of the Nineteenth Century*. London: George Allen.

SCHNEER, J. 1999. *London 1900*. New Haven and London: Yale University Press.

SHANES, E. 1994. *Impressionist London.* London: Abbeville Press.

SHAW, W. N. 1901. The London Fog Inquiry. *Nature* LXIV: 649–50.

SHELLEY, P. B. 1819. *Peter Bell the Third*, Part 3: Hell, Verse 1.

STRADLING, D. 1999. *Smokestacks and Progressives: Environmentalists, Engineers and Air Quality in America, 1881–1951.* Baltimore: Johns Hopkins University Press.

THORNES, J. E. 1979. Landscape and Clouds. *Geographical Magazine* LI(7): 492–499.

—— 1999. *John Constable's Skies.* Birmingham: University of Birmingham Press.

THORNES, J. E. and G. R. McGREGOR. 2003. 'Cultural Climatology', in *Contemporary Meanings in Physical Geography*, pp. 173–197. Edited by S.T. Trudgill and A. Roy. London: Arnold.

TUCKER, P. H. 1989. *Monet in the '90s.* Exhibition Catalogue. Boston: Museum of Fine Arts.

WHEELER, M. 1995. 'Environment and Apocolypse'. In *Ruskin and Environment.* Edited by M. Wheeler, pp. 165–186. Manchester and New York: University of Manchester Press.

WILDE, O. 1889. *The Decay of Lying.* In *The Works of Oscar Wilde.* 1987 Edition. Leicester: Galley Press.

WILDENSTEIN, D. 1996. *Monet.* Vols. I–IV. Taschen: Wildenstein Institute.

WILTON, A, 1979. *The Life and Work of J.M.W. Turner.* London: London Academy Edition.

–9–

Changing Earth and Sky:
Movement, Environmental Variability,
and Responses to El Niño in the
Pio-Tura Region of Papua New Guinea[1]
David M. Ellis

The central problem of this chapter is the effects of a drought on people of the Pio-Tura region of Papua New Guinea, caused in parts of the Pacific by the El Niño Southern Oscillation in 1997.[2] The chapter proceeds from an outline of social life, weather and climate in the Pio-Tura region to an ethnographic account of the 1997 drought and its aftermath there. Seasonality and environmental change are then considered with regard to history and mythology in the Pio-Tura region. Further connections are discussed concerning local perceptions of development and the national and international response to the drought in terms of humanitarian aid. A broader set of linkages and questions is considered in the conclusion about the role of ethnography in documenting changes in weather and climate. It is argued that ethnographic narratives move between different registers of time and place and make valuable connections in the study of complex human and ecological phenomena.

Pawaia People and the Pio-Tura Region

The lands of people often referred to collectively as Pawaia stretch from the southern parts of the Karimui plateau and mountainous valleys on the edge of the New Guinea highlands to the 'piedmont' (Egloff and Kaiku 1983) and 'riparian' (Hall 1983) areas through which the Purari River flows on its way to the Papuan coast (see Figure 9.1). They also straddle the boundaries of three provinces within Papua New Guinea – Gulf, Simbu and Eastern Highlands – and vary in altitude from less than 100 meters to over 3000 meters above sea level. I use the term 'Pio-Tura region' to refer to a portion of these lands – an area of approximately 1950 square kilometres on the northwest side of Pawaia territories.[3] There were about 1086 men, women and children living there in late 1999.[4] Population density was

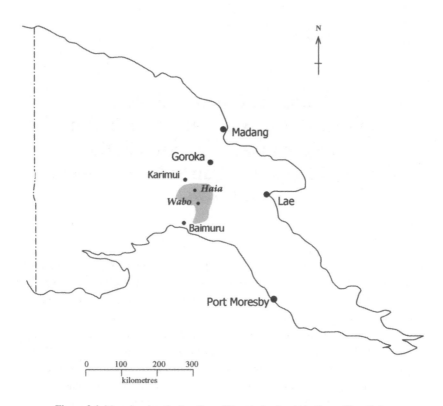

Figure 9.1 Map showing the location of Pawaia lands within Papua New Guinea.

therefore about 0.56 people per square kilometer. The region is largely forested and much of it is considered by biologists to be pristine.

Forms of contact and development in the region have centred on Haia village. They have included a New Tribes Mission since 1973, a grass airstrip since 1975, the provision of health care through the mission and later through a government-run health sub-center, and a primary school. In 1999, while a high percentage (97.1) of people had a base in one or more of the villages in the region (Haia, Iabalamaru, Joraido and Uheino), mobility was an important dynamic of social life. Most people divided their time between different bases in the villages and the forests of the region,[5] undertaking a diverse set of subsistence activities and social obligations. In the 1990s, these activities included the cultivation of sago and production of sago flour as a staple food, swidden gardening, the cultivation of yielding trees and palms, pig husbandry, hunting and trapping of wild animals and birds, fishing in rivers and small lakes, and collection of wild foods and materials in the forest. Game hunted included wild pigs, cassowaries, tree kangaroos, wallabies, cuscus, bandicoots, rats, snakes, lizards, edible frogs, flying foxes, megapodes and their eggs, birds, occasionally echidna and, at lower altitudes, turtles and their eggs. Sago, cooked in bamboo cylinders in the fire, was the main staple food, accompanied usually by green leaves of aibika[6] (*Abelmoschus manihot*) and meat, fish or highly valued sago grubs or tree grubs, if available. Tubers (sweet potato, manioc, taro and yam) were also important.

Among the range of different ecological/altitudinal zones and variations in emphasis in subsistence practices across Pawaia territories, comparable data exist for three points – Iuro on the Karimui plateau, Haia in the Pio-Tura region and Wabo in the Upper Purari area, as seen in Table 9.1. Historically, Pawaia social life and human ecology have been influenced by relations between people across extensive territories stretching from the edge of the highlands to the lowlands approaching the Papuan coast. These relations, including marital alliance, ritual practice, and violent conflict, lent themselves to the movement of people, narratives, and myths. Both Wagner (1972: 164–5) and Hide (1984: 28–9) write of ritual innovation in the region. Styles of dancing, prophecy, rhythms of movement, subsistence, and housing have also been subject to innovation.

The myth of a hero-creator figure called Souw[7] has also travelled across the region, just as he himself is said to have moved across the landscape. Wagner has

Table 9.1 Regional variation on Pawaia lands.

Name of settlement	Altitude (ASL)	Approximate annual rainfall	Features of landscape/ environment	Subsistence and human ecology
Iuro	1150m	<4000mm[a]	Karimui plateau. Edge of highlands.	Gardening and sweet potato more important; sago less so. Some hunting, fishing, gathering.
Haia	740m	>6000mm[b]	Ranging from edge of highlands to foothills. Rugged terrain.	Sago production most important. Hunting, gathering, fishing and gardening also important. High mobility between villages, other settlements and forest.
Wabo	150m	>9000mm[c]	Purari River, lowlands. Crocodiles and turtles in larger rivers.	Sago, hunting, gathering and fishing most important. High mobility between villages, other settlements and forest. More travel by river in canoes.

[a] See Hide (1984: 15).

[b] New Tribes Mission, personal communication, 1999.

[c] See Evesson (1983: 16–19); Petr (1983: xiii).

written extensively on the myth (e.g. 1967, 1972, 1978) and its ontological significance for neighboring Daribi people. Daribi and Pawaia people have similar versions of the myth, and it can also be 'tracked' across the landscape to Polopa people and others much further afield (Wagner 1996).

In the late 1990s, narratives moved across the region in many ways. People sometimes travelled great distances, on foot and by canoe. Stories, myths, and discourses about the past and the present were articulated both privately and publicly, between family members or in speeches delivered at the market or in discussions on the airstrip. People also heard news bulletins on radios operated by batteries brought in occasionally by small aircraft. These aircraft also brought and fetched people – local people, politicians canvassing for electoral support, missionaries, development practitioners, conservation biologists, occasional tourists, and others. Narratives arrived from towns and other centers of settlement across the region in this way. There was also another kind of radio – a two-way radio linking Haia with some of the other villages within a nationally protected 'Wildlife Management Area' and with the office of the conservation organization whose staff administered the conservation project in the highlands town of Goroka.

While narratives in the 1990s and at other points in history moved across spaces of the region, they also moved through time, changing as they went. Equally, the landscape (and perceptions of it) changed, in both space and time, echoing the creation of its forms. Movement and change, in both physical and ideational terms, could be said to be integral to Pawaia experiences and expressions of the world.

Weather, Climate, and Human Ecology in the Pio-Tura region

High rainfall has a marked influence on the weather, climate and landscape of the Pio-Tura region. Pio-Tura lands are at the heart of the Purari River catchment, the third largest in Papua New Guinea after the Sepik and Fly Rivers (Pain 1983; Petr 1983: xiii; Pickup and Chewings 1983: 123). Water flows through the landscape in an intricate network of rivers and streams. These range from lethal torrents to small creeks where children can play and catch small fish.

Variations in altitude, rainfall and emphasis placed on particular subsistence practices across Pawaia lands are also marked out in terms of climate. Hide (1984: 15) writes of a predominant pattern in south Simbu of 'a minimum [rainfall] between May and August during the southeast season, and a maximum between December and March during the northwest season'. He also notes the much higher rainfall in Wabo on the Purari River and the reversal of the seasonal pattern there. Evesson (1983) notes the effect of topography on seasonal airstreams, leading to widespread variations. Seasonal patterns in Haia seem to differ from those of both Iuro and Wabo. The rainiest month in Haia is usually July.

Water is a particularly significant technology for subsistence in the Pio-Tura region on account of the prominence of sago in the local diet. Readily available flowing water is required to wash pulp produced from each palm and thereby extract the valuable carbohydrate. Sago palms are dependent on swampy, marsh-like areas. Fishing in rivers and small lakes is also important in the human ecology of the region. Dugout canoes are used to travel along stretches of the larger rivers.

Crossing rivers is a daily feature of moving across the landscape. The capacity and velocity of the rivers fluctuate, often on an hourly basis, depending on rainfall up-river in the catchment area. This is often unpredictable. Rivers might rage even if there is no rain nearby. The larger rivers are chameleon-like. They might be a rich turquoise and deep green on a dry sunny day, a dark green in overcast weather, or a muddy red laced with white torrents after heavy rains.

Heavy rains sometimes last incessantly for several weeks. During these periods, I noticed that many people became quite agitated and morose, preferring the freedom to move across the landscape and attend to work and social relations. Heavy rains were restrictive in that they caused the rivers to swell to perilous levels, becoming both non-navigable and impossible to cross. They also rendered the land cold,[8] wet, and grey. Torrential rains have a deleterious effect on crops, turning green leaves yellow or even inflicting damage on land and crops. The sound and tremor of landslides during heavy rains are familiar to people who live there.

In this rainy environment, it only takes a few days of consistent sunshine for people to start speaking of a 'good time' or a 'dry season' (in either their own language or in Tok Pisin). A week or more of predominantly dry weather tended to produce a collective sense of freedom and well-being.

The Long Dry Season of 1997

Although people's lives were generally not threatened in the Pio-Tura region by the 1997 drought as in some areas of the country, its effects were dramatic on a number of levels. By early September, many people had already taken advantage of the dry weather to stay in encampments on their own lands, and to fish. It was said that people liked to dance in the dry season and there were many evenings of dancing on the airstrip and elsewhere in Haia, to local folk music and to tapes of Papua New Guinean pop music. These were attended mainly by children and young people in their teens and twenties.

By the middle of September, reports began to filter through of extensive water shortages and related problems in the highlands. A drought assessment team, including a VSO volunteer, flew into Haia airstrip on Sunday September 28, 1997. Aeroplane landings were unusual at the weekend. Based out of Kundiawa, the capital of Simbu Province, the team had been flying around the province all day assessing the state of the water shortage, and accompanying damage to gardens and crops. This was their last visit of the day, to the furthest reaches of the province. They walked to a garden close to the airstrip and soon declared that it was the best place they had seen all day. They had seen places with no water and food. In these severe cases, reports had to be made to the Simbu provincial government and then to Australia for aid. Their assessment, part of the National Phase 1 Assessment, graded the Pio-Tura region as category 2 on a scale of 1 to 5 (5 being the most severe). This meant that Haia and the surrounding region were considered not to be in great danger and no aid was recommended. Before they left, team members told people to plant food close to large rivers and to boil water, and they spoke of scientific predictions that there would be no substantial rains for months.

People in Haia were sobered by this and we sat and spoke about it for a long time after the team had left. People said that they would be the last to die, thanks to sago and wild game on their lands. For them, there was a sense that the wettest place would be the last to be affected and would survive all but the most pernicious of droughts. At that point, however, people began to worry about the forecasts of a prolonged drought. Predictions broadcast on the radio also suggested that it could last well into the following year, possibly until March or even May 1998.

On Monday September 29, Anatuae,[9] a man in his fifties, spoke to me of a 'dark time' when the sun had been eclipsed. He told me the next day that it was in 1962. His memory of this and the current onset of drought did not seem to be unrelated.

That night the heavens opened in a brief respite from the dryness, though their effect was not lasting. The rains worked their way down the ridges around Haia village and set in from the south, a course often predicted by Samuel, a man in his thirties who was an accomplished forecaster of the weather. At the beginning of October there was also a little rain, although as before, its effects on land, crops and water courses were not prolonged.

On October 10, it seemed from accounts from elsewhere that the effects of the drought were edging nearer. People returning from Baimuru, the district center far to the south in Gulf Province, said that people there were obliged to dig holes for their water and the quality was poor. The Pio River, several hours' walk to the south of Haia, was very low. It was usually traversable only by canoe but at that point it was possible to wade across and the water came up to waist level. It had turned a dark reddish colour.

The sun was fierce during mid-October. The ground had dried and the water table dropped quite rapidly. The previous short-lived rains gave way to very light rain or no rain at all. Liset, a woman from the Eastern Highlands who married a man from the region, told me that her husband's mother had said that a singing cricket was prophesying a long and hard dry season. Although sunny conditions were a welcome respite from heavy rains which make the crops turn yellow, the ground had become too dry to dig in some parts.

By October 13, the nights were becoming colder and clearer and the moon was becoming larger. At this point, I started to hear reports of the withering of some food crops. Reports of places beyond the region continued to convey a deteriorating situation everywhere. Jonathan, the missionary pilot who often flew the planes which landed in Haia, said that there had been no water in the town of Goroka in the Eastern Highlands, where he was based, for three days. Staff of the conservation organization which worked in the Pio-Tura region and whose office was in Goroka were clocking off earlier than usual due to the crisis. Liset's husband returned from the national capital Port Moresby with similar news.

Herowana, about two days' walk away to the northeast of Haia, on the edge of the highlands, was also reported to be in a bad state. Moae, a young man in his twenties, returned from Herowana with accounts of sickness and death. Six people were said to have died the previous week and two people, a man and child, had been buried in the same grave.

People continued to comment that the Pio River to the south had turned red. The colour of the rivers at that time was different to the hue resulting from heavy rainfall. It was a slower, deeper, more stagnant red. The Nimi River closest to Haia had turned into a smaller and slower river than usual but it did not seem to drop below that level. Small streams in the bush had dried up, however. The worst effects had not reached Haia. The topsoil was dry but there was still moisture beneath the surface. Nevertheless, it was clear by then that the drying of the small streams would have a detrimental effect on sago production, as it would restrict which palms could be felled and where the pith could be processed. I wondered at that stage if stocks near to Haia might diminish as a result, given that the best climatic conditions in the region at the time seemed to be where most people were concentrated.

On October 16, the latest news by word of mouth from Karimui, the district centre in Simbu Province about two days' walk away, was that all the streams and small rivers there had dried up and that greens had withered and died. On October 27, the sky became dull and oppressive after a pattern of light nocturnal showers died away, leaving little impact on the dry landscape. Everyone was hoping for substantial rains. There were stories in the international news on the radio of starvation from lack of rain, food and water in parts of Papua New Guinea. The reports we heard indicated that half a million people, said to be one eighth of the population, were severely affected. Accounts of the drought and its effects around the country and the region were becoming increasingly perturbing. People in Haia were also starting to make prophecies and forecasts, ranging from the meteorological to the biblical.

On November 1, Mark, a man in his late twenties, told me that the commandments of custom were the same as those of the Bible – they were about not stealing, about treating your neighbour well, respecting your parents, not committing murder and adultery and so on, he said. The so-called 'community work' to maintain the grass airstrip, so often poorly attended, was well supported two days later. It was around that time that we first heard of extensive fires raging in Maimafu to the north. This and other fires were the cause of the oppressive grey skies.[10] We were beneath a smoke haze, the likes of which had been reported in the international media as a result of the fires raging in Indonesia and other parts of southeast Asia. I spent a long time one afternoon in the beating sun carrying water across the village with members of the family I lived with to try to extinguish a fire that had taken hold near their houses. Fortunately, no larger fires took hold in Haia.

I was working on a detailed census in October and November, and this often involved being inside people's houses and eating with them at mealtimes if appropriate. From this I could tell that food was not short. The staple foods, sago and greens, were still available, though people were beginning to worry about supplies. During this period, food was still available at the early morning market on Tuesdays and Fridays, although not as abundantly as usual.

As people were buying produce on November 4, the sun rose, red and large through the smoke haze. It was an unreal sunrise. Tsenape, an influential man in his sixties, made a speech, addressing himself to anyone who would listen. He said that only the Big Man (God) could know what would come, but that there was still food. He beamed a broad smile and preached custom. He said that women must look after their children well, that people must not complain, and that everyone must try to get on and be at peace. He felt that this would assuage the drought and people's growing fears. Given that he had long since become a Christian himself, his 'commandments' of custom were linked with biblical commandments. This was a time of making such codes explicit, in such a manner that the interplay between custom and Christianity was also apparent, as Mark had pointed out to me three days before. The suggestion was that people had to improve themselves morally in order that the overall situation should improve. There was something prophetic about Tsenape's speech. It contained an unspoken speculation of what might happen if people did not take heed of such teachings.

In subsequent days, serious effects of the drought had reached areas within a day's walk from Haia. People spoke of animals starting to die due to lack of water in the bush, of areas completely infested with mosquitoes, and of resulting illness and death in some places, especially through malaria. These accounts came especially from the settlements to the west of Haia, including Iabalamaru and Joraido. Women in Haia were beginning to say that it was no longer possible to process sago, not just because of the shortage of water to wash the pulp and produce the starch, but because the inside of the palm was dry, hard, and stringy.[11]

Although no one expected to see aeroplanes at that point due to the smoke haze, an aircraft landed on Monday November 11 to pick me up on a ticket I had booked previously. I was due to visit colleagues in Sandaun Province before returning to the UK for Christmas and then coming back to Haia in the New Year. It was an eerie flight to Goroka in high winds and thick smog. Before I left Haia I spoke with people at length about what they envisaged might happen if rains did not commence. There were no signs of rains at the time, according to both local predictions and scientific weather forecasts. At least two women, two men, and one child were said to have died as a result of high levels of malaria in other parts of the Pio-Tura region, perceived by local people to be a symptom of the drought, and many were said to be chronically ill. People told me that they could envisage that food would run out in another two to three weeks. They asked me to write down their assessment of the situation as a request for food aid, which appeared to me as urgent as it did to them. I did this and distributed it to NGO staff working in conservation and development who were coordinating communication with the drought relief teams. I also communicated it to colleagues working on the Future of Rainforest Peoples Programme who used it to issue a press release on the drought in Papua New Guinea.

After my departure from Haia, I witnessed some of the variations across the country. I travelled from Goroka to Vanimo in the northwest of the country near the border with the Indonesian province referred to then as Irian Jaya. The situation there was almost unaffected by the drought. The capital, Port Moresby, on the other hand, was badly affected. When I left Papua New Guinea for the UK on November 23, circumstances in drought-affected areas were continuing to worsen.

The Height of the Drought in Haia and its Aftermath

I returned to Port Moresby from the UK on Friday January 9, to Goroka in the Eastern Highlands the following Friday, and into Haia on Thursday January 22 after being delayed by heavy rains. In Goroka I learned that Haia had been graded 3 in the National Phase 2 Assessment of the drought which had taken place in December. The worsening situation had therefore been acknowledged, but Haia was still considered to be far better off than other places worse hit by the drought.

There had been no significant rains in Haia from the point of my departure in November until late December. Rain had come on Christmas Day and had continued to fall regularly since then. It had been seen as a great blessing on that day. The staple foods, sago and greens, had become available again almost immediately. New gardens were planted at this time. Sweet potatoes were not abundant at that point, as would be expected given that they take a number of months to grow depending on the altitude and climate. I asked many questions about conditions people had experienced between mid-November and the end of December when I returned in January. The members of the family I lived with said that there was a space of about a week before the rains came when they had almost nothing to eat as sago had become almost impossible to produce and other regular food-stuffs had been exhausted. They had spent all they could on store goods and they managed with what foods they could find.[12]

So conditions in Haia were completely different by January 22 when I returned in comparison with when I left on November 11. It might help our understanding of the drought to see it in a number of distinct phases which merge into each other but which nonetheless demonstrate how it took new turns. From mid-September until mid-November, there was a gradual deterioration in terms of the effects of water shortage on crops, animals, people and the spread of illness, especially malaria. Mid-November until late December was the most severe period of the drought when conditions continued to worsen to levels where people were short of food. From late December, when rains began again, into early January there was a dramatic reversal of the food shortages caused by the drought as sago could be processed freely as usual and greens soon became abundant. In 1998, people began gradually to reap the benefits of the planting they had undertaken as rains continued. People also commented on how fertile the soil seemed and how abundantly everything grew in the wake of the drought.[13]

By late January, there was little trace of the drought that had caused so much concern just weeks before (cf. Dwyer and Minnegal 2000). In the ensuing months, people soon started to complain of the rain again whenever it returned for prolonged periods.

A planeload of rice arrived in Haia as food aid in mid-January before my return. Missionaries and local people decided that three further planeloads offered at the time should be turned down as there were so many places where people were in greater need.[14]

On Wednesday February 11, I observed the arrival of three further consignments of food aid. The first one, a silver plane from Kundiawa, the capital of Simbu Province, brought thirty-four bags of brown rice weighing 25 kilograms each. The second landing was the same plane laden with flour and cooking oil. The final landing was a bright orange helicopter owned by an expatriate entrepreneur who had married and settled in the district center of Baimuru in Gulf Province. He brought two boxes filled with tinned fish, rice, flour, and cooking oil to give to the people he knew. Each arrival was also said to come from the provincial government to help people in the time of drought.

This occurred some two months after the height of the drought in the Pio-Tura region at a point when it seemed that the drought and its ill effects had long since passed.[15] There was a sense of excitement, even humor, when the planes and helicopter arrived. In addition to the usual fascination with planes and helicopters, these arrivals brought a free gift to be divided among over a thousand people. A line of men passed and threw the thirty-four bags of rice swiftly out of and away from the plane. Men, women, and children milled around excitedly and a crowd of children gathered around the growing pile of rice. Everyone knew that they did not need this food, as they were not going hungry, but it was clearly welcome.

Later in the day there was confusion and dispute about how to divide the rice, first between the larger groups and then among smaller social groupings and families. As people tended to prefer white rice to brown, their enthusiasm for the brown rice quickly waned over the ensuing days. It took quite a while to eat, both because they preferred white rice and because they had sufficient provisions of their preferred staple foods.

Perceptions of Seasonality and Environmental Change

The following extract from a discussion in <u>Tok</u> <u>Pisin</u> with three men in their early twenties on August 23, 1999 throws light upon how people interact with seasonal and climatic cycles in the course of their subsistence activities. It also highlights how these cycles are perceived by them to be changing.

There is a season for bandicoot <u>marita</u>.[16] When leaves come on the <u>galip</u>[17] trees, the <u>tulip</u>[18] season starts. But this year the <u>tulip</u> has not started yet. It is supposed to be the dry season now, but we are having heavy rains at the moment. Now old wise men are troubled with thoughts of this. In the past, there was a clear dry season, but now it has changed. Is it that the sky and the earth are going to end? We also think that it is the 'last time'[19] now and all kinds of things are going to happen. They could happen at any time. Now is the time of the dry season but we are getting rain.

The bandicoot <u>marita</u> season is like this: in the fifth month [i.e. May], . . . [the <u>marita</u> fruit] starts, in the sixth month it starts, in the sixth month it falls and in the eighth month it is finished. If it falls in the sixth month, it finishes in the seventh month; if it falls in the seventh month, it stops in the eighth month.

Now [i.e. August] is the cassowary time. The baby cassowary will eat this <u>marita</u> fruit as well. But when we go around the bush at the moment, we don't see baby cassowaries yet. The fifth month and the sixth month are times for laying and watching eggs. When the bandicoot <u>marita</u> falls, it has a long fruit, about six centimeters across. It looks like <u>marita</u>. The seeds fall down from the middle. At this time, cassowary eggs break and babies come out. This year, bandicoot <u>marita</u> is late and it is only just starting to fall. The cassowaries must be in their eggs.

When the sun holds them, the shoots of the <u>tulip</u> tree come and we eat <u>tulip</u>. When the sun comes, all <u>tulip</u> trees will bear flowers and new leaves. Now the rain has got them, the <u>tulip</u> trees in the bush have not made new leaves either. On the ones near the house, one or two are starting to grow.

In the fifth month we usually find <u>mausgras</u> fish. All the fish come and meet at a place where . . . [the water] is deep and there is white sand. Now, they are all over the place, hiding beneath stones. In the fifth month there are lots of them. This year they came in the fifth month. The seventh month [July] is the normal time for rain. In the sixth month it rains occasionally, and usually falls into the pattern of morning sun and afternoon rain.

In 1987 it was just about alright. We used to sleep in the bush because we knew it would not rain. From 1990 onwards it changed. In 1997 there was a big drought or dry season. Since then it has been rain, then dry season, then rain, then dry season and now it is not too good. Rain, rain . . .

Flora and fauna are connected in a seasonal interplay by which people mark time and plan their subsistence. Yet the prominent view in the Pio-Tura region seems to be that seasons have changed significantly and tend to merge into each other now and cause confusion. In October 1999, for example, I was told by a range of men of different ages and social groups that there used to be clear seasons in the past for the behavior of fauna (including possums, cuscus, tree kangaroos, cassowaries and other game, and fish) and that this is how people knew when to hunt. I heard countless comments by both men and women on the theme of changing seasons.

In August 1999, I also asked a group of women at the market if, whilst going about their work, they had noticed any changes in the seasons. Arinau, a woman in her forties, replied: 'Some seasons do not come at the right time. In the past, we used to plant by the seasons. But now it has changed, in the last few years. When we plant greens it gets dry, and dries our sweet potatoes and bananas. Prolonged droughts are bad for growing food, and so are heavy rains.'

Oral history and mythology in the Pio-Tura region suggest that ancestors and their landscapes and climates also underwent a series of transformations. I heard a number of accounts describing a period after creation in the time of the first ancestors when there was no rain and people slept at the foot of trees. Origin stories of people in the Pio-Tura region sometimes depict a substantially different landscape from that in which people live now. They evoke a formless earth, without trees or rain.[20] Some accounts state that there was no forest a long time ago. Earth and water were combined. The mountains did not have trees. After the ancestors came and brought the forebears of the current generation into the world, then there were trees and grass. According to accounts I heard, such a time was about eight generations ago.

Ancestors also underwent metamorphoses from generation to generation. In some cases, beings which were half human and half animal gave birth to humans, while in other cases, different generations of descendents were different sizes. There was a period when people were much larger and stronger than they are now and everything in the landscape, including both flora and fauna, was in greater abundance.

Until the arrival of the mission in Haia in 1973, Souw was said to have created the components of the environment and also, through his impetuous actions, the forms of the landscape.[21] He laid a curse on people which offers an explanation of subsequent suffering and strife.

If we think of the earth and the sky changing in an apocalyptic sense, as the commentators on changing seasons have done above, then we might also look to other events in history and mythology when the earth and the sky are believed to have changed.

Between the 1930s and 1970s, an ecstatic religious movement occurred across a broad region stretching at least from the edge of the highlands to the lower Purari River, incorporating both the Pio-Tura area and Karimui. It was connected to the prophetic words of a Pawaia man from the Purari River area called Koriki who had worked with the colonial government as a police constable and patrol guide (Wagner 1979). People are said to have looked to the sky, believing that God was there and that floods and earthquakes would come. The time of darkness referred to above by Anatuae, when the sun was eclipsed, was during this period.

Contact, Development, and Aid

The reasons which compelled white men to visit the lands of Pawaia people reflected the colonial experience in general in Papua, although the Pio-Tura region was among the last places to be visited. Such areas were considered particularly remote and inaccessible parts of the 'Papuan hinterland' (Schieffelin and Crittenden 1991). White men came on expeditions, prospecting for gold, coal, oil and sites for hydroelectric power generation. They also came on colonial government patrols, on Christian missions, and on medical research patrols and for other development and research-oriented reasons, including, from the 1980s, conservation. 'Contact' was gradual, as outsiders ventured progressively further into the region, first from the south and later from the north.

By the late 1990s, most attempts at development in the region appeared to have failed, both to local people and to outsiders. Although a grass airstrip had been completed manually by 1975, it was often perceived that this had not brought the development it should have. Health and education services often failed to run effectively in the late 1990s. Stories of large-scale development, such as petroleum, mining, and logging operations were abundant in the 1990s and must have started much earlier in the century when prospectors became active in the region.

There was a sense in the Pio-Tura region during the 1997 El Niño event that the drought, like development, occurred elsewhere. Accounts of the drought travelled into the region, largely by word of mouth, from outside. They came from visitors who walked to Haia or people returning from other settlements in the region or from town, from pilots who flew into Haia, on the two-wave radio, and from radio news broadcasts. Stories of development took similar routes into the region and they always seemed to happen elsewhere.

The ill effects of the drought were also reminiscent of narratives about the deleterious effects of certain kinds of development, most notably logging. On seeing pictures in August 1999 of a landscape like his own which had been logged,[22] Jacob, a man in his late forties, likened what he saw to a time of drought and a 'last time' scenario:

> Pigs will not roam in this kind of place. They will get hot and run away. In the dry season they do not roam. They have to be in good forest. If everywhere, even places in the mountains, becomes like this, everything will be ruined. The earth and the mountains will fall and the rivers will be ruined and there will be landslides. Everything will meet its end . . .

These thoughts show how landscape, weather, and the well-being of people and other species are intricately interlinked.

As planeloads of food aid were distributed on the basis of population figures, pilots and relief officials asked people upon landing what their population was and how they divided themselves into 'clans'. This is reminiscent of helicopter and plane visits by other 1990s development officials, notably conservation practitioners trying to establish a mandate for protecting the region and logging and mining company representatives.

At an international level too, responses to changes in weather and climate are linked to development. Transnational donors respond to natural disasters such as drought and earthquakes with development aid. On the other hand, particular policies and practices of development and consumption have induced widespread environmental change on a global scale.

Conclusion: Ethnography and Registers of Time and Space

In this chapter, I have discussed the importance of movement in the human ecology and social life of people of the Pio-Tura region of Papua New Guinea. I have described climatic conditions there, the course of the 1997 drought, perceptions of seasonality and environmental change in terms of history and mythology, and the 1998 relief operation with regard to the history of contact and development in the region. What kinds of connections might be discerned in all of this?

We might deduce that changes and transformations in the landscape and in social practices are nothing new in the Pio-Tura region. The data also suggest that perceptions of environmental change can be seen in the context of historical and mythological thinking. Tsenape's speech at the market in 1997 connected the drought with moral behavior, interpreting it in terms of both custom and Christianity.[23] In 1999, Tsenape gave me his account of the story of Souw and how it had changed over time, particularly with regard to Christianity. Like God, Souw both created everything and laid a curse on humankind. Tsenape told me the story of the curse and also depicted a previous era in which people were happy and felt secure in their knowledge that Souw had created the land and all living beings. Although Tsenape had become a devout Christian, he noted that Christianity had effected a spoiling of Souw, revealing his powers of creation as lies. In his 1999 narrative, it is implied that environmental change is a symbol of uncertain times following the succession of the omnipotence of Souw by God and Jesus.

Allen (2000: 111) critiques disaster relief on the grounds that disasters tend to be perceived as isolated incidents. Minnegal and Dwyer (2000) suggest that events need to be placed in historical and local contexts when designing aid programmes. If we take a temporal view of the ethnography presented in this chapter, we might note that the whole chapter moves between different registers of time and space. On the one hand, the narrative moves between different localities – Haia, Iabalamaru, and Goroka, for example – and different scales of space, from the local to the regional to broader frames of reference – Haia, the Pio-Tura region, Pawaia territories, Simbu Province, the state of Papua New Guinea, and the global environment. In terms of time, as well as space, the chapter moves between different registers which are not homologous. I refer to micro-events during the 1997 drought, to particular days, months and years, to periods spanning several years and to historical and mythological pasts in the Pio-Tura region.

The study of weather gives rise to multiple linkages in space and time.[24] I want to suggest in conclusion that this is also what ethnography does. At the outset of the chapter, I presented a discussion of movement as an underlying physical and conceptual principle for people of the Pio-Tura region. Ethnography also moves between different localities and frames of time.

Yet these broader ethnographic readings also suggest a diffraction of responsibilities of the ethnographer to different groups and goals. In the context of transnational conservation and development, people of the Pio-Tura region have often been considered to be a threat to biodiversity and an obstacle to conservation. Contemporary narratives of changing environmental conditions and historical and mythological accounts of depleting flora and fauna might be interpreted as justification for such representations.

Narratives of environmental change in the Pio-Tura region cannot be taken at face value by Euro-American climatologists, conservation practitioners, or anthropologists. I have endeavored to show a range of frames for thinking about environmental change in the Pio-Tura region. In order to see the 1997 drought and its aftermath in context, we need to consider day-to-day experiences of that period, the social and subsistence practices of people of the region, contemporary understandings and histories of development, and mythological narratives. If we could integrate these aspects of social life in the Pio-Tura region with perspectives from humanitarian aid or climatology,[25] we might be able to view climatic events and patterns with regard to local practices and ways of conceptualizing the world.

Notes

1. I would like to thank the people of Haia and the Pio-Tura region; pilots and staff of Mission Aviation Fellowship and New Tribes Mission; colleagues at the National Research Institute; and staff of the Research and Conservation Foundation and the Wildlife Conservation Society. Robin Hide gave encouragement to write this chapter, assistance with references, and ongoing insights and commentary. Thanks are also due to Cynthia Fowler, Christin Kocher Schmid, Ben Orlove and Sarah Strauss for comments on earlier drafts of this chapter, and to Paige West for reading an earlier version in my absence at the AAA meetings in 2001. Funding came from the European Commission DGVIII through the Future of Rainforest Peoples Programme (L'Avenir des Peuples des Forêts Tropicales – APFT).
2. See Chappell and Grove (2000) for an overview of this phenomenon.
3. While the combined administrative census divisions of 'Pio' and 'Tura' form the southeast corner of Simbu Province, my use of the term extends beyond the provincial boundary. This is intended to reflect the importance of mobility for people of the region, some of whom are the custodians of land beyond the Simbu boundary.
4. These figures are based on a census I carried out with people of the Pio-Tura region between 1997 and 1999.
5. Camps were constructed in specific locations, sometimes for just an overnight shelter, and sometimes for several weeks or months while sago was produced or gardens made. Most people also had houses of varying degrees of permanence on their own lands in the forest.
6. Words in Tok Pisin, a lingua franca of Papua New Guinea, are underlined.
7. The spelling Souw is used here in English in order to correspond to other works, most notably Wagner (e.g. 1967). There are many regional differences in pronunciation.
8. Typical daily temperatures in Haia range from a high of 28.5 degrees Celsius during the day to a low of 20 degrees at night. The highest temperature I recorded was 30 degrees and the lowest 17 degrees. 17 degrees in persistent heavy rains felt cold, both to local people and to others.
9. Actual names are not used.
10. By November 1997, there were also fires in the Karimui area of Simbu Province (see Allen and Bourke 2001: 157).
11. A number of commentators on the drought elsewhere in Papua New Guinea, including Allen (2000: 109), note the difficulties of processing sago due to the drying up of small creeks. I have not heard other reports similar to those from Haia that describe difficulties in processing due to changes in the texture of the inside of the palm.

12. People resorted to varying degrees to so-called famine foods, including banana corms (see Allen and Bourke 2001: 159, 163) and wild tubers, such as wild yams. Allen (2000) emphasizes the ingenuity of people and their social relations as a key factor in their survival during this period, as opposed to popular perceptions that people were saved by food aid (Dwyer and Minnegal 2000: 251).

13. Bourke (2000: 155) notes that there was a flush of nutrients, particularly nitrogen, into the soil after the rains. While this might explain the fertility experienced in 1998 in the Pio-Tura region, it has also been seen as a reason for 'poor tuberisation' (ibid.) of crops planted in late 1997 in the highlands.

14. Karimui, for example, about two days' walk away on the edge of the highlands, was struck more severely. Many parts of the highlands and other areas of the country were affected yet more severely. Karimui was still affected badly in mid-February and for some months after this. At that point, people returning to Haia from Karimui said that there was only corn to eat and no sweet potato, the staple in those parts. It seems that the production of sago recovered as soon as there was water, while it took several months for new sweet potato crops to yield. People had planted faster-yielding crops, such as corn, in large quantities in the meantime.

15. Allen and Bourke (2001: 158) write: 'In a number of provinces . . . rice continued to be supplied long after the worst food shortage was over, mainly because, although it had been ordered during the height of the drought, funds for its purchase and distribution took months to reach the provinces.'

16. This is a kind of marita pandanus whose fruit is eaten by bandicoots but is inedible for humans.

17. *Terminalia sp.* The Tok Pisin term 'galip' usually refers to *Canarium.*

18. *Gnetum gnemon*, a tree whose young leaves are an important green vegetable and whose fibres beneath the bark are woven by women into string to make string bags.

19. This is a biblical reference to the book of *Revelation* (cf. Eves 2000). Teachings of the New Tribes Mission in Haia suggested that the last time would come at an indeterminable point and that we should be on our guard for it.

20. Comparisons with the biblical account of creation in the book of *Genesis* were made explicit to me on one occasion: 'In the beginning God created the heavens and the earth. Now the earth was formless and empty' (International Bible Society 1988: 4).

21. See also Dwyer and Minnegal (2000: 261–263) on the creation of features in the landscape of Bedamuni people in the lowlands of Western Province by mythological figures, including the comparison the authors make with Duna and Huli mythologies. They write of how Bedamuni people read the drought in a number of ways, one of them according to such mythologies. These

interpretations, Dwyer and Minnegal suggest, were the most satisfying, coherent, and tangible ones for Bedamuni people.

22. I recorded perceptions of logging and the process of logging negotiations across the region in the late 1990s. One of the methods I employed was to show people visual materials depicting logging and to discuss and note their reactions.

23. Note similarities with Eves (2000) on the prophecy and exegesis of the 1997 drought in southern New Ireland. The account of Dwyer and Minnegal (2000: especially 252) on Bedamuni people is also reminiscent of this, though in a more secular millenarian context.

24. Anthropological studies of time have also noted the complexity of con-ceptualizations of time and space (Adam 1990; Gell 1992; Munn 1992).

25. A correlation of the data presented here with historical data on rainfall and climate in the region might provide a valuable study, for example.

References

ADAM, BARBARA. 1990. *Time and Social Theory*. Cambridge and Oxford: Polity Press.

ALLEN, B. J. 2000. 'The 1997–98 Papua New Guinea Drought: Perceptions of Disaster,' in *El Niño – History and Crisis: Studies from the Asia-Pacific Region*. Edited by R. H. Grove and J. Chappell, pp. 109–122. Cambridge, UK: The White Horse Press.

ALLEN, B. J. and R. M. BOURKE. 2001. 'The 1997 Drought and Frost in PNG: Overview and Policy Implications', in *Food Security for Papua New Guinea. Proceedings of the Papua New Guinea Food and Nutrition 2000 Conference.* Edited by R. M. Bourke, M. G. Allen and J. G. Salisbury, pp. 153–163. Canberra: Australian Centre for International Agricultural Research.

BOURKE, R. M. 2000. 'Impact of the 1997 Drought and Frosts in Papua New Guinea', in *El Niño – History and Crisis: Studies from the Asia-Pacific Region*. Edited by R. H. Grove and J. Chappell, pp. 149–170. Cambridge, UK: The White Horse Press.

CHAPPELL, J. and R. H. GROVE. 2000. 'Introduction. ENSO: A Brief Over-view', in *El Niño – History and Crisis: Studies from the Asia-Pacific Region*. Edited by R. H. Grove and J. Chappell, pp. 1–4. Cambridge, UK: The White Horse Press.

DWYER, PETER, and MONICA MINNEGAL. 2000. El Niño, Y2K and the 'Short, Fat Lady': Drought and Agency in a Lowland Papua New Guinea Community. *The Journal of the Polynesian Society* 109(3): 251–272.

EGLOFF, B. J. and O. KAIKU. 1983. 'Prehistory and Paths in the Upper Purari River Basin', in *The Purari – Tropical Environment of a High Rainfall River Basin*. Edited by T. Petr, pp. 475–91. The Hague: Dr. W. Junk Publishers.

EVES, RICHARD. 2000. Waiting for the Day: Globalisation and Apocalypticism in Central New Ireland, Papua New Guinea. *Oceania* 71(2): 73–91.

EVESSON, D. T. 1983. 'The Climate of the Purari River Basin,' in *The Purari – Tropical Environment of a High Rainfall River Basin*. Edited by T. Petr, pp. 9–26. The Hague: Dr. W. Junk Publishers.

GELL, ALFRED. 1992. *The Anthropology of Time: Cultural Constructions of Temporal Maps and Images*. Oxford: Berg.

HALL, A. J. 1983. 'Health and Diseases of the People of the Upper and Lower Purari,' in *The Purari – Tropical Environment of a High Rainfall River Basin*. Edited by T. Petr, pp. 493–507. The Hague: Dr. W. Junk Publishers.

HIDE, ROBIN L. Editor. 1984. *South Simbu: Studies in Demography, Nutrition and Subsistence. The Research Report of the Simbu Land Use Project, Volume VI*. Boroko, Papua New Guinea: Institute of Applied Social and Economic Research.

INTERNATIONAL BIBLE SOCIETY. 1988. *Disciple's Study Bible: New International Version,* Nashville, TN: Holman Bible Publishers.

MINNEGAL, MONICA, and PETER DWYER. 2000. Responses to a Drought in the Interior Lowlands of Papua New Guinea: A Comparison of Bedamuni and Kubo-Konai. *Human Ecology* 28(4): 493–526.

MUNN, NANCY. 1992. The Cultural Anthropology of Time: A Critical Essay. *Annual Review of Anthropology* 21: 93–123.

PAIN, C. F. 1983. 'Introduction to the Purari River Catchment', in *The Purari – Tropical Environment of a High Rainfall River Basin*. Edited by T. Petr, pp. 1–7. The Hague: Dr. W. Junk Publishers.

PETR, T. (Ed.). 1983. *The Purari – Tropical Environment of a High Rainfall River Basin*. The Hague: Dr. W. Junk Publishers.

PICKUP, G. and V. H. CHEWINGS. 1983. 'The Hydrology of the Purari and its Environmental Implications', in *The Purari – Tropical Environment of a High Rainfall River Basin*. Edited by T. Petr, pp. 123–139. The Hague: Dr. W. Junk Publishers.

SCHIEFFELIN, EDWARD and ROBERT CRITTENDEN (Eds.). 1991. *Like People You See in a Dream: First Contact in Six Papuan Societies*. Stanford: Stanford University Press.

WAGNER, ROY. 1967. *The Curse of Souw: Principles of Daribi Clan Definition and Alliance in New Guinea*. Chicago and London: University of Chicago Press.

—— 1972. *Habu: The Innovation of Meaning in Daribi Religion*. Chicago and London: University of Chicago Press.

—— 1978. *Lethal Speech: Daribi Myth as Symbolic Obviation*. Ithaca and London: Cornell University Press.

—— 1979. The Talk of Koriki: A Daribi Contact Cult. *Social Research* 46: 140–165.

—— 1996. 'Mysteries of Origin: Early Traders and Heroes in the Trans-Fly', in *Plumes from Paradise: Trade Cycles in Outer Southeast Asia and their Impact on New Guinea and Nearby Islands until 1920*. Edited by P. Swadling, pp. 285–298. Waigani: PNG National Museum, and Coorparoo, Queensland: Robert Brown and Associates.

–10–

Meteorological Meanings: Farmers' Interpretations of Seasonal Rainfall Forecasts in Burkina Faso

Carla Roncoli,[1] Keith Ingram, Christine Jost, and
Paul Kirshen

The Making of Understanding

Recollections of the past, observations of the present, and expectations for the future shape our experience of climate phenomena and our understanding of climate information. Research shows that people filter and absorb scientific knowledge in terms of pre-existing cultural models and aspirations for a desired future (Thompson and Rayner 1998; Kempton et al. 1995). Assessments of El Niño-based rainfall forecasts in Latin America illustrate the shifts in meaning that information takes as it circulates among various groups, according to their collective memories of drought, perceptions of available options, and conflicting agendas and aspirations (Broad 2000; Nelson and Finan 2000; Otterstrom 2000). It is essential to elucidate this cognitive framework in order to ensure that risk communication leads to appropriate actions.

In this chapter we reflect on a case of seasonal rainfall forecast dissemination to farmers in the Sahel-Sudan region. As in most of sub-Saharan Africa, rural households in this region depend largely on rainfed agriculture for food and income and, due to scarcity of productive resources and economic opportunities, they are highly vulnerable to climate variability and change (O'Brien and Leichenko 2000). Recent developments in climate predictions have triggered hopes that forecasts may help farmers to better manage climate risk (Washington and Downing 1999; Hammer et al. 2001). Yet, many have noted that this potential hinges on the development of viable communication approaches that enable rural producers to understand seasonal rainfall forecasts, particularly their probabilistic nature (O'Brien et al. 2000; Patt and Garata 2002; 2002, Ingram et al. 2002). In the case of climate forecasts, farmers' interpretations are anchored in their remembrance of desirable or dreaded situations they lived through, their observations about the conditions that brought them about, and their assessments of how they managed through them.

First, we provide a concise description of the diversity of environmental and social contexts in which farmers of Burkina Faso live and work. Second, we present an account of how the 2000 seasonal rainfall forecast was communicated to farmers in our research sites. Third, we discuss farmers' assessments of the 2000 rainy season as well as their expectations prior to its onset. Finally, we examine how farmers remembered and interpreted the messages presented to them and how they responded to them in making production decisions. Our aim is to contribute to a better understanding of the relationship between context and meaning in the communication of scientific information.

Present Configurations of Risk and Livelihood

The Sahel-Sudan climatic zone is characterized by a strong gradient of decreasing annual rainfall from south to north, with most rainfall occurring during a single wet season, lasting from May–June to September–October. Total seasonal rainfall ranges from 100 to 650 mm in the semi-arid Sahel, and from to 650 mm to over 1000 mm in the semi-humid Sudan (Sivakumar and Gnoumou 1987). Rainfall in the region is characterized by considerable inter- and intra-annual variation among seasons. Adverse effects of climate variability are further exacerbated by prolonged droughts that last for several years or decades, alternating with relatively wetter periods (Nicholson 1985). These dry periods have caused widespread famines in the 1910s, 1940s, mid-1970s, and mid-1980s (Nicholson 1986).

Given that the large majority of the population in the region subsists on rainfed agriculture and livestock production, climate variability remains a powerful constraint to sustainable development. Therefore, recent advances in climate prediction science have generated a great deal optimism among donors and policy makers for the potential role of climate information, particularly rainfall forecasts, in improving production and livelihood systems in the region. Seasonal rainfall forecasts are based on the principle that sea surface temperatures (SST) influence global atmospheric circulation. In West Africa, seasonal forecasts predict total rainfall during July, August, and September, the three-month period at the core of the rainy season during which 80 percent of annual rains fall. These seasonal rainfall forecasts are developed before the onset of the rainy season, in May, and are presented as the probability of the rainfall being in the high, middle, or low tercile of the total mean seasonal rainfall in the region over the historic period for which weather records are available.

How to present probabilistic forecasts to potential users and rural producers in ways that enable them to understand them and use them to better cope with climate variability remains an unanswered research question (Orlove and Tosteson 1999; Stern and Easterling 1999; O'Brien et al. 2000; Patt 2001). Addressing this question is the goal of the Climate Forecasting and Agricultural Resources project, a multidisciplinary research partnership of the University of Georgia and Tufts University.[2] The project team combines expertise in agro-meteorology, agricultural systems, pastoralism, water resource management, and environmental anthropology in order to better understand how households and institutions of the Sahel–Sudan region could use seasonal precipitation forecasts to improve agricultural production and livelihood security.

Burkina Faso was selected as a research area because it has a range of agro-ecological zones representative of the region. Between 1998 and 2001, research was conduced in three sites that correspond to the three main climatic areas of the country (Ingram et al. 2002). The village of Bouahoun is located in a commercial cotton area in the southwest, with an average annual rainfall of 900–1,000 mm. The village of Bonam is in a rainfed cereal farming area in the Central Plateau, with an average annual rainfall of 600–700 mm. In the Sahel, which has an average annual rainfall of 400–500 mm, two villages, Koria and Sambonaye, were selected to represent two ends of the agro-pastoralism continuum, with agriculture dominating as a source of livelihood in Koria and pastoralism in Sambonaye.

Each of the communities has about 2,000-3,000 residents and is located within 30 km of a provincial administrative center. In the southwest site, the indigenous *Bwa* community is being increasingly outnumbered by *Mossi* immigrants. Some *Fulbe* immigrants, who historically have tended locally owned cattle, have also chosen a more settled lifestyle in the area due to increasing restrictions on herd movement and shrinking pasture areas. In the Central Plateau site, *Mossi* farmers coexist with *Fulbe* households who have taken up residence in the bushy areas surrounding villages. In the Burkinabé Sahel, *Fulbe* are historically and demographically the dominant group and identify themselves as pastoralists, while formerly enslaved *Rimaibé* and *Bellah* and the indigenous *Gurmantché* have always been agriculturalists.

In all sites, agricultural production depends largely on seasonal rainfall. Producers concur that drawing a livelihood from the natural environment, whether by farming or by herding, has become increasingly arduous and risky during the last two to three decades due largely to greater frequency of water-deficit years, late onset of the rainy season, premature end of rains, and anomalous rainfall distribution during the season. Crop production strategies strive to manage risks and reduce losses by diversifying field locations, soil types, and crop mixes. Farmers expand cultivation in lowland or upland fields according to their expectations of seasonal rainfall, but land shortage limits this strategy, especially in the Southwest site.

Agricultural systems center on cultivation of sorghum (*Sorghum bicolor*) and millet (*Pennesitum glaucum*), and other crops, such as peanut (*Arachis hypogea*), bambara nuts (*Vigna subterrenea*), cowpea (*Vigna unguiculata*), and sesame

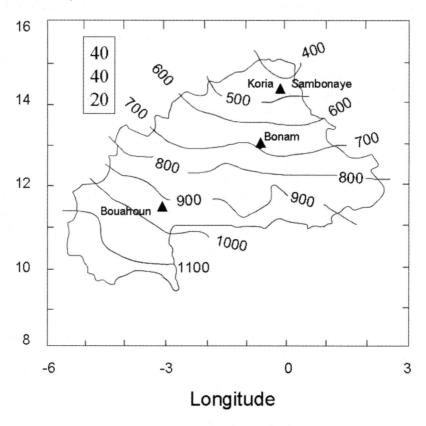

Figure 10.1 Map of Burkina Faso showing the location of research sites, mean average annual rainfall, and 2000 seasonal rainfall forecast.

(*Sesamum indicum*). Most production is for household consumption, with some surpluses being sold on local markets. Among staple grains, sorghum prevails in the Central Plateau site, complemented by smaller acreages of millet, maize (*Zea mays*), rice (*Oryza sativa*), and other crops. Farmers have responded to increased occurrence of drought and shortening of the rainy season by shifting from traditional varieties of sorghum and millet that had a longer (120- to 150-day) growth duration to those that have medium (70- to 90-day) or short (50- to 60-day) durations.

Millet is the staple of choice in the Sahel, and is grown mostly in sandy soils. But 70- to 90-day sorghum varieties, which ripen before local millet, are being planted more often, especially in valley bottoms and in rainy years on clayey soils that were previously used for pasture. Expansion of agriculture and declining rainfall make it more difficult for *Fulbe* households to make a living on livestock production alone, so many households combine transhumant pastoralism with some crop production during the rainy season. At the same time, agriculturalists are diversifying into livestock production. In the southwest, cotton farming has reduced the diversity of cropping systems, although its returns are too low for farmers to abandon household food production. Most farmers grow similar acreages of cotton and maize, with small fields of rice, sorghum, peanut, sesame, and beans. Varieties of food crops are often poor quality derivatives of 'improved' varieties, which the extension service makes available for purchase, though availability is erratic.

Commercial agriculture has enabled southwest farmers to have far greater market orientation and access to technology, inputs, and credit, which are channeled through SOFITEX (Societé des Fibres Textiles), a semi-private Burkinabé–French commercial partnership that purchases, processes, and exports cotton, the primary export and earner of foreign exchange for the country. In the southwest, a few wealthy farmers have tractors and most farming households own at least one plow and pair of oxen. In contrast, less than one-fourth of households in the Central Plateau site own plows, while Sahelian households do not use plows because the topsoil layer is too shallow and the subsoil too rocky to allow plowing.

In the Central Plateau and in the Sahel sites, farmers apply manure and organic matter to selected fields, whereas southwest farmers use large quantities of chemical fertilizers, herbicides, and insecticides. Inputs are bought on credit from SOFITEX through producers' groups, and the costs are subtracted from cotton sales revenues after harvest. The amount of money farmers owe to the company is a major factor in farming decisions: farmers need to plant cotton to obtain inputs (which they use for both cotton and maize) and cash, even in climatic and agronomic conditions that might be more suited for other crops.

Bringing Forecasts to Farmers

In 2000, the CFAR project, in collaboration with the meteorological service of Burkina Faso and the national agricultural and environmental research institution of Burkina Faso, organized the experimental dissemination of forecasts to farmers and herders in its three sites. Initially, a provisional forecast was presented to a small group of farmers from the CFAR sites that participated in the 2000 PRESAO (Prévisions Saisonnières pour l'Afrique de l'Ouest) Forum in Ouagadougou (Roncoli et al. 2000). This forum is held in May each year (since 1998), before the onset of the rainy season. The goals of the forum are to develop a 'consensus forecast' for the West Africa region by combining results from global circulation models with statistical analyses of long-term rainfall data, and to bring together forecast producers and users to discuss potential application. But given the experimental nature of the methodology and the modest predictive skill of the forecast, the information is still not widely publicized.

The 2000 PRESAO forecast for Burkina Faso indicated a 40% probability that seasonal rainfall fall would be in the higher tercile, 40% for the middle tercile (referred to as 'near average'), and 20% in the lower tercile for all three climatic zones of Burkina Faso. This forecast was revised on the basis of updated SST data at the end of June, and minor changes made (35% for the higher, 45% for the middle, 20% for the lower tercile in all three zones).

Differences in the agenda and concerns of key players shaped how the forecast was presented to the general public. At the end of the PRESAO Forum, the director of Burkina Faso's meteorological service held a press conference, which was broadcasted by the national radio, announcing a 'good probability of at least average rainfall'.[3] He did not announce the quantitative probabilities, instead giving a more cautious general interpretation in order to avoid adverse political consequences that might ensue if the forecast was perceived to be wrong about an issue of such economic importance. On the other hand, independently from the meteorological service, SOFITEX publicized 'a strong probability of abundant rainfall' during a weekly radio program that the company sponsors to reach farmers in cotton production areas. The announcement encouraged farmers to continue planting cotton well into the season, a strategy that helps SOFITEX to meet production quotas and client commitments, but is risky because the late-planted cotton will fail if the rains end prematurely.

In mid-July 2000, a team of researchers from the national meteorological and agricultural research services traveled to the CFAR research sites to present the updated forecast to farmers. In the course of purposely convened village meetings, the researchers informed the population that, based on their studies, they expected rainfall in 2000 to be in the 'middle range'. In particular, they predicted rainfall to be less than that of 1999, which was a year of abundant rainfall, but more than that of 1997, which was a year of drought. The team also explained that: (a) the forecast is 'probabilistic', meaning that there is a margin of uncertainty; (b) forecasts are for 'zones' and do not predict rainfall in a specific village or a field; (c) forecasts relate only to July, August, and September rainfall; (d) the forecast cannot predict when the rains would begin and end, or how they would be distributed during the season.

In January and February 2001, the CFAR research team returned to the field to assess how farmers had understood the forecast and how they had used the information in their production choices. We spent from one to two weeks in each site doing semi-structured interviews and focus groups, including samples of villagers who had and had not attended the meeting with the visiting team in July. Between five and fifteen group and individual interview sessions were conducted in each village. While the small size, non-random, and heterogeneous nature of the samples limits the analyses that can be done with the data, it made it possible to obtain in-depth ethnographic information from farmers, some of who have known and worked with the team for several years.

In the effort to contact those who had attended the forecast dissemination meeting in July, it became clear that village politics, ethnic identity, and gender roles had contributed to excluding certain groups. Information about the meeting was not passed on to *Fulbe* herders living on the margin of villages in the Central Plateau and southwest sites, who are not considered to be part of the resident community. In the Sahel, village sections inhabited by low caste families and by families opposing the village leader were also not informed. *Fulbe* women had been unaware of the meeting, and cultural norms would have prevented them from mixing with men in public events. Such norms are more relaxed among lower castes, so that several *Rimaibé* women did attend. But where meetings occurred in the late afternoon, women were unable to participate because they were busy with dinner preparation.

Predictions and Performance: the 2000 Rainy Season

Despite the strong prediction for average or above average seasonal rainfall, and despite a good start of the rains in some areas of the country, all three sites experienced a drier than average 2000 rainy season (Table 10.1). The water deficit was serious in the Sahel, and especially devastating in the Central Plateau, where total seasonal rainfall was less than half the long-term average: the lowest in forty years.

As a measure of the gravity of the situation, farmers in the Sahel and in the Central Plateau related how every component of their carefully diversified production systems had failed. Sorghum and millet yields were very poor, especially in upland fields and in clayey soils. Maize, which plays an important role in relieving hunger before the harvest of sorghum and millet, also failed. Most

Table 10.1 Total 2000 seasonal rainfall and long-term average rainfall for CFAR sites.

Rainfall station	2000 seasonal rainfall	Long-term average 1959–1998
Dori (Koria and Sambonaye)	301 mm	485.7 mm
Boulsa (Bonam)	312 mm	688.5 mm
Houndé (Bouahoun)	705 mm	930.5 mm

Source: Direction de la Météorologie Nationale, Ouagadougou, Burkina Faso.

secondary crops, such as cowpea, sesame, sorrel, peanut, and bambara nut produced very little, and nothing at all if planted later in the season. Many households
had no seed for the new farming season. In the Central Plateau, farmers reported
harvesting only between 10% and 30% of normal annual grain production. In the
Sahel, both crops and pasture did poorly: grass and water were extremely scarce,
which exacerbated tensions over pastures among neighboring communities.

By January–February 2001, only three months after the harvest, households in
the Sahel and in the Central Plateau were facing severe food shortages, and were
already rationing the daily intake of food and selling livestock and other assets to
buy grain. Pastoralists were migrating towards southern more humid areas at a
greater rate than usual, but some animals were already too weak from insufficient
grazing to be able to travel. In the Sahel, most able-bodied men moved to gold
panning sites in nearby areas and across the border in Niger to gain money to buy
food for their families.

The situation was slightly better in the Southwest. Cotton performed better than
maize, which needs more rain, but lack of rain reduced its weight and quality,
which resulted in lower financial returns to producers. Yields for maize and other
crops varied according to the date of planting, because a water deficit in September
injured crops that had been planted after early July. In some areas, late October
downpours damaged ripened maize that had already dried and was waiting to be
harvested.

As we returned to the sites to evaluate the impacts of the forecast, we were
concerned about how farmers would react to the 'failure' of the forecast to predict
the actual rainfall situation. In fact, few farmers seemed surprised, despite being
deeply troubled by the prospects of a protracted famine. Obviously, villagers may
have refrained from challenging the visiting foreigners and government officials
out of hospitality and deference. But their assessment of the 'accuracy' of the
forecast was also a function of their attitudes towards the possibility of knowing
the future and their understanding of the forecast, which in itself was shaped by
what they expected and what they were most interested in knowing.

Views of the Future: Farmers' Expectations for the 2000 Rainy Season

The notion of uncertainty is not new to farmers, although whether they can or do
quantify probabilities remains to be established. Uncertainty is a defining feature
of farmers' environment and experience as well as a building block of local
systems of thought, which stress that human knowledge is inherently partial and
provisional as a 'work in progress' that unfolds through time (Roncoli et al. 2002).
This perspective enables them to appreciate that science as well as local knowledge

can at best provide incomplete information, and that actual outcomes may always differ from those expected and may always be altered by divine intervention. No attempt is made to reconcile pieces of information derived from the plurality of knowledge systems that are at work locally into a unified coherent picture. Full knowledge is considered to be God's exclusive domain in which humans cannot, and should not, venture.

Local forecasting draws from an assortment of phenomena and indicators that appear in the landscape and in the spiritual world (Roncoli et al. 2002). Environmental forecasting knowledge tends to be available to most farmers. Specialists in spiritual forecasting either inherit their skills or acquire them through initiation. Adherence to local forecasts varies widely among and within sites according to age, literacy, religion, and ethnicity. Knowledge or ignorance of forecasting was often invoked to define relationships of authority or social identity. Younger respondents deferred to the knowledge of elders, immigrants to that of original residents, and commoners to that of priestly lineages. At the same time, some people also denied knowing about local forecast so as to show a higher level of education, modernity, or religious orthodoxy. Very few farmers in the Southwest, where the influence of cotton-related extension has been stronger, reported knowing about local forecasts. In the Sahel, *Fulbe* herders, who are strict Muslims, condemn ritually based forecasts as idolatry.

Environmental indicators become available for observation at different times of the year, from the end of one rainy season until the onset of the subsequent one. The most often cited indicators relate to temperatures during the dry season and production of leaves and fruits of local trees. Farmers believe that the duration and intensity of cold and hot temperatures during the earlier and later periods of the dry season (respectively December–February and February–April) correspond to the intensity and duration of rainfall. A clear-cut transition between the two periods is associated with a favorable season, while a less defined shift in temperature is considered a bad sign. At the onset of the rainy season (May–June), farmers observe the production of fruits or flowers by certain local trees, such as the sheanut tree (*Butyrospermum parkii*) and the raisinier (*Anogeissus leiocarpus*). Abundant production is believed to predict good rainfall. Temperatures were mentioned in about half of the interviews in the Sahel and in the Central Plateau. About half of the Central Plateau farmers and a few Sahelian farmers also referred to trees. Several pastoralists in the Sahel also referred to the strength and direction of winds during the dry season and at the onset of the rainy season, and to fluctuations in water sources. Some elders also predict the nature of the season and determine time planting or herding decisions on the basis of star and moon movements. In the Central Plateau site a diversity of cultural and ritual specialists predict rains on the basis of ritual practices or from visions and dreams. They include elders, diviners, soothsayers, and *marabouts*, who mix local and Islamic practices.

Observations of various local forecasting indicators generate hypotheses or expectations about the future, but most farmers do not use them in making decisions. Rather, they wait to corroborate forecasts with what happens at the onset of the rainy season, which is considered to be the most reliable predictor for the coming season. They closely scrutinize the timing and direction of rainfall onset during and shortly after planting: if rains begin early, from the south, and are followed by regular rains, farmers expect a good rainy season, while rains that begin late, from the north, and are followed by erratic rainfall lead farmers to expect a drought. Based on the short duration and relative mildness of the cold during the previous dry season, as well as other indicators, farmers in the Central Plateau expected low seasonal rainfall and the delayed onset of rains confirmed these expectations. On the other hand, in the Sahel local forecasts were mixed, some predicting a poor season, others a good season. But after the rainy season had begun regularly and promisingly, farmers who had anticipated poor rains were reassured and prepared for a good rainy season.

Views of the Past: Farmers' Recollections of the 2000 Rainy Season

To understand what aspects of seasonal rainfall are most relevant to farmers, we asked respondents to describe in detail the 2000 rainy season. Overall, farmers' evaluations reflected an understanding of rainfall as a process, inseparable from its temporal dimension, rather than a quantity, abstracted into a set of static categories such as the terciles of seasonal precipitations forecasts. Confirming findings from our previous research (Ingram et al. 2002), the main parameters farmers used to characterize the rainy season were associated with the *duration* of the season (the timing and nature of the onset and end of the rains) and the *distribution* of rainfall during the season (the number of 'important' rain events, and the timing and duration of dry spells at key points of growth for crops and pasture). In all their observations, farmers defined rainfall events and water deficits in terms of their observations of plant–climate interactions, rather than by precipitation measures *per se*.

The 'duration' of the season is key to farmers' perceptions and adaptations, but their definitions of what constitutes the 'beginning' and the 'end' of the season differ from those of meteorologists.[4] For instance, in the Southwest, early May rains were not counted as marking the onset of the season as they were judged to be insufficient for planting. Producers talk about a 'false start' if the first rains are followed by a prolonged dry spell that causes seedlings to die, resulting in a loss of seed and labor by the farmer. May rains enable farmers to begin planting lowland fields before planting upland fields; their failure causes farmers to plant all fields at once in June. Hence, when all fields are planted at the same time, farmers expect an unfavorable season.

In all three sites, farmers elaborated in great detail on the onset of the rainy season, a crucial time when they must make key productive decisions. Most respondents in the Sahel described the early rains that fell in mid-June as timely, abundant, and widespread, enabling crops and pastures to emerge well and leading them to expect a favorable season. Unfortunately this auspicious rainfall pattern ended shortly after planting. In the Central Plateau, the onset was about three weeks late, in late June, followed by weak, scattered rains. This meant that farmers were unable to plant lowland fields in May as they normally do, but had to wait until late June to plant lowland and upland fields at the same time. Farmers strive to stagger planting to reduce the risk of exposure of crops to water deficits and to spread labor demands, so that they can spend more time preparing the soil to facilitate rainwater infiltration. Because the early rains were followed by a long dry period, those farmers who were unable to finish planting all their fields because of insufficient labor had to replant up to four times. In the Southwest, rains started about ten days late, in early- to mid-June, but were generally adequate.

In the Sahel and in the Central Plateau sites farmers emphasized the number of 'good' or 'large' rains (number of rains was less salient in the Southwest, where rains are more frequent). In particular, half of the farmers interviewed in the Central Plateau complained that only 3 or 4 good rains fell during the whole season, compared to 8 or 10 in normal years. Farmers do not consider all rains to be positive phenomena, but evaluate them according to their impact on farm work and plant growth, which is also a function of time. Rains may be 'useless' rains if they come too late, are too far apart, are negligible in quantity, or are followed by hot wind that dries the soil. Rains may even be 'harmful' if accompanied by much thunder and lightning that kill animals and destroy crops and homes, or if they fall with very large drops that damage flowers or grain heads.

'Good' rains begin at night and fall steadily till the morning, are widespread rather than localized, and are not accompanied by a lot of wind, thunder, or lightening. They last at least 3 or 4 hours so that rainwater infiltrates the soil rather than being lost as runoff, as in the case when heavy rain occurs in a short time. The key parameter whereby farmers distinguish rains is the number of days they leave the soil moist. This criterion varies according to when rains occur during the season. A 'good' rain at planting time should leave the soil most, but not soaked as to impede cultivation, for up to one week in upland fields and two weeks in lowland fields. Later in the season, 'large' rains should fill streams, ponds, and valley bottoms. These rains are particularly needed in July when farmers plant maize, and in August when grain crops are forming seed heads. At this time 'large' rains should fall every few days, alternating with sunny days that trigger flowering of crops and grasses. But farmers in the Sahel and in the Central Plateau reported that in 2000 most of these rains failed to occur.

The occurrence of water deficit periods is another key evaluation criteria in farmers' accounts of seasonal rainfall. This was especially true in the Southwest, where the main crops, cotton and maize, are more vulnerable to water deficit than sorghum or millet. Farmers define water deficit periods operationally, as periods that injure crops because there is no rain or because rains are too light and infrequent to wet below the soil surface. The impact of dry spells varies according to the stage of plant growth, soil types and field location, and previous rainfall patterns. For instance, while crops planted in lowland fields can withstand up to three weeks without rain, those planted in upland fields will suffer after one week without rain. Likewise, Koria's sandy soils retain moisture even after a two or three weeks' dry period, while Sambonaye's clay fields become hot and hard after only one week without rain. In the Sahel and in the Central Plateau, the effect of September droughts were particularly severe because it had not rained much in August, which is normally the wettest time of the year.

In the Sahel, farmers reported two severe water deficit periods, one after planting and the other during seed heading. In some areas the drought after planting lasted up to four weeks, causing farmers to replant their clayey fields two or three times. Some continued planting until late August, when the viable planting time had already passed. In the Central Plateau, the combined effect of exceptionally low seasonal rainfall and several water deficits, each lasting up to three weeks, injured crops beyond their capacity to recover. In the Southwest, a three-week drought in September damaged cotton and maize and other crops, especially those that had been planted late and in upland fields.

In all three sites, farmers assessed the premature end of the rains to be the most problematic feature of the 2000 rainy season since crops, whose growth had been slowed by drought, failed to reach maturation. Farmers consider the season to end with the last rain that has any significance for crops. Therefore, many considered the season to have ended in August. This was the case in the Central Plateau, even though a large rain was registered at the end of September, when crops were already too dried to benefit from it. It was also the case in the Southwest, even though three big rains fell in mid- to late-October. Those rains, which were very heavy as well as localized, caused damage where they fell, shattering the dry maize kernels, causing them to germinate, and spoiling the quality of cotton, thereby reducing its price.

Contextual Comprehension: Farmers' Interpretations of the Forecast

Farmers' perceptions and priorities affected how they understood and what they remembered of the information received from the forecast dissemination team or from radio broadcastings. Farmers seemed to retain (correctly or incorrectly) pieces of information to the extent that they addressed their concerns as well as their anxieties that had been building up at the onset of the season. Expectations formed on the basis of observations of the rain onset appear to have led farmers to emphasize negative or positive elements of the forecast. For instance, where the onset was regular, farmers understood the forecast to predict an average season, while where the onset was late they thought the forecast indicated the possibility of a drought.

In the Sahel, where the season had begun promisingly, most respondents understood that the forecast predicted a relatively favorable ('average' or 'regular') season, although tempered with a few qualification that rains would be 'not abundant', 'not many', and 'less than 1999'. Some understood that the team said the onset would be early, that it would rain till the end of the season, and that it would rain throughout the region. On the other hand, in the Central Plateau, where the onset had been late and anomalous, the large majority of farmers retained the perception that rainfall would be 'not too much', 'not heavy', and 'less than 1999'. Half of the farmers interviewed remembered that the rainy season would be 'not long' and marked by 'not many big rains', which would be widely spaced. But some also believed that, while modest, rains would be sufficient. In the Southwest, where rains had begun a bit late but continued regularly through June, the forecasts provided at the meeting and on the radio were interpreted as indicating a probability of moderate rainfall, but 'average', 'adequate', 'sufficient', for most crops. Several farmers understood that the season would be 'good', but a few farmers perceived the forecast to mean that rainfall, or the number of rains, would not be substantial. The few farmers who heard the SOFITEX broadcast expected abundant seasonal rainfall.

Clearly there were questions on the farmers' mind when the forecast dissemination team arrived and those appear to have influenced their retention of information. The main question in the Sahel and in the Central Plateau concerned the length of the season. This parameter is so salient to farmers' decisions and so vital to crop performance that a 'good' or 'poor' season is most often used interchangeably with adequate or deficient length. Although scientific forecasts only provide an estimate of total quantity of seasonal rainfall, a reference to 'duration' was made when the forecast dissemination team explained that 'seasonal' forecasts relate to rainfall in July, August, and September. In most cases, farmers interpreted this notion as a prediction that the rainy season duration would last about, or no more than, three months. This was particularly the case in the Central Plateau, where a three-week delay in the onset of the rains might have fueled fears that crops might not have time to mature before the end of the season. Some farmers in the Sahel also remembered that the team said that it would rain for three months. Given that three months is a relatively short season in the Central Plateau but a normal season in the Sahel, the belief that the forecast had predicted a season of three months might have shaped expectations for a poor season in the Central Plateau and for a good season in the Sahel. In the Southwest, the length of the season was mentioned less frequently than the possibility of floods or water deficit periods.

Most farmers in the Southwest and in the Central Plateau remembered hearing that rainfall would be less than 1999, when exceptionally heavy rains in August caused flooding, destroyed homes, and damaged crops in those areas. Several farmers in the Southwest also reported, incorrectly, that the team had discussed water deficit periods, an aspect of seasonal rainfall that has significant implications for crop performance in the area. About half of them remembered that the team, who had arrived during a dry period, reassured them that 'the rains will come'.

Another element of information provided by the team related to the notion of 'climatic zone'. As with the reference to the three-month forecast, the idea of a zone had been introduced as a way of explaining some of the limitations of the seasonal rainfall forecast, that is the fact that forecasts relate to a regional rather than localized scale. Some farmers, especially where it had already started raining in nearby areas but not locally, understood it as a prediction that rains would be spatially localized, another key aspect of climate variability often mentioned in farmers' recollections of the 2000 season. A few farmers retained the general idea of 'zone' without specifically remembering what had been said, while others mistook information relative to other zones as applying to their own.

Farmers' evaluation of the scientific forecast reflected local understandings of knowledge as temporary and fragmented. Rather than making general statements of overall accuracy, comments referred to the forecast's ability to predict some aspects of seasonal rainfall and its failure to predict others. The Imam (Muslim cleric) of Bonam commented: 'Of what they said, some things were true and some things were untrue. We also have only some of the truth.' Farmers in the Sahel stated that what the team had predicted (modest but adequate rainfall) seemed true at first but it turned out to be wrong as the season unfolded. In the Southwest, farmers perceived that the forecast correctly predicted that it would rain less than in 1999, that it would rain more in some areas than in others, that rains would pick up again after the dry period during which the team came to the village, and that it would rain till October, which was true although the October rains came too late to benefit the crops.

Putting Predictions into Practice: Farmers' Responses to the Forecast

Farmers' responses to the forecast reflected how they understood the information provided to them, even more than their verbal statements.[5] In the Sahel farmers responded to expectations for average-to-good rains, while in the other sites farmers anticipated a less than average seasonal rainfall. This was especially true in the Central Plateau, where a three-week delay of rain onset fueled fears of an impending drought.

In the Sahel, farmers rehabilitated old fields, established new fields, expanded cultivated areas, and worked harder to ensure that no gaps were left in planting. These adjustments occurred especially in clayey areas, which had been gradually abandoned because of greater frequency of drought, but where sorghum produces well in years of good rainfall. Some farmers selected longer-duration varieties of sorghum and peanut, whose taste is preferred but which require more rain than shorter-duration varieties. Other farmers bought seed and planted more secondary crops, such as peanut, cowpea, sesame, sorrel, and maize, which are grown mostly by women. Those who could do so increased manure application, especially in sandy fields, to take advantage of the good rains. If farmers expect drought they apply less manure to avoid scorching the crops. In general, pastoralists did not change their livestock production strategies in response to the forecast, because they make migration and management choices as a result rather than in anticipation of the rains. But, since most pastoralists in Burkina Faso combine livestock and crop production, they used the information in their farming decisions, particularly in determining the optimal amounts of manure to apply to their fields.

In the Central Plateau, farmers also made adjustments in terms of types of fields, size of planted area, and crop varieties, but their responses were in preparation for drought. As the season progressed, most farmers replaced longer-duration varieties with shorter-duration varieties they had first planted as the former failed to establish. Some farmers planted lowland fields, which they had abandoned because of flooding in 1999. Others increased the planted area to make up for the shortfall in yields and to have more flexibility in terms of where and what to plant. Some also expected to be able to cultivate a larger field because low rainfall would produce fewer weeds.

Likewise, in the Southwest, farmers also prepared for less than average seasonal rainfall by choosing shorter varieties of sorghum and maize, and, in some cases, replacing maize and rice with sorghum, which is less vulnerable to water deficit. Farmers responded by adjusting the timing of farming operations, plowing and planting as quickly as possible to ensure crops were established as early as possible and were able to mature in case the rains stopped prematurely. One farmer planted directly after plowing without ridging to save time, while another stopped planting in early July in order to have time to thoroughly hoe and weed the fields he had planted so far. Farmers who had heard an earlier radio broadcast of the forecast or who had participated in the PRESAO Forum changed the orientation of ridges in ways that helped retain rainwater in the fields. Several farmers also bought or applied less fertilizer, pesticides, and herbicides partly to reduce their debt burden in case of poor yields, and partly because they expected weed and pest infestation to be less severe with low rainfall.

Applying the forecast information to field selection was less feasible in the Southwest than in the other sites because cotton and maize fields account for much of the cultivable land near the village. But some of the farmers who had abandoned their lowland fields because of the 1999 floods brought them back into cultivation upon hearing the forecast. In contrast, one farmer who had heard on the radio that 'abundant rainfall' was expected abandoned negotiations for borrowing a lowland field and planted on higher ground instead, because he expected that lowlands would be flooded as in 1999. He estimated that his maize production from the upland field was 30% less than he would have obtained from the lowland field.

Notably, most of the 'losses' associated with application of forecasts were reported in the Sahel, where the forecast had been interpreted 'accurately' as predicting average or above average seasonal rainfall. On the other hand, in the Southwest, and especially in the Central Plateau, where the forecast had been 'misunderstood' as referring to low-to-moderate rainfall and a shortened season, farmers' responses helped them prepare for a water deficit season. In some cases, farmers' ability to contextualize the scientific forecasts with short-term observations of crop–climate interactions and with their long-term experience in making farming decisions in a highly uncertain environment, helped mitigate the risk of negative impacts of a probabilistic forecast that failed to accurately predict seasonal rainfall.

Conclusions: Meanings that matter

The production of climate forecasts in West Africa is occurring in a diverse and dynamic context that shapes the livelihood strategies and risk mitigation options available to rural households, and, therefore, their ability to utilize forecasts. This context encompasses the landscape as well as the ways it is perceived, understood, experienced, and managed by the communities that interact with it. Both biophysical and socio-cultural dimensions of the environment are always in motion, as they adjust to pressures that emanate from local tensions and global trends. Farmers in Burkina Faso perceive that the overall climate has become more variable, seasonal precipitation has decreased, and the rainy season has shortened, on account of the later onset and premature end of the rains. At the same time, declining availability and productivity of land, increasing price of productive inputs, lack of cash-earning opportunities, and chronic food insecurity are limiting the range of risk management strategies that may be enacted by farmers. Therefore, most rural producers are open to and interested in receiving scientific information because they perceive their own forecasting knowledge to have become less reliable in predicting rainfall patterns and crop performance. In the words of a Central Plateau farmer, 'nowadays farming is like playing the lottery'.

Preliminary analyses indicate that farmers' perceptions of increased climate variability are consistent with meteorological records (West 2001), in contrast to other cases in which local and scientific assessments of environmental change diverge (Gray 2000). The extent to which farmers' empirical observations match the 'reality' of scientific data is an intriguing question that is attracting considerable attention in climate science circles. Perhaps the more interesting question is how farmers' knowledge and experience shape the meaning that scientific information acquires in their midst and how it is integrated in their cognitive landscape. In the case of seasonal rainfall forecasts, this landscape is constituted not only by the meteorological phenomena, but also by the accumulated experience of previous climate events and by conflicting hints, hopes, and fears about the upcoming season.

The case study presented here suggests that farmers' interpretation of scientific forecasts is influenced by how farmers think about rainfall and what they are most interested in knowing. The analysis underscores that scientific and technical knowledge is not a 'product' that can be pre-packaged and delivered to 'users' without its being altered by its incorporation into a different set of meanings and relations from those that produced such knowledge. The pieces of information retained by Burkina Faso farmers were not necessarily the entire and the same message intended to be conveyed by the meteorological service. But because they were grounded in farmers' own observations and experience in coping with a highly variable climatic environment, these 'misunderstandings' helped reduce the risks entailed in probabilistic forecasts. Discontinuities in meaning between climate science and farmers' understandings must be looked at as more than unfortunate failures to convey or to grasp information across cultural or linguistic frameworks. They subsume adaptive mechanisms that build on time-honored farming competence, keen awareness of subtle shifts in environmental conditions, and scrupulous management of scarce resources in view of an uncertain future.

The risks and responsibilities associated with the provision of probabilistic information to subsistence farmers should be given serious consideration. However, these risks are not only a function of rainfall variability, but also of resource constraints. Structural constraints are also powerful contextual factors that shape the interface between what people know and what people do (Patt 2002; Nelson and Finan 2000; Broad 2000; O'Brien et al. 2000). Some of these constraints are culturally and politically difficult to overcome (i.e. land shortage), but others, such as plowing animals and equipment, viable seeds for short cycle varieties, chemical or organic fertilizer, and agricultural credit are key enabling factors that can help translate climate information into appropriate action. Improving farmers' access to these resources, i.e. their ability to cope with risk and recover in case of failure, is as important as improved communication of forecasts.

Notes

1. Corresponding author: Sustainable Agriculture and Natural Resource Management CRSP, University of Georgia, 1422 Experiment Station Road, Watkinsville, GA 30677, ph: (706) 769-3792, fx: (706) 769-1471, email: carlaroncoli@ yahoo.com.
2. The CFAR project is funded by the Office of Global Programs of the U.S. National Oceanic and Atmospheric Administration and implemented by Tufts University and the University of Georgia in collaboration with the Burkina Faso national meteorological service (Direction de la Météorologie Nationale), the national agricultural and environmental research service (Institut National de l'Environnement et des Recherches Agricoles), and Plan International, an international non-governmental development organization.
3. Most Southwest households own radios, and televisions are common in wealthy households. About one-third of households in the Central Plateau site and in the Sahel sites own radios and very few have televisions. The Southwest site receives Radio Nationale du Burkina (RNB), which is relayed from Bobo-Dioulasso, where several private FM stations also operate. The Central Plateau site receives RNB from Ouagadougou. The Sahel sites lay outside of RNB reach but a private FM station in Dori has over 100 km coverage and is widely listened to.
4. The national meteorological service of Burkina Faso marks the onset of the rainy season on the first day after May 1 when it begins raining and at least 20 mm of rain fall during 3 consecutive days that are not followed by a dry period of more than a week. The end of the rainy season is marked on the day after September 1 after which no more than 2 mm of rain are recorded over a period of 20 days.
5. The limited size and purposive nature of the sample precludes our ability to estimate what proportion of the farmers who heard the forecast considered it in making decisions, but our data shows that at least some did. In about half of the cases, respondents who had received a forecast during the team visit or from a radio announcement reported using the information.

References

BROAD, KENNETH. 2000. El Niño and the Anthropological Opportunity. *Practicing Anthropology* 22: 20–23.

GLANTZ, MICHEAL. 1996. *Currents of Change: El Niño's Impact on Climate and Society.* Cambridge: Cambridge University Press.

GRAY, LESLIE. 2000. Reconciling Local Knowledge with Western Scientific Notions of Soil Fertility Decline in Southwestern Burkina Faso. Paper presented at the *African Studies Association* Annual Meeting, Nashville: 15–19 November 2000.

HAMMER, G. L., J. W. HANSEN, J. G. PHILLIPS, J. W. MJELDE, H. HILL, A. LOVE, and A. POTGIETER. 2001. Advances in Applications of Climate Predictions in Agriculture. *Agricultural Systems* 70: 515–533.

INGRAM, KEITH, CARLA RONCOLI, and PAUL KIRSHEN. 2002. Opportunities and constraints for farmers of West Africa to use seasonal precipitation forecasts with Burkina Faso as a case study. *Agricultural Systems*, 74: 331–349.

KEMPTON, W., BOSTER, and J. HARTLEY. 1995. *Environmental Values in American Culture*. Cambridge, MA: MIT Press.

NELSON, DONALD and TIMOTHY FINAN. 2000. The Emergence of a Climate Anthropology in Northeast Brazil. *Practicing Anthropology* 22: 6–10.

NICHOLSON, SHARON. 1985. Sub-Saharan Rainfall 1981–84. *Journal of Climate and Applied Meteorology* 24: 1388–1391.

—— 1986. 'Climate, Drought and Famine in Africa', in *Food in Sub-Saharan Africa*. Edited by A. Hansen and D. McMillan, pp. 107–128. Boulder: Lynne Rienner.

O'BRIEN, KAREN and ROBIN LEICHENKO. 2000. Double Exposure: Assessing the Impacts of Climate Change within the Context of Economic Globalization. *Global Environmental Change* 10: 221–232.

O'BRIEN, K., L. SYNGA, K. NAESS, R. KINGAMKONO, and B. HOCHOBEB. 2000. *Is Information Enough? User Responses to Seasonal Climate Forecasts in Southern Africa.* Report to the World Bank, AFTE1-ENVGC. Adaptation to Climate Change and Variability in Sub-Saharan Africa, Phase II.

ORLOVE, BENJAMIN and JOSHUA TOSTESON. 1999. *The Application of Seasonal to Interannual Climate Forecasts based on El Niño-Southern Oscillation (ENSO) Events: Lessons from Australia, Brazil, Ethiopia, Peru, and Zimbabwe.* WP 99–3, Berkeley: Institute of International Studies, University of California.

OTTERSTROM, SARAH. 2000. Variation in Coping with El Niño Droughts in Northern Costa Rica. *Practicing Anthropology* 22: 15–19.

PATT, ANTHONY. 2001. Understanding Uncertainty: Forecasting Seasonal Climate for Farmers in Zimbabwe. *Risk Decision and Policy* 6: 105–119.

PATT A. and C. GWATA. 2002. Effective Seasonal Climate Forecast Applications: Examining Constraints for Subsistence Farmers in Zimbabwe. *Global Environmental Change: Human and Policy Dimensions* 12(3): 185–195.

RONCOLI, CARLA, KEITH INGRAM, and PAUL KIRSHEN. 2000. Can farmers of Burkina Faso use rainfall Forecasts? *Practicing Anthropology* 22: 24–28.

—— 2001. The costs and risks of coping with drought: livelihood impacts and farmers' responses in Burkina Faso. *Climate Research* 19: 119–132.

—— 2002. Reading the Rains: Local Knowledge and Rainfall Forecasting in Burkina Faso. *Society and Natural Resources* 15: 411–430.

SIVAKUMAR, M. V. K. and F. GNOUMOU. 1987. *Agroclimatology of West Africa: Burkina Faso.* Information Bulletin n. 23, Patancheru, India: International Crops Research Institute for the Semi-Arid Tropics.

STERN, P. C. and W. E. EASTERLING. 1999. *Making climate forecasts matter.* Washington: National Academy Press.

THOMPSON, MICHAEL and STEVE RAYNER. 1998. 'Cultural Discourses', in *Human Choice and Climate Change: The Societal Framework.* Edited by S. Rayner and E. Malone, pp. 265–343. Columbus: Battelle.

WASHINGTON, RICHARD and THOMAS DOWNING. 1999. Seasonal Forecasting of African Rainfall: Prediction, Responses, and Household Food Security. *The Geographical Journal* 165: 255–274.

WEST, COLIN. 2001. *Testing Farmers' Perceptions of Climate Variability with Meteorological Data: Burkina Faso and the Sulphur Springs Valley, Arizona.* M.A. Thesis, Department of Anthropology, University of Arizona, Tucson.

GENERATIONS

Climate Science and the Policy of Drought Mitigation in Ceará, Northeast Brazil

Timothy J. Finan

The Discourse of Drought

One can parody a somewhat weathered witticism with reference to Northeast Brazil by saying that everyone talks about climate, but politicians do something about it.[1] In terms of public discourse, climate – the pattern of seasonal rainfall – dominates the collective social and political consciousness of Northeast Brazil's inhabitants from December 13, St. Lucia's Feast, through the symbolic harvest day, June 24, St. John's Feast. Early in December, discussions of the impending rainy season, which normally starts in January or February, penetrate local conversations as well as print and electronic media. And throughout the unfolding of the season, sometimes abundantly clear in its definition, sometimes painstakingly uncertain, the public discourse about this year's season and its impacts on people's lives constitutes an annual drama, replete with theme and subplot. Climactic tension builds until the St Joseph's Feast (March 19) at which point no recovery is possible from a 'weak winter' (*inverno fraco*). Then, during the next months, the discourse focuses on the joy of bounty or the hard reality of emergency relief. During this six-month period of the year, nearly everyone talks about climate.

Politicians, on the other hand, feel compelled to *do* something about the climate. In the Northeastern state of Ceará, drought-based policymaking occupies much of the attention of the governor's office and the secretariats of agriculture, of water resources, and of social action. At the local level of the *município*, drought relief management is the major reoccurring policy challenge. History shows that drought-related policy is not always motivated by humanitarian concerns or by constituency demand, but rather becomes both a discourse and a stratagem for consolidating political power and, in many cases, accumulating personal wealth. Nonetheless, policymakers have clearly staked out a public domain in the general discourse on climate, one in which they use science to champion the cause of drought's victims.

So it is that the discourse of drought reconstructs itself annually in a culturally patterned fashion. The collective anxiety begins to grip rural society as augurs of the upcoming season appear. On the public side, climate information generated in and disseminated from the state capital provides an official, 'scientific' forecast; while locally, rain prophets (*profetas de chuva*) ply their skills reading what signs 'nature' has manifest in the behavior of stars, plants, birds, and animals (Finan 1999). This chapter intends to show how a climate discourse is embedded in traditional forms of political interaction within a highly stratified, paternalistic society. Particularly, the appropriation by policymakers of science as a means of solving drought (Nelson 2000), a key component of the discourse, imbues 'objective' information with cultural meaning. I argue that in the context of heightened uncertainty and anxiety, policymakers assert a privileged access to knowledge thus ennobling and legitimizing their political status. To be a '*dono da verdade*' ('owner of truth') is to play at God, thus reinforcing the paternalistic cultural model that has dominated the region since colonization. The chapter will trace the emergence of science as a integral part of climate discourse in Ceará and demonstrate how the value of climate forecast information has been reduced and compromised by its manipulation in the political culture of the region. Finally, a suggestion for fuller realization of the potential of climate forecasts is offered.

Ceará: Vulnerability in a Semi-arid Environment

The state of Ceará, located squarely in Northeast Brazil, presents all the climatological characteristics of a semi-arid environment. The majority of annual rainfall occurs during the period January–April, but is widely distributed spatially and temporally. Although the state-wide historical average precipitation is around 700 mm, regional patterns vary from 500 mm to 1200 mm. Even within a region, rainfall in any given year may favor one local site over another. There is a general consensus in rural areas that the level of annual rainfall has tended to diminish. While droughts were commonly considered to occur one out of ten years, during the last decade, five years of drought crisis were recorded. Along with this high inter-annual variation, there is also strong intra-annual oscillation. Thus, heavy rains at the beginning of the season, followed by an extended dry period (*veranico*) can be as economically devastating as an insufficient total amount of annual rainfall.

Drought is what stimulates the annual public obsession with climate. It was first recorded in the 1500s soon after European settlement and has occurred with regularity ever since; however, recent patterns (five drought years out of the last ten) suggest an increase in both frequency and intensity. Of the more than 6 million inhabitants of Ceará, 35 percent live in rural areas, and 40 percent of the economically active population are employed in agriculture. However, this segment of the population generates only 6 percent of the state domestic product, a strong indicator of the impoverishment of rural families. The primary agricultural activity is the subsistence production of corn and beans, which depends solely upon rainfall. Some rainfed cash cropping in cotton, cashew nut, and coconut is found in localized areas. The state does not have a natural surface water source, although one river valley has an annual flow from a network of upstream reservoirs.

The social sciences – particularly geography and anthropology – have widely documented that climate variability is not the principal determinant of climate vulnerability (Blaikie et al. 1994; Bohle et al. 1994; Adger and Kelly 1999). Rather, socio-economic conditions, particularly the uneven distribution of assets and entitlements, define profiles of vulnerability within the *context* of climate variability. In Northeast Brazil, this argument is both historically and presently substantiated. Today's rural economy in Ceará, as well as in the rest of the *sertão nordestino*, manifests the consequences of a colonial settlement pattern that concentrated land and other assets in the hands of a few privileged families and created the socio-economic distinctions that still predominate. The landed class obtained its labor first from enslaved Amerindians, then Africans, then from the landless poor – both resident sharecroppers and *corvée* laborers. The Ceará described by Johnson (1972) over three decades ago retains most of the same patron–client characteristics today. Traditionally the vast majority of rural residents were landless farmers, dependent not only upon the rainfall but upon the largesse of large landowners who ultimately control the destinies of their sharecroppers. From the beginning of the sugar economy along the coast of the Northeast in the 1500s and especially after the rise of cotton production during the American Civil War, an economic pattern emerged in which large *fazendeiros* preoccupied themselves with cattle, while their sharecroppers produced subsistence food crops (one third usually to the landowner) and cotton (one half to the landowner). Historically land established wealth and prestige, and landownership attracted wealthy families from urban areas, such as Fortaleza. Merchants and professionals alike invested in *fazendas* as a source of wealth *and* power.

Today the demographic shift toward an urban population has altered the rural economy and the social ecology. The declining profitability of cattle raised under traditional technologies and the virtual disappearance of cotton have dried up investment in rainfed agriculture and ranching. Once-prominent rural families now sell their *fazendas* to purchase residential apartments in Fortaleza, where all their children reside. Nonetheless, the land tenure pattern remains concentrated in largeholdings (albeit smaller than they once were), and the percentage of landless and, now, independent smallholder farmers continues to be extremely high. Even for those with larger amounts of owned land (500–1000 ha, for example), the operational farm size (the amount of cultivated land in any year) remains highly limited by existing rainfed technologies and the growing scarcity of city-bound labor. Thus while the economic non-viability of largeholdings is increasingly apparent, the large army of landless farmers still makes up the vast majority of the rural population.

While access to land is one determinant of vulnerability, the lack of alternative income is the other. Cotton was considered to be the 'salary' crop to poor farming families. While highly exploitative, cotton production did produce a small annual income to cover non-food costs and emergencies. As cotton fell victim to globalization and the boll weevil, no other source of income appeared to take its place. The rather successful strategy of industrialization around the capital of the state has neither spread to the interior regions nor expanded sufficiently to absorb the rural exodus.

Thus, in one essential sense, the rural economy has not changed over three decades or more. It is constituted of people without land, without cash, and without technological alternatives, and herein lies the source of their vulnerability. Without land, these families cannot diversify into small livestock activities (such as small ruminants), and they have no collateral to obtain credit for investment. Equally unavailable is access to part-time labor employment that is climate-neutral. Under these conditions, survival is based on patron largesse, emigrated children, and government subsidies such as rural pensions and drought relief programs.

Our research in the state has spanned five years and includes a survey of 484 households in 1998, followed by a survey of 120 households during the 1998–99 El Niño event. We also conducted an exhaustive institutional analysis of the public sector involved in drought relief and drought management.[2] The initial survey generated a vulnerability classification of the sampled farmers according to levels of the production of food crops and income from agricultural and livestock activities (Finan and Nelson 2001). Outside income sources were treated as exogenous to the classification and treated as types of coping mechanisms (see Corbett 1988). This analysis resulted in three classes of vulnerability, with forty-four of the sample households located in the most vulnerable category and nearly 80 percent in the two most vulnerable categories.

Since agricultural production is a function of land size under existing technologies, it cannot be taken as an single indicator of vulnerability. Nonetheless, the form of land tenure is an independent measure, and the analysis showed that, as expected, the most vulnerable classes cultivated less land, but also that the most vulnerable households tended to be the landless. Only one household in the most vulnerable category had access to any irrigated land. The asset base of these households was also significantly reduced with respect to livestock ownership, particularly cattle. With regard to off-farm income, the most vulnerable categories clearly relied on off-farm income as a coping mechanism, and the vulnerable households had an average of 2.5 sources of off-farm employment. While total off-farm income for the vulnerable classes is only slightly lower than for the least vulnerable groups in absolute terms, the proportion of off-farm income in total household income is much greater. Nonetheless, the 1997 total per capita income of the most vulnerable group (about US$ 450) is nearly one-fourth that of the least vulnerable households (US$ 1690).

Such vulnerabilities help explain the dire consequences of climate extremes. When drought occurs, crop production is decimated and these families cannot feed themselves. While drought may be pronounced regionally (i.e. at the level of the state), it is felt locally – on farms and in *comunidades*. In a typical crisis, the majority of *municipios*, but not all, will receive either inadequate or poorly distributed rains. As a crisis unfolds, farmers will plant and replant their crops and attempt to locate moisture soils (*baixios*), but most do not have a drought technology on hand – neither resistant seeds nor emergency irrigation sources. As importantly, drought usually reduces much of the income-generating potential of the more vulnerable and landless households, such as manual labor on larger farms. In Ceará, the larger landowners pasture their herds over large expanses of the unique native vegetation called *caatinga*. During drought not only do the rangeland grasses disappear, but water holes dry up, leaving the cattle to die of both thirst and hunger. Some of the least vulnerable cattlemen, those with other sources of permanent income, are often able to move their herds to other less-affected regions or to provide sources of supplementary feed. The more vulnerable livestock owners do not have these options and are often forced to sell their herds.

One of the most urgent impacts of drought is the loss of water for human consumption. The *município*, the basic administrative unit, is roughly a county-like geographical area with a relatively small urban center and a number of surrounding settlement concentrations called *comunidades*. Each *comunidade* has a water source, usually a small reservoir which provides water for all human (and animal) uses. In the majority of cases, these reservoirs cannot survive a period of drought, and the water soon becomes concentrated in salts and unfit for human consumption. Even the larger urban centers are vulnerable to severe water shortage. In the case of drought, both rural and urban populations depend upon the public distribution of water in tanker trucks.

Thus does one characterize the components of climate vulnerability in rural Ceará. The potential loss of food and feed production, the high level of livestock mortality, and the overall shortage of drinking water engender the exceedingly public apprehension that accompanies the spectre of drought. Duly encoded in song, literature, and language, drought is a stark reality in Ceará and the rest of the Northeast, and it establishes the very identity of the people who suffer it. The national cultural image of the backlander, the *sertanejo*, is one of suffering and endurance.

What Politicians do about Climate

I have argued elsewhere that in Northeast Brazil *politics* and *policy* are distinguished neither in language nor in practice (Finan 1999). They have intimately enmeshed meanings that are only understood within the context of a highly class-based society. Beginning with the original distribution of the most valued factor of production, land, the social formation of the Northeast was steeped in inequity. Large landowners first used slaves to produce their sugar cane, their food, and their cattle; then after slavery, landless sharecroppers occupied the lowest rungs of the class ladder. Until recently in Ceará, local strongmen (*coronéis*) and their families controlled fief-like regions where they ruled imperiously, the basis of their support derived from a system of patronage and clientilism that even today is a dominant form of social control. Landless families depend upon the powerful to obtain land for planting, to secure an emergency safety net in times of crisis, and to protect them from other sources of threat. In return, the landless provide a docile labor force and complete political support for the *patrão* and the powerful.

Politician commitments to local constituencies have followed this same patron–client framework, since in fact most state-level politicians come from these powerful rural families. Progressive ideas about the responsibilities of people in public power and the essential rights of a voting populace have never made strong inroads in the rural Northeast. Political relationships continue today to be highly personalized and based not on a broader sense of public service response to constituent needs but on a desire to maintain hegemonic power relationships. One has only to visit a local politician's home or office and observe the daily line of 'voters' with petty requests for money or medicine to understand how strongly clientilistic institutions are embedded in this system of patronage. And, of course, drought is very much part of this cultural fabric.

A History of Drought Response

Climate first achieved national attention in the 1877–79 extended drought in which 500,000 *cearenses* perished due to starvation and smallpox (Davis 2001: 79–90; Souza and Filho 1983: 34). During this crisis, the federal government, stung by accounts of unprecedented suffering, spent the equivalent of 4 million pounds sterling to provide emergency food and relief. From that time forward, the federal government began to take responsibility for the climate-based plight of the populations of the Northeast and, in effect, to develop an 'environmental policy' with regard to climate variability. Within the context of this chapter, it is important to emphasize that drought itself was seen as a climatic phenomenon rather than a socio-economic one related to the acute vulnerability of the rural population (Sen 1981;

Watts 1983). Thus, the government looked to 'science and technology' to solve the nagging riddle of climate variability. Since the problem was framed in terms of the lack of rainfall, the initial public response was to stockpile water. The first large dam was constructed in 1906 and, since the creation of the precursor of today's Department for Works Against Drought (DNOCS) at that time, more than 275 dams have been built throughout the Northeast (many in Ceará) with a capacity to hold 14 billion cubic meters (Magalhães 1993: 193). The strategy of water storage was to provide adequate supplies to urban populations in the interior of the region and to create the infrastructure for irrigated agriculture. It still astounds the uninformed to fly over the state of Ceará and witness the quantity of water stored in reservoirs compared to the modest amount of irrigated agriculture.

While the policy set designed to permanently eliminate drought recruited the aid of science and technology, the policy set for drought alleviation was traditionally based on emergency relief, ex post factum. In 1959 (the year following the worst drought of the century), the Superintendency for the Development of the Northeast (SUDENE) was created by the federal government to concentrate development efforts and coordinate investment programs. Its role in drought relief was to coordinate and finance the program of '*frentes de trabalho*', an emergency public works program comprised of labor gangs drawn from the families of drought victims. In this program, politics and policy became inextricably enmeshed, as local politicians used the available funds to spread the gospel of clientilism and patronage (Pessoa 1987). In Ceará, the 10 percent of the landowners who own 90 percent of the land regularly directed relief funds toward improvements on their *fazendas*. Corruption was rife, as long-dead and non-existent workers, even babies, were commonly enrolled in the work front programs and paid their deadman's wages. Through this and other avenues, public relief funds were converted into actual income for largeholders or into an army of labor that became a source of private (no cost) investment for their *fazendas*. This widespread and cynical exploitation of intense misery has been labeled the 'drought industry', considered one of the most lucrative of the Northeast. Souza and Filho (1983: 97–98) cite the deposition of the president of the Federation of Rural Workers in Ceará published in a local newspaper saying: 'The large landholder and the politician monopolized the Emergency Program, while we workers, who sustain the Nation, continue impoverished' [author translation].

Consistent with historical patterns, it is still the level of human suffering (with the concomitant social unrest) that prompts emergency response. When the situation becomes intolerable, local politicians inform state politicians who then inform the federal government. Funds are appropriated at the federal level and move back down the pipeline to local *municípios* and *comunidades*. Emergency funds are traditionally allocated to three relief activities – provisioning of public employment, food deliveries, and water deliveries. The public work salaries are set at basic survival levels, and the actual projects are selected according to criteria that include the improvement of local infrastructure.[3] The distribution of food is in the form of 'basic market baskets' that contain a month's supply of essential staples (beans, oil, sugar, dried milk, etc.) for an average family. Water is delivered to local communities through tanker trucks. In the drought of 1998–99, these three components cost approximately 450 million dollars in the state of Ceará, and over 250,000 families participated in the emergency program. Certainly at the level of emergency relief, drought has offered, and to some extent still offers, the opportunity for local-level politicians to accrue great political, if not financial, advantage from the suffering of their constituencies.

The Recruitment of Climate Science against Drought

Along with emergency relief, there is still the commitment to the permanent reduction of drought vulnerability. This effort once again demonstrates how politics and policy can become confused, when the legitimizing power of science is appropriated by the politician/policymaker. The most notable recruitment of science to the mitigation of drought was the establishment of a climate forecasting agency in Ceará – FUNCEME (Fundação Cearense de Meteorologia). The current version of FUNCEME has its roots in the 1970s, when it was thought that the technology of cloud-seeding could obviate drought. The agency maintained a small fleet of planes and regularly ran cloud-seeding operations during the rainy season months. While cloud-seeding did not produce the desired results, there was a widespread acceptance of the role of science as the ultimate answer to drought vulnerability. This acceptance emboldened policymakers and imbued them with a sense of privileged access to information considered nearly divine, the political implications of which were immediately realized.

In the late 1980s, FUNCEME developed its forecasting capacity with a broad base of support from both Brazil's meteorological community and the international climate science community (Lemos et al. 2002). The climatic patterns of Northeast Brazil display a robust El Niño signal, and droughts generally correlate with strong El Niño events (such as 1877 and 1998). With a state-of-the-art forecasting capacity, the Ceará was internationally perceived as a laboratory for the application of forecasts in drought mitigation. The governor of the state, who himself projected a modernist, strong executive image, wished to demonstrate that science could serve as handmaiden to policymaking, and he consequently used his influence to attract resources to the new forecasting agency. Following the work of Weiss (1978), a knowledge-based model of policymaking occurs when science – in the pursuit of knowledge – makes a discovery. Once policymakers are made aware of the new knowledge, they seek ways of applying it to their policy challenges. In the case of

Ceará, climate science had made new and important advances in discerning and modeling the El Niño Southern Oscillation (ENSO) patterns; now state policy-makers were challenged to see how this science could be applied in their particular problem-solving contexts.

FUNCEME gained international attention in 1992, when during the previous December it announced the likelihood of drought. According to the legend and literature (Glantz 1996: 80–81; Golnaraghi and Kaul 1995: 42; Orlove and Tosteson 1999: 12–15), this forecast unleashed a set of measures that included the provisioning of 'drought-tolerant' seed, the opening of credit lines, and a whistle-stop journey throughout the interior by the then-governor Ciro Gomes, to urge farmers to participate in the program. The purported result of this effort was a table of numbers published in the international literature comparing two drought years, one with forecast, one without, both with similar levels of precipitation, but with 85 percent of average harvest in the forecast year compared with only 15 percent of average harvest in the other. These figures have been cited regularly to promote the value of climate information; however, this success story also laid the ground-work of a major crisis for FUNCEME and diverted attention from the areas of environmental policymaking where climate information could be most valuable.

It is still intriguing that the international community so readily accepted this case as confirmation of the value of climate forecasts. In our research in Ceará, we have attempted to use a time series (1975 to the present) of production and precip-itation data published as official state statistics to recreate these figures in the table, and no set of assumptions regarding the composition of the harvest provides comparable figures (Nelson 2000). Even if the numbers are accepted, however, there are alternative explanations to explain the temporal differences. As all climate scientists warn us, the semi-arid tropics are characterized by high levels of spatial and temporal variability in rainfall. For the years in question, 75 percent of average precipitation is a meaningless figure, if the distribution of rainfall is not taken into consideration. Rainfall in a given year can exceed the average, but farmers actually experience drought, as defined by harvest losses. Equally, the production potential of the state is not spread evenly across the landscape; rather some areas have particularly appropriate soils for rainfed production, while in other regions, soils are thin and lacking in fertility. Thus, specific local conditions also determine production outcome of precipitation.

In effect, this story illustrates the co-optation of science by politicians in the sense that political benefits outstripped the actual economic gains from the fore-cast. In a manner very similar to the way local politicians and powerful landowners had distorted the emergency relief programs, the state level policy system had sought to gain privileged control over knowledge so that it could be used to promote political agendas and reinforce power relations. Much as a local politician might distribute medicine to the destitute poor as if it came from his/her own pocket, FUNCEME had sought to reinforce its power base by doling out knowledge (science) to clients extremely vulnerable to climate extremes. If the climate science product had higher levels of certainty, this advantage might have been maintained. In 1992, FUNCEME reached the zenith of its popularity; however, in 1993, the agency's release of an inaccurate forecast provided the first indication of the difficulties of applying climate forecast data. A widespread crisis in credibility experienced by FUNCEME cast doubts on the value of climate science as a tool to mitigate drought-related effects on rainfed agriculture. In the media, where many public perceptions are formed, the FUNCEME forecast came to be seen as failed mockery of reality.

As suggested above, the FUNCEME forecast was incorporated into other sectors of policymaking within the state government. The program *Hora de Plantar* (It's Time to Plant) was an improved seed distribution program that linked access to quality seed varieties to appropriate timing of planting. Seeds would be released only when FUNCEME's forecast had determined that the rains had in fact arrived. Farmers traditionally plant as soon as the first rains wet the soil to a depth of about 25 cm, and they need their seeds at that point. However, when such rains were deemed by FUNCEME to be anomalous, the government would not release the seeds, and the banks would not provide production credit, thus frustrating expectant farmers. These situations caused the forecast to be perceived not so much as relevant information but as a constraint and a hindrance to the local system. As the lack of credibility in FUNCEME increased, so did the distrust of science. This of course undermined the political advantage that had been sought so intensely.

Climate Science and Climate Anthropology

As anthropology defines an agenda for the understanding of the relationship between climate science and policy, the Ceará case study provides important insights. In our interviews with all the policy system stakeholders and with rural households, several salient issues were identified that are perhaps valid across different societies. The first and perhaps most prominent lesson from this research is that policymakers – in their eagerness to appropriate the political benefits of science and knowledge – did not fully understand the limits of the knowledge product itself. In effect, a seasonal forecast is a probabilistic statement of expected annual precipitation within a historical distribution of past rainfall. In a given year, a forecast cannot be judged wrong; one can only say that the actual outcome was likely or not likely to occur. When politicians in the state presented probabilities as certainties (i.e. it *will* rain this year) or allowed the media to do so, the limits of the science were exceeded. Moreover, the targeted constituency (e.g. farmers) recognized that such excess had occurred, that it had occurred for political reasons, and condemned FUNCEME for the sin of hubris. As a result the forecasts them-selves came to be dismissed, even when – within scientific discourse – they were actually correct. It is clear that the application of this science is in a learning phase. Neither farmers nor policymakers nor any other stakeholders in Ceará fully understand quite how to structure their decisions around probabilistic information, not so much because it is probabilistic but rather because it is new. As the limits of risk related to different probabilities become better understood, the forecast potential will increase.

This analysis of the relationship between science and policy has also indicated that climate forecast information, even if it were precise and robust, would not offer a benefit to the majority of the rural population of Ceará. First of all, there is no neutral and indisputable body of evidence demonstrating that the dissemination of climate information has had any impact on levels of food crop production throughout the state – either in drought or normal years. The survey of 484 households suggests that climate information in general – and FUNCEME's product in particular – does not affect planting, crop choice, or use of technology on most farms. The expectation that climate information itself would stimulate behavioral changes in farmers and improve their buffering capabilities is a mis-guided one that serves primarily to reap political benefit. In reality, the farmers in this study present vulnerability profiles so extreme that their flexibility in decision-making is highly constrained. In other words, farmers do not have the technological options to respond to one forecast or another. Thus, the science by itself is rendered useless, until the more fundamental problems of vulnerability are corrected (through the policy system).

It is important to note that FUNCEME is not the only purveyor of climate information in the state. Over the second half of the 1990s, the media significantly enhanced the visibility of the empirical rain prophets, and in fact annual confer-ences of the empirical forecasters coincided with the launching of the FUNCEME forecast, suggesting, to the delight of the press, that the rural farmers could choose between science and local empiricism in their decision-making. Our survey again reveals that while most farmers know of and acknowledge the *profetas* and their forecasts, such information does not orient planting decisions, but seems more valuable as a liniment for the collective psyche. In fact, all farmers have their set of observations that they correlate with a good or bad winter; however, regardless of the signs when the rains wet the soil, they plant. One farmer told us wryly: 'when it comes to forecasting the winter rains, each of us is a *profeta*'.

Finally climate anthropology is equipped with the tools to explore where climate forecasts might best be applied within a complex socio-economic and political context. Just as vulnerability is not determined by climate variability itself, but rather by a set of socio-economic conditions, so too is the process of science application constructed within a dynamic social system with its cultural meanings, its polity, and its diverse livelihoods. The challenge to the anthropologist in the case of Ceará is to discover where climate science can successfully mitigate the traditional afflictions of drought.

Conclusion: Where Science May Improve Policymaking (and Political Ethics)

As enlightened policymakers seek to understand (or exploit) climate science more objectively, the Ceará case offers a possible path. The main challenge is whether science can be used to break the historical bonds of patronage and clientilism that have made drought an economic boon to local powermongers. The current research in Ceará has hypothesized that local governments, those most susceptible to corruption and mismanagement, are the ideal focal points for forecast applications. The research results show conclusively that most farmers do not have the means to respond to forecasts. Such, however, is not the case with local *município* governments and local leaderships. An intrepid leader with advance knowledge of the onset of drought has a range of response options, if conditions obtain. First, there must be an objective assessment of the differing vulnerabilities within the *município*, which have been neutrally and 'scientifically' analyzed in terms of the causes and magnitude of that vulnerability. This assessment becomes a tool for proactive drought planning, the second condition. In Ceará at the state level there is a growing recognition that drought is not an anomaly but a reality of the semi-arid environment. Such a shift in mentality is critical to promote a process of local-level, participatory planning based on an 'objective' depiction of the needs of the constituency. Such a proactive plan would enhance the value of a forecast, since it would specify prior sets of mitigating interventions rather than awaiting human suffering to trigger a response. In this way, the value of patronage would be reduced. Patronage requires personal and private negotiation; while drought planning requires public and transparant negotiation based upon a reality that all accept. To the extent that science can be made accessible to all participants in society, it stops serving but a few.

Within the complex political system of Ceará, the local use of climate forecasts requires not only the substitution of an engrained patronage system, but also readjustments at the state and perhaps national level. Fortunately in Ceará, as Tendler (1997) has documented and as the rest of Brazil has recognized, a new sense of objective, rational professionalism has supplanted the system of *coronéis*, and the delivery of government services to the state has been held to new, account-able standards. For local *prefeituras* to successfully integrate probabilistic climate science into drought planning, the state government must embrace the innovation, since most drought relief funds are either centralized in state coffers or mobilized at the federal level through state mediation. State planning to reduce the impacts of drought must be based on the preparation and implementation of local-level plans. This creation of a wider state and local partnership provides FUNCEME and its climate product with a clear venue and marks a new era of sophistication in ongoing efforts to adapt to the realities of a severe, semi-arid environment.

Notes

1. In this chapter, climate is a seasonal phenomenon, thus one can say: 'the climate of northwest Brazil has a well-defined rainy season which begins in February'. Weather, by contrast, is the immediate phenomenon. As some say, climate is what you expect, weather is what you get.
2. This research has been funded by the National Oceanic and Atmospheric Administration and is being carried out by a multidisciplinary team from the University of Arizona, Federal University of Ceará, and the Government of Ceará.
3. A recent innovation has been to pay adults this salary to attend literacy classes. During 1998–99 around 30,000 people participated in this program.

References

ADGER, W. N. and P. M. KELLY. 1999. Social Vulnerability to Climate Change and the Architecture of Entitlements. *Mitigation and Adaptation Strategies for Global Change* 4(3/4): 253–266.

BLAIKIE, P., T. CANNON, I. DAVIS, and B. WISNER. 1994. *At Risk: Natural Hazards, People's Vulnerability, and Disaster*. New York: Routledge.

BOHLE H. G., T. E. DOWNING, and M. J. WATTS. 1994. Climate Change and Social Vulnerability: Toward a Sociology and Geography of Food Insecurity. *Global Environmental Change* 4(1): 37–48.

CORBETT, J. E. M. 1988. Famine and household coping strategies. *World Development* 16(9): 1099–1112.

DAVIS, MIKE. 2001. *Late Victorian Holocausts: El Niño Famines and the Making of the Third World*. London: Verso.

FINAN, TIMOTHY J. and DONALD R. NELSON. 2001. Making roads, making rain, making do: public and private response to drought in Ceará, Northeast Brazil. *Climate Research* 19: 97–108.

FINAN, TIMOTHY J. 1999. Drought and Demagoguery: A Political Ecology of Climate Variability in Northeast Brazil. Paper presented to the Carnegie Foundation, New York September 1999

GLANTZ, M. 1996. *Currents of Change: El Nino's Impact on Climate and Society*. Cambridge: Cambridge University Press.

GOLNARAGHI, M. and R. KAUL. 1995. The Science of Policymaking: Responding to El Nino. *Environment* 37(4): 16–44.

JOHNSON, ALAN. 1972. *Sharecroppers of the Sertão*. Palo Alto: Stanford University Press.

LEMOS, M. C., T. J. FINAN, R. W. FOX, D. R. NELSON, and J. TUCKER. 2002. The Use of Seasonal Climate Forecasting in Policymaking: Lessons from Northeast Brazil, *Climatic Change* 55: 479–507.

MAGELHÃES, A. R. 1993. Drought and Policy Responses in Northeast Brazil, in *Drought Assessment, Management, and Planning: Theory and Case Studies*. Edited by D. A. Wilhite. Boston: Kluwer Academic Publishers.

NELSON, DON. 2000. Solving for Drought: Science and Policy in Northeast Brazil. MA Thesis, University of Arizona.

ORLOVE, BENJAMIN S. and JOSHUA L. TOSTESON. 1999. The Application of Seasonal to Interannual Climate Forecasts Based on El Niño-Southern Oscillation (ENSO) Events: Lessons from Australia, Brazil, Ethiopia, Peru, and Zimbabwe. Working Papers in Environmental Politics 2. Berkeley: UC Berkeley WP 99–3.

PESSOA, DIRCEU. 1987. Drought in Northeast Brazil: impacts and government response, in *Planning for Drought: Toward a Reduction of Societal Vulnerability*. Edited by D.A. Wilhite and W. Easterling. Boulder, CO: Westview Press.

SEN, AMARTYA. 1981. *Poverty and Famines: An Essay on Entitlement and Deprivation*. Oxford: Oxford University Press.

SOUZA, ITAMAR DE and JOÃO MEDEIROS FILHO. 1983. *Os Desagregados Filhos da Seca: Uma análise sócio-política das secas do Nordeste*. Petrópolis: Editora Vozes.

TENDLER, J. 1997. *Good Government in the Tropics*. Baltimore: Johns Hopkins University Press.

WATTS, MICHAEL J. 1983. *Silent Violence: Food, Famine, and Peasantry in Northern Nigeria*. Berkeley: University of California Press.

WEISS, C. H. 1978. Improving the Linkage between Social Research and Public Policy, in *Knowledge and Policy: The Uncertain Connection*. Edited by L. E. Lynn. Washington, D.C, National Academy of Sciences.

–12–

Climate and Culture in the North: The Interface of Archaeology, Paleoenvironmental Science, and Oral History

Anne Henshaw

The eastern Canadian Arctic as a region and as a homeland to Inuit peoples provides a unique opportunity to examine human understandings of, and responses to, meteorological phenomena involving both short-term weather events and long-term climatic patterns. Studies examining the interface between weather, climate and culture are not new in Arctic anthropology or archaeology and have often formed the explanatory basis for understanding the temporal dimensions of changing landscapes, resources, societies, and economies in the north. This is mainly due to the fact that the Arctic is a place of high seasonal variability, where the amplification of weather and climatic extremes can produce dramatic effects and consequences for northern peoples. In recent years, there has been a surge of climate–culture interaction studies in light of our global concerns about climate change and its regional impacts. Increasingly, social scientists and natural scientists are turning to northern peoples to gain an understanding of their unique relationship with the environment as a way to create more culturally informed and effective climate change policies (Fenge 2001; Fox 2000; McDonald et al. 1997; Riedlinger 2001; Craver 2001). However, with the exception of Julie Cruikshank's (1981, 1984, 2001) research, most recent studies focus on shorter-term weather and climate phenomena (on the time scale of days, months, and years), where long-term change (decades and centuries) and human response are given a low profile.

This chapter explores how we can contextualize contemporary perceptions of weather and climate within a greater temporal framework by linking archaeology and paleoenvironmental science with Inuit oral traditions. Specifically, I argue that by examining climate-sensitive places on the landscape and seascape from a multidisciplinary perspective, social scientists can broaden the current methodologies they employ to collect and document the range of adaptive strategies used by people in the past and present. The knowledge associated with such an adaptive range is important for understanding how northern peoples may choose to respond to climatic changes predicted for the future. In order to explore the linkages between past and present, I focus on one key climate-sensitive environmental feature in the north, sea ice. Sea ice dominates the Inuit seascape for most of the calendar year and is highly sensitive to weather conditions as well as longer-term climate change. This chapter builds on previous research by combining long-term Inuit–sea ice interactions with preliminary oral history place-name research on southern Baffin Island (Henshaw 1999, 2000, 2003).

Indigenous Knowledge and Climate Change

The study of cultural perceptions and classifications of the environment has a long history in the field of anthropology, and more specifically in the subfield of ethnoecology (Conklin 1969; Ellen 1982; Hardesty 1977; Ingold 1996; Milton 1996). In the Arctic, indigenous knowledge (IK), which encompasses what is referred to as traditional ecological knowledge (TEK) or Inuit Qaujimajatuqangit (IQ),[1] has increasingly been used in contemporary resource management, environmental impact assessment, and for establishing land claims agreements (Caulfield 1997; Cohen 1997; Freeman 1976; Freeman and Carbyn 1988; Riewe 1992; Riewe and Oakes 1992; Sallenave 1994; Stevenson 1996).[2] Many of these studies show that Inuit have a holistic understanding of their environment that extends well beyond descriptive biology. Such knowledge not only helps us to understand how different components of ecosystems interrelate, but also provides specific information on the behavior, movements, and health of animals in relation to their surrounding environment (Usher and Wenzel 1987; Freeman 1992). Increasingly these studies have focused on indigenous understandings of weather and climate as a way to highlight local manifestations of global climate change at scales relevant to human activity.

Recent work carried out in the Hudson Bay region documented the regional environmental changes observed by Inuit and Cree relating to animal behavior and range, sea ice conditions, weather patterns, and ocean currents (MacDonald et al. 1997). A broad range of Inuit and Cree environmental knowledge is clearly demonstrated in this study and many of the observations described point to greater variability and unpredictability in the general climate system. Similarly, studies from the Inuvialuit community of Sachs Harbor as well as several communities in the eastern Canadian Arctic and Alaska describe weather and seasons that are increasingly unpredictable, especially with respect to sea ice, making 'traditional' weather forecasting techniques no longer useful and travel a high risk activity (Riedlinger 2001; Fox 2000). Recent research has also been devoted to the responses of individuals and communities to the changes they observe. For example, amongst the Inuvialuit Riedlinger (2001: 97) identified five strategies community residents employed to cope with environmental change and fluctuation, including: '1) modifying the timing of harvest activity; 2) modifying the location of harvest activity; 2) modifying the method of harvest activity; 4) adjusting the species harvested; and 5) minimizing risk and uncertainty.' While such responses testify to the flexible nature of Inuvialuit lifeways, there still exist a number of conceptual challenges to conducting this type of research.

With the exception of Cruikshank's (2001) recent work documenting Athapaskan, Eyak and Tlingit glacier-related knowledge back to the Little Ice Age, most studies focus on contemporary perceptions while the temporal depth often associated with indigenous oral traditions remains elusive. This is not to say such time depth (beyond one lifetime) does not exist but more likely that our methodologies to collect and document such knowledge need to be carefully re-examined. The apparent lack of temporal depth may be related to cultural constructions of time and linguistic nuances that may not be picked up in translations.[3] From the outset, as Nadasdy (1999) and Cruikshank (2001) have pointed out, much of the discourse relating to climate change is biased toward western scientific terminology that do not easily translate in the languages or cultural practices of aboriginal people. Therefore climate change inquiries often do not adequately reflect the unique cultural lens in which such knowledge is constructed. Additionally, much of the current research attempting to document indigenous forms of climatic knowledge are done in a workshop format that lasts one or two days. While such workshops have certain advantages, they often do not allow for an in-depth understanding of a region afforded through other methodologies including participant observation and oral history research.

In general, IK in the form of oral tradition has also been underutilized in fields such as historical ecology and paleoenvironmental reconstruction (Crumley 1994). Researchers have used the archaeological record in combination with various environmental data sets to trace anthropogenic impacts on the landscape and human responses to climate change, but relatively few studies have used oral testimony from indigenous peoples to address similar issues (Crumley and Marquardt 1990; McGovern 1994; Kirch 1997; Ogilvie 1984, 1990; Spink 1969). Oral tradition, when used as a basis for reconstructing past environments, is characterized by both strengths and weaknesses (Cruikshank 1981). Persistence, consistency, the integration of historical events, and the long duration of observations are considered some of its greatest strengths. However, problems associated with cultural misinterpretations, translation, specific literary styles, symbolism, temporal and spatial distortions, non-empirical phenomena, and the qualitative nature of the data have often prevented researchers from using oral testimony for gaining insight into human–environment interactions in the past (Arima 1976a, 1976b; Burch 1971; Cruikshank 1981). The weaknesses that have been identified, however, can be minimized when research is conducted in a culturally sensitive manner that takes into account indigenous lifeways and attempts to contextualize symbols and potential distortions where they exist.

In order to capture this unique lens and the depth of knowledge that exists, social scientists need to focus on topics that resonate with northern communities and knowledge that is encoded in ways that persist through time and can have meaning within western scientific climate change narratives. I argue that if we use archaeological sites and Inuit place-names or toponyms as a common reference point, we may be able to broaden our current understandings of how Inuit environmental knowledge transforms from practice and experience to memory, and where important adaptive behaviors can be passed from one generation to the next.

Bridging the Gap: Information 'Capture' and Inuit Flexibility

In order to help bridge the gap between archaeology and oral tradition, I employ a model proposed by Joel Gunn (1994) in a paper entitled 'Global Climate and Regional Biocultural Diversity'. This model, in part, revolves around the concept of information capture and how cultures encode climatically relevant information and its 'attendant' adaptive behavior so that it can be passed across generations and invoked during appropriate times. A culture's comprehension of its regional climates, or its repertoire of 'captured information', depends on the duration of the culture in a particular location. According to Gunn (1994: 86), 'captured' knowledge is 'packaged' when it has been formulated into folk tales, ritual and calendrical ceremonies, and other religious practices in a manner appropriate to each culture. A culture's tolerance of change will grow with time as it experiences more episodes of regional climate and accumulates a broader repertoire of climatic knowledge. Further, Gunn (1994) suggests, the sensitivity of a region to climate determines the range of climatic variation a culture will experience through time. In a region such as the Arctic, where climate change is often amplified, cultures would be expected to have a vast repertoire of knowledge pertaining to a variety of climate regimes important to their survival and overall socio-economic flexibility.

The implications this model holds for the Arctic are instructive for thinking about how we interpret the archaeological record and how we investigate contemporary Inuit perspectives on climate change. The ancestors of modern Inuit, archaeologically known as the Thule, arrived in the eastern Canadian Arctic about 1,000 years ago. According to Gunn's (1994) model, Inuit from Baffin Island should possess a broad repertoire of climatic knowledge kept alive through a culture rooted in oral tradition. By tracing Inuit–sea ice interactions through time, we can begin to see how these cultural abstractions manifest themselves archaeologically and through the place names used by contemporary Inuit on south Baffin Island.

Inuit–sea ice Interactions in Long-Term Perspective: Paleoecology and Archaeology

The reconstruction of climate–culture interaction in temporal scales that span centuries requires multiple lines of evidence involving both the archaeological and paleoenvironmental records. Over the last millennium, groups in the region have experienced a range of climatic regimes, including two global phenomena: (1) the Medieval Optimum, a warm period spanning roughly AD 1000–1400; and (2) the Little Ice Age (LIA), a cool period spanning about ca. AD 1400–1850 (IPCC 2001; Overpeck et. al., 1997). These global phenomena, however, were not synchronous across space or time, so that regional indicators are important for establishing the effects of climate change at the local level. In this case study, the reconstruction of proxy sea ice conditions, modern records of sea ice extremes, and archaeological site distribution provide a framework for examining variability of regional climate in relation to human settlement patterns. More importantly, the temporal depth afforded by the archaeological and paleoenvironmental records provides a measure with which to gauge some of the present climatic conditions being experienced by northern peoples.

Recent studies conducted on the Penny Ice Cap (PIC) on Cumberland Peninsula, Baffin Island, by Grumet et al. (2001) have shown an inverse correlation between marine aerosols (namely sea salt) and sea ice extent in the Labrador Sea/Baffin Bay region. Through this correlation and through the ice core melt data from the same core, a proxy record for spring sea ice conditions has been generated for the last 1,000 years. According to these records, sea ice over the past millennium shows a great deal of variability, and it is this variability I argue that provides the foundation for Inuit knowledge pertaining to sea ice. Specifically, the data indicate that the period between ca. AD 1500–1740 had increased ice severity with the exception of the mid-sixteenth century. More severe conditions again go into effect ca. AD 1800–75 with a trend towards ameliorating sea ice conditions through the twentieth century. One noted exception relates to the last thirty years where some temperature data continue to rise while sea ice conditions deteriorate (Grumet et al. 2001). The study also finds that the sea ice severity recorded over the last fifty years in this region falls within the range of conditions that would have been in effect during the LIA. However, because the temporal resolution of the PIC is much greater than what can be detected archaeologically, it is difficult to reconstruct the human response to specific changes in sea ice conditions through time.

In order to track the relationship between sea ice variability with human settlement and subsistence over the last 1,000 years, archaeological sites representing different cultural periods from south Baffin Island were plotted in relation to modern sea ice extremes from the same region using Geographic Information

Systems (Henshaw 1999, 2003). Three cultural phases characterize the last millennium including: (1) Classic Thule (c. AD 1000–1200), (2) Developed Thule (c. AD 1200–1600), and (3) Historic Inuit (c. AD 1600–1850) (e.g. Schledermann 1975; Maxwell 1985; Sabo 1991; Stenton and Rigby 1995). Modern sea ice extremes spatially analyzed from Frobisher Bay and Cumberland Sound show a clear difference in land fast ice extent in relation to sites representing different time periods. During the sea ice minimum (February 1981) the floe edge extends much farther up the bays while during the sea ice maximum (March 1983) the floe edge extends much farther out from the coastline (Henshaw 2000, 2003). Despite these differences, archaeological sites occupied during both Thule and Historic Inuit times show no clear association with specific ice conditions, which suggests that groups were able to accommodate and adapt to a variety of ice conditions. The data also provide an important framework for thinking about how key environmental knowledge might be tied to archaeologically significant places where ice extremes may have been witnessed in the past.

Inuit environmental knowledge also may be tied to places on the landscape that afforded some measure of predictability in a climatic region often characterized by pervasive uncertainty. Archaeological excavations located in outer Frobisher Bay provide a case in point. Two general time periods of historic Inuit habitation were identified in the region, including: (1) protohistoric Inuit (ca. AD 1350–1850), characterized by intermittent contact between Inuit and early European explorers; and (2) late historic Inuit (ca. AD 1850–1930), which consisted of prolonged interaction between Inuit and a triad of fur trappers/traders, Royal Mountain Canadian Police (RCMP), and missionaries who worked in the region (Henshaw 1999). Throughout the periods, Inuit groups living in outer Frobisher Bay appear to have strategically located their sites in relation to a polynya. Polynyas are generally defined as non-linear areas of open-water surrounded by ice which vary greatly in size and shape and appear to be caused by a combination of factors including wind, oceanic upwelling, tidal fluctuations, and currents (Stirling 1980, 1997; Smith and Rigby 1981). Recurring polynyas, which are very sensitive to climate change, fall into two types: 'those which are open throughout the winter and those which may be ice covered only during the coldest months in some years but which can be relied upon to have at least some open-water early in spring, usually by late March or early April, when the first migrating marine mammals and birds arrive' (Stirling 1997: 10). A recurring polynya similar to the first type described occurs in outer Frobisher Bay (Figure 12.1), and as I have discussed elsewhere (Henshaw 1999, 2000, 2003; Woollett et al. 2000), it is probably less sensitive to climatic variability and therefore represents a more predictable feature in the seascape in this area.

Such predictability in the past can be measured, at least in part, through the faunal remains recovered from Kamaiyuk (AD 1300–1850), Kussejeerarkjuan

(AD 1920–30) and Kuyait (AD 1850–1930) (Figure 12.1). These three sites represent typical Arctic archaeological sites and consisted of a variety of cultural features including habitation structures, caches, burials, qarmaqs (late historic Inuit habitation structures), and stone tent rings. From these sites, a total of thirteen habitations were excavated between 1990 and 1992. A total of 20,399 bones were recovered from the three sites. Of these, 6,351 were identified to genus and/or the species level, representing 31 percent of the total assemblage. The results of the faunal analysis show that Inuit from this area, ethnographically known as the Nugumiut, practiced a consistent mixed strategy of procuring ice-sensitive and open-water adapted species. Largely ringed seal dominated small phocids comprising between 47.4 and 61.2 percent of the house assemblages for both early and late historical periods. Modern population studies of ringed seals show that different age classes segregate between landfast ice and the floe edge; juveniles concentrate primarily along the floe edge, while mature and yearling seals congregate in birthing lairs in the landfast ice (Smith, 1973). The tooth section analyses from all three sites revealed that juveniles and yearlings were captured

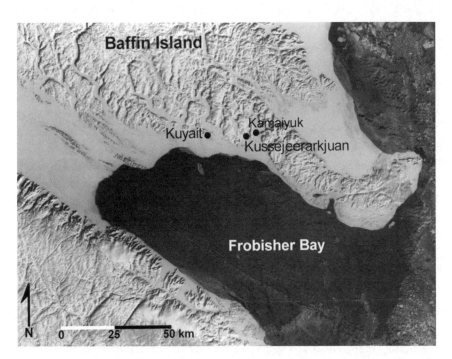

Figure 12.1 LANDSAT4 image taken on March 26, 1983 shows the outer Frobisher Bay polynya during a severe sea ice year in relation to archaeological sites. The polynya is the area of open water at the mouth of the bay, to the southeast of the ice at the head of the bay. The upper and lower left portions of the image show snow-covered land. The uneven gray portions along the right edge show sea ice.

during winter, which suggests that both floe edge and landfast ice were important habitats used by Inuit hunters (Henshaw 1999, 2000, 2003).

The relative proportions of ringed seal procured in relation to open-water species including walrus and bearded seal provide additional information on the importance of ice edge habitats to Nugumiut hunters. Ratios calculated by house for the protohistoric period represented at Kamaiyuk are low and range from 1: 3.25–1: 6.5. During the late historic period for houses dating between 1910 and 1930, there is also a high degree of consistency, with the exception of House 12 at Kuyait with a ratio of 1: 13.5, and House 2 at Kussejeerarkjuan with a ratio of 1: 40 suggesting an overwhelming preference for ringed seals over bearded seal or walrus. The overwhelming number of ringed seals represented in these particular houses could indicate particularly severe ice years during which Inuit hunters had to adapt quickly to expanding landfast ice conditions (Henshaw, 2003).

Zooarchaeological data from the head of Frobisher Bay also testify to the flexibility of Thule and Historic Inuit subsistence and settlement strategies to changing ice conditions (Jacobs and Stenton 1985; Stenton 1987; Stenton and Rigby 1995). At the multicomponent sites of Peale Point and Tungatsivvik, ringed seal also dominate the assemblages, but caribou are consistently represented as the major terrestrial resource. According to faunal data from these two sites, caribou comprised up to 25 to 30.2 percent of the faunal species identified from structures dating between c. AD 1200 and 1850 (Jacobs and Stenton 1985). Incremental studies of ringed seal canines have produced no evidence of winter kills at the Peale Point site, which suggests that breathing hole sealing, a technique developed to harvest ringed seals in their landfast ice habitat, was never an important means of procuring resources (Stenton 1987). As the terrestrial environment became less productive and sea ice conditions deteriorated, Jacobs and Stenton (1985) suggest, the area was abandoned around 1850 when people probably moved to outer Frobisher Bay to access the floe edge, implying that mobility as well as subsistence shifts formed an important cornerstone of Thule and Historic Inuit adaptability. On the basis of these findings and those of the settlement pattern studies presented earlier, I argue that environmental knowledge pertaining to different ice conditions and human responses to changes in the seascape may be locked up in the memories and 'captured' information that relate to specific places where a host of different sea ice environments were experienced.

Contemporary Inuit Perspectives on Sea Ice: Methodological Considerations

Increasingly, Arctic social scientists have shown that Inuit environmental knowledge does not occur in a cultural vacuum, but that such knowledge is embedded within broader cultural contexts which are often shared in the form of stories, ritual and other folklore (Stevenson 1996; Cruikshank 1998, 2001). In the context of the Arctic, where climatic variability is the norm rather than the exception, I would argue that 'packages' of information key to the environmental capturing described by Gunn (1994) are retained in the form of Inuit toponyms. By conducting oral history in the context of particular sites sensitive to climatic variability, we might be able to better illuminate Inuit mental maps that are important for understanding how landscapes and seascape have changed through time. As other studies have shown, such knowledge is no doubt encoded in the language, where toponyms represent an important repository for aboriginal collective memory relating to ecology (including climatic indicators), geography, subsistence activities, myth-ology, and local history that persist through time; toponyms also form an important spatial frame of reference for navigating and traveling safely on the land (Müller-Wille 1983, 1985; Basso 1988; Cruikshank 1990; Rankama 1993; Peplinski 2000).

A recent example of such encoding comes from Mark Nuttall's research in West Greenland where he interprets the landscape as an active memoryscape that reveals a complex and rich repository of local knowledge used in the cultural construction of community (Nuttall 1992: 38). Similarly, Cruikshank (1990; 2001) discusses how Eyak, Athapascan, and Tlingit place names encapsulate ecological infor-mation that 'reflect changes in the landscape or in movements of plants and animals' (1990: 63). For example, the Tutchone (descendents of Athapascan peoples) living along the Alsek River in the Yukon Territory gave the name *Naludi* or 'fish stop' to a glacier that interrupted salmon migrations to the interior when it surged (Cruikshank 2001: 380). The South Baffin Island Placename Project is providing additional insight into similar types of climatically relevant infor-mation (Peplinski 2000). The toponyms described in this study make reference to a variety of environmental indicators (nesting areas for birds, seal birthing areas, location of polynyas) as well as other referential types of information. For example, *Pitsiulaaqsit* in Frobisher Bay is described as a place where guillemots nested in the past but do not currently; *Qasigiaraajuk*, the same location as Kussejeerarkjuan (the archaeological site referred to in the present study) is referred to as a place that was a good place to hunt harbor seals in the past (Peplinski 2000: 63).

Current oral history research I am conducting in the Nunavut community of Kinngait located on southwest Baffin Island is providing similar types of know-ledge. Of particular interest are the toponyms linked to the high concentration of small polynyas (or *saava*) in this region which are associated with the strong ocean currents characterizing the island chains situated along the south coast of Baffin Island. Many of the names that have been documented thus far provide important knowledge for Inuit navigating the dangerous waters that polynyas are associated. For example, *Niiniq* is referred to as a place of strong currents that push ice toward the land or *Kalikatsilik*, the island that looks like it is dragging in the water because of the strong currents. Future research I will be undertaking in this community will continue to focus on climate sensitive 'places', such as polynyas, and to explore the ways in which toponyms form important repositories of mythical knowledge and related stories that represent the more detailed kind of 'packaging' initially described by Gunn (1994).

The Future of Inuit Collective Knowledge and Flexibility

Inuit collective knowledge as it relates to the environment continues to play a vital role in helping Inuit meet the challenge of climatic variability. Although many Inuit are increasingly living more sedentary lives, spending time on the land hunting and camping away from the community continues to form a critical component to their cultural livelihood and identity. Currently, Inuit environmental knowledge is being constructed in the context of rapid social and technological change. By embedding such knowledge within a greater temporal framework, collective knowledge can be mobilized to help meet present concerns related to issues of climatic unpredictability and variability. Together with community-based oral history initiatives, a key to this mobilization effort is to expand land-based experiential learning within the local school curriculum. Unless individuals experience the land firsthand and retain that knowledge through the construction of living oral histories and 'memoryscapes', the sustainability of Inuit socio-economic flexibility that have defined generations will remain uncertain. Given the fact that the ancestors of contemporary Inuit persisted in the north for over 1,000 years, the depth of their experience, preserved in the form of oral tradition, serves as a guidepost for enabling Inuit to adapt to the severe weather and long-term climate variability predicted for the next millennium. How well people in the north respond to climate change will depend on passing the knowledge and experience of their elders down through successive generations of Inuit.

Acknowledgements

This material is based upon work supported by the National Science Foundation under Grant No. 9906701.

Notes

1. *Inuit Qaujimajatuqangit* (IQ) is an all-encompassing Inuktitut term used to denote the knowledge associated with Inuit language, culture, and oral

tradition. IQ is commonly used by the government of Nunavut to describe Inuit 'traditional knowledge'.

2. For the purposes of this chapter I use the term Indigenous Knowledge (IK) as apposed to TEK and IQ because knowledge construction is a dynamic process that is highly contextual and occurs within a broader cultural framework, not within an environmental framework exclusively (Stevenson 1996).

3. Interpreters are commonly used in the Canadian Arctic because most Inuit elders are monolingual Inuktitut speakers.

References

ARIMA, EUGENE. 1976a. 'An Assessment of Reliability of Informant Recall', in *Inuit Land Use and Occupancy Project*, vol. 2. Edited by Milton Freeman, pp. 31–38. Ottawa: Department of Indian and Northern Affairs.

—— 1976b. 'Views on Land expressed in Inuit Oral Tradition', in *Inuit Land Use and Occupancy Project*, Vol. 2. Edited by Milton Freeman, pp. 217–222. Ottawa: Department of Indian and Northern Affairs.

BASSO, K. H. 1988. 'Speaking with Names': Language and Landscape among the Western Apache. *Cultural Anthropology* 3(2): 99–130.

BIELAWSKI, ELLEN. 1992. Inuit Indigenous Knowledge and Science in the Arctic. *Northern Perspectives* 20(1): 5–8.

BURCH, ERNEST. 1971. The Nonempirical Environment of the Arctic Alaska Eskimos. *Southwestern Journal of Anthropology* 27: 148–165.

CAULFIELD, RICHARD A. 1997. *Greenlanders, Whales and Whaling*. Hanover, NH: University Press of New England.

COHEN, STUART. 1997. Mackenzie Basin Impact Study (MBIS) Final Report. Minister of Supply Services, Environment Canada, Ottawa. Internet address: (http: //www1.tor.ec.gc.ca/mbis/mackenzie.htm).

CONKLIN, HAROLD. 1969. 'An Ethnoecological Approach to Shifting Agriculture,' in *Environment and Cultural Behavior*. Edited by Andrew P. Vayda, pp. 221–233. Garden City, NY: American Museum of Natural History [by] the Natural History Press.

CRAVER, AMY. 2001. Impact of Climate Change on Alaska Native Subsistence Lifestyles, Paper presented at the American Anthropological Association meeting, November, 2001. Washington D.C.

CRUIKSHANK, JULIE. 1981. Legend and Landscape: Convergence of Oral and Scientific Traditions in the Yukon Territory. *Arctic Anthropology* 17(2): 67–93.

—— 1984. Oral Tradition and Scientific Research: Approaches to Knowledge in the North. In *Social Sciences in the North: Communicating Northern Values*. Occasional Publication No. 9, Association of Canadian Universities for Northern Studies.

—— 1990. Getting the Words Right: Perspectives on Naming and Places in Athapascan Oral History. *Arctic Anthropology* 27(1): 52–65.

—— 1998. *The Social Life of Stories: Narrative and Knowledge in the Yukon Territory*. Lincoln, NB: University of Nebraska Press.

—— 2001. Glaciers and Climate Change: Perspectives from Oral Tradition. *Arctic* 54(4): 377–393.

CRUMLEY, CAROL. 1994. *Historical Ecology: A Multidimensional Ecological Orientation*. Edited by Carole Crumley, pp. 1–16. Sante Fe: School of American Research Press.

CRUMLEY, CAROL and WILLIAM MARQUARDT. 1990. 'Landscape: A Unifying Concept in Regional Analysis', in *Interpreting Space: GIS and Archaeology*. Edited by Kathleen Allen, Stanton Green, and Ezra Zubrow, pp. 73–79. Bristol, PA: Taylor and Francis.

ELLEN, ROY. 1982. *Environment, Subsistence, and System: The Ecology of Small Scale Social Formations*. New York: Cambridge University Press.

FENGE, TERRY. 2001. The Inuit and Climate Change. *Isuma* 2(4): 79–85.

FOX, SHARI. 2000. *When the Weather is Uggianaqtuq: Inuit Knowledge of Climate Change in the Eastern Canadian Arctic*. Poster presented at the HARC, Arctic Weather Workshop, 5–9 November 2001, moderated by John Walsh and Henry Huntington. (http: //arcus.zeroforum.com/).

FREEMAN, M. M. R. (Ed.). 1976. *Inuit Land Use and Occupancy Project*, Vs 1–3. Ottawa: Supply and Services Canada.

FREEMAN, M. R. 1992. The Nature and Utility of Traditional Ecological Knowledge. *Northern Perspectives* 20(1).

FREEMAN, M. R. and L. N. CARBYN (Eds.). 1988. *Traditional Knowledge and Renewable Resources Management in Northern Regions*. Occasional Paper 20, Boreal Institute for Northern Studies, University of Alberta.

GRUMET, N. S., C. WAKE, P. A. MAYEWSKI, G. ZIELINSKI, S. I. WHITLOW, R. M. KOERNER, D. A. FISHER, and J. WOOLLETT. 2001. Variability of Sea-ice Extent in the Baffin Bay over the Last Millennium. *Climate Change* 49: 129–145.

GUNN, JOEL. 1994. 'Global Climate and Regional Biocultural Diversity', in *Historical Ecology: Cultural Knowledge and Changing Landscapes*. Edited by Carole Crumley, pp. 67–98. Sante Fe: School of American Research Press.

HARDESTY, D. L. 1977. *Ecological Anthropology*. New York: John Wiley and Sons.

HENSHAW, ANNE. 1999. Location and Appropriation in the Arctic: An Integrative Zooarchaeological Approach to Historic Inuit Household Economies. *Journal of Anthropological Archaeology* 18: 79–118.

—— 2000. Central Inuit household economies: zooarchaeological, environmental, and historical evidence from outer Frobisher Bay, Baffin Island, Canada. *British Archaeological Reports, International Series* 871. Oxford: Archaeopress.

—— 2003. Polynyas and Ice Edge Habitats in Cultural Context: Archaeological Perspectives from Southeast Baffin Island. *Arctic* 56(1): 1–13.

INGOLD, TIM. 1996. 'Hunting and Gathering as Ways of Perceiving the Environment', in *Redefining Nature: Ecology, Culture and Domestication*. Edited by Roy Ellen and K. Fukui, pp. 117–156. London and New York: Berg Publishers.

IPCC (Intergovernmental Panel on Climate Change). 2001. *Climate Change 2001: A Scientific Basis*. Edited by J. T. Houghton, Y. Ding, D. J. Griggs, M. Noguer, P. J. van der Linden, and D. Xiaosu. Cambridge: Cambridge University Press.

JACOBS, JOHN and STENTON, D. 1985. Environment, Resources and Prehistoric Settlement in Upper Frobisher Bay, Baffin Island. *Arctic Anthropology* 22(2): 59–76.

KAPLAN, S. A. and WOOLLETT, J.M. 2000. Challenges and choices: Exploring the interplay of climate, history and culture on Canada's Labrador coast. *Arctic, Antarctic and Alpine Research* 32(3): 351–359.

KIRCH, PATRICK. 1997. Microcosmic Histories: Island Perspectives on 'Global Change'. *American Anthropologist* 99(1): 30–42.

MAXWELL, MOREAU. 1985. *Prehistory of the Eastern Arctic*. New York: Academic Press.

MCDONALD, MIRIAM, LUCASSIE ARRAGUTAINAQ, and ZACK NOVALINGA. 1997. *Voices from the Bay: Traditional Ecological Knowledge of Inuit and Cree in the Hudson Bay Bioregion*. Ottawa: Canadian Arctic Resources Committee and Environmental Committee of the Municipality of Sanikiluaq.

MCGHEE, ROBERT. 1981. 'Archaeological Evidence of Climate Change during the Last 5000 Years', in *Climate and History: Studies in Past Climates and their Impact on Man*. Edited by T. Wigley, M. J. Ingram, and G. Farmer, pp. 162–179. Cambridge: Cambridge University Press.

McGOVERN, T. 1991. Climate, Correlation, and Causation in Norse Greenland. *Arctic Anthropology* 28(2): 77–100.

—— 1994. 'Management for Extinction in Norse Greenland', in *Historical Ecology: Cultural Knowledge and Changing Landscapes*. Edited by Carol Crumley, pp. 127–154. Santa Fe: School of American Research Press.

MILTON, KAY. 1996. *Environmentalism and Cultural Theory: Exploring the Role of Anthropology in Environmental Discourse*. London: Routledge.

MÜLLER-WILLE, L 1983. Inuit toponymy and cultural sovereignty. In *Conflict in the development in Nouveau-Quebec*, pp. 131–150. Edited by L.M. Müller-Wille. Centre of Northern Studies and Research at McGill University.

—— 1985. une methodologie pour les enuêtes toponymiques autochthones: le répertoire inuit de la region de kativik et de sa zone côtière. *Etudes/Inuit/Studies* 9(1): 51–66.

NADASDY, P. 1999. The Politics of TEK: Power and the 'Integration' of Knowledge. *Arctic Anthropology* 36(1–2): 1–18.

NELSON, RICHARD. 1969. *Hunters of the Northern Ice*. Chicago: University of Chicago Press.

NUTTALL, MARK. 1992. *Arctic Homeland: Kinship, Community and Development in Northwest Greenland*. Toronto: University of Toronto Press.

OGILVIE, ASTRID. 1984. The Past Climate And Sea-Ice Record From Iceland. *Climate Change* 6: 131–152.

——1990. Climate Changes in Iceland C. AD 865–1598. Acta Archaeologica 61: 232–251.

OVERPECK, JONATHAN, K. HUGHEN, D. HARDY, R. BRADLEY, R. CASE, M. DOUGLAS, B. FINNEY, K. GAJEWSKI, G. JACOBY, A. JENNINGS, S. LAMOUREUX, A. LASCA, G. MACDONALD, J. MOORE, M. RETELLE, S. SMITH, A.WOLFE, and G. ZIELINSKI. 1997. Arctic Environmental Changes of the Last Four Centuries. *Science* 278: 1251–1256.

PEPLINSKI, LYNN. 2000. Public Resource Management and Inuit Typonomy: Implementing Policies to Maintain Human-Environmental Knowledge In Nunavut. M.A. Thesis, Royal Roads University, Victoria, B.C., Canada.

RANKAMA, T. 1993. Managing the Landscape: A Study of Sàmi Place-names in Utsjoki, Finnish Lapland. *Etudes/Inuit/Studies* 17(1): 47–67.

RIEDLINGER, DYANNA. 2001. Responding to Climate Change in Northern Communities: Impacts and Adaptations. *Infonorth* 54(1): 96–98.

RIEWE, RICK. 1992. *Nunavut Atlas*. Canadian Circumpolar Institute and Tungavic Ferderation of Nunavut, Edmonton.

RIEWE, RICK and JILL OAKES (Eds.). 1992. *Human Ecology: Issues in the North*. Edmonton: Canadian Circumpolar Institute.

SABO, GEORGE. 1991. *Long Term Adaptations among Arctic Hunter-Gatherers: A Case Study from Southern Baffin Island*. New York: Garland Publishing, Inc.

SALLENAVE, J. 1994. Giving Traditional Ecological Knowledge its Rightful Place in Environmental Impact Assessments. *Northern Perspectives* 22(1): 16–19.

SCHLEDERMANN, PETER. 1975. *Thule Eskimo Prehistory of Cumberland Sound, Baffin Island, Canada*. Archaeological Survey of Canada Paper 38. Ottawa: Nation Museums of Canada.

SMITH, T. G. 1973. *Population Dynamics of the Ringed Seal*. Fisheries Research Board of Canada, Bulletin 181.Ottawa.

SMITH, M. and B. RIGBY. 1981. Distribution of Polynyas in the Canadian Arctic. In *Polynyas in the Canadian Arctic*. Edited by I. Stirling and H. Cleator, pp. 7–28. Occasional Paper 45. Ottawa: Canadian Wildlife Services, Environment Canada.

SPINK, JOHN. 1969. Historic Eskimo Awareness of Past Changes in Sea Level. *Musk-Ox* 5: 37–40.

STENTON, DOUGLAS. 1987. Recent Archaeological Investigations in Frobisher Bay, Baffin Island, N.W.T. *Canadian Journal of Archaeology*, 11: 13–48.

STENTON, D. R. and RIGBY, B. G. 1995. Community-based Heritage Education, Training, and Research: Preliminary Report on the Tungatsivvik Archaeological Project. *Arctic* 48(1): 47–56.

STEVENSON, MARC. 1996. Indigenous Knowledge and Environmental Assessment. *Arctic* 49(3): 278–291.

STIRLING, I. 1980. The Biological Importance of Polynyas in the Canadian Arctic. *Arctic* 33(2): 303–315.

—— 1997. The Importance of Polynyas, Ice Edges, and Leads to Marine Mammals and Birds. *Journal of Marine Systems* 10: 9–21.

USHER, P. J. and G. WENZEL. 1987. Native Harvest Surveys and Statistics: A Critique of their Construction and Use. *Arctic* 40: 145–160.

WOOLLETT, J., A. S. HENSHAW, and C. P. WAKE. 2000. Palaeoecological Implications of Archaeological Seal Bone Assemblages: Case Studies from Labrador and Baffin Island. *Arctic* 53(4): 395–413.

–13–

Testing Farmers' Perceptions of Climate Variability: A Case Study from the Sulphur Springs Valley, Arizona

Colin Thor West and *Marcela Vásquez-León*

Introduction

As debates on global climate change become more public and political, the gap between the global perspectives of scientists and the local perspectives of stakeholders becomes more evident. Climatologists tend to focus on climatic fluctuations that affect large regions and restrict their analyses to long-term records on the scale of centuries and millennia. Agriculturists tend to be more interested in how climate varies locally and in time-scales of several years to perhaps a few decades. These contrary concerns involving time and space often result in the dismissal by scientists of local perceptions of climate change. In their work *Environmental Values in American Culture*, for example, Kempton et al. state: 'It is effectively impossible for laypeople to accurately discern a climate trend from their own casual observations of local weather' (1997: 81). Bryant et al.'s (2000) study of Canadian agricultural adaptations to climate variability also casts doubt on whether farmers can accurately detect climate variability. In citing a report contracted by their research team (Granjon 1999), the authors state that '70% of his 30 farmer respondents claimed to have observed "climatic change" over the last 20 years, these "changes" were for the most part related to specific events over a period of one or two years (e.g. two consecutive years of droughty conditions and the 1998 ice storm)' (Bryant et al. 2000: 192).

These assertions are symptomatic of the epistemological divide between 'descriptive' and 'interpretive' research (Malone and Rayner 2001). The descriptive perspectives of Bryant et al. (2000) and Kempton et al. (1997) privilege external data such as meteorological records over the interpretive perspectives of actors and their internal observations of local climate patterns. A few examples of more interpretive perspectives, mostly from research in Africa, indicate that farmers and pastoralists can and do detect long-term trends in rainfall (Ovuka and Lindqvist 2000; Sollod 1990). Our study borrows insights from studies among subsistence farmers and herders and applies them to North American farmers and ranchers. By comparing statements of a changing climate with empirical evidence, we also attempt to bridge the gap between the descriptive and the interpretive.

Our research tested perceptions of climate variability among farmers and ranchers in the Sulphur Springs Valley (SSV) of southeastern Arizona.[1] This region, where aridity has been the fundamental constraint in the evolution of ranching and farming, is characterized by extremely variable and low annual precipitation, high temperatures, and scarce water resources. Perceptions were compared to meteorological data with the intention of making a preliminary assessment of the long-term dynamics between oscillations in rainfall and the ways in which humans view these changes. This has important implications since perceptions of climate variability and their impacts on human populations often translate into adaptations that seek to decrease societal vulnerability to particular events and/or long-term climatic changes (Dagel 1997; Finan et al. 2002). We therefore sought to document local perceptions of climate variability and establish their empirical validity.

As discussed below, our work with ranchers and farmers strongly indicates that some perceptions held by these stakeholders correspond to local trends in rainfall on the order of at least decades. In fact, we contend that particular perceptions of rainfall variability held by farmers and ranchers in the SSV strongly correlate with long-term meteorological patterns. We hesitate to categorize these local perceptions as perspectives on 'climate change'. Our results, however, indicate that rural producers in the arid Southwest United States can and do accurately detect climate variability.[2] Before discussing specific perceptions, these must first be contextualized in terms of anthropological theory, the physical and demographic setting, the regional climate, and the historical development of agriculture in the SSV.

Anthropological Understandings of Human Perceptions and Environmental Change

Aridity allows us as anthropologists to pursue Julian Steward's cultural core analytical paradigm where 'cross-cultural regularities are thus conceived as recurrent constellations of basic features . . . which have similar functional inter-relationships resulting from local ecological adaptations and similar levels of sociocultural integration' (1972: 6). Clifford Geertz elaborated the cultural core concept for contemporary societies and extended it beyond functional relationships that exist between human behavior and the environment. In *Agricultural Involution: The Processes of Ecological Change in Indonesia*, he writes:

One conceives of the techniques of swidden agriculture as an integral part of a larger whole which includes alike the edaphic and climatological characteristics of tropical forest landscapes, the social organization of a labor force which must be shifted continually from field to field, and the empirical and nonempirical beliefs which influence the scattered and varied land resources.

(1963: 10)

Accordingly, ecological and climatological conditions shape particular patterns of belief, which induce people to place more value on specific natural phenomena than others. In the case of rural producers in the SSV, rain becomes one of the most salient of the entire constellation of environmental indicators that grant it with particular potency or meaning. In terms of climate, differences in seasonal rainfall are the key symbols to which farmers focus and it is here that we look to test their perceptions of climate variability.

The relationship between people and climate in the American West has been well investigated by a range of social scientists. Historian Walter Prescott Webb's *The Great Plains* (1931), for example, describes the 98th meridian as an 'institutional fault' because rainfall beyond it was inadequate for rain-fed agriculture. Thus, agriculture beyond this longitude required significantly greater institutional, technological, and organizational investment than those areas east of it. In *Arizona: A History* (1995) anthropologist Thomas Sheridan discusses how climate shaped ranching and farming in Arizona. He concludes that 'technological development and government subsidies have buffered people against floods, droughts, and other natural disasters' to the point where 'many of us no longer feel that nature is a significant factor' (1995: 361).

Despite these institutional and technological buffers, farmers and ranchers in the SSV remain vulnerable to climate. Droughts increase the costs of production and decrease cattle forage. Excessive rain leads to widespread flooding that, in turn, decreases harvests. Enter any breakfast café early in the morning in Elfrida, Willcox or Douglas and rainfall will be *the* topic of conversation at every table where locals sit.

The Physical and Demographic Setting

The SSV lies approximately 100 miles (160 km) southeast of Tucson in the Basin and Range physiographic province of Arizona. The valley trends northwest to southeast and is ringed by mountains (Figure 13.1). Two hydrological units, the Willcox and Douglas Basins, underlie the SSV. Because the valley has no permanent sources of surface water, these aquifers provide all water for domestic and agricultural use. The Willcox Basin is enclosed by mountains and has no outlet. This fact causes rainfall to accumulate on the valley floor south of Willcox and

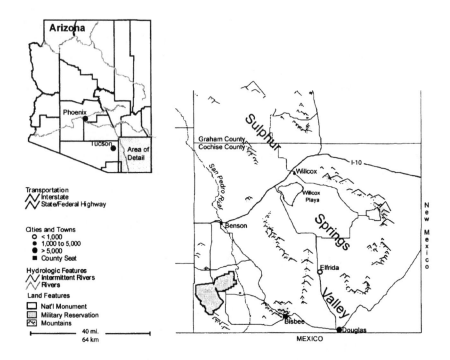

Figure 13.1 Map of the SSV and Arizona.

form a vast and shallow seasonal lake, the Willcox Playa. The Douglas Basin drains southward into the Yaqui River watershed of northern Mexico. Groundwater recharge in these basins is largely a function of rainfall and temperature. Winter rains are particularly important, as they are the main source of aquifer recharge, including snowmelt from the surrounding mountain ranges, which is transported to the valley by streams and washes (ADWR 1994).[3]

The SSV is classified as semi-arid. Average temperatures range from a minimum of 25°F (–4°C) in December to a maximum of 94°F (34.4°C) in July (WRCC 2001). Because of its latitude and elevation, winter temperatures can drop below freezing and snow is not uncommon – particularly in the mountains. Elevation makes the area cooler in the summer than the surrounding desert region of southeastern Arizona. Annual rainfall totals a mere 12.28 inches (272 mm) and precipitation occurs mostly in the summer and winter months. Spring and fall are normally drought-like although heavy rains can occur in the early fall and cause widespread flooding. Droughts occur frequently and, as discussed in more detail below, the region is characterized by extreme interannual rainfall variability (Figure 13.2).

Even though these physical and climatological constraints have not allowed for the development of rain-fed farming, irrigated agriculture thrives in the SSV. Lying

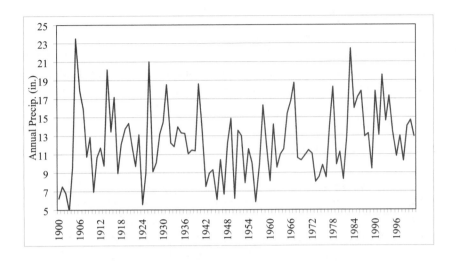

Figure 13.2 Annual precipitation for Willcox, AZ, 1900–2000. (*Source*: WRCC.)

within Cochise County, the SSV leads Arizona in the production of corn, apples, and chile, and it is also the largest producer of range cattle in the state (Vásquez-León et al. 2002). The region is predominantly rural and only two towns have more than 4,000 inhabitants, Douglas and Willcox. Approximately 422 farms are spread out across the SSV along the valley floor (Vásquez-León et al. 2002). These operations are relatively small (around 1000 acres) and are typically family-owned and operated. Farming in the SSV is characterized by its diversity. Farms range from intensive corn, cotton, chile, and hay farms to fruit and nut orchards. The SSV also contains a few tomato greenhouses, Christmas tree and squash farms, and U-Pick vegetable and fruit orchards.

Family-owned ranches dot the mountain slopes and encompass thousands of acres of private and public land. Although today ranching is seen as economically marginal, historically it has been key to the economic development and cultural identity of the region. Farming and ranching operations are generally separate activities, although some farmers may run a few head of cattle on the side either as a hobby or, in the case of the most marginal farmers, as a source of security during difficult times.[4] Even though around 55 percent of the population of the SSV is Mexican or of Mexican descent, more than 80 percent of commercial ranchers and farmers are Anglo-American. Mexicans and Mexican-Americans constitute a small percentage of farm and ranch owners, and provide most of the labor force as seasonal workers or as ranch and farm managers (Vásquez-León et al. 2002).

From a technological perspective, while some operations are highly sophisticated, use computer-driven irrigation systems and expensive harvesting machinery, others use low-tech flood-furrow irrigation and hand-labor for harvesting. The latter types are also the most marginal and concentrate in the southern end of the SSV. Most Hispanic farmers are in this category (Vásquez-León et al. 2002). This diversity of crops, ethnicity, and technology make the SSV an ideal field-site for investigating perceptions of climate variability because a wide range of perspectives can be gathered through brief visits.

A History of Agriculture in the SSV

The SSV has a long and discontinuous history of agriculture and settlement that has been largely limited by both the aridity of the region and the lack of permanent sources of surface water for irrigation. Archaeological evidence indicates that settled agriculturists were probably present in the SSV by around AD 500 (Kayser and Fiero 1970) but abandoned the area by AD 1450 (Woosley et al. 1987: 151). Early attempts at intensive and extensive farming did not begin until Anglo-American settlers arrived in the 1870s.

The first pioneers focused on ranching which was seen as a much more viable livelihood given the arid conditions and lack of surface water (Schultz 1980: 17). Yearly rainfall between 1905 and 1907, however, was well above the long-term average. Perceptions of a 'wet' climate played a key role in the early settlement of the region as word of this ample rain reached farmers in the Midwest and Eastern United States. The belief that 'rain followed the plow' encouraged an influx of farmers (Clark and Dunn 1997: 11). By 1908 annual rainfall returned to its measly average of around 12 inches and residents of the SSV soon realized that rain-fed farming was impossible in the region. Farming families either left, turned to ranching, or developed ditches and catchments for raising beans. Ranching became the dominant economic activity.

Commercial farming did not take off until 1940, when large-scale groundwater extraction from the Douglas and Willcox Basins became possible with the establishment of the SSV Electrical Cooperative. The availability of pumps, inexpensive electrical power and an increased wartime demand for cotton led to the rapid expansion of irrigated acreage. Irrigated acreage in Cochise County, most of which concentrated in the SSV, tripled from 8,260 in 1944 to 25,297 in 1949 (Schultz 1980 [1964]: 93).

Although groundwater withdrawal began to exceed recharge as early as 1960, good commodity prices, government subsidies, and cheap energy prices allowed irrigation to prosper and expand. A harsh drought in the 1950s wiped out many ranchers, and induced adaptations such as the adoption of windmills and inexpensive piping to extend water resources over rangeland (Finan et al. 2002). Farming commodities such as corn, cotton and sorghum remained profitable up through the early 1970s. This changed in the latter-half of the 1970s. Droughts between 1974 and 1978 negatively affected the water table and farmers recall 'chasing water' with their wells. This meant that they frequently moved or deepened their wells in order to obtain sufficient amounts for irrigation. Furthermore, commodity prices plummeted as a result of the grain embargo on the USSR. Simultaneously, the Energy Crisis of 1976 drastically increased the cost of pumping. One farmer recounted how his monthly pumping costs increased from $300 to $3,000 in only six months (Vásquez-León et al. 2002).

These climatological, economic, and hydrological circumstances led to a massive exodus of farmers. The area around Elfrida lost approximately 80 percent of its agricultural families. Irrigated acreage in Cochise County declined by 39 percent from 157,480 to 95,860 acres between 1975 and 1981 (Vásquez-León et al. 2002). Farmers and ranchers who were able to remain in the SSV started experimenting with water-efficient irrigation technologies. Center pivot and drip irrigation became essential to the continuation of farming in this arid environment. As farmers often emphasized, these technologies double irrigation efficiency and ultimately reduce the costs of production. During these crises SSV farming also began diversifying into vegetable, fruit, and nut operations. Unable to compete with more traditional markets as a result of high water costs, farmers sought niche markets for specialty crops. By 1990, some abandoned farmland began going back into production. Technological innovation and diversification have made farming again viable and profitable. Most farmers, however, would tell you that profit is not their motive. They variously state that farming is a 'way of life' or, as one corn farmer wryly stated, 'it's a disease'.

Today, the fundamental constraint on agriculture in the SSV continues to be access to groundwater. Local farmers are aware of the importance of winter precipitation for aquifer recharge. Noting the unexpected torrential rains that occurred during the fall of 2000 and the visible snow on the nearby mountains, one local farmer commented: 'We're tickled to death with all this winter moisture.' This link between seasonal rainfall, aquifer recharge, and irrigation costs forms the functional relationship between perceptions of climate variability and agricultural production.

Climate and Agriculture in the SSV

The region is characterized by a bimodal pattern of precipitation, with most rain falling from July through September and from December to February. As Figure 13.3 demonstrates, winter and summer rains differ in amounts and also in kind. Winter precipitation is typified by occasional storms that bring widespread, gentle rain and sometimes snow (Sheppard et al. 1999: 7). These frontal storms pass

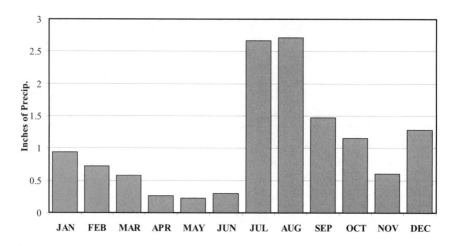

Figure 13.3 Mean monthly distribution of precipitation, Willcox, AZ, 1961–1990 (adapted from West 2001: 38).

through the region at the same time that temperatures are moderate or low, which facilitates groundwater recharge.

Summer rains are quantitatively and qualitatively different from those in winter. They are highly localized and often violent convection storms. These thunderstorms roll in from the south and can deliver large amounts of rain in a short period of time. These storms are the result of the North American Monsoon (NAM) which causes a shift in the prevailing winds from west to south (Sheppard et al. 1999: 13). Moist air from the Eastern Pacific and Gulf of California are brought into the Southwest by these winds. As these moist parcels of air pass up and over the mountain ranges surrounding the SSV, convective currents occur and thunderstorms erupt. The spatial distribution of these storms varies widely and it is not unusual for one farmer to receive several inches of rain during the summer while his neighbor one mile away receives none.

The consequences of these general conditions for agriculture are profound. The bimodal distribution of rain leads to ample spring and summer grass for livestock. Low winter temperatures provide an adequate number of chilling days required by pecan, pistachio, peach, and apple trees to bud during the spring. The milder summer temperatures, relative to other parts of southern Arizona, permit alfalfa hay to grow more slowly and contain greater amounts of protein. Corn, chile, and other vegetable crops also grow well under these mild conditions with less heat stress than the same varieties in other parts of Arizona. Cooler temperatures in the spring and summer permit the agricultural calendar to be extended into the fall and some crops such as onions, chile, squash and lettuce enter the market at precisely the time when these same products are scarce in other parts of the world and they fetch higher prices.

But climate also imperils agricultural production. Decreased winter rainfall reduces the amount of edible grasses and shrubs available to cattle. Under these conditions, ranchers are forced to purchase supplemental feed in the form of hay, which increases costs. For farmers, winter droughts cause the soil to become particularly hard and they must invest additional time, fuel and labor into ripping this crust open in order to plant. Under these conditions, farmers also have to irrigate more heavily prior to planting in order to assure adequate sub-moisture for the germination of seeds. Most importantly, consecutive years of winter drought can lead to a decline in the water table and have major long-term impacts on irrigated farming.

Summer droughts dry up water sources for cattle and likewise decrease the quantity of edible grasses. Ranch operations respond to droughts at this time of the year by purchasing hay, hauling water or culling herds at precisely the time when cattle prices are low. Lack of summer rain requires that farmers apply more irrigation water, which in turn increases costs. Over the years, the added costs associated with winter or summer droughts have forced farmers and ranchers out of business (Vásquez-León et al. 2002).

These functional relationships between agricultural production and seasons cause perceptions of ranchers and farmers to converge on seasonal differences between years. Interannual temperature variation within the same season is slight and it is difficult for humans to perceive (see Sarewitz and Pielke 2000). However, variation in seasonal precipitation is noted, recorded, and talked about by numerous informants.

Climate Change, Climate Variability, and Events

Our principal question concerning local perceptions is whether these are based on climatic trends or on short-term events. By definition, events encompass short-term meteorological phenomena on the order of days, weeks, months, and perhaps one year. Climate, on the other hand, encompasses long-term meteorological trends to the order of two or more years. Our research tested whether particular perceptions of climate variability were consistent with meteorological data on ten-year time-scales.

First of all, is climate changing? The answer from the physical science community is 'unequivocally "Yes"' (Allbritton and Filho 2001: 25). The most definitive example of global climate change is the increase by 0.6°C of mean surface temperatures since 1900 (Allbritton and Filho 2001: 26). However, participants in our study hardly mentioned increased temperatures. Only one person commented that the previous summer (1999) had been extremely hot. Perhaps this is due to the fact that it is always warm in this part of the Southwest. Or, as Pielke and Sarewitz point out, 'People can't directly sense global warming, the way they can see a clear-cut forest or feel the sting of urban smog in their throats . . . people and ecosystems experience local and regional temperatures, not the global average' (2000: 56). This observation leads us to assess the case for climate variability at the regional scale.

In terms of regional climate variability, two trends appear. First of all, physical scientists on the CLIMAS Project determined that 'During the 20th century, the Southwest experienced wet years in the early part of the century (1905 to 1930), a mid-century dry period (1942–1964), and warm, wet winters and erratic summers since 1976' (Sheppard et al. 1999: 24). Second, the same authors state: 'The most obvious feature of the multi-decadal variation is the current increase in temperature to an extent unprecedented in the last four hundred years. This feature has been noted even at the global scale . . .' (1999: 27). Nowhere within this report do the authors make any claim that these trends indicate 'climate change' but the scientific evidence for increased surface temperatures and increased winter precipitation in the Southwest is clear. To what extent do local farmers and ranchers perceive these trends?

Methodology

For the purposes of this chapter, we combined ethnographic analysis with quantitative rainfall data from local meteorological stations to test local perceptions of climate variability. Interview data from 71 stakeholders, all rural residents of the SSV, was gathered during fieldwork by CLIMAS researchers in the summer, fall, and winter of 2000 through 2001 (Vásquez-León et al. 2002). Many of the farmers and ranchers interviewed can trace their family's presence in the SSV back to 1896. This fact is important in that, as Dagel (1997) indicates, participants who have resided in an area longer tend to have more reliable perceptions of climate. Consequently, our fieldwork purposively sought out persons whose families had lived in the area for periods greater than ten years. Among those who fit in this category, we specifically asked for their opinions of climate change in the SSV. For those interviewees who responded affirmatively to this question, we then asked them to specify what kinds of changes they had observed.

Informants were also selected to represent the wide variety of crop and livelihood strategies found in the SSV which are all impacted differently by climatic events. Taken together, both of these criteria, residence and crop, mean that one is more likely to capture a wide range of observations of different phenomena over time intervals that span more than one generation. Our strategy was to move from the general to the specific and we avoided asking leading questions such as: 'What kinds of changes have you observed in terms of summer rain?' All of this information was obtained through interviews using topical outlines, which were in turn typed into searchable word-processing programs.

A few participants expressed a strong belief in local climate change. However, most interviewees believed that any change was just part of a cycle and not permanent – e.g. observed changes were examples of climate variability. These statements about climate change or variability were coded from the interview transcripts and catalogued. Monthly precipitation totals, against which we tested farmers' perceptions, were obtained via the Western Regional Climate Center (WRCC) website for the Willcox meteorological station. The Willcox station provides the longest and most complete record of the seven other stations found in the SSV. Missing data for any month were obtained from other station records in the SSV. Perceptions were tested using both descriptive and statistical software.

Analysis

All responses concerning climate change differed slightly and, because we were using an open-ended topical outline, they were difficult to compare. To overcome this problem we identified six perception types and then matched each respondent's specific perception into one of these categories. Table 1 summarizes these results.

Two types of perception had the highest frequency among those participants who discussed some observation of climate variability and/or change (Category 3 participants). The most common perception is that the area was becoming increasingly arid or that droughts were becoming more frequent (Perception A). As an example, one chile farmer stated: 'In the last five years it has been drier and drier.' A retired cotton farmer told us: 'We used to get a lot of rain, but in the past six years there has been no rain. We got some rain, but real spotty.' The next most frequently stated perception is that concerning oscillations in the ratio of winter and summer precipitation. As an example of the latter, one rancher stated: '[We] are shifting more and more to winter-dominant moisture as opposed to summer. We have drier summers and wetter winters.' He also conceded that the last two winters, 1999 and 2000, were exceptions to this pattern.

Because these two perceptions were the most common and since they lend themselves to comparison with the meteorological data, we chose them for our empirical tests. To test the perception that rainfall is declining, we measured the departure of each individual year's annual precipitation from the 1961 to 1990 mean (see Lamb 1985). We also plotted the five-year moving average (Figure 13.4).

Table 13.1 Summary of respondent perceptions of climate variability.

Interviewee Category and Perception Category	No.	Percent of Cat. 1 interviewees	Percent of Cat. 2 interviewees	Percent of Cat. 3 interviewees
Total interviews	71	*	*	*
Cat. 1. Total interviewees	61	100	*	*
Cat. 2. Long-term residents (>10 years)	35	57.4	100	*
Cat. 3. Interviewees who expressed some perception of climate variability and/or change	19	31.1	54.3	100
Perception A. Interviewees who expressed observations of increasing aridity or drought occurrences	14	23.0	40.0	73.7
Perception B. Interviewees who expressed observations of oscillations in summer and winter precipitation	11	18.0	31.4	57.9
Perception C. Interviewees who expressed observations of current drought	10	16.4	28.6	52.6
Perception D. Interviewees expressing observations of increased spottiness of monsoonal precipitation	4	6.6	11.4	21.1
Perception E. Interviewees expressing a belief in cycles of drought	2	3.3	6	10.5

The chart indicates that there is a trend towards decreased annual rainfall as evinced by the five-year moving average. However, as one counts backwards from 1999 in Willcox, only two of the last five years and two of the last ten years represent negative departures from the 30-year mean. The five-year moving average suggests a trend towards declining annual rainfall, but this is not consistent over the last ten years, in which more years have had above average rain than below. Thus, our test does not conclusively demonstrate a trend towards increased aridity. Next, we tested the perception that winter precipitation was becoming more dominant than summer. On average, winter (December–February) precipitation accounts for 22.5 percent of annual rainfall whereas summer (July–September) accounts for 53 percent (West 2001: 51). For testing, we plotted the percentage of winter and summer precipitation to the annual total for the 'water year', October 1 through September 30, of each year (Figure 13.5).

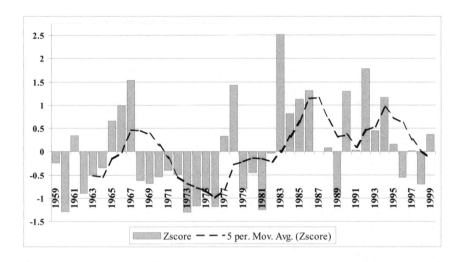

Figure 13.4 Annual departures from 1961–1990. Mean Rainfall, Willcox, AZ, 1959–1999. (*Source*: West 2001: 50.)

Figure 13.5 points out that the meteorological station at Willcox rarely receives more winter moisture than summer. Between 1900 and 1974, this occurred only four times. However, between 1975 and 2000, winter precipitation exceeded summer precipitation in seven different years. Over the last decade, 1991 to 2000, this anomaly occurred in five years (1991, 1992, 1993, 1995 and 1998), which is

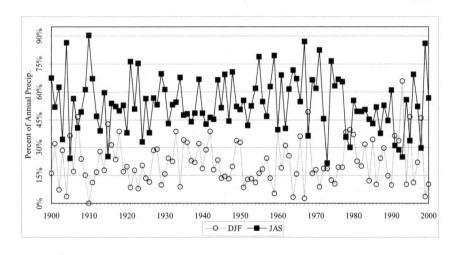

Figure 13.5 Ratio of winter and summer precipitation, Willcox, AZ, 1900–2000. (*Source*: West 2001: 52.)

unprecedented for any other decade in the instrumental record. Thus, the perception that precipitation is becoming more frequent in winter than in summer correlates strongly with meteorological evidence.

Overall, the above analyses indicate that one of the perceptions of precipitation variability can be meteorologically substantiated. Of greater interest is the fact that this variability can be seen on ten-year (decadal) or greater scales. As shown above, annual rainfall in Willcox shows little or no substantial trend regarding the last ten years (1990–99) and perceptions of declining yearly precipitation have little validity in the meteorological record. However, perceptions of seasonal variability are borne out through analyses of the instrumental record. Precipitation data from Willcox verifies the increasing dominance of winter precipitation observed by SSV farmers and ranchers. SSV residents register intra-annual variability in rainfall on time-scales of at least a decade. Furthermore, this perception closely mirrors the same climatic trend – 'wetter winters, and more erratic summers' – observed by physical scientists. Last, rural producers of the SSV indeed perceive multi-year rainfall patterns rather than just events.

Conclusion

The conclusion drawn by other researchers that farmers' perceptions of climate variability are influenced by events rather than trends requires revision. Climate has myriad facets to which humans could attune such as temperature, precipitation, seasonality, types of storms, and other long-term weather phenomena. However, agriculturists in the SSV discussed mostly variation in seasonal precipitation. These particular perceptions are linked to the underlying vulnerabilities of farming and ranching in semi-arid environments.

The prevailing wisdom among SSV agriculturists is that winter snow and rain recharge the regional aquifers even though the summer monsoons provide greater amounts of moisture. These same informants state that increased winter precipitation raises the water table and decreases pumping costs. Similarly, they attribute lower water levels to decreased winter precipitation and overdraft. Ultimately, the long-term viability of farming in this region and most of the Southwest United States depends on the availability of groundwater. Once these aquifers run out as they have in the Imperial Valley of California, then agriculture will fail as well. Ranchers in the area are also affected by differences in seasonal precipitation. Winter snow and rain provide moisture for edible winter annuals and shrubs, and the abundance of such forage permits ranchers to forego purchasing supplemental feed, which is a considerable expense (Conley et al. 1999: 16).

These results have a practical bearing on the interdisciplinary nature of climate vulnerability research. Most anthropologists currently doing such studies are part of larger research teams investigating the potential of using seasonal climate forecasts (Broad 2000; Nelson and Finan 2000; Orlove et al. 2000; Roncoli et al. 2000). Testing the perceptions of farmers, fisherman, and other groups affected by climate variability allows us to elucidate their concerns. The hope is that this effort will give ethnographic accounts more explanatory 'weight' among colleagues in the natural and physical sciences and assist these scientists in orienting their research around the concerns of stakeholders. It seems very probable that these fluctuations in seasonal precipitation have their roots in larger climate phenomena such as El Niño-Southern Oscillation (ENSO) and Pacific Decadal Oscillation (PDO) sea surface temperature (SST) patterns. Investigating the relationship between the climate trends observed by farmers and ranchers and SSTs could result in seasonal forecasts that have greater relevance for their decision-making.

The results presented in this chapter have significance for the social sciences as well. As Sarewitz and Pielke (2000) suggest, the discourse on 'global warming' has the potential to be used, misused, and even abused. It is unlikely that global warming in and of itself threatens farmers in the semi-arid regions of the world. However, increased temperatures and other changes in climate patterns such as seasonal rainfall could have severe positive or negative repercussions for agriculturists around the world. In fact, the IPCC has noted that there may be links between global warming and the occurrence of sea surface temperature fluctuations that drive regional climate change (Allbritton and Filho 2001: 52). Moreover, there is evidence that El Niño events are increasing in frequency and that this is connected to climate change (Burton 1997: 187). El Niño has a strong influence on increased winter precipitation in the Southwest (Sheppard et al. 1999: 10–11). El Niño's increased frequency may manifest itself as a switch to winter rainfall dominance in terms of how it would be felt by people 'on the ground'. Our study indicates a path that social scientists can take for bridging scientific and local discourses concerning climate.

Previous research in North America casts doubt on the ability of human beings to discern between changes in weather with changes in climate. The results presented here, however preliminary, empirically demonstrate that perceptions of climate variability held by farmers and ranchers in the Southwest closely correlate with rainfall in the meteorological record. Thus, the people we interviewed key into changes in *climate* as opposed to just meteorological *events*. These perceptions are embedded within the larger physical context of seasonality and within the material conditions of vulnerability that climate imposes on agriculture in the Southwest. This empirical insight helps bolster the importance of local perspectives in debates about climate change.

Notes

1. This study is part of the larger Climate Assessment for the Southwest (CLIMAS) Project sponsored by the National Oceanic and Atmospheric Administration (NOAA) Office of Global Programs (OGP) and based at the University of Arizona. CLIMAS combines the interdisciplinary expertise of physical and social scientists in defining the entire range of human and natural systems' vulnerabilities to climate variability for the U.S. Southwest.
2. Burton (1997) draws a distinction between climate variability and climate change. He suggests that climate variability, or 'normal climate', is composed of extreme weather events such as storms, droughts, blizzards, and other phenomena. Climate change, on the other hand, entails an increased frequency in the occurrence of such events. For the purpose of this study, climate change is overly complex; thus we focus instead on climate variability.
3. Abundant summer rainfall does not contribute to aquifer recharge for two reasons: first, high temperatures increase evaporation rates, which average 67 inches per year, and second, clay and silt layers that characterize the greater part of the upper basins' fill impede downward percolation of water, making recharge from rainfall and irrigation water on the valley floor negligible (ADWR 1994).
4. Only one family in the SSV engaged in both farming and ranching on a commercial scale. Their neighbors refer to them as the 'cowboy farmers', indicating the rarity of such a combination.

References

ALLBRITTON, D. L. and L. G. MEIRA FILHO. 2001. *Climate Change 2001: The Scientific Basis – Technical Summary.* Contribution of Working Group I to the Third Assessment Report of the Intergovernmental Panel on Climate Change. Accessed on 2/15/2002 at http: //www.ipcc.ch/pub/wg1TARtechsum.pdf.

ARIZONA DEPARTMENT OF WATER RESOURCES (ADWR). 1994. *Arizona Water Resources Assessment: Inventory and Analysis.* Department of Water Resources Report, Volume I. Phoenix: ADWR.

BAHRE, CONRAD J. 1991. *A Legacy of Change: Historic Human Impact on Vegetation in the Arizona Borderland.* Tucson: University of Arizona Press.

BROAD, KENNETH. 2000. El Niño and the Anthropological Opportunity. *Practicing Anthropology* 22: 20–23.

BRYANT, C. R., B. SMIT, M. BRKLACICH, T. R. JOHNSTON, J. SMITHERS, Q. CHIOTTI, and B. SINGH. 2000. Adaptation in Canadian Agriculture to Climatic Variability and Change. *Climatic Change* 45: 181–201.

BURTON, IAN. 1997. Vulnerability and Adaptive Response in the Context of Climate and Climate Change. *Climatic Change* 36: 185–196.

CLARK, LEE and DOUGLAS DUNN. 1997. *Cochise County Agriculture*. Cooperative Extension Report. Tucson: University of Arizona College of Agriculture.

CONLEY, JULIE, HALLIE EAKIN, THOMAS E. SHERIDAN, and DIANA HADLEY. 1999. *CLIMAS Ranching Case Study: Year 1*. CLIMAS Report Series CL3-99. Tucson: Institute for the Study of Planet Earth, University of Arizona.

DAGEL, KENNETH C. 1997. Defining Drought in Marginal Areas: The Role of Perception. *Professional Geographer* 49: 192–202.

FINAN, TIMOTHY J., COLIN THOR WEST, DIANE AUSTIN, and THOMAS MCGUIRE. 2002. Processes of Adaptation to Climate Variability: A Case Study from the U.S. Southwest. *Climate Research,* forthcoming.

GEERTZ, CLIFFORD. 1963. *Agricultural Involution: The Processes of Ecological Change in Indonesia.* Berkeley: University of California Press.

GRANJON, D. 1999. *Enquêtes et Resultants sur l'Adaptation de l'Agriculture aux Différents Types de Stress: Le Cas de la Zone de Napierville.* Research report submitted to B. Singh and C.R. Bryant as part of a research contract with Atmospheric Environnement Services. Downsview: Environnement Canada.

KAYSER, DONALD C. and DAVID W. FIERO. 1970. Pipeline Salvage near Willcox, Arizona. *The Kiva* 35: 131–137.

KEMPTON, WILLETT, JAMES S. BOSTER, and JENNIFER A. HARTLEY. 1997. *Environmental Values in American Culture.* Cambridge, MA: The MIT Press.

LAMB, PETER J. 1985. Rainfall in Subsaharan West Africa during 1945–83. *Zeitschrift für Gletscherkunde und Glazialgeologie* 21: 131–139.

MALONE, ELIZABETH L. and STEVE RAYNER. 2001. Role of the Research Standpoint in Integrating Global-scale and Local-scale Research. *Climate Research* 19: 173–178.

NELSON, DONALD R. and TIMOTHY J. FINAN. 2000. The Emergence of a Climate Anthropology in Northeast Brazil. *Practicing Anthropology* 22: 6–10.

ORLOVE, BENJAMIN S., JOHN C. CHIANG, and MARK A. CANE. 2000. Forecasting Andean Rainfall and Crop Yield from the Influence of El Niño on Pleiades Visibility. *Nature* 403: 68–7.

OVUKA, MIRA and SVEN LINDQVIST. 2000. Rainfall Variability in Murang'a District, Kenya: Meteorological Data and Farmers' Perceptions. *Geografiska Annaler* 82: 107–119.

RONCOLI, CARLA, KEITH INGRAM, and PAUL KIRSHEN. 2000. Can Farmers of Burkina Faso use Seasonal Rainfall Forecasts? *Practicing Anthropology* 22: 24–28.

SAREWITZ, D. and J. ROGER PIELKE. 2000. Breaking the Global Warming Gridlock. *The Atlantic Monthly* 286: 55–64.

SCHULTZ, VERNON B. 1980 [1964]. *Southwestern Town: The Story of Willcox, Arizona.* Tucson: University of Arizona Press.

SHEPPARD, PAUL R., ANDREW C. COMRIE, GREGORY D. PACKIN, KURT ANGERSBACH, and MALCOLM K. HUGHES. 1999. *The Climate of the Southwest.* CLIMAS Report Series CL1-99. Tucson: Institute for the Study of Planet Earth, University of Arizona.

SHERIDAN, THOMAS E. 1995. *Arizona: A History.* Tucson: University of Arizona Press.

SOLLOD, ALBERT E. 1990. Rainfall Variability and Twareg Perceptions of Climate Impacts in Niger. *Human Ecology* 18: 267–281.

STEWARD, JULIAN HAYDEN. 1972 [1955]. *Theory of Culture Change: The Methodology of Multilinear Evolution.* Urbana: University of Illinois Press.

VÁSQUEZ-LÉON, MARCELA, COLIN THOR WEST, JANE M. MOODY, BARBARA WOLF, and TIMOTHY J. FINAN. 2002. *Vulnerability to Climate Variability in the Farming Sector: A Case Study of Groundwater Dependent Agriculture in Southeastern Arizona.* CLIMAS Report Series forthcoming. Tucson: Institute for the Study of Planet Earth, University of Arizona.

WEBB, WALTER PRESCOTT. 1931. *The Great Plains.* Boston: Ginn and Company.

WEST, COLIN THOR. 2001. Testing Farmers' Perceptions of Climate Variability with Meteorological Data: Burkina Faso and the Sulphur Springs Valley, Arizona. M.A. thesis, Department of Anthropology. Tucson: University of Arizona.

WESTERN REGIONAL CLIMATE CENTER (WRCC). 2001. Monthly Precipitation Totals for Willcox, AZ. Data accessed 01-04-2001 at http: //www.wrcc.dri.edu/cgi-bin/cliMAIN.pl?azwill.

WOOSLEY, ANNE I., TIM PRICE, and D. CAROL KRIEBEL. 1987. *Archeological Survey of the Sulphur Spring Valley, Southeast Arizona.* Dragoon: The Amerind Foundation, Inc.

Mood, Magic, and Metaphor: Allusions to Weather and Climate in the *Sagas of Icelanders*[1]

Astrid E. J. Ogilvie and Gísli Pálsson

> . . . like the dark mists that are drawn up out of the ocean, dispersing slowly to sunshine and gentle weather, so did these verses draw all reserve and darkness from Thordis' mind and Thormod was once again bathed in all the brightness of her warm and gentle love.
>
> (*The Saga of the Sworn Brothers*, vol. II, p. 355)[2]

Culture, Fiction, and Historical Truth

In 1783, when modern scientific understanding as we know it was very much in its infancy, a massive volcanic eruption took place in the Lakagígar area in south-east Iceland. Not only did the ash from the eruption settle on pastures throughout Iceland, it was also carried over great distances, covering the Northern Hemisphere like a large veil. The summer of 1783 was characterized by a phenomenon described by contemporaries as the 'great dry fog', in areas as far apart as many countries in Europe, Alaska, Labrador, Newfoundland, Tunisia, Asia Minor, and possibly China (Demarée and Ogilvie 2001). Icelanders carefully observed the eruption, which occurred at a time when the Enlightenment had brought new methods of scientific description to Iceland; and indeed, they could hardly fail to see where the ash came from. It was only months later, however, when the merchant ships of the Danish monopoly arrived in Copenhagen with the news from Iceland, that the larger world learned about the actual origin of the 'fog'. Meanwhile, continental Europeans remained puzzled, eagerly commenting upon the causes of the fog as well as its implications. For some, it signified the end of the world. Many interpreters rushed to conclusions. These were later judged to be unfounded, even bizarre, freely mixing myth, theology, and natural science. The contemporary discussion surrounding the Lakagígar event underlines important general points: first, environmental and climatic events are frequently not confined to the local domain; second, they sometimes have massive repercussions throughout economies and societies; and, finally, their interpretation is critically dependent on cultural context and the information available at any given point in time.

In this chapter, we consider how descriptions of one specific natural phenomenon, the weather, are used in a particular genre of medieval literature, the *Sagas of Icelanders*.[3] It is of course, sometimes difficult to separate 'weather' from 'climate'. While we focus here on weather, we do also allude to a very few descriptions in the sagas which may more appropriately be defined as referring to climate. Before proceeding further, the term 'weather' may be defined as 'short-term climate', something that lasts for a relatively brief time; on the scale of days to months and seasons, possibly even over a few years. 'Climate' is the longer-term sum of 'weather' averaged over time.

The *Sagas of Icelanders*, prose works not dissimilar to the modern novel, are undoubtedly the most well-known type of written source from Iceland. Also known as the *Icelandic Family Sagas*, they are concerned with prominent Icelandic families during the early settlement period of Iceland (ca. AD 871–930) and the so-called 'Saga Age' (ca. AD 930–1050). They comprise about one hundred sagas and shorter stories (*sögur* and *þættir*). They are not contemporary accounts but were compiled in Iceland mainly in the thirteenth and fourteenth centuries. To what extent they are works by individual authors, and how much they draw on oral tales, has long been debated by saga scholars. Although the sagas feature known historical characters, current scholarship places them in the realm of literature rather than history or ethnography (Kristjánsson 1988). Nevertheless, in spite of their limitations as historical evidence, the sagas contain a rich reservoir of social information, and are hence a potentially valuable source for the understanding of Icelandic society and history during the time in which they were written (Durrenberger 1992, Pálsson 1995, Ólason 1998). Among other things, they include many interesting references to weather events and climatic conditions. Many of these descriptions must be seen in the context of literary fiction. Some, however, may reflect a real event. Others may be a mixture of the two and it is not always possible to unravel one from the other. We shall argue that, while the weather and climate accounts of the *Sagas of Icelanders* may be far from strictly factual, they provide a wealth of information on the cultural significance of weather. In the sections that follow we divide weather descriptions into three categories: those that are likely to be factually correct; those that may be fictitious in part but which may contain an element of truth; and those which are almost certainly wholly fictitious and which are used as a literary device, for example as a metaphor, or to create a mood, or in connection with the use of weather in the making of magic. In the final analysis, of course, we can never be sure beyond a shadow of a doubt that we have placed a description in the correct category. For that kind of certainty, we would have to travel back in time and consult our saga informants.

Typical sea-ice limit in a mild summer
Typical sea-ice limit in a severe winter

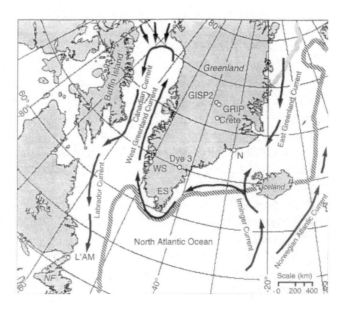

Figure 14.1 Data-location points and areas mentioned in the text.

In the sections which follow below, our examples are taken from these individual sagas: *Egil's Saga*; *Njal's Saga*; *The Saga of the People of Laxardal*; *The Saga of the Sworn Brothers*; *Eirik the Red's Saga*; *The Saga of the Greenlanders*; *Gisli Sursson's Saga*; *The Saga of the People of Eyri*; *The Saga of Havard of Isafjord*; *The Saga of Bjorn, Champion of the Hitardal people*; *Viglund's Saga*; *The Saga of the People of Vopnafjord*; *Hen-Thorir's Saga*; and *The Saga of the People of Vatnsdal*. Prior to our discussion of different types of weather descriptions in the sagas, we present recent research on the climate of Iceland from settlement times to ca. 1430 (at which time the medieval phase of Icelandic literature and historiography may be said to have come to an end). We note the evidence provided by reliable written records, marine-sediment data, and the analyses of ice cores. Figure 14.1 shows data-location points and areas mentioned in the text.

Drilling in Time: Reading Documents, Ice, and Marine Cores

Twentieth-century advances in climate research have included the development of historical climatology – the use of written documentary evidence to infer variations

in climate in the past. This gained momentum with the realization by climatologists, environmental historians, anthropologists, and others, that climate is not
a fixed constant, but is continually changing (Lamb 1956; Ellen 1982; Crumley
1994). The value of 'proxy' climate data from written records rests on the use of
information that adheres to the criteria of contemporanaeity and propinquity, and
is judged to be factual and reliable (Bell and Ogilvie 1978).

For much of its 1,000-year history, Iceland is unusually rich in both the quality
and quantity of its documentary information on climate (Thórarinsson 1956;
Ogilvie 1991, 1992; Ogilvie and Jónsson 2001; Jónsson and Garðarsson 2001).
One reason for this is that in this marginal environment, the climate has always
played a crucial role in the economic life of the country. The simple fact that the
climate has generally made cereal growing difficult or impossible, meant that, until
the development of the fisheries in the late nineteenth century, livestock farming
was the main economic activity. The most important annual agricultural crop has
therefore been the grass and hay on which the livestock were dependent. In the
past, it frequently happened that a failure of the hay crop led to livestock deaths,
and this, in turn, led to famine and deaths among the human population (Ogilvie
2000). It is undoubtedly the interest in the weather (on which lives could depend),
together with the tradition of writing that was established on Iceland from early
times, that has led to the proliferation of documents that contain descriptions of the
weather and climate.

The earliest contemporary written records in Iceland date from the mid-twelfth
century. These give descriptions of mild and severe seasons, and other weather
details such as heavy snowfalls and unusual rains and droughts, as well as accounts
of the Arctic sea ice which is periodically brought to Iceland by the East Greenland
Current. Circumstantial evidence (such as the fact that the settlers seem to have
maintained a reasonable lifestyle for several centuries and the fact that they were
able to grow barley – a practice which later ceased) suggests that, on the whole, a
relatively favourable climate (similar perhaps to that of the late twentieth century)
prevailed for the first few centuries of settlement. However, the much-vaunted term
the 'medieval warm period' is not necessarily appropriate as it serves to obscure the
fact that the medieval climate of Iceland was also highly variable with many cold
episodes (Ogilvie 1991; Ogilvie and Jónsson 2001). Figure 14.2 shows occurrences of mild and cold seasons and sea ice reported in historical documents from
Iceland covering the period ca. AD 865–1598.

Cores taken of marine sediments may also be used as proxy indicators of past
climatic regimes, and may be regarded almost as 'time machines' (Mayewski and
White 2002). For example, two high resolution marine-sediment cores from
Nansen Fjord off eastern Greenland have been analysed by Jennings and Weiner
(1996). These show evidence of changes in oceanographic and sea-ice conditions
from AD 730 to the present. The changes are inferred from two different lines of

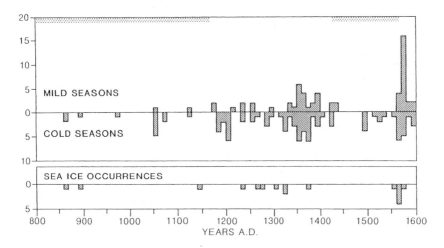

Figure 14.2 Occurrences of mild and cold seasons and sea ice reported in historical documents from Iceland covering the period ca. AD 865–1598. Top shaded area indicates sparse data.

proxy evidence for environmental change. These are variations in lithofacies (types of marine sediments) and *foraminifera* (microscopic fauna with shells). For the period AD 730–1100, the foraminiferal evidence suggests that relatively mild Atlantic Intermediate Water was the predominant water mass on the Nansen Fjord floor. The implication is a period of fairly mild and stable conditions, conducive to Viking expeditions and the settlement of Iceland and Greenland, as well as voyages of exploration to the New World. As a corollary to this, it is possible that there was less Arctic sea ice to trouble travelers at sea than is often the case. The sediment record suggests a similar picture. Both these types of evidence also suggest two cold intervals dominated by Polar Water culminating in AD 1150 and AD 1370 (see Ogilvie et al. 2000 for further details of these proxy climate records).

Although central Greenland lies far from the island of Iceland, ice-core isotopic records from various sites on Greenland may give us some hints regarding the past climate of the North Atlantic region. By analyzing the chemical composition of cores taken in the ice (especially the changes in oxygen isotope ratios) it is possible to build up a detailed record of environmental change that extends thousands of years into the past. Such records suggest a warmer time period variously interpreted as between AD 700 and 1100 (Dansgaard et al. 1975) or between AD 900 and 1350 (Stuiver et al. 1995) depending on smoothing and averaging techniques applied to the data. Borehole temperatures from central Greenland ice cores show a period warmer or as warm as today between AD 900 and 1200. According to the ice-core evidence, the founding of the Eastern and Western Settlements in Greenland in the late tenth century by Icelanders may have been favored by mild climate. The loss of these settlements (dated by historical documents to ca. 1360 for the

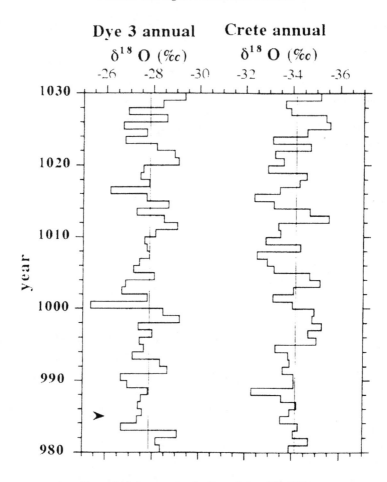

Figure 14.3 Ice-core data for the period AD 980–1030.

Western Settlement and perhaps ca. 1450 for the Eastern Settlement) was due to a combination of factors, but there seems little doubt that the climate of that time played a part (Barlow et al., 1997; Ogilvie et al., 2000). Figure 14.3 shows ice-core data for the period AD 980 to 1030.

The Sagas as 'Field Notes'

The ethnographic and historical usefulness of the sagas has already been noted by Turner. The sagas, he said, 'read like exceptionally well-filled ethnographic records and diaries' (1971: 371), 'full of the very materials that anthropologists rejoice in when vouchsafed to them by informants in the field' (ibid.: 351). More recently, several historians and anthropologists have pointed out through more systematic analyses that many saga narratives parallel ethnographic descriptions from other parts of the world (see, for instance, Miller 1990, Durrenberger and Pálsson 1999).

If we regard the sagas as field notes, as more or less reliable statements *about* medieval realities, a guided package-tour into the past, what can we do with them? Just as anthropologists approach their field notes with differing questions, so saga scholars bring differing perspectives to their texts. A general ethnographic and historical view of the sagas allows for a number of problems and approaches and different authors are unlikely to agree on details. Some saga studies concentrate on the search for abstract semiotic systems, emphasizing ideational, normative codes ('culture'). Structural analyses of the sagas have indeed been developed by some anthropologists (Hastrup 1985). Several scholars have adopted a different approach, attempting to regain life from the text. There are important differences between saga and life, the written and the oral, and, of course, students of the saga age and medieval Scandinavia do not have the advantage of the fieldworker, who is able to arrive on the scene and participate in social life. We simply cannot 'go back', as fieldworkers often do, to re-examine the praxis of the 'natives'. Nevertheless, the 'world out there' presented in our second-hand field notes, in this case, the *Sagas of Icelanders*, often gives the distinct impression of active persons, not of norms and rules.

We know that the *Sagas of Icelanders* were written long after the events they purport to describe. Scholars have debated the relative importance of the pre-Christian period and the early Commonwealth, on the one hand, and, on the other, the later society of state hegemony and Christianity, the contemporary society of those who wrote the sagas. We have good reason, then, to doubt the value of our sources. To make things even more complicated, at times our ethnographer-informants have been deliberately cheating. Not only did they withhold information, they also invented or distorted the 'facts', sometimes for the purpose of justification and entertainment (Tout 1934).

Even though in one sense the sagas do *not* provide the kinds of analyses we now count as proper ethnography, there are sound reasons for juxtaposing saga 'fiction' and anthropological description. Some scholars suggest that the making of ethno-graphies is 'creative' writing, a kind of 'saga'. Even if events do not occur as written, nonetheless the assumptions of how the social context ought to work (how it is represented) is reflective of the writer's own history and reality. Every saga contains echoes from a distant discourse. If the factual and fictive go hand in hand, and any text or utterance is necessarily a collaboration of generations of writers and speakers, the boundary between literary studies and linguistics, on the one hand, and anthropology and history, on the other, is not as important as is often implied (Pálsson 1995). The chief aim of saga scholars trained in anthropology and history is indeed to extract social information from the sagas to reveal the culture and dynamics of early Iceland and similar societies elsewhere, in medieval Scandinavia or beyond.

Astrid E. J. Ogilvie and Gísli Pálsson

Weather and Climate in the *Sagas of Icelanders*

New Players on an Empty Stage

When the early settlers began to colonize Iceland in the last decades of the ninth century, they came to a brave new world formed, by volcanic activity, probably some fifteen or so million years ago (Einarsson 1985). They traveled, of course, by ship, for the sea was their natural highway. The country must have appeared fertile, attractive, and highly suitable for settlement. Vegetation had remained undisturbed for centuries. Early accounts, in particular the *Íslendingabók*, or 'Book of the Icelanders', imply that there was extensive vegetation, including trees, when the settlers first arrived (Benediktsson 1968). This is corroborated by recent research which suggests that 30 percent of Iceland's land mass was forested at that time. The current wooded area is 1.3 percent (Blöndal and Gunnarsson 1991). There were no native inhabitants on Iceland, and the fertile land around the coasts was thus there for the taking. With the arrival of the settlers and their grazing animals, the environment was radically changed. Much of the birch forest was soon gone: cut down for firewood or building, or destroyed by the settlers' livestock. Erosion, which remains a serious problem, soon set in. Nevertheless, the new society that was Iceland continued to exist, despite a harsh environment. Unlike the Norse Greenlanders, the Icelanders lived to tell their tales.

There are very few descriptions of climatic events and environmental features (as opposed to references to 'weather') in the *Sagas of Icelanders* that are likely to be completely factually correct. Indeed, there are very few such descriptions at all. However, there are some which may well come very close to the truth, and these are extremely interesting. As the major focus here is on weather used in a metaphorical sense, only one example of climatic/environmental description will be given. This is taken from *Egil's Saga*, which dates possibly from the early thirteenth century. Here is found an account of the natural environment from the time when Egil's father, Skallagrim, first settled in the western part of Iceland. This description refers to a period some 300 years or so before the saga may have been written. We might well suspect a nostalgic harking back to a Golden Age on the part of the saga writer were it not for the fact that the passage quoted reflects a reality deduced not only from written sources but also from palaeoenvironmental evidence (Ogilvie and McGovern 2000).

> He always kept many men with him and gathered all the resources that were available for subsistence, since at first they had little in the way of livestock to support such a large number of people. Such livestock as there was grazed free in the woodland all year round. Skallagrim was a great shipbuilder and there was no lack of driftwood west of Myrar. He had a farmstead built on Alftanes and ran another farm there, and rowed out

from it to catch fish and cull seals and gather eggs, all of which there were in great abundance. There was plenty of driftwood to take back to his farm. Whales beached there, too, in great numbers . . . the animals were not used to man and would never flee. He owned a third farm by the sea on the western part of Myrar. This was an even better place to gather driftwood, and he planted crops there and named it Akrar (Fields).

(Egil's Saga, vol. I, p. 60)

This account seems likely to be accurate in many ways. When the settlers first reached Iceland, there was undoubtedly an abundance of useful commodities such as driftwood, marine mammals and birds' eggs. It is also extremely interesting that it is written that the livestock 'grazed free in the woodland all year round'. As stated above, the fact that trees and shrubs existed on Iceland in the early days of settlement is known from historical evidence as well as pollen analysis. The account also implies that the climate was mild enough to enable the livestock to be out all year. This is in stark contrast to the more typical situation when livestock needed to be housed during the winter, and which is illustrated in the section below. Finally, regarding this account, it is made clear that it was possible to grow 'crops'. These were undoubtedly barley. We know from a variety of sources that the early settlers cultivated barley; however, in later centuries this became unviable (Thórarinsson 1956).

Famines and Forecasts: Grains of Truth

Other accounts in the *Sagas of Icelanders* discuss short-term weather events and impacts on farming and subsistence that may or may not reflect real situations or events. As stated above, from early times, the Icelandic economy was based on livestock farming, and the most important task associated with this was to harvest enough hay to keep the livestock alive during the winter. Some accounts describe this situation clearly:

That summer there was very little grass for fodder, and the quality was not good because it could not dry. People had a very poor hay harvest . . . Summer passed and winter came. North of Hlid there were severe shortages early on, and provisions were few. Life got hard. It went on like that until Yule, and when the *Thorri* month [mid-January to mid-February] came, people were really hard pressed and many of them just could not go on.

(Hen-Thorir's Saga, vol. V, p. 242)

There are also many references to particular seasons, especially the impact of the weather on the harvesting of the hay and associated events such as severe winters, which would have negative implications for domestic livestock and humans:

The winter was exceedingly harsh far and wide across the country. Livestock died and farming conditions were difficult. Many men went north to Strandir to hunt whales.

(*The Saga of the Sworn Brothers*, vol. II, p. 343)

This passage is interesting in that it refers to the hunting of whales. Marine mammals formed a supplementary food source which was added to the diet whenever possible, especially in times of famine (Ogilvie 2000). In subsistence farming and fishing, the reliability of environmental knowledge and weather forecasts was often critical. This is underlined again and again in saga texts:

'I can't give you any advice other than what I do myself,' replied Ulfar. 'I am going to have the scythes brought out today and have as much grass as possible cut all through this week because I think it might become rainy, but after that my guess is that we will have good drying weather for the next fortnight.'

It turned out just as he had said, for it was often the case that he could predict the weather better than others. Then Thorolf went home and ordered his many farm-workers to get to work at once on the meadows. The weather turned out exactly as Ulfar had said.

(*The Saga of the People of Eyri*, vol. V, p. 167)

That morning Atli woke up early and got out of bed . . . He went outdoors and checked on the weather. The weather was cold and well below freezing.

(*The Saga of Havard of Isafjord*, vol. V, p. 339)

Early on the morning of Maundy Thursday Thorkell made preparations to leave.

Thorstein tried hard to dissuade him, saying, 'It looks like unfavourable weather is brewing'.

Thorkell said the weather would serve him fine, 'and don't attempt to advise me against it, kinsman, for I intend to be home before Easter'.

(*The Saga of the People of Laxardal*, vol. V, p. 116)

By ill luck he began to speak, and talked away looking at the sky: 'The weather is very changeable today. This morning it seemed to me somewhat snowy and it was very cold, but now it seems to me to be as likely that it may thaw.'

Bjarni said, 'Thawing will never cease if this becomes a thaw'.

(*The Saga of the People of Vopnafjord*, vol. IV, p. 328)

The sagas occasionally refer to events such as famines or dearths which may well have been climate-related. In the epic late thirteenth-century *Njál's Saga*, for example, it is said of one of the main female characters, Hallgerd, that she offers her guests food during a time of famine: 'Hallgerd brought food to the table, including cheese and butter' *Njál's Saga*, vol. III, p. 57). Realizing that they did not have such provisions in stock and that they therefore must have been stolen, her husband, Gunnar, orders this food to be removed: Everything was taken off the table and meat brought in instead' *Njál's Saga*, vol. III, pp. 57–8). This episode is said to have taken place during a 'great famine' in Iceland. This is a case in point where we cannot be sure if there was a grain of historical truth in the occurrence of this famine or if it is used as a literary device to create a mood of unpleasantness which serves to highlight one of Hallgerd's less desirable characteristics: her dishonesty.

In the examples given above, the allusions to weather are used as literary devices, creating tension and drama in the narrative. It is possible, however, that some of these accounts may contain more than a grain of truth and may reflect memories of actual events.

The Sea and Sailing

The section above dealt with farming, subsistence, and life on land. The marine element was of equal importance in the lives of the people described in the sagas. In nearly all of the *Sagas of Icelanders*, the sea and sailing are woven in to form a constant backdrop. To say that the Vikings were sailors is something of a tautology, and the settlement of Iceland and subsequent relations with the 'mother country' of Norway must be seen in the context of the Viking voyages west. During the 'saga age' traffic between Iceland and Norway, and indeed also to Greenland and the New World, was vital for both subsistence and for communication. The importance of the sea and sailing in daily life, and how far they were engrained in the psyche of the early Icelanders, is reflected in the large role they play in mythology and the supernatural. The god of the sea was called Aegir or Hler, and the goddess of the sea was Ran. In the accounts which describe them they are given attributes which reflect the twofold nature of the sea: an element which both gives to humans (it provides them with a means of travel and with subsistence in the form of fish and marine mammals) but is also a despoiler of human life; storms rage on the ocean and lives are lost. Those who kept company with Aegir in his hall under the sea (which parallels Odin and Valhalla) were mainly drowned seafarers. Egill Skallagrimsson, in his poem *Sonatorrek* ('Lament for his Sons') gives what must be one of the most eloquent examples in literature of a description of the cruelty of the sea. Here the sea, in the role of the sea gods and goddesses, is cast in the role of his bitter enemy:

> But the lord of the sea,
> brewer of storms
> seems to oppose me,
> his mind set.
> I cannot hold
> my head upright,

the ground of my face,
my thoughts' steed.

(*Egil's Saga*, vol. I, p. 155)

The dual nature of the sea, as giver and taker, is also illustrated in this account from *The Saga of the Sworn Brothers*:

> Thorgeir and Thormod prepared to set sail to hunt and to fish at Strandir in the north, but just as they were ready to start out the wind turned against them and made it impossible for them to leave the fjord . . . When winter arrived, a fair breeze allowed them to set sail out of Isafjord in good weather. However, it was too calm for them to make much headway, and when they had sailed for a while the weather first began to thicken and then it started to snow. By the time they were out of the fjord, the weather turned against them. They were so beset with squalls that blustered and blew around them in the freezing cold that they could no longer see their course . . . The daughters of the sea-goddess, Ran, tried to embrace them, but they managed to make their way into a fjord . . .

(*The Saga of the Sworn Brothers*, vol. II, pp. 336–7)

During the winter, there was little traffic across the highways of the North Atlantic. The sailing season began in spring when the worst of the winter storms were over and continued until the autumn: 'When spring came and the weather began to improve, they launched their boat and made ready to sail' (*The Saga of the Sworn Brothers*, vol. II, p. 340). To sail during the winter was to risk bad weather and shipwreck:

> Egil was slow in getting ready, and by the time he put to sea it was too late for favourable winds, with autumn and bad weather approaching. They sailed north of Orkney. Egil did not want to stop there since he assumed King Eirik was ruling the islands. They sailed southwards along the coast of Scotland in a heavy storm and crosswinds, but managed to tack and head south of Scotland to the north of England. In the evening, when it began to get dark, the storm intensified. Before they knew it, the waves were breaking on shoals both on their seaward side and ahead of them, so the only course of action was to make for land. They did so, running their ship aground in the mouth of the Humber. All the men were saved and most of their possessions, except the ship. It was smashed to pieces.

(*Egil's Saga*, vol. I, p. 116)

Indeed, many journeys did end in shipwreck. It is said of Eirik the Red's original colonization of Greenland that twenty-five ships set out but only fourteen reached Greenland. (Some of the others were wrecked and the rest were driven back to Iceland.) Travel by ship was dependent on the winds and fair weather and the intended destination was sometimes elusive:

After this they set sail and the weather, which had been favourable when they set out, changed. The favourable wind dropped and they were beset by storms, so that they made little progress during the summer . . . The sea swelled and the boat took on much water but, despite many other hardships, they made land in Greenland at Herjolfsnes at the Winter Nights.

(*Eirik the Red's Saga*, vol. I, p. 5)

Another account from *Egil's Saga* describes how seafarers could be at the mercy of the winds and the waves. This time it is the coast of Iceland that is hard to reach:

In the spring, when the seas became calmer, Bjorn launched his ship and prepared it for sailing in great haste. When he was ready to set out and a favourable wind got up, he sailed out to the open sea. Driven by a powerful gale, they were only at sea for a short while before they neared the south of Iceland. The wind was blowing from the land and carried them west of Iceland and back out to sea. When a favourable wind got up again they sailed towards land. None of the men on board had ever been to Iceland before.

(*Egil's Saga*, vol. I, p. 71)

Eirik the Red's Saga and the *Saga of the Greenlanders* are collectively known as the 'Vínland Sagas' as they tell very similar stories concerning the exploration of the northeastern seaboard of the continent of North America, and the country named by the would-be settlers 'Vínland' ('Wineland' after the wild grapes they found growing there). One of the attempted voyages to Vínland was also foiled by unfavourable winds.

Thorstein Eiriksson now wished to sail to Vínland to retrieve his brother Thorvald's body and made the same ship ready once more. He selected his companions for their strength and size, taking with him twenty-five men and his wife Gudrid. Once they had made ready, they set sail and were out of sight of land. They were tossed about at sea all summer and did not know where they had gone.

(*The Saga of the Greenlanders*, vol. I, p. 26)

Ice on the sea, whether ice that drifted to the shores of Iceland on the East Greenland current or ice that formed on the water, was a danger at worst and a hindrance at best. The presence of ice meant, among other things, that ships could not approach the coast freely.

After the burial, the weather worsened. It became very cold and snow started to fall. Ice covered a large part of the fjord and no ship could approach Olafsdal.

(*The Saga of the Sworn Brothers*, vol. II, p. 370)

The winter had been a cold one and there was a thick layer of ice along the shore and far out into the bay of Breidafjord, preventing ships from setting out from the coast of Bardastrond . . . The following day the weather was mild and calm.

(*The Saga of the People of Laxardal*, vol. V, p. 102)

The marine environment and the weather associated with it are described very frequently in the sagas; indeed, more so than weather on land. It is likely, however, that the descriptions above parallel those associated with land-use in that they are clearly used to set a scene and to create a mood, but there may well have been an element of truth to a description, or a long-kept memory of the weather associated with a certain event.

Moods, Metaphors, and the Making of Magic

As we have seen, saga writers used natural events to set scenes and to create moods for dialogues and social events. In the two previous sections, we refer to weather descriptions which were used for this purpose, but which could conceivably also have their origins in real weather events. In other cases, it seems likely that a weather description is used purely as a literary device. In this section we consider weather references which we believe are likely to belong to this latter group. For this discussion it is necessary to refer to elements of the plots of the sagas.

It was the kind of weather where the air is very still, but there was also a heavy frost.

(*Gisli Sursson's Saga*, vol. II, p. 44)

Gisli Sursson's Saga tells of Gisli Sursson, a man who is drawn unwittingly into a sequence of events which lead to his being declared an outlaw. This is a common theme in the *Sagas of Icelanders*. Gisli is no lawless malcontent, however, rather a tragic hero, unable to escape another frequent element in the sagas, his fate. The quotation above mirrors events in a certain stage of the saga and serves to create a mood of foreboding and unease. It is said that 'Gisli stayed home that summer, and all was quiet.' Then things begin to change: 'on the last night of summer, Gisli could not sleep.' The weather description that follows these sentences artfully mirrors the suggestion that things appear quiet on the surface ('very still') but that trouble will soon occur: 'there was also a heavy frost'. Sure enough, Gisli is soon set upon by a group of his enemies and loses his life. The 'heavy frost' thus also foreshadows the chill of death. It is said of Gisli: 'Thus Gisli's life came to an end, and although he was deemed a man of great prowess, he never had much luck' (vol. II, p. 47).

It had been a bright day with a good deal of sunshine, but as Thormod reached the booth the weather began to thicken. Thormod looked by turns up at the sky and then down at the ground in front of him.

Egil said, 'What are you doing that for?'

Thormod answered, 'Because both the sky and the earth indicate that a great blow is imminent'.

Egil said, 'And what does such a great blow usually mean?'

Thormod replied, 'Such blows always portend important tidings. Now, should you hear a sound then you must do what you can to keep out of harm's way. Run back to the booth as fast as you can and take refuge there.'

As they were speaking, there was a great shower of rain, a downpour that no one had expected, so that they all ran to their booths.

(The Saga of the Sworn Brothers, vol. II, p. 377)

The Saga of the Sworn Brothers probably dates from around the latter part of the thirteenth century. It concerns two friends, Thorgeir and Thormod, who, believing they were likely to die fighting, swore an oath that whoever survived the other would avenge his death. It is said in the saga: 'Their rise to fame was fast. They roamed far and wide about the land but were far from being popular' (vol. II, p. 331). The quotation above has a parallel with *Gisli Sursson's Saga*, mentioned above, in that there is a change from calm or favorable weather to cold or temp-estuous (unfavorable) weather that presages events in the narrative and thus helps to establish a mood or feeling. The precursor to this apparent weather description is an incident that takes place in Greenland in which it is made clear that Thormod feels that his friend Thorgeir has been insulted by a man named Thorgrim. Know-ing this, the saga-reader senses that the fact that the day has been 'bright' with sunshine but that the weather is now starting to 'thicken' suggests that events in the human world are also about to turn unpleasant. In this case, there is also a play on the word 'blow'. When Thormod says that 'the earth and the sky indicate that a great blow is imminent', it soon becomes apparent that he is not only referring to the weather. A few minutes after this conversation, Thormod struck Thorgrim 'on the head, splitting him to the shoulders'. The word 'blow' is used again: 'When Egil heard the great blow that Thormod dealt Thorgrim, he ran back' (vol. II, p. 378), and this time the meaning is not meteorological.

This was what their night's lodging was like: some of them got themselves out of their breeches, which hung, frozen, overnight on the partition, and they lay down to sleep. Early in the morning Bjorn got up and looked at the weather, shutting the door when he came in. Thorstein asked what the weather was like. Bjorn said it was good weather for brave men. Thorstein called to his companions and told them to make ready, and so they did . . . But when Thorstein went out the weather was abominable.

He said, 'Bjorn isn't choosy about weather on our behalf; he doesn't know how short of heroism we are.'

Bjorn heard what he said: 'Yet it is fit weather for a begging journey to Husafell', he said.

Thorstein grew angry at this response, went out to the main room and joined Thorfinna. There was one other woman there. They were quiet and said little; Bjorn had come in too. Frost followed the great storm, and at times there were bright patches in the sky.

(*The Saga of Bjorn, Champion of the Hitardal People*, vol. I, p. 291)

The Saga of Bjorn, Champion of the Hitardal People is one of a group of sagas concerning poets and has as its focus a love triangle. The 'action' takes place in England, Russia, and the Borgarfjord district in western Iceland. In the account quoted above, the weather is used to enhance the narrative and to echo the conflicts amongst the protagonists. Angry responses, the 'storms', are followed by 'frost', but 'bright patches' of disquiet remain.

The examples of weather serving to amplify and enhance the narrative given above have mostly referred to fighting and violent events. However, weather is also used metaphorically to suggest powerful human emotions. Thus, the epigraph of this chapter, from *The Saga of the Sworn Brothers*, likens dark thoughts of the mind to 'dark mists that are drawn up out of the ocean' and the 'brightness of her warm and gentle love' to 'sunshine and gentle weather' (vol. II, p. 355). This statement powerfully evokes the intermingled joys and sorrows of human sexual love.

Many saga accounts discuss the manufacture of dangerous weather through witchcraft, *gerningaveður* (literally 'performative weather' or 'weather acts'). Making weather, a branch of 'ancient arts', was often seen as women's business:

There was a man named Gamli . . . He was an excellent hunter and fisherman, and was married to a woman named Grima, an ill-tempered woman but one with many talents. She was a good healer and quite well versed in the ancient arts.

(*The Saga of the Sworn Brothers*, vol. II, pp. 382–3)

Grima sat on the threshold, span some yarn and hummed something that the others did not understand.

(*The Saga of the Sworn Brothers*, vol. II, p. 384)

That winter Thorodd paid Thorgrima Magic-cheek to bring out a wild storm while Bjorn was crossing the heath. One day Bjorn went over to Froda, but when he left to go home that evening, the sky was overcast and it had started to rain, and he was rather late getting going. By the time he came up to the heath, the weather had turned very cold and there were snow drifts. It was so dark that he could not see the path in front of him. After that a blizzard blew up with so much force that he could hardly stand up.

(The Saga of the People of Eyri, vol. V, pp. 181–2)

The cloud quickly scudded across the sky and when it was over the farm at Froda it grew so dark that people could not see beyond the home meadow, and they could scarcely distinguish their own hands. So much rain fell from the cloud that all the hay lying on the ground became soaked. The cloud suddenly drew past and the weather cleared up. People could then see that blood had rained down in the shower.

(The Saga of the People of Eyri, vol. V, p. 197)

The sagas seem to assume two aspects of witchcraft, the ritual act itself, or the performance of witchcraft, and the magical spell of the word. *Gisli Sursson's Saga* provides an example of the former:

She walked several times withershins around the outside of the house, sniffing in all directions. As she did this, the weather broke and a heavy, blustering snow storm started up. This was followed by a thaw in which a flood of water gushed down the hillside and sent an avalanche of snow crashing into Berg's farmhouse. It killed twelve men. The traces of the landslide can be seen to this day.

(vol. II, p. 22)

Many accounts emphasize infliction through the act of speaking: chants (*söngvar, seiðir*) and libels (*ákvæði, áhrínisorð, níð*). Usually words and actions seem to have gone together. In some acts of witchcraft speech was dominant, in others not.

Ulfhedin was a great friend of Dueller-Starri, and men say that, when Thorarin the Evil challenged Starri to a duel, Ulfhedin accompanied him to the duelling place; and on that journey the weather turned foul, and they believed it was a witch's storm.

There was a man called Bard who was called the Peevish; he also went with them. They asked him to call off the bad weather because he had the wisdom of a wizard. He asked them to join hands and make a circle; he then went round backwards three times, spoke in Irish, and bade them all say 'yes' out loud – and this they did. He then waved a kerchief at the mountain and the weather relented.

(The Saga of the People of Vatnsdal, vol. IV, pp. 64–5)

There was a man named Bjorn who was one of the farmhands of Thorgrim the Elegant. He was such a bold sailor that no matter how terrible the weather, he was not afraid to sail. He always said that he did not worry about the size of the swells . . .

It happened in the autumn that both of Bjorn's fishing companions got sick because of Kjolvor's magic. All the men were employed at haymaking when Bjorn wanted to row out for fish and he asked the brothers Viglund and Trausti to row out with him for the day. They did so, since the weather was fine and they were good friends of his. Kjolvor knew all about this and climbed up on the house and waved her hood in an easterly direction, and all at once the weather turned bad. When the three had reached the fishing banks, there were quite a few fish, but then they saw a cloud rising in the east-north-east.

Viglund said, 'I think it advisable to head for land. I don't like the look of the weather.'

Bjorn said, 'We're not going to do that until the boat is full.'

'You're the one who's in charge,' said Viglund.

The cloud approached quickly, accompanied by wind and frost, and such heavy seas that the water was very rough and pelted them as though with grains of salt. Bjorn now said that they should head for land.

(*Viglund's Saga*, vol. II, p. 422)

These accounts underline a folk theory of speech acts. Poetry was one way of influencing events through language. Some poets, particularly the so-called *kraftaskáld* ('power poet' or 'magic poet'), were believed to be charged with greater powers than others (Bauman 1992, Pálsson 1995). Such an idea seems to have been entertained by Icelanders for centuries, even up to recent times.

For early Icelanders, runic inscriptions had a magical quality, with important consequences for the people involved, positive or negative, depending on the point of view.[4] In the early days of writing, when the art of writing was only known to a few, the old Norse term 'rune' was extended to embrace any kind of powerful 'text'. Theoretically, any piece of text might alter the course of events and, thereby, affect people's lives. For Icelanders, the text, whether it be a runic inscription, a work on grammar, a legal text, or a saga, had a force of its own.

Discussion

Recently, anthropologists, social historians, and archaeologists have been exploring the value of an approach that takes heed of the importance of historical veracity but which carefully uses literary texts to gain insights into the culture in which a particular work was written. Bauman notes that 'if we can turn literary models to the study of society, we should find it equally productive to apply sociological perspectives to literary texts' (1986: 134). As we have seen, the *Sagas of Icelanders* provide a range of information on the ways in which the saga age presented weather events. The saga-writers, we have suggested, may well be regarded as anthropological informants, bridging the temporal gap between their reality and ours, between the past and present. While medieval Icelandic texts were rooted in Western discourse, they must somehow mirror the culture, needs, and circumstances of those who produced them. We have focused on four themes prominent in saga discussions of weather: sailing and the sea; references to the all-important subsistence and farming; the use of weather as a metaphor and to create a mood; and the manipulation and creation of weather though witchcraft and magic. Some accounts seem likely to be accurate in many ways as they resonate with what is known from historical and archaeological evidence. Other accounts, however, including descriptions of the manufacture of storms by magic, were deliberate fiction, rhetorical devices reflecting the constraints of storytelling by the time the sagas were written.

While some narratives of weather events may be mere literary devices – for setting scenes, tensions, and emotional states, for making a good story – they must also reflect the ways in which medieval Icelanders thought and talked about the environment and their place within it. Thus, in the *Sagas of Icelanders*, the *natural* landscape, with the backdrop of the annual cycle of seasonal events, is closely intertwined with the *cultural* landscape, the internal and external lives of the saga characters. This suggests that in medieval Iceland there was no radical separation of nature and society. As Gurevich argues, in ancient Scandinavia 'man thought of himself as an integral part of the world . . . His interrelation with nature was so intensive and thorough that he could not look at it from without; he was inside it' (1992: 207). Much of the saga text also underlines the irrelevance of the category of the 'supernatural', echoing the modern condition of post-modernity (Descola and Pálsson 1996). Weather magic was just as 'natural' or down-to-earth as weather events and weather forecasts.

Ellen (1982: 11) suggests that among environmental factors, meteorological phenomena are generally those that are 'least likely to be directly affected by local human activity'. While this perhaps fails to acknowledge the driving forces behind pollution and the recent phenomenon of anthropogenically induced global warming, it seems valid for most of human history. Climate, on the other hand, has obviously been important for human society throughout history; for some societies, however, more than others. Leach (1961: 9) points out, in his work on a village in Ceylon, that 'the inflexibility of topography – of water and land and climate – . . . most of all determines what people shall do', adding that the 'interpretation of ideal legal rules is at all times limited by such crude nursery facts as that water evaporates and flows downhill' (ibid.). While water is a necessity for any social formation (see, for instance, Geertz (1972), for an interesting early analysis of the 'wet and the dry'), what people make of it varies from one context to another. Even in extreme arid conditions, water is culturally represented in various ways (Pálsson 1990). As a result, statistics on precipitation, on their own, are not particularly informative for students of human societies.

The sagas are obviously limited in many respects, but are they *all* we have got? As we have seen, an important theme in recent scholarship juxtaposes life and text. For some scholars writing in this genre, the sagas *constitute* medieval culture. Thus Meulengracht Sörensen suggests there is no medieval Icelandic culture outside the sagas. For him 'there are no longer any roads to reality outside the actual sagas' (1992: 28). Such claims are overstatements informed by the linguistic turn. Research on other, normative and economic documents, combined with modern ethnography, archaeology, and economics significantly adds to latent contextual information in the sagas. Frye makes a useful comparison between saga studies and biblical scholarship:

> we cannot get an inch further without new archaeological evidence, and such evidence would carry the authority that we have ceased to assign to the sagas themselves. Similarly, for the historian of the Biblical period, the primary historical authority is not the Bible but what (the written sources having been exhausted long ago) archaeology can still dig up in the way of acceptable evidence.
>
> (Frye 1982: 43)

In the saga case, recent studies of ice cores, archaeological remains, and pollen analysis have added extensively to our understanding of the conditions of the saga age. After all, temporality is 'written' in the material products of generations of humans and other living organisms.

The perceived wisdom regarding the climate of Iceland during medieval times is that it generally provided a mild and favorable background to the golden 'Saga Age'. As we now know from studies of a variety of climate proxy data, the reality was undoubtedly more complex, with a high level of climatic variability. The true nature of the climate of this time is also heavily obscured by the fact that the settlers to Iceland came to an untouched landscape; a 'natural capital' of pristine soils, grass, and birch forests. This undoubtedly provided a 'buffer' against inclement weather. Later economic difficulties may have had as much, or more, to do with environmental degradation than an unfavorable climate (Ogilvie and McGovern 2000).

Long-term climatic change is, by definition, usually beyond the observation of single generations; thus, while the *Sagas of Icelanders* have much to say about weather events and their manifold implications they are relatively silent (with exceptions such as the passage quoted above from *Egil's Saga*) on long-term change. As Cronon (1996: 47) points out, much of our knowledge of atmospheric change (including our current understanding of anthropogenic global warming and the development of the ozone hole) must be virtual since we cannot 'observe' it in any real sense. Combining folk and scientific narratives (see, for example, Cruik-shank 2001) may, however, yield powerful insights into environmental history and human–environment relations. The *Sagas of Icelanders*, as a vivid backdrop to sober studies of climate and weather using modern tools such as ice-core, marine-core, and other palaeoenvironmental data, are a telling example of such an exercise.

Notes

1. The chapter draws upon related discussions in some of our earlier research. Work on this chapter has been generously supported by the National Science Foundation (USA), the Leverhulme Trust (UK), the University of Iceland, and the Stefansson Arctic Institute, Akureyri. Rósa Signý Gísladóttir and Kristín Erla Harðardóttir provided valuable help in searching for descriptions of weather events in the digitalized concordance, *The Sagas of Icelanders* ed. Bergljót S. Kristjánsdóttir, Eiríkur Rögnvaldsson, Guðrún Ingólfsdóttir, and Örnólfur Thorsson (Reykjavík: Mál og Menning, 1996). We thank Lisa Barlow for permission to use Figure 14.3. We are grateful to Trausti Jónsson and Trond Woxen for helpful comments on the manuscript.
2. All page references to the sagas are to *The Sagas of Icelanders*, vols. I–V. Reykjavík: Leif Eiriksson 1997.
3. Other categories of medieval Icelandic prose include: the 'Sagas of Norwegian Kings' (*Heimskringla*); *Fornaldarsögur* or 'Sagas of the Past', and legal texts, notably *Grágás* ('Grey Goose') and *Jónsbók* ('The Book of Jón'). Furthermore, there are extensive poetic texts, including the *Poetic Edda*.
4. The word 'rune' (*rún*) referred both to a letter of the indigenous alphabet and to a secret symbol with magical qualities. The latter meaning is probably the original one. Thus particular symbols (*stafir, tákn*) were seen to influence fishing success, others would affect loss of livestock, and still others might insure or prevent love relationships.

References

BARLOW, L. K., J. P. SADLER, A. E. J. OGILVIE, P. C. BUCKLAND, T. AMOROSI, J. H. INGIMUNDARSON, P. SKIDMORE, A. J. DUGMORE, and T. H. MCGOVERN. 1997. Interdisciplinary Investigations of the End of the Norse Western Settlement in Greenland. *Holocene* 7: 489–499.

BAUMAN, R. 1986. Performance and Honor in 13th-century Iceland. *Journal of American Folklore* 99: 131–50.

—— 1992. 'Contextualization, Tradition, and the Dialogue of Genres: Icelandic legends of the *kraftaskáld*', in *Rethinking Context: Language as an Interactive Phenomenon*. Edited by A. Duranti and C. Goodwin, pp. 125–145. Cambridge: Cambridge University Press.

BELL, W. T. and A. E. J. OGILVIE. 1978. Weather Compilations as a Source of Data for the Reconstruction of European Climate during the Medieval Period. *Climatic Change* 1: 331–348.

BENEDIKTSSON, J. 1968. Íslendingabók. Landnámabók. *Íslenzk Fornrit I*. Reykjavik: Hið Íslenzka Fornritafélag.

BLÖNDAL, S. and S. B. GUNNARSSON. 1991. *Íslands skógar: hundrað ára saga*. Reykjavik: Mál og Mynd.

CRONON, W. (Ed.). 1996. *Uncommon Ground: Rethinking the Human Place in Nature*. New York: W.W. Norton & Company.

CRUIKSHANK, J. 2001. Glaciers and climate change: Perspectives from oral tradition. *Arctic* 54(4): 377–395.

CRUMLEY, C. (Ed.). 1994. *Historical Ecology: Cultural knowledge and changing landscapes*. Santa Fe: School of American Research Press.

DANSGAARD, W., S. J. JOHNSON, N. REEH, N. GUNDESTRUP, H. B. CLAUSEN, and C. U. HAMMER. 1975. Climatic Changes, Norsemen and Modern Man. *Nature* 255: 24–28.

DEMARÉE, G. R. and A. E. J. OGILVIE. 2001. 'Bons baisers d'Islande: Climatic, environmental, and human impacts of the Lakagígar eruption (1783–1784) in Iceland', in *History and Climate: Memories of the Future*. Edited by P. D. Jones, A. E. J. Ogilvie, K. R. Briffa, and T. D. Davies. Dordrecht: Kluwer Academic/ Plenum Publishers.

DESCOLA, P. and G. PÁLSSON (eds). 1996. *Nature and Society: Anthropological Perspectives*. London: Routledge.

DURRENBERGER. E. P. 1992. *The Dynamics of Medieval Iceland: Political economy and literature*. Iowa City: University of Iowa Press.

DURRENBERGER, E. P. and G. PÁLSSON. 1999. 'The Importance of Friendship in the Absence of States, According to the Icelandic Sagas', in *The Anthropology of Friendship: Beyond the Community of Kinship*. Edited by S. Bell and S. Coleman, pp. 59–77. Oxford: Berg Publishers.

EINARSSON, Th. 1985. *Jarðfræði* ('Geology'). Fifth ed. Reykjavík: Mál og menning.

ELLEN, R. 1982. *Environment, Subsistence, and System: The Ecology of Small-scale Social Formations*. Cambridge: Cambridge University Press.

FRYE, N. 1982. *The Great Code: The Bible and Literature*. New York and London: Harcourt Brace Jovanovich, Publishers.

GEERTZ, C. 1972. The wet and the dry: Traditional irrigation in Bali and Morocco. *Human Ecology* 1(1): 73–89.

GUREVICH, A. 1988. *Medieval Popular Culture: Problems of Belief and Perception*. Translated by J. M. Bak and P. A. Hollingsworth. Cambridge: Cambridge University Press.

—— 1992. *Historical Anthropology of the Middle Ages*. Ed. J. Howlett. Oxford: Polity Press.

HASTRUP, K. 1985. *Culture and History in Medieval Iceland: An Anthropological Analysis of Structure and Change*. Oxford: Oxford University Press.

JENNINGS, A. E. and N. J. WEINER. 1996. Environmental Change in Eastern Greenland during the Last 1300 Years: Evidence from Foraminifera and Litho-facies in Nansen Fjord, 68°N. *Holocene* 6: 179–191.

JÓNSSON, T. and H. GARÐARSSON. 2001. 'Early Instrumental Meteorological Observations in Iceland', in *The Iceberg in the Mist: Northern Research in Pursuit of a 'Little Ice Age'*. Edited by A. E. J. Ogilvie and T. Jónsson, pp. 169–187. Dordrecht: Kluwer Academic Publishers.

KRESS, H. 1987. Bróklindi Falgeirs: Fóstbræðrasaga og hláturmenning miðalda. *Skírnir* 161: 271–86.

KRISTJÁNSSON, J. 1988. *Eddas and Sagas: Iceland's Medieval Literature*. Translated by Peter Foote. Reykjavík: Hið íslenska bókmenntafélag.

LAMB, H. H. 1956. The Early Medieval Warm Epoch and its Sequel. *Palaeogeography, Palaeoclimatology, Palaeoecology* 1: 13–37.

LEACH, E. 1961. *Pul Eliya: A Village in Ceylon*. Cambridge: Cambridge University Press.

MAYEWSKI, P. A, and F. WHITE. 2002. *The Ice Chronicles: The Quest to Understand Global Climatic Change*. Hanover, NH: University Press of New England.

MEULENGRACHT SÖRENSEN, P. 1992. 'Some Methodological Considerations in Connection with the Study of the Sagas', in *From Sagas to Society: Comparative Approaches to Early Iceland*. Edited by G. Pálsson, pp. 17–42. Enfield Lock: Hisarlik Press.

MILLER, W. I. 1990. *Bloodtaking and Peacemaking: Feud, Law, and Society in Saga Iceland*. Chicago and London: The University of Chicago Press.

OGILVIE, A. E. J. 1991. 'Climatic Change in Iceland AD c. 865 to 1598', in *The Norse of the North Atlantic* (Presented by G. F. Bigelow). *Acta Archaeologica* 61: 230–251.

—— 1992. 'Documentary Evidence for Changes in the Climate of Iceland, AD 1500 to 1800', in *Climate since AD 1500*. Edited by R. S. Bradley and P. D. Jones, pp. 92–117. London and New York: Routledge.

—— 2000. 'Climate and farming in Iceland, ca. 1700–1850,' in *Aspects of Arctic and Sub-arctic History*. Edited by I. Sigurðsson and J. Skaptason, pp. 289–299. Reykjavík: University of Iceland Press.

OGILVIE, A. E. J., L. K. BARLOW, and A. E. JENNINGS. 2000. North Atlantic climate c. AD 1000: Millennial reflections on the Viking discoveries of Iceland, Greenland and North America. *Weather* 55: 34–45.

OGILVIE, A. E. J. and T. JÓNSSON (Eds.). 2001. '"Little Ice Age" Research: A Perspective from Iceland', in *The Iceberg in the Mist: Northern research in pursuit of a 'Little Ice Age'*. Edited by A. E. J. Ogilvie and T. Jónsson, pp. 9–52. Dordrecht: Kluwer Academic Publishers.

OGILVIE, A. E. J. and T. H. McGOVERN. 2000. 'Sagas and Science: Climate and human impacts in the North Atlantic,' in *Vikings: The North Atlantic Saga*. Edited by W. W. Fitzhugh and E. I. Ward, pp. 385–393. Washington D.C.: Smithsonian Institution Press.

ÓLASON, V. 1998. *Dialogues with the Viking Age: Narration and Representation*. Translated by Andrew Wawn. Reykjavík: Mál og menning.

PÁLSSON, G. (Ed.). 1990. *From Water to World-making: African Models and Arid Lands.* Uppsala: Scandinavian Institute of African Studies.

—— 1992. *From Sagas to Society: Comparative Approaches to Early Iceland.* Enfield Lock: Hisarlik Press.

—— 1995. *The Textual Life of Savants: Ethnography, Iceland and the Linguistic Turn.* Chur: Harwood Academic Publishers.

THE SAGAS OF ICELANDERS, vols. I–V. 1997. Reykjavík: Leif Eiriksson.

STUIVER, M., P. M. GROOTES, and T. F. BRAZUNIAS. 1995. The GISP2 18º climate record of the past 16,500 years and the sun, ocean and volcanoes. *Quaternary Research* 44: 341–354.

THÓRARINSSON, S. 1956. *The Thousand Years Struggle against Fire and Ice.* Reykjavík: Bókaútgáfa Menningarsjóðs.

TOUT, T. F. 1934. 'Mediaeval Forgers and Forgeries', in *The collected papers of Thomas Frederick Tout* vol. III, Historical Series, No. LVXI, Publications of the University of Manchester No. CCXXI. Manchester: Manchester University Press.

TURNER, V. 1971. 'An Anthropological Approach to the Icelandic Saga', in *The Translation of Culture: Essays to E.E. Evans-Pritchard.* Edited by T.O. Beidelman, pp. 349–374. London: Tavistock.

AFTERWORD

–15–

Domesticating Nature: Commentary on the Anthropological Study of Weather and Climate Discourse

Steve Rayner

The essays collected in this volume attest to the resurgence of anthropological interest in weather and climate that has occurred during the past decade. This interest appears to have been driven by, or at least to have accompanied, a growing concern about climatic change and variability among scientists and the wider society.

Margaret Mead was probably the first anthropologist to address the societal threats of anthropogenic climate change, joining forces with meteorologist William Kellogg to convene a scholarly workshop on the topic as long ago as 1976 (Kellogg and Mead 1976). To the best of my knowledge, the first time the issue was addressed at a meeting of the American Anthropological Association was a paper entitled *Risk Management and the Global Commons: A Cultural Approach to Decision Making*, which I delivered at the annual meeting in Phoenix in 1988. In 1995, anthropologist Willet Kempton and his colleagues published a significant study of *Environmental Values in American Culture,* in which people's perceptions of climate and climatic change is the central theme. A new scientific focus on climatic variability and its policy implications has grown in parallel with the extension of anthropological inquiry into climate-related beliefs and behaviors around the world. Subsequently, Ben Orlove, Kenny Broad, Tim Finan, and Carla Roncoli have been at the forefront in establishing the related issue of climatic variability within the community of applied anthropologists. Now, largely as a result of efforts by the editors of this book, it seems that a meeting of the AAA would be incomplete without a topical panel on the anthropology of climate and weather. New terms have entered the anthropological lexicon: 'ethnoclimatology' and 'ethnometeorology'.

My own slant on the topic of climate and society has been heavily influenced by my undergraduate studies in philosophy. I was very taken by the fact that the great philosophers in the Western tradition almost invariably applied themselves to two apparently distinct areas of intellectual endeavor, a theory about the way the world is (an inquiry into nature and our knowledge of it) and a theory about the way the world ought to be (a theory of politics or ethics). I cannot claim that this was an original observation. Indeed, it echoed that of Bertrand Russell's popular history of the subject published some thirty years earlier (Russell 1945). However, I was soon preoccupied by a further refinement of this observation that seemed of relatively little interest to philosophers. That is the fact that a philosopher's theory about nature always seemed to provide a natural underpinning or justification for his theory about society. Thus, Plato, who favored a stable polity ruled over by a hereditary caste of Guardians, also proposed that the phenomena we observe in daily life are but ephemeral projections of a world of perfect unchanging forms. On the other hand, Marx and Engels squandered many hours in a pub near the British Museum getting very excited about the fact that liquid water absorbs heat without any change of physical form until it reaches boiling point, at which it immediately turns into gas. Thus, they reasoned, socialist revolution was 'only natural'.

The general absence of professional reflexivity about the dual nature of philosophers' musings was one of the factors that drove me to anthropology as a graduate discipline. There I found that my observation was not confined to the rarefied world of philosophers. In fact, the ethnographic record suggested that the buttressing of moral or political beliefs by appeals to nature is a universal phenomenon. Thus, in certain traditional African societies, leprosy was viewed as a natural consequence of adultery. Cattle disease was merely a natural consequence of violating the traditional sexual division of labor (Douglas 1966). Nature is a direct source of moral feedback for behavior, desirable or undesirable.

In the mid-1980s, I had the opportunity to collaborate with one of the pioneers of environmental anthropology, the University of Minnesota anthropologist Luther Gerlach. It seemed to us that what was, at that time, the sleeping issue of climate change presented a promising research site for a research program to explore the relationship between nature and culture. We proposed this program to the senior management of the Oak Ridge National Laboratory, where I was then working. A senior economist on the staff, a former deputy administrator of EPA, dismissed our proposal. He pronounced that climate change would never be a significant public policy issue for three reasons. First, it was too far in the future to engage public attention. Second, there was no easily identifiable single villain. And third, the science was too uncertain. Our response was that these characteristics were precisely the ones that made climate the ideal issue on which a wide variety of social actors could, and would, hang social disputes about the good life, the relationship of humans to nature, the nature of human nature (pursuing profit or perfection), etc. Fortunately, senior managers at the Laboratory decided to take a risk on our proposal. With the advent of the 1988 drought and heat wave in the United States, climate hit the front pages and the congressional hearing rooms. The rest, as they say, is history.

Climate change has become a prominent site of disputation about competing social values and epistemologies (Thompson and Rayner 1998). As such, it is perhaps more closely linked with adjacent issues than our colleagues in the natural sciences are comfortable with. For example, scientists generally would have us make clear distinctions between climate and weather, although the emerging field of climate variability is beginning to fudge that once clear distinction. Most scientists take the public's apparent confusion, or conflation, of climate change and stratospheric ozone depletion as evidence of public misunderstanding of science. Some people's attribution of global warming to the ozone hole was reported in Kempton et al. (1995) and has been replicated in succeeding public opinion surveys.

However, this may not be the simple case of scientific error that it seems on the surface. Applying an anthropological perspective, we can see that, rather than a simple category error, the claim that stratospheric ozone depletion and climate change are the same thing may be a sensible and salient one from a public perspective. In seeking to make sense of the puzzling Nuer claim that 'twins are birds' (not that twins are like birds, but that they actually are birds) Evans-Pritchard (1956) argued that claims of sameness or identity between two items are often only comprehensible in relation to a third, unstated or implicit, item. Thus twins are birds in the sense that, for the Nuer, both twins and birds are especially close to god. Viewed from this perspective, we might see the apparent equation of climate change and ozone depletion as an assignment of both phenomena to an unstated category of 'industrial insults to the atmosphere'. In that sense, two quite different scientific issues are the same thing from a public perspective. The precise scientific etiology of the ozone hole or a global temperature rise is simply not salient to this audience. The identity of climate and stratospheric ozone seems even more justifiable when seen through the lens of proximate causation, in that human production of chlorofluorocarbons (CFCs) is known to be a significant cause of both the ozone hole and global warming.

The essays in this collection attest to the importance of climate as a site for anthropological investigation of the relationship between ideas of nature and moral and political life. As a whole they describe a spectrum of experience ranging from subsistence rain-fed agriculture to irrigated commercial farming; from Nordic Argonauts plying the North Atlantic in tiny sailboats without wireless or weather forecasts to contemporary Chesapeake Bay watermen; from medieval to post-modern; from folk knowledge to scientific weather prediction.

At one end of this spectrum, the elements are directly experienced. Ogilvie and Pálsson's account of the attention to weather in Icelandic sagas certainly suggests that climate and weather, especially anomalous weather, were closely observed. In extreme climates, or those subject to sudden change, as in many mountain regions, such as the Swiss village described by Strauss, attention to weather conditions and knowledge of the signs of change seem to be obvious survival skills. The disastrous consequences of inattention to weather conditions may be immediate, as in the case of Ogilvie and Pálsson's medieval seafarers; delayed, as they may be for Brazilian farmers encouraged by scientific forecasts to ignore the onset of early season rain as described by Finan; or both, as exemplified in Paolisso's account of contemporary watermen of the Chesapeake Bay, whose crab population may be vulnerable to the highly variable hydrology for which the bay is well known.

Where weather is directly experienced it is also a strong focus of ritual, as among the Ihanzu, described by Sanders, and mythology, as illustrated by Ogilvie and Pálsson. Anomalous weather events attest to the importance of events or the superhuman characteristics of the heroes and villains of Icelandic sagas.

At the other end of the spectrum, in the modern industrialized world, our experience of nature is seldom so direct. It is invariably mediated by science. Nature as lived-in milieu has been thoroughly domesticated. Even in its wildest forms it has become 'the environment'. In the United States, where the prototype of nature is untouched wilderness, even that wilderness is domesticated by its legal designation as a reserve, which precludes most citizens from any possibility of experiencing it directly. In Europe, nature is domesticated as countryside – a cultural landscape owing as much to human artifice as anything else.

The mediation of our experience of nature is not confined to our external lives; it is characteristic of our knowledge of our biological selves. In the post-Prozac world, not only our bodies, but also our emotions and cognitive capacities have become thoroughly medicalized. Information about the state of our biological selves is now more likely to be derived from urine and blood tests or other diagnostic technologies than from self-awareness or even from communicable clinical craft skills.

Weather has not escaped this trend. For urbanites (and that is now half of the world's population) the impacts of extreme weather tend to be buffered by infrastructure, including housing, roads, and storm drainage systems. Information about weather is not derived from personal observation, but from mass media communications based (presumably) on observations using scientific instruments and analyzed with the aid of computers.

One way or another, humans have attempted to domesticate weather, climate, and their consequences for millennia. Some methods of domestication have relied heavily on material culture and infrastructure. Both clothing and traditional dwelling designs evolved to mediate people's experience of weather by providing shade and shelter from sun, wind, and rain. Irrigation systems exemplify early human attempts to domesticate climatic variability by regularizing the irregular occurrence of rainfall, flood, or snowmelt for agriculture. In the 1950s, publications with such now politically incorrect titles as *The Boy's Bumper Book of Science* would have been incomplete without a vivid illustration of how 'by the end of the 20th century cities will be built under domes to protect them from the weather'.

Although this extreme infrastructural innovation shows no sign of becoming reality, we have become separated from the need or desire to pay close attention to weather signs or weather lore. Strauss provides a clear example of this in her description of contemporary Leukerbad. In contrast with the role of weather in Icelandic sagas, anomalous weather in the twenty-first century has become spectacle. Although the strong representation of British case studies in this book seems to confirm the popular stereotype of an insular nation obsessed with the weather, it is in fact in the United States where this obsession has reached its highest or, depending on your point of view, its lowest point. Americans are treated to a monthly magazine devoted to the weather. The Weather Channel broadcasts 24 hours a day, interspersing weather forecasts with live and recorded coverage of extreme weather events, such as storms, floods, and droughts. The commercial breaks offer videotapes of hurricane, tornado, and flood footage that John Seabrook (2000) writing in the New Yorker has dubbed 'Weatherporn'. At least in the industrialized world, 'The more weather we watch on TV the less time we spend in it.'

We seem to have reached at least a temporary limit to our infrastructural domestication of climate and weather. In parts of the United States, the Army Corps of Engineers is actually seeking permission to dismantle dykes and levees along the Mississippi River. Currently human efforts at taming the weather focus on technologies of prediction and control. The accounts in this book of Swiss traditional *Bauernregeln*, British weather lore, and the various folk indicators of weather used by farmers in Burkina Faso remind us that ethnoclimatology and ethnometeorology are probably as old and as widespread as humanity itself.

The modern scientific era of weather prediction emerged, as Golinski relates, in the eighteenth century. It has brought enormous benefits, in terms of improved agricultural yields and lives saved from flooding and shipwrecks. But from its beginning, scientific forecasting has also raised moral dilemmas. For example, recent debates about the unfair competitive advantage that access to El Niño forecasts give to commercial fishing fleets at the expense of artisanal fishermen (Pfaff et al. 1999), were foreshadowed by the advent of weather forecasting in nineteenth-century America. Thus, in his exemplary historical study *Americans and Their Weather*, William Meyer (2000), a cultural geographer, describes contemporary concern about how the advent of the telegraph enabled news of rain traveling from west to east across the United States to be transmitted from Philadelphia to New York, bestowing a competitive advantage on, among others, well-connected umbrella salesmen.

Contemporary computer-based technologies for predicting both climate change and climate variation may appear to bring us closer to nature by generating expectations of how natural systems will behave. In other words, they purport to provide people with information about the future on timescales of months to decades, so that farmers may plan planting and harvesting, or dam builders can anticipate changes in the characteristics of watersheds, and so forth. In the case of climate change, scientists and policymakers view general circulation models as vital sources of information to guide long-term energy policy. However, as revealed by ethnographic research methods in the field of STS (Science and Technology Studies), such models do not merely represent nature, they are also ways of creating 'other' simulated natures at the same time as 'naturalizing' the social world (Jasanoff and Wynne 1998).

General circulation models (GCMs) have been the focus of most of the past decade's scientific and political controversy about the extent and even reality of climate change. The assumption justifying their use in both science and policy is that they more or less accurately reproduce significant behaviors of the earth's climate system. One way in which scientists test these models is to run them backwards to see how well they 'predict' past climates. But there are some problems with this method of validation. The observational data to which the model is compared are themselves informed by theoretical assumptions that may not be transparent either to the modeller or the user of the model-based information. As Jasanoff and Wynne (1998) note, the reconstruction of past climates is an act of 'heterogeneous archaeology' that combines analysis of physical data, such as polar ice cores, fossilized pollen, and tree rings with at least superficially incommensurable social artefacts such as parish records. Translating such data and artefacts into measures of past climate, in turn, depends heavily on theory and inference.

At least some of the data used to validate climate models are themselves model outputs. GCMs are one of the resources used to construct time-series data sets of past climates accessible only through the sort of proxies described above. Moreover, the past climate that models are expected to reproduce is defined by data such as sea-surface temperatures, atmospheric pressures, and precipitation. Such data themselves reflect implicit choices about what is important to measure, how and where data are collected, what standardization measures are applied, etc. Thus the data used as a standard against which the model is evaluated may not be wholly independent of the model or at least the assumptions shaping it.

The stability of some of the model-based predictions of future climate may be due as much to institutional factors influencing the modelers as to properties of the models themselves. As Cartwright (1983) observes more generally, models are creative endeavors in which some properties ascribed to objects will be authentic, but others will be properties of convenience or necessity. Certainly the development of GCMs has been characterized by a certain degree of intellectual incestuousness among the modelers.

Institutional factors appear to be instrumental in establishing the stability of predictions of the range of global average temperature changes for a doubling of atmospheric carbon dioxide concentrations from preindustrial levels, which for many years was consistently given as 1.5–4.5 degrees C. If this estimate were a product of GCMs, it would be reasonable to expect a probability distribution across the range with a most likely value (say 2.5 degrees C) somewhere in the middle, tailing off to low values at the extremes. In practice, however, this value was not derived deterministically from the formal models but was the result of diffuse expert judgment and negotiation among climate modellers (van der Sluijs 1997; Shackley et al. 1998). Commentators disagree about the extent to which the negotiated stability of the projected temperature range represents a consensus about the scientific credibility of the values or a more hybrid consensus that takes account of what policy makers find credible and potentially manageable (Rayner 2000). Whichever is the case, the emergent stability has been an important factor in domesticating climate change as a seemingly tractable problem for both science and policy (Jasanoff and Wynne 1998).

Clearly, the goals of climate modelers and the expectations of policymakers converge. Both seek more accurate prediction on a finer scale, but while the scientific community is rigorous in its attempts to deal with explicit scientific uncertainties and communicate them to policymakers, the latter continue with an unrealistic expectation of scientific capabilities. Furthermore, the nature of what we refer to as uncertainty in climate prediction often lies outside of the GCM modeling framework – for example, inherently unpredictable thresholds for rapid climate destabilization, such as the so-called 'runaway greenhouse effect'.

Thus, not only do climate-related models mediate between humans and nature, they are also instruments of political mediation, incorporating and establishing assumptions about human agency and institutional capacity. This aspect of models becomes even more important as their scope moves beyond the climate system itself, to incorporate potential ecological impacts of climatic change and variation (Jasanoff and Wynne 1998). Taylor's analysis of a systems model of African pastoralist ecology is instructive in this respect. Following the droughts of the early 1970s, international aid agencies commissioned this model to identify the kinds of management policies that could be adopted to avoid regional desertification, economic collapse, and starvation. As Taylor (1992: 123) notes, the model did not simply represent the nature of the system, but was rather 'a science of representing in relation to someone's conception of possible interventions.' The boundaries of the model simply took for granted external factors such as international trade rules and the scope of intervention available to international aid agencies. The behavior of the pastoralists themselves was assumed to be a homogeneous stimulus-response dynamic, identical in principle to modeling of the natural system. Thus the model served to mediate and naturalize a particular set of political relationships and options for ecosystems management.

Outside of laboratories and government agencies, people seem to be a bit more ambivalent about both the achievability and the desirability of prediction. Whereas the scientific authors of America's Accelerated Climate Prediction Initiative (1998) were uncompromising in their promise of better policy through finer grained climate prediction, the Chesapeake Bay watermen and farmers in Burkina Faso, described in this volume, appear to share a conviction that complete knowledge of the future is a divine not a human prerogative. Golinski spots the same ambiguity in eighteenth-century Britain, in which 'we recognize a reflection of our own ambivalence about enlightenment and modernity. Thinking about the weather obliges us to acknowledge the incompleteness of modernity, even its questionable value as an ideal . . . the eighteenth century had already perceived some of the limitations of the project to order the weather and was by no means as uniformly enlightened as we have sometimes assumed' (p. 32). Another, perhaps more rationalist interpretation is that invoking the divine prerogative is a way of coming to terms with the disappointments of modernism. Despite our rational pretensions we are forced to manage our lives with not just imperfect, but imperfectable information.

There may also be more mundane reasons for ambivalence about the value of prediction among non-scientists. In the course of research on the use of short-term climate forecasts that I conducted with Helen Ingram and Denise Lach, some interviewees described how they used the existing uncertainty in weather and short-term climate forecasts to meet organizational, political, or operational goals. They were concerned that improved information about future weather conditions could limit their decision space (Rayner et al. 2002). For instance, the construction manager of one California utility described additional erosion protection measures that he is required to implement if a storm is forecast. These measures are very disruptive of construction schedules. However, if an unforecast event occurs, he is not held responsible for failing to 'button down the site'. His perceived self-interest suggested to him that he would be happier with less, rather than more, skilful forecasting. He could then claim that uncertainty in the forecasts means that they don't provide adequate information to prepare for weather events. Thus, the construction industry can transfer the erosion problem away from its current practices and attach it to the issue of forecast reliability. Similarly, in the Chesapeake Bay, forecasts could, in principle, be used to control the timing of fertilizer or manure spreading on fields to avoid the runoff that occurs when heavy rain falls on freshly applied nutrients. While this would be beneficial for those seeking to reduce nutrient loading in the bay, farmers do not necessarily welcome the loss of autonomy.

These findings were part of a larger study examining the question of why water resource managing institutions in the United States do or do not use probabilistic forecast information about seasonal and inter-annual climate variability in their planning. The study sought to describe water resource decision-making processes in sufficient detail to enable us to identify the institutional conditions under which increased use could be made of probabilistic climate forecasting information to benefit society as a whole. However, our findings suggested that humans don't always welcome more information about weather and climate, even in highly sensitive areas such as resource management.

According to the most popular social science model of decision-making, the rational choice perspective, decision-makers (particularly in the private sector) are strongly motivated – by the desire to optimize performance – to readily incorporate research results and forecast information into their decision making. Failure to incorporate such information is characterized merely as an exogenous barrier or remediable market imperfection.

However, we discovered that water resource managers universally gauge their success by a single indicator – their own invisibility to consumers and political authorities. They are driven by a clear hierarchy of values – security of water supply, quality of water delivered, and (coming in a distant third) cost. Hence, they tend to be very conservative in making changes to their decision-making procedures and criteria, especially if the potential for increased efficiency is accompanied by any prospect of increased risk to continuity of supply or even transitory changes in water quality. This conservatism suggests that water resource managers are using an implicit payoff matrix (see Table 15.1) leading to extreme reluctance to incorporate improved climate forecast information.

Table 15.1 Implicit payoff matrix for water resource managers to incorporate new climate forecast information.

	Established Procedures	*Innovative Methods*
Desirable outcome	Low visibility 'Business as usual'	Low visibility 'Why bother?'
Undesirable outcome	Moderate visibility 'Soon forgotten'	High visibility 'Heads will roll'

Beyond infrastructure and forecasting, humans have sought to impose order on the weather by direct intervention in weather processes. Since the Second World War there have been extensive efforts to change the weather through cloud seeding (Kwa 2001). Most of these were inconclusive attempts to stimulate rain in arid environments or at times of drought. However, throughout the 1960s and 1970s Project Stormfury addressed the possibility of weakening hurricanes through cloud seeding. The idea was to seed a hurricane's bands of thunderstorms in a way that would make the eye expand. If the eye grows larger across, the winds spiralling into it would slow down. The results were inconclusive and, finally, in 1980,

Project Stormfury was brought to a close. Sanders' case of rainmaking rituals among the Ihanzu reminds us, that these modern attempts to control weather, especially stimulating rain in arid and semi-arid regions, are part of a long tradition. It is not clear, however, that Ihanzu rituals are any more or less effective than cloud seeding.

It is fair to say that all of the essays in this collection affirm the link between moral and political ideas and ideas about nature represented by weather and climate. However, they are less unanimous about the direction of causation. Do weather and climate shape culture or are our ideas about weather, climate, and seasons shaped by human organization and behavior? The climate–society relationship has been a topic of scholarly interest since Herodotus and Hippocrates. Mostly it has been dominated by various versions of climatic determinism. Nineteenth-century writers on the topic were nearly unanimous in equating hot weather with the tendency of a culture towards indolence and low productivity. Temperate zones were thought to lead nations to be industrious and productive. Of course these writers were all convinced that the climate of their own location was the one most likely to promote the ideal level of intellectual activity. In this volume, Golinski tells us that already in the eighteenth century the British weather diarists viewed the temperate character of British weather as an example of God's particular favor.

Such a chauvinistic approach led scholars throughout the twentieth century to ignore the climate–society relationship altogether. As a result, there is an eighty-year gap in the social science research record on this topic. When attention returned to the issue late in the century, largely because of concerns about global warming and climate variability, the result has been a tendency towards a static view of climate that assumed that the earth's current state represents some kind of optimum that ought to be preserved. In this last respect, Golinski's essay is a nice reminder that the current concerns about global climate change are not as entirely unprecedented as they are often hyped up to be by scientists, activists, and the media. He shows how eighteenth-century scientific concern about weather in Britain emerged out of a broader set of worries about the effects of industrial development on nature. This led, for the first time, to the emergence of an ideally stable 'national' weather, foreshadowing the emergence of an ideally stable 'global climate' two centuries later.

A rare departure from the social sciences' lack of concern with the climate-society relationship throughout the twentieth century was Mary Douglas' (1966) comparison of Lele and Bushong economies. Douglas observed a stark difference in the levels of development and climatological perception of these neighboring peoples, who were separated by the Kasai River, and subject to only minor variations in ecological conditions. Whereas the more economically developed Bushong viewed the summer as hot, dry, and unpleasant, the technologically and artistically inferior Lele regarded it as a pleasant season of relaxation. Douglas suggested that the ability of the monogamous Bushong to earn status through their own industriousness provided more stimulus to cooperative economic effort than the polygamous Lele. The latter could only acquire status, along with wives, through age. Hence, Bushong were hard at work herding throughout the summer while their Lele counterparts were able to kick back in the shade drinking palm wine. According to this account, social relations exert a strong influence on ideas about the weather.

Contributors to the present volume seem divided. For example, several appear to see perceptions of climate and weather as determined by natural conditions of aridity. Indeed, there are echoes of climatic determinism in West's claim that 'ecological and climatic conditions shape particular patterns of belief, which induce people to place more value on specific natural phenomena than others' (p. 235). On the other hand, Finan emphasizes 'how a climate discourse is embedded in traditional forms of political interaction within a highly stratified, paternalistic society' (p. 204). Orlove and Harley seem positively Douglasian in their descriptions of how seasons are anchored in cultural stereotypes associated with calendrical time. In turn, the attempt to establish an empirical relationship between climatic seasonality and time is at the core of Golinski's discussion of the emergence of eighteenth-century weather science, which we can see as a modernist attempt to replace a temporality determined by an ordinal scale climatology with a climatology defined by an interval-scale temporality.

The currently fashionable resolution of the dilemma of causation in nature-society relations is *coproduction*. That is to say, for example, that conditions of aridity will lead the inhabitants of a region to focus on precipitation and temperature, but the particular way in which they express that focus will be culturally shaped and that both processes are tightly linked in mutually reinforcing iterative loops. In all fairness, I expect that all of the contributors to this book would readily embrace some version or another of this explanation over the extremes of climatic or cultural determinism. That is fair enough, so far as it goes, but it does leave us with some explanatory dilemmas that cannot merely be dismissed as historical contingency. For example, we learn from the papers collected here that aridity leads farmers to focus on the weather in Arizona, Burkina Faso, and Tanzania. Apparently the British are weather-obsessed because they do not experience weather extremes but rather rapid variation in weather within a rather temperate range of conditions. Weather among the British is a resource for polite conversation, because it does not require intimate conversational disclosure that would breach class lines and social conventions, but Ihanzu rainmaking involves explicit sexual imagery and conversation that would make a well-bred Briton blush.

Golinski tells us that British weather talk should be understood as 'phatic' communication. That is to say, it is an act of social bonding, rather than the transmission of information. However, despite their explicitly instrumental purpose of making rain, Ihanzu weather rituals are also, by definition, about social bonding. The coproduction idea may tell us how climate and culture are intertwined. But it merely pushes back the need for explanation to another level. Interestingly, despite the contrast between the studied politeness of British weather talk and the vulgar sexuality of Ihanzu rainmaking discourse, both seem to be about temporarily dissolving rigid social structures. As Sanders writes, 'In the ritual realm of rain-making . . . Disputes over the relative statuses and powers of the genders are temp-orarily resolved' (p. 86). Do the British talk about the weather because their ordered patterns of social relationships impel them to domesticate natural variability through a discourse that safely transcends social class? Or is it merely that variable weather is so ubiquitous that it forces itself on the attention of the national psyche in such a way that its discussion does not threaten the social order? My own answer is undoubtedly conditioned by the experience of returning to the UK after an absence of two decades. I have been struck by both the erosion of the social class system and the decline in casual conversation about the weather!

Whatever position the authors take on causation in the culture-climate relation-ship, the driving question underlying the entire collection is how to understand the selective incorporation of scientific ideas of weather and climate forecasting into social practice among farmers, watermen, and other citizens. Here the authors seem to speak with almost a single voice on two counts. First, that people in a wide diversity of climatological and cultural circumstances all exhibit some degree of ethnometeorological or climatological competence derived from a combination of experience of past weather patterns, occupational or survival skills, and social organization. Second, that these existing levels of competence lead to the operation of a cultural analogue of the *confirmation bias* known to psychologists. Put simply, this states that we tend to incorporate new information that is compatible with our existing views and reject that which is irrelevant to or in conflict with them.

Thus, Paolisso insists that Chesapeake watermen demonstrate effective weather craft skills based on wider cultural models that locate water pollution in the context of values about religion, nature, morality, work, independence, and responsibility combined with empirical ecological and economic knowledge. Roncoli, discussing the dissemination of probabilistic seasonal prediction forecasts among rain-fed farmers of the Sahel-Sudan Region, demonstrates that forecasts are interpreted through the lens of their own concerns and do not necessarily receive the message intended by the forecasters. Finan's description of the Northeast Brazilian 'drought industry' shows how climate discourse is embedded in traditional forms of political interaction, including a system of clientalism, which regulates the provision of water and food deliveries and public employment, and provides a framework of incentives through which any scientific information has to be processed. Unfort-unately, in this instance, science has often been used to legitimize corruption in infrastructure provision for drought resistance.

Even West's finding that farmers in Southwest Arizona have accurate recollections of precipitation and rainfall patterns close to the statistical records does not contradict this general principle, especially since the only other source they have is pumped groundwater, so annual and monthly irrigation costs are likely to serve as an independent reminder of seasonal weather conditions each year. Hence, the Southwest Arizona case should not be interpreted as invalidating the rather robust findings of Kempton et al. (1995), Meyer (2000), and reiterated in this volume by Harley, that people's recollections of past weather patterns are usually unreliable.

In the end it does seem, as Harley and Orlove indicate, that our memories of past climates depend very heavily on idealized stereotypes of seasonal conditions. We still expect to see snowmen on seasonal greetings cards although, as Harley points out, there has not been a White Christmas in Lowland Britain since 1970. This reinforces my confidence in the findings of my own research on the resistance of water resource managers to climate forecasts. It seems that climate information appears to offer no exception to the general rule 'I'll see it when I believe it!' Far from being a natural background to or constraint upon human behavior, both climate and weather emerge as important social constructs mediating people's experience of and interaction with nature and with each other. Perhaps we might consider a more symmetrical approach than Proust's claim that 'A change in the weather is sufficient to recreate the world and ourselves.' We could add that 'A change in ourselves and the world is sufficient to recreate the weather.' That might be an appropriate thought for a world reportedly on the brink of global climate change.

References

ACCELERATED CLIMATE PREDICTION INITIATIVE. 1998. *The Accelerated Climate Prediction Initiative: Bringing the Promise of Simulation to the Challenge of Climate Change.* Pacific Northwest National Laboratory. PNNL-11893. Richland, WA.

CARTWRIGHT, N. 1983. *How the Laws of Physics Lie.* Oxford: Oxford University Press.

DOUGLAS, M. 1962. 'Lele Economy compared with the Bushong: A Study of Economic Backwardness', in *Markets in Africa.* Edited by P. Bohannan and G. Dalton, pp. 211–233. Evanston: Northwestern University Press. Reprinted 1982 in M. Douglas, *In the Active Voice*, pp. 148–173. London: Routledge and Kegan Paul.

DOUGLAS, M. 1966. *Purity and Danger: Concepts of pollution and taboo.* London: Routledge & Kegan Paul.

EVANS-PRITCHARD, E. E. 1956. *Nuer Religion.* Oxford: Oxford University Press.

JASANOFF, S. and B. WYNNE. 1998. 'Science and Decisionmaking', in *Human Choice and Climate Change, Volume 1: The Societal Framework.* Edited by S. Rayner and E. L. Malone, pp. 1–88. Columbus, OH: Battelle Press.

KELLOGG, W. W. and M. MEAD (Eds). 1976. *The Atmosphere: Endangered and Endangering.* Fogarty International Center Proceedings No. 39, Washington D.C.: Department of Health, Education, and Welfare Publications.

KEMPTON, W. M., J. S. BOSTER, and J. HARTLEY. 1995. *Environmental Values in American Culture.* Cambridge, MA: MIT Press.

KWA, C. 2001. The Rise and Fall of Weather Modification. In *Changing the Atmosphere: Expert Knowledge and Environmental Governance.* Edited by C. A. Miller and P. N. Edwards, pp. 135–66. Cambridge, MA: MIT Press.

MEYER, W. 2000. *Americans and their Weather.* New York: Oxford University Press.

PFAFF, A., K. BROAD, and M. GLANTZ. 1999. Who benefits from Climate Forecasts? *Nature* 397: 645–646.

RAYNER, S. 2000. 'Prediction and Other Approaches to Climate Change Policy', in *Prediction: Science, Decision Making, and the Future of Nature.* Edited by D. Sarewitz, R.A. Pielke Jr., R. Byerly Jr., pp. 269–296. Washington D.C.: Island Press.

RAYNER, S., D. LACH, H. INGRAM, and M. HOUCK. 2002. *Weather Forecasts are for Wimps: Why Water Managers Don't Use Climate Forecasts.* Report to the Office of Global Programs, National Oceanic and Atmospheric Administration. www.ogp.noaa.gov/mpe/csi/econhd/fy98/raynerfinal.pdf.

RUSSELL, B. 1945. *A History of Western Philosophy.* London: George Allen & Unwin.

SHACKLEY, S., P. YOUNG, S. PARKINSON, and B. WYNNE. 1998. Uncertainty, Complexity, and Concepts of Good Science in Climate Change Modelling: Are GCMs the Best Tools? *Climatic Change* 8: 159–205.

SEABROOK, J. 2000. Selling the Weather. *New Yorker*, April 3.

TAYLOR, P. 1988. 'Re/constructing Socioecologies: System Dynamics Modelling of Nomadic Pastoralists in Sub-Saharan Africa', in *The Right Tools for the Job.* Edited by A. Clarke and J. Fujimura, pp. 115–148. Princeton: Princeton University Press.

THOMPSON, M. and S. RAYNER. 1998. 'Cultural Discourses', in *Human Choice and Climate Change, Volume I: The Societal Framework.* Edited by S. Rayner and E.L. Malone, pp. 265–344. Columbus, OH: Battelle Press.

VAN DER SLUIJS, J. 1997. *Anchoring amid Uncertainty: On the Management of Uncertainties in Risk Assessment of Anthropogenic Climate Change.* Leiden: Ludy Fein.

Index

absolute time, 23
Accelerated Climate Prediction Initiative, 284, 289
Ackroyd, P., 149, 158
Addison, Joseph, 19, 29
addresses to spirits, 90–6
'Adventure of the Bruce-Partington Plans, The' (Doyle), 150
Aegir (god of the sea), 261
Africa
    pastoralist ecology model, 283
    Sahel-Sudan region, 181–3
    See also Burkina Faso
Agricultural Involution (Geertz), 234–5
agricultural seasons, 127
aibika, 163
air pollution, 141, 143, 145–6, 156
    See also London, England, fog
Alaska, 218
alfalfa, 237, 240
algorithms for weather prediction, 44–5
Allen, B. J., 175, 178
almanacs, 28, 43–5, 49, 55, 59
Amazing Tempest, The, 26
American Anthropological Association, Anthropology and Environment Section, 11, 277
American Meteorological Society, 45
Americans and Their Weather (Meyer), 281, 289–90
ancestors, 89, 172–3
anemometers, 51
animals
    behavior, 50, 218
        captured in place names, 225
    classification systems, 124–5
    effected by climate and weather, 62, 168
    faunal analysis, 223
annual cycles. *See* seasons
anthropologists, 4

Anyampanda (royal leaders), 90
apples, 237
Appletree, Thomas, 21
aquifer recharge with winter precipitation, 239, 246
Arbuthnot, John, 29
    Essay Concerning the Effects of Air on Human Bodies, 22, 34
archaeological sites, 222–5
Arctic (Canada), 217–18, 220, 225
    See also Inuit
Aristotle, *Meteorologica*, 144
Arizona: A History (Sheridan), 235, 250
Arizona, Sulphur Springs Valley, 234–8
    climate and agriculture, 238–41
    local perception of variability, 233–4, 236, 241–7, 289
Army Corps of Engineers, 281
artworks portraying atmospheric effects, 4, 141–3, 149–56
assumptions, cultural-environmental, 77
astronomy, 144
Athapaska, 219
    place names, 225
Atlantic Intermediate Water, 255
atmospheric effects in art works, 4, 141
atmospheric scientists, 4
avalanches, 47

Baffin Island, 220
    archaeological sites, 221
    South Baffin Island Placename Project, 225
Baganda, 127
Bakiga, terms for seasons, 133–4
bambara nuts, 183, 188
Bantu language, 87
barley, 259
barometers, 27, 45
Barr, R., 'Doom of London, The ,' 150, 158
Baudelaire, Charles, 142

Index

Baudrillard, Jean, 32, 57n15
Bauern-Praktik (almanac), 49
Bauernregeln (farmer's rules), 40, 48–51, 53–5
Bauman, Richard, 268, 271
Bauman, Zygmunt, 52, 58
BBCAC (Bi-State Blue Crab Advisory
    Committee), 69–70
beans, 185, 205
bearded seal, 224
Bedouin, terms for seasons
    in Libya, 135
    in Saudi Arabia, 136
beer brewing, 88
beliefs
    about procreation, 89, 94, 96
    cultural, 63, 115
    elite vs. vernacular, 24–5
    moral and political, buttressed by laws of
        nature, 278
Bellah, 183
Benson, E. F., 149, 158
Bentham, Jeremy, 41, 52
Bergmann, Matti (informant pseudonym), 40,
    51–2
Berlin, Brent, 123, 132
    Ethnobiological Classification, 124–5, 137
biodiversity, 175
bioethics, 5
biomedicine vs. folk medicine, 43
Bi-State Blue Crab Advisory Committee
    (BBCAC), 69–70
Bjerknes, Vilhelm, 145
Blacking, John, 5, 12
blue crab
    effects of humans on, 75
    effects of weather on, 62, 67–9, 71–2, 74, 78
    integrating scientific and watermen's
        knowledge about, 75–6
blue crab fishery, 61, 63–5
    cultural model, 62–3, 66–7, 72–8
    harvesting gear, 63–4
    regulations, 69–72, 74
Bolivia, traditional forecasting methods, 122
Bonacina. L. C. W., 141, 158
Bonam, Burkina Faso, 183–4, 187
Book of the Icelanders (*Íslendingabók*), 258
borrowed days, 27
Bosavi, 126

Bouahoun, Burkina Faso, 183–4, 187
Boyle, Robert, 21, 34
Boy's Bumper Book of Science, The, 280
Brazil
    Caboclo, terms for seasons, 133
    See also Ceará, Brazil
Brimblecombe, P., 150, 158
British Association of Social Anthropologists, 5
British Empire, 143
Broad, Kenneth, 277
Brodie, F. J., 147, 158
Bryant, C. R., 233, 248
Burkina Faso
    environmental and social context, 182–5
    probabilistic forecasts of seasonal rainfall,
        185–90, 194–7
    farmers' interpretations, 181–2, 192–4
    farmers' recollections, 190–2
Bushong, economic comparison with Lele,
    286–7
Bwa, 183

Caboclo, terms for seasons, 133
calendars, 126
    agricultural, 127
    civic, 18–19, 22–4, 28
    ecclesiastical, 27, 49
    indigenous, 122
    political, 127
    ritual, 127
    See also borrowed days
calendrical ceremonies, 220
Campbell, John, 28
Canadian Arctic, 217–18, 220, 225
    See also Inuit
carbon dioxide atmospheric concentrations,
    global average changes, 282–3
caribou, 224
Carpenter, Alfred, 148
Cartwright, N., 282, 289
cashew nuts, 205
cash income, 206
    See also cotton, as a cash crop
Ceará, Brazil
    drought relief management
        based on emergency aid, 175, 209–10
        drought-based policymaking, 203–4,
            208–10, 214–15

God's favor/disfavor reflected in the weather, 19, 21, 144, 150, 286

God's guidance of nature, 20–5, 30–1

God's omens as weather events, 20

God's omnipotence, 168, 175, 189, 204

God's stewardship of nature, 44, 63, 71–6, 78

Gomes, Ciro, 211

government subsidies, 235

grandchildren (classificatory), participation in rainmaking rituals, 83, 90–3

Granjon, D., 233, 249

Great Britain
  climate
    in 1947, 116n6
    as a reflection of national character, 17–19, 22, 142
    conversation about weather, 19, 25, 28–9, 103
    extreme weather events, obsession with, 31, 106, 108–9, 111, 114
    See also Great Storm (1703)
    journalism about weather, 25–6, 31
    nostalgic remembrance of weather, 109–15
    weather diaries, 21–5, 31–2
    weather newsgroups, data collection from, 104–8

Great Flood (Old Testament), 4

Great Freeze (1962-1963), 111

Great Plains, The (Webb), 235, 250

Great Storm (1703), 19–22, 26, 31

greenhouse gases, 11, 14, 283

Greenland, 225, 255

Gregorian calendar, 18, 23, 28

Grice, H. P., 105, 117

Grinker, Roy Richard, 123, 137

groundhog day, 27

Grumet, N. S., 221, 228

guillemot, 225

Gundjeihmi, terms for seasons, 130–1

Gunn, Joel, 'Global Climate and Regional Biocultural Diversity,' 220, 225–6, 228

Gurevich, A., 269, 272

Gurmantché, 183

Haia, Papua Territory, New Guinea, 162–4, 176n8

Halmahera, Indonesia, 121

harbor seal, 225

Hen-Thorir's Saga, 259

Hide, Robin L., 163–4, 179

Hillary, William, 24, 36

historical climatology, 253–4, 282

Hler (god of the sea), 261

Hofer, Johannes, 109

Holland, Dorothy, 66, 81

Hooke, Robert, 21, 36

Hora de Plantar (It's Time to Plant) program, 212

hot months, definition, 112

household surveys, 206, 213

Houses of Parliament, Sunset (Monet), 156

Howard, Luke, *Climate of London, The*, 29–31, 36

Hudson Bay, 218

Human Relations Area Files, 127–8

humans
  emotions, weather as a metaphor for, 266
  human nature, 278
  interrelation with nature, 4–6, 75–6, 269
  knowledge, limits of, 188–9, 194
  perception, 5
    of climate change, 171–4, 197, 233–5, 241–3
    of climate variability, 233–4, 236, 241–7, 289
    eyesight, 3
    skin receptor cells, 3
    weather intervention, 285–6

humidity, 50

hurricanes, 72

Huxham, John, 23

hydrological seasons, 133

ice-core data, 8, 253, 270
  isotopic records, 255–6

Iceland
  climate and economy, 253–6
  sea ice, 263–4
  volcanic eruptions, 26, 251
  See also Sagas of Icelanders

Icelandic culture, 252

Icelandic Family Sagas. See Sagas of Icelanders, The

Idler, The, 150

Ihanza, Tanzania, 83

Index

Index